Principles of Constraint Programming

Krzysztof R. Apt

CWI, Amsterdam, The Netherlands

CAMBRIDGE
UNIVERSITY PRESS

CAMBRIDGE UNIVERSITY PRESS
Cambridge, New York, Melbourne, Madrid, Cape Town, Singapore,
São Paulo, Delhi, Dubai, Tokyo

Cambridge University Press
The Edinburgh Building, Cambridge CB2 8RU, UK

Published in the United States of America by Cambridge University Press, New York

www.cambridge.org
Information on this title: www.cambridge.org/9780521125499

First published 2003
This digitally printed version (with minor corrections) 2009

A catalogue record for this publication is available from the British Library

ISBN 978-0-521-82583-2 Hardback
ISBN 978-0-521-12549-9 Paperback

To Alma and Daniel

Contents

Acknowledgements

I took to constraint programming late. In fact, I can be more precise. In the summer of 1995, when travelling to a conference, I stopped by at Joxan and Jennifer Jaffar's house in upstate New York. Joxan was working then at the IBM Research Heights and they were moving to Singapore. I still recall the half packed boxes in their hall and a pleasant evening spent on their terrace. I was discussing with Joxan research on constraint logic programming and was confused at that time that constraint programming is the same as constraint logic programming. But he showed me the book Tsang [1993]. Most of this material was new to me, though some isolated concepts I encountered earlier in the most useful book Van Hentenryck [1989].

One year later I thought I should give a course on the subject to learn it better. Providentially, in December 1996, during my visit to Israel, Rachel Ben Eliyahu from the University of Beer-sheva 'sent me over' to Rina Dechter who was staying then on sabbatical at the Tel-Aviv University. A two hour discussion with Rina helped me enormously. Moreover, over the next few months Rina patiently replied to all my, often stupid, questions and provided me with most useful pointers to the literature. This helped me to enter this subject and to start doing research on it.

In the course of the next five years I learned a lot on constraint programming by talking to many colleagues. In addition to those mentioned above I recall in particular illuminating conversations on this subject with Maarten van Emden (during his visits at CWI and my visit at the University of Victoria, Canada, in the summer of 1999), with Andrea Schaerf (during his visits at CWI in the period 1996–1998), François Fages (during the POPL '97 conference in Paris), with, unfortunately deceased in 2000, Igor Shetsov (in the bus to the hotel during the CP '97 conference and later, in 2000, in Amsterdam), François Puget (during a flight from Linz to Frankfurt after the CP '97 conference), Philippe Codognet (during his two short visits in

Amsterdam in, I believe, 1996 and 1999), Alexander Semenov (during his visit to Amsterdam in 2001), and last, but not least, Eric Monfroy, who worked at CWI in Amsterdam from 1996 until 2000.

In 2003 the circle closed, since I finished this book while visiting the National University of Singapore, where Joxan is now Dean of the School of Computing. While in Singapore, I also profited from useful conversations on constraint programming with Martin Henz and Roland Yap. Martin kindly provided me with the tests summarised in Table 9.1 in Chapter 9, obtained using the Oz Explorer. I would like to thank here all those mentioned above for their help in my understanding of the subject.

In addition, I appreciated most helpful comments, corrections and suggestions on various parts of the manuscript sent to me by Sebastian Brand, Karen Chong Sau Leng, Chen Chunqing, Radosław Cymer, Maarten van Emden, Pierre Flener, Rosella Gennari, Martin Henz, Willem Jan van Hoeve, Victor Marek, Pedro Meseguer, Eric Monfroy, Cristina Mota, Zsofi Ruttkay, Kees Vermeulen, Sebastian Voigt, Kazunori Ueda, Roland Yap, and Peter Zoeteweij. Also, I have greatly benefited from giving a course based on this material at the School of Computing of the National University of Singapore. Several students in my course, namely Lim Min Kwang, Cui Hang, Wen Conghua, Dong Xiaoan, Ma Lin, Xu Cheng and Damith Chatura Rajapakse provided useful comments. I also taught on this subject for a couple of years at the University of Amsterdam. Strangely, the only comment I ever got on the continuously growing manuscript was from a student who found that I should replace somewhere in the text 'We now get' by 'We get now'. [1]

Finally, Liu Jiang Hong kindly prepared the figures using the Dia drawing program. Nicola Vitacolonna modified the `skak` package in a way that allowed me to take care of the chess board drawings in Chapters 8 and 9 and Hugh Anderson helped me to insert them in the text as .epsi files. Also it is a pleasure to acknowledge the help I received from David Tranah of the Cambridge University Press throughout the production of this book.

And last, but not least, I would like to thank my family, Ruth, Alma and Daniel, for their patience with me during writing this book. Alma (now 7) kindly offered to proofread the book but fortunately it's not needed: this book no errors. Daniel (now 10) got interested in the Dia program. Who knows: perhaps he will be willing to make drawings for my next book?

---

[1] Fortunately, worse comments can happen. Peter Medawar, a recipient of the Nobel Prize in Physiology or Medicine in 1960 mentions in his memoirs that he gave once a lecture during an open day at his University and the only question he got was 'Where is the women's toilet?'

PS. A comment about the cover: Alma likes penguins very much.

1

Introduction

1.1 Basic characteristics of constraint programming

THIS BOOK IS about *constraint programming*, an alternative approach to programming which relies on a combination of techniques that deal with *reasoning* and *computing*. It has been successfully applied in a number of fields including molecular biology, electrical engineering, operations research and numerical analysis. The central notion is that of a constraint. Informally, a *constraint* on a sequence of variables is a relation on their domains. It can be viewed as a requirement that states which combinations of values from the variable domains are admitted. In turn, a *constraint satisfaction problem* consists of a finite set of constraints, each on a subsequence of a given sequence of variables.

To solve a given problem by means of constraint programming we first formulate it as a constraint satisfaction problem. To this end we

- introduce some variables ranging over specific domains and constraints over these variables;
- choose some language in which the constraints are expressed (usually a small subset of first-order logic).

This part of the problem solving is called *modeling*. In general, more than

1

one representation of a problem as a constraint satisfaction problem exists. Then to solve the chosen representation we use either

- domain specific methods,

or

- general methods,

or a combination of both.

The **domain specific methods** are usually provided in the form of implementations special purpose algorithms. Typical examples are:

- a program that solves systems of linear equations,
- a package for linear programming,
- an implementation of the unification algorithm, a cornerstone of automated theorem proving.

In turn, the **general methods** are concerned with the ways of reducing the search space and with specific **search methods**. The algorithms that deal with the search space reduction are usually called **constraint propagation algorithms**, though several other names have been often used. These algorithms maintain equivalence while simplifying the considered problem. They achieve various forms of **local consistency** that attempt to approximate the notion of (global) consistency. The (top down) search methods combine various forms of constraint propagation with the customary backtrack and branch and bound search.

The definition of constraint programming is so general that it embodies such diverse areas as Linear Algebra, Global Optimization, Linear and Integer Programming, etc. Therefore we should stress one essential point. If domain specific methods are available they should be applied *instead* of the general methods. For example, when dealing with systems of linear equations, the well-known linear algebra algorithms are readily available and it does not make sense to apply to these equations the general methods.

In fact, one of the aims of constraint programming is to look for efficient domain specific methods that can be used instead of the general methods and to incorporate them in a seamless way into a general framework. Such a framework usually supports

- domain specific methods by means of specialised packages, often called **constraint solvers**,
- general methods by means of various built-ins that in particular ensure or facilitate the use of the appropriate constraint propagation algorithms and support various search methods.

Once we represent a problem as a constraint satisfaction problem we need to solve it. In practice we are interested in:

- determining whether the chosen representation has a solution (is consistent),
- finding a solution, respectively, all solutions,
- finding an optimal solution, respectively, all optimal solutions w.r.t. some quality measure.

After this short preview we can formulate the following basic characteristics of constraint programming:

Two Phases Approach: The programming process consists of two phases: a generation of a problem representation by means of constraints and a solution of it. In practice, both phases consist of several smaller steps that can be interleaved.

Flexibility: The representation of a problem by means of constraints is very flexible because the constraints can be added, removed or modified. This flexibility is inherited by constraint programming.

Presence of Built-ins: To support this approach to programming several built-in methods are available. They deal with specific constraint solvers, constraint propagation algorithms and search methods.

An additional aspect brought in by constraint programming is that modeling by means of constraints leads to a representation of a problem by means of relations. This bears some resemblance to database systems, for instance relational databases. In fact, constraints are also studied in the context of database systems. They are useful in situations where some information, for instance the definition of a region of a map, needs to be provided implicitly, by means of constraints on reals.

The difference is that in the context of database systems the task consists of efficiently querying the considered relations, independently on whether they are defined explicitly (for instance by means of tables) or implicitly (for example by means of recursion or inequalities). In contrast, in constraint programming the considered relations are usually defined implicitly and the task consists of solving them or determining that no solution exists. This leads to different methods and different techniques.

1.2 Applications of constraint programming

Problems that can be best solved by means of constraint programming are usually those that can be naturally formulated in terms of requirements, general properties, or laws, and for which domain specific methods lead to overly complex formalisations. Constraint programming has already been successfully applied in numerous domains including:

- interactive graphic systems (to express geometric coherence in the case of scene analysis),

- operations research problems (various optimization problems, in particular scheduling problems),

- molecular biology (DNA sequencing, construction of 3D models of proteins),

- business applications (option trading),

- electrical engineering (location of faults in the circuits, computing the circuit layouts, testing and verification of the design),

- numerical computation (solving polynomial constraints with guaranteed precision),

- natural language processing (construction of efficient parsers),

- computer algebra (solving and/or simplifying equations over various algebraic structures).

More recent applications of constraints involve generation of coherent music radio programs, software engineering applications (design recovery and code optimization) and selection and scheduling of observations performed by satellites. Also, constraint programming proved itself a viable approach to tackle certain computationally intractable problems.

While an account of most of these applications cannot be fit into an introductory book, like this one, an interested reader can easily study the research papers on the above topics, after having acquainted himself/herself with the methods explained in this book.

The growing importance of this area can be witnessed by the fact that there are now annual conferences and workshops on constraint programming and its applications that consistently attract more than one hundred (occasionally two hundred) participants. Further, in 1996 an (unfortunately expensive) journal called 'Constraints' was launched. Also, several special issues of computer science journals devoted to the subject of constraints have appeared. But the field is still young and only a couple of books on this subject have appeared so far. This led us to writing this book.

1.3 A very short history of the subject

Before we engage in our presentation of constraint programming, let us briefly summarise the history of this subject. It will allow us to better understand the direction the field is heading.

The concept of a constraint was used already in 1963 in an early work of I. Sutherland on an interactive drawing system SKETCHPAD. In the seventies various experimental languages were proposed that used the notion of constraints and relied on the concept of constraint solving.

The concept of a constraint satisfaction problem was also formulated in the seventies by researchers in the artificial intelligence (AI). They also identified the main notions of local consistency and the algorithms that allow us to achieve them. Independently, various search methods were defined. Some of them, like backtracking can be traced back to the nineteenth century, while others, like branch and bound, were defined in the context of combinatorial optimization. The contribution of constraint programming was to identify various new forms of search that combine the known techniques with various constraint propagation algorithms. Some specific combinations were already studied in the area of combinatorial optimization.

In the eighties the first constraint programming languages of importance were proposed and implemented. The most significant were the languages based on the logic programming paradigm. This led to a development of *constraint logic programming*, an extension of logic programming by the notion of constraints. The programming view that emerged led to an identification of *constraint store* as a central concept. Constraint propagation and various forms of search are usually available in these languages in the form of built-ins.

In the late eighties and the nineties a form of synthesis between these two developments took place. The researchers found various new applications of constraint programming, most notably in the fields of operations research and numerical analysis. The progress was often achieved by identifying important new types of constraints and new constraint propagation algorithms. One also realised that further progress may depend on a combination of techniques from AI, operations research, computer algebra and mathematical logic. This turned constraint programming into an interesting hybrid area, in which theoretical work is often driven by applications and in turn applications lead to new challenges concerning implementations of constraint programming.

1.4 Our approach

In our presentation of the basic concepts and techniques of constraint programming we strive at a streamlined presentation in which we clarify the nature of these techniques and their interrelationship. To this end we organised the presentation around a number of simple principles.

Principle 1: Constraint programming is about a formulation of the problem as a constraint satisfaction problem and about solving it by means of domain specific or general methods.

This explains our focus on the constraint satisfaction problems and constraint solvers.

Principle 2: Many constraint solvers can be naturally explained using a rule-based framework. The constraint solver consists then of a set of rules that specify its behaviour and a scheduler. This viewpoint stresses the connections between rule-based programming and constraint programming.

This explains our decision to specify the constraint solvers by means of proof rules that transform constraint satisfaction problems.

Principle 3: The constraint propagation algorithms can be naturally explained as instances of simple generic iteration algorithms.

This view allows us to clarify the nature of the constraint propagation algorithms. Also, it provides us with a natural method for implementing the discussed constraint solvers, since a rule scheduler is just another instance of a generic iteration algorithm.

Principle 4: (Top down) search techniques can be conceptually viewed as traversal algorithms of the search trees.

This explains why we organised the chapter on search around the slogan:

Search Algorithm = Search Tree + Traversal Algorithm,

and why we explained the resulting algorithms in the form of successive reformulations.

1.5 Organisation of the book

The above explained principles lead to a natural organisation of the material. Here is a short preview of the remaining chapters. In **Chapter 2** we discuss several examples of constraint satisfaction problems. We stress there that in many situations several natural representations are possible. In **Chapter 3** we introduce a general framework that allows us to explain the basics of constraints programming. We identify there natural ingredients of this framework. This makes it easier to understand the subject of the subsequent chapters.

Then, in **Chapter 4**, we provide three well-known examples of complete constraint solvers. They deal, respectively, with solving equations over terms, linear equations over reals and linear inequalities over reals. In turn, in **Chapter 5** we introduce several notions of local consistency and characterise them in the form of proof rules. These notions allow us to study in **Chapter 6** in more detail a number of incomplete constraint solvers that involve Boolean constraints and linear and arithmetic constraints on integers and reals.

In **Chapter 7** we study the constraint propagation algorithms that allow us to achieve the forms of local consistency discussed in Chapter 5. The characterisation of these notions in the form of proof rules allows us to provide a uniform presentation of these algorithms as instances of simple generic iteration algorithms. Next, in **Chapter 8**, we discuss various (top down) search algorithms. We present them in such a way that one can see how these algorithms are related to each other. Finally, in **Chapter 9**, we provide a short overview of the research directions in constraint programming.

Those interested in using this book for teaching may find it helpful to use the transparencies that can be downloaded from the following website: `http://www.cwi.nl/~apt/pcp`.

Constraint satisfaction problems: examples

T HE AIM OF this chapter is to discuss various examples of constraint satisfaction problems (CSPs [2] in short). The notion of a CSP is very general, so it is not surprising that these examples cover a wide range of topics. We limit ourselves here to the examples of CSPs that are simple to explain and that illustrate the use of general methods of constraint programming. In particular, we included here some perennial puzzles, since, as it has been recognised for some time, they form an excellent vehicle to explain certain principles of constraint programming.

As already mentioned in Chapter 1 the representation of a problem as a CSP is usually called *modeling*. The selected examples clarify a number of aspects of modeling. First, as we shall see, some of the problems can be formalised as a CSP in a straightforward way. For other problems the appropriate representation as a CSP is by no means straightforward and relies on a non-trivial 'background' theory that ensures correctness of the

---

[2] For those knowledgeable in other areas of computer science: constraint satisfaction problems have nothing do to with Communicating Sequential Processes, a programming notation for distributed processes introduced by C.A.R. Hoare and also abbreviated to CSP.

adopted representation. Also for several problems, more than one natural representation exists.

When presenting the CSPs it is useful to classify them according to some criterion. In general, the techniques used to solve CSPs depend both on the domains over which they are defined and on the syntax of the used constraints. In most examples we use some simple language to define the constraints. Later, in Chapters 4 and 6, we shall be more precise and shall discuss in detail specific languages in which the constraints will be defined. But now it is too early to appreciate the role played by the syntax. So we rather classify the CSPs according to the domains over which they are defined. This explains the structure of this chapter.

First, we formalise in Section 2.1 the notion of a constraint and of a CSP. Then, in Section 2.2 we introduce some well-known problems and puzzles that can be naturally formalised as CSPs with integer domains. In Section 2.3 we consider examples of problems the formalisation of which leads to CSPs with variables ranging over reals. In turn, in Section 2.4 we consider **Boolean CSPs**. These are CSPs in which the variables range over the integer domain $[0..1]$ or, equivalently, {**false, true**} and in which the constraints are expressed by means of Boolean expressions.

An important class of CSPs are the ones in which the variables range over non-numeric domains. We call them **symbolic CSPs**. They are considered in Section 2.5. In case we are interested in finding an optimal solution to a CSP we associate with each solution an objective function that we want to minimise or maximise. This leads to a modification of a CSP that we call a **constrained optimization problem**. They are considered in Section 2.6.

2.1 Basic concepts

As explained in the previous chapter constraint satisfaction problems, or CSPs, are a fundamental concept in constraint programming. To proceed we need to define them formally. The precise definition is completely straightforward. First we introduce the notion of a constraint.

Consider a finite sequence of variables $Y := y_1, \ldots, y_k$ where $k > 0$, with respective domains $D_1, \ldots, D_k$ associated with them. So each variable y_i ranges over the domain D_i. By a **constraint** C on Y we mean a subset of $D_1 \times \cdots \times D_k$. When $k = 1$ we say that the constraint is **unary** and when $k = 2$ that the constraint is **binary**. By a **constraint satisfaction problem**, or a **CSP**, we mean a finite sequence of variables $X := x_1, \ldots, x_n$ with respective domains $D_1, \ldots, D_n$, together with a finite set $\mathcal{C}$ of constraints, each on a subsequence of X. We write such a CSP as $\langle \mathcal{C} \; ; \; \mathcal{DE} \rangle$, where

$\mathcal{DE} := x_1 \in D_1, \ldots, x_n \in D_n$ and call each construct of the form $x \in D$ a **domain expression**. To simplify the notation we omit the '{ }' brackets when presenting specific sets of constraints $\mathcal{C}$.

We now define the crucial notion of a solution to a CSP. Intuitively, a solution to a CSP is a sequence of legal values for all of its variables such that all its constraints are satisfied. More precisely, consider a CSP $\langle \mathcal{C} ; \mathcal{DE} \rangle$ with $\mathcal{DE} := x_1 \in D_1, \ldots, x_n \in D_n$. We say that an n-tuple $(d_1, \ldots, d_n) \in D_1 \times \cdots \times D_n$ **satisfies** a constraint $C \in \mathcal{C}$ on the variables $x_{i_1}, \ldots, x_{i_m}$ if

$$(d_{i_1}, \ldots, d_{i_m}) \in C.$$

Then we say that an n-tuple $(d_1, \ldots, d_n) \in D_1 \times \cdots \times D_n$ is a **solution** to $\langle \mathcal{C} ; \mathcal{DE} \rangle$ if it satisfies every constraint $C \in \mathcal{C}$. If a CSP has a solution, we say that it is **consistent** and otherwise we say that it is **inconsistent**.

Note that in the definition of a constraint and of a CSP no syntax was assumed. In practice, of course, one needs to define the constraints and the domain expressions. In what follows we assume that they are defined in some specific, further unspecified, language. In this representation it is implicit that each constraint is a subset of the Cartesian product of the associated variable domains. For example, if we consider the CSP $\langle x < y ; x \in [0..10], y \in [5..10] \rangle$, then we view the constraint $x < y$ as the set of all pairs (a, b) with $a \in [0..10]$ and $b \in [5..10]$ such that $a < b$.

Let us illustrate these concepts by a simple example. Consider the sequence of four variables x, y, z, u ranging over natural numbers and the following three constraints on them: $x^3 + y^3 + z^3 + u^3 = 100$, $x < u$, $x + y = z$. According to the above notation we write this CSP as

$$\langle x^3 + y^3 + z^3 + u^3 = 100, \ x < u, \ x + y = z \ ; \ x \in \mathcal{N}, y \in \mathcal{N}, z \in \mathcal{N}, u \in \mathcal{N} \rangle,$$

where $\mathcal{N}$ denotes the set of natural numbers.

Then the sequence $(1, 2, 3, 4)$ is a solution to this CSP since this sequence satisfies all constraints. Indeed, we have $1^3 + 2^3 + 3^3 + 4^3 = 100$, $1 < 4$ and $1 + 2 = 3$.

Finally, let us clarify one simple matter. When defining constraints and CSPs we refer to the sequences (respectively subsequences) of variables and *not* to the sets (respectively subsets) of variables. Namely, given a CSP each of its constraints is defined on a *subsequence* and not on a *subset* of its variables. In particular, the above constraint $x < y$ is defined on the subsequence x, y of the sequence x, y, z, u.

Also, the sequence z, y is not a subsequence x, y, z, u, so if we add to the above CSP the constraint $z = y + 2$ we cannot consider it as a constraint on z, y. But we can view it of course as a constraint on y, z and, if we wish, we can rewrite it as $y + 2 = z$. The reliance on sequences and subsequences of variables instead of on sets and subsets will allow us to analyse in a simple way variable orderings when searching for solutions to a given CSP. So this presentation does not introduce any restrictions and simplifies some considerations.

2.2 Constraint satisfaction problems on integers

The remainder of this chapter is devoted to a presentation of various examples of constraint satisfaction problems. We begin with examples of CSPs with integer domains.

Example 2.1 *SEND + MORE = MONEY.*

This is a classic example of a so-called **cryptarithmetic problem.** These are mathematical puzzles in which the digits are replaced by letters of the alphabet or other symbols. The problems dealing with valid sums are called **alphametic** problems. In the problem under consideration we are asked to replace each letter by a different digit so that the above sum, that is

$$
\begin{array}{r}
SEND \\
+ \ MORE \\
\hline
MONEY
\end{array}
$$

is correct. Here the variables are S, E, N, D, M, O, R, Y. Because S and M are the leading digits, the domain for each of them consists of the integer interval $[1..9]$. The domain of each of the remaining variables consists of the integer interval $[0..9]$. This problem can be formulated as the equality constraint

$$
\begin{aligned}
& 1000 \cdot S \ + \ 100 \cdot E \ + \ 10 \cdot N \ + \ D \\
+ \ & 1000 \cdot M \ + \ 100 \cdot O \ + \ 10 \cdot R \ + \ E \\
= \ 10000 \cdot M \ + \ & 1000 \cdot O \ + \ 100 \cdot N \ + \ 10 \cdot E \ + \ Y
\end{aligned}
$$

combined with 28 disequality constraints $x \neq y$ for x, y ranging over the set $\{S, E, N, D, M, O, R, Y\}$ with x preceding y in, say, the presented order.

A minor variation on the above representation of this problem as a CSP is obtained by assuming that the domains of all variables are the same, namely the interval $[0..9]$, and by adding to the above constraints two disequality constraints:

$$
S \neq 0, \ M \neq 0.
$$

Yet another possibility consists of additionally introducing per column a 'carry' variable ranging over $[0..1]$ and using instead of the above single equality constraint the following five, one for each column:

$$D + E = 10 \cdot C_1 + Y,$$

$$C_1 + N + R = 10 \cdot C_2 + E,$$

$$C_2 + E + O = 10 \cdot C_3 + N,$$

$$C_3 + S + M = 10 \cdot C_4 + O,$$

$$C_4 = M.$$

Here, $C_1, \ldots, C_4$ are the carry variables.

In turn, the disequality constraints can be replaced by a single constraint that stipulates that the variables are pairwise different. Given a sequence of variables $x_1, \ldots, x_n$ with respective domains $D_1, \ldots, D_n$ we define

$$\texttt{all\_different}(x_1, \ldots, x_n) := \{(d_1, \ldots, d_n) \mid d_i \neq d_j \text{ for } i \neq j\}.$$

Then we can replace the above 28 disequality constraints by a single constraint $\texttt{all\_different}(S, E, N, D, M, O, R, Y)$.

Yet another way to deal with these disequality constraints is to follow a standard method used in the area of Integer Linear Programming, the objective of which is to find optimal integer solutions to linear constraints. For each pair x, y of different variables from $\{S, E, N, D, M, O, R, Y\}$ we introduce a variable $z_{x,y}$ ranging over $[0..1]$ and transform the disequality $x \neq y$ to the following two constraints:

- $x - y \leq 10 - 11 z_{x,y},$
- $y - x \leq 11 z_{x,y} - 1.$

Note that $x \neq y$ is equivalent to the disjunction $x < y$ or $y < x$ which is equivalent to $x - y \leq -1$ or $y - x \leq -1$, which in turn is equivalent to the disjunction

$$(x - y \leq 10 - 11 z_{x,y} \text{ and } z_{x,y} = 1) \text{ or } (y - x \leq 11 z_{x,y} - 1 \text{ and } z_{x,y} = 0).$$

So to satisfy the constraint $x \neq y$ it is equivalent to satisfy one of the above two constraints on x, y and $z_{x,y}$. The disadvantage of this approach is that we need to introduce 28 new variables.

The above problem has a unique solution depicted by the following sum:

$$9567$$
$$+\ 1085$$
$$\overline{10652}$$

As a consequence, each of the above representations of it as a CSP has a unique solution, as well. □

Example 2.2 *The n Queens Problem.*

This is probably the most known CSP. One is asked to place n queens on the $n \times n$ chess board, where $n \geq 3$, so that they do not attack each other. Figure 2.1 shows a solution to the problem for $n = 8$.

One possible representation of this problem as a CSP uses n variables, $x_1, \ldots, x_n$, each with the domain $[1..n]$. The idea is that x_i denotes the position of the queen placed in the ith column of the chess board. For example, the solution presented in Figure 2.1 corresponds to the sequence of values $(6,4,7,1,8,2,5,3)$, since the first queen from the left is placed in the 6th row counting from the bottom, and similarly with the other queens.

The appropriate constraints can be formulated as the following disequalities for $i \in [1..n-1]$ and $j \in [i+1..n]$:

- $x_i \neq x_j$ (no two queens in the same row),
- $x_i - x_j \neq i - j$ (no two queens in each South-West – North-East diagonal),
- $x_i - x_j \neq j - i$ (no two queens in each North-West – South-East diagonal).

Using the `all_different` constraint introduced in the previous example we can replace the first set of $\frac{n \cdot (n-1)}{2}$ disequalities by a single constraint `all_different`$(x_1, \ldots, x_n)$. In Section 2.4 we shall discuss another natural representation of this problem. □

Example 2.3 *The Zebra Puzzle.*

As another example consider the following famous puzzle of Lewis Carroll. A small street has five differently coloured houses on it. Five men of different nationalities live in these five houses. Each man has a different profession, each man likes a different drink, and each has a different pet animal. We have the following information:

The Englishman lives in the red house.

The Spaniard has a dog.

The Japanese is a painter.

The Italian drinks tea.

Fig. 2.1. One of 92 solutions to the 8 queens problem

The Norwegian lives in the first house on the left.
The owner of the green house drinks coffee.
The green house is on the right of the white house.
The sculptor breeds snails.
The diplomat lives in the yellow house.
They drink milk in the middle house.
The Norwegian lives next door to the blue house.
The violinist drinks fruit juice.
The fox is in the house next to the doctor's.
The horse is in the house next to the diplomat's.
The question is who has the zebra and who drinks water?

An interesting aspect of this puzzle is that in its data neither zebra nor water is mentioned and yet it has a unique solution. To formulate it as a CSP we first try to determine the variables and their domains. Note that this puzzle involves:

- five houses, which we number from left to right: 1, 2, 3, 4, 5,
- five colours, namely red, green, white, yellow, blue,
- five nationalities, namely English, Spanish, Japanese, Italian, Norwegian,
- five pets, namely dog, snails, fox, horse, and (implicitly) zebra,
- five professions, namely painter, sculptor, diplomat, violinist, doctor,
- five drinks, namely tea, coffee, milk, juice, and (implicitly) water.

To solve this puzzle it suffices to determine for each house its five characteristics:

- colour,
- nationality of the owner,
- pet of the owner,
- profession of the owner,
- favourite drink of the owner.

So we introduce 25 variables, five for each of the above five characteristics. For these variables we use the following mnemonic names:

- 'colour' variables: `red, green, white, yellow, blue,`
- 'nationality' variables: `english, spaniard, japanese, italian, norwegian,`
- 'pet' variables: `dog, snails, fox, horse, zebra,`
- 'profession' variables: `painter, sculptor, diplomat, violinist, doctor,`
- 'drink' variables: `tea, coffee, milk, juice, water.`

We assume that each of these variables ranges over [1...5]. If, for example, `violinist = 3` then we interpret this as the statement that the violinist lives in house no. 3. After these preparations we can now formalise the given information as the following constraints:

- The Englishman lives in the red house: `english = red`,
- The Spaniard has a dog: `spaniard = dog`,
- The Japanese is a painter: `japanese = painter`,
- The Italian drinks tea: `italian = tea`,
- The Norwegian lives in the first house on the left: `norwegian = 1`,
- The owner of the green house drinks coffee: `green = coffee`,
- The green house is on the right of the white house: `green = white + 1`,
- The sculptor breeds snails: `sculptor = snails`,
- The diplomat lives in the yellow house: `diplomat = yellow`,
- They drink milk in the middle house: `milk = 3`,
- The Norwegian lives next door to the blue house: `|norwegian − blue| = 1`,
- The violinist drinks fruit juice: `violinist = juice`,
- The fox is in the house next to the doctor's: `|fox − doctor| = 1`,
- The horse is in the house next to the diplomat's: `|horse − diplomat| = 1`.

Additionally, we need to postulate that for each of the characteristics the corresponding variables are different. This means that we introduce fifty disequality constraints, ten for each characteristics. For example `red` ≠

white is one of such disequalities. Alternatively, instead of postulating these fifty disequality constraints we can employ the all_different constraint introduced in Example 2.1 and postulate instead

$$\text{all\_different}(\text{red}, \text{green}, \text{white}, \text{yellow}, \text{blue}),$$

$$\text{all\_different}(\text{english}, \text{spaniard}, \text{japanese}, \text{italian}, \text{norwegian}),$$

$$\text{all\_different}(\text{dog}, \text{snails}, \text{fox}, \text{horse}, \text{zebra}),$$

$$\text{all\_different}(\text{painter}, \text{sculptor}, \text{diplomat}, \text{violinist}, \text{doctor}),$$

$$\text{all\_different}(\text{tea}, \text{coffee}, \text{milk}, \text{juice}, \text{water}).$$

Now, it turns out that there is exactly one assignment of values to all 25 variables for which all constraints are satisfied. Because of this the puzzle has a unique solution Indeed, the puzzle is solved once we find in this unique assignment for which 'profession' variables

$$x, y \in \{\text{painter}, \text{sculptor}, \text{diplomat}, \text{violinist}, \text{doctor}\}$$

we have

$$x = \text{zebra and } y = \text{water}.$$

The answer is $x = \text{japanese}$ and $y = \text{norwegian}$, which means that the Japanese has the zebra and the Norwegian drinks water.   □

2.3 Constraint satisfaction problems on reals

Let us move now to the case of CSPs the variables of which range over reals.

Example 2.4 *Spreadsheets.*

Spreadsheet systems, such as Excel, are very popular for various office-like applications. These systems have in general a number of very advanced features but their essence relies on constraints.

To be more specific consider Table 2.1. It represents a spreadsheet, in which the values for the cells D4, D5, E7 and E8 are computed by means of the formulas present in these cells.

Equivalently, we can represent the spreadsheet of Table 2.1 by means of a CSP that consists of nine variables: B1, B4, B5, C4, C5, D4, D5, E7 and E8, each ranging over real numbers, and the following nine constraints:

B1 = 0.17,
B4 = 3.5,

	A	B	C	D	E
1	**Tax**	0.17			
2					
3	**Product**	**Price**	**Quantity**	**Total**	
4	tomatoes	3.5	1.5	= B4 * C4	
5	potatoes	1.7	4.5	= B5 * C5	
6					
7				**Grand Total**	= D4 + D5
8				**Final Amount**	= E7 * (1 + B1)

Table 2.1. A spreadsheet

	A	B	C	D	E
1	**Tax**	0.17			
2					
3	**Product**	**Price**	**Quantity**	**Total**	
4	tomatoes	3.5	1.5	5.25	
5	potatoes	1.7	4.5	7.65	
6					
7				**Grand Total**	12.9
8				**Final Amount**	15.093

Table 2.2. Solution to the spreadsheet of Table 2.1

B5 = 1.7,

C4 = 1.5,

C5 = 4.5,

D4 = B4 * C4,

D5 = B5 * C5,

E7 = D4 + D5,

E8 = E7 * (1 + B1).

A spreadsheet system solves these constraints and updates the solution each time a parameter is modified. The latter corresponds to modifying a numeric value v in a constraint of the form $x = v$, where x is a variable. For example, a modification of the C5 field corresponds to a modification of the right-hand side of the constraint C5 = 4.5.

In the case of the spreadsheet of Table 2.1 the solution is represented by the spreadsheet of Table 2.2. □

Example 2.5 *Finding zeros of polynomials of higher degree.*

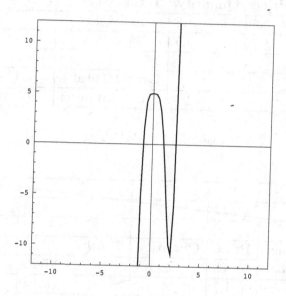

Fig. 2.2. The diagram of the polynomial $2 \cdot x^5 - 5 \cdot x^4 + 5$

Consider the polynomial $2 \cdot x^5 - 5 \cdot x^4 + 5$ represented in Figure 2.2. Suppose we wish to find its zeros. The difficulty lies in the fact that in general, by the celebrated Galois' theorem, the zeros of polynomials of degree higher than four cannot be expressed as radicals, that is by means of the four arithmetic operations and the root extraction. In fact, $2 \cdot x^5 - 5 \cdot x^4 + 5$ is one of such polynomials, found in the nineteenth century by the Norwegian mathematician Niels Henrik Abel. Another complication is that the real numbers cannot be faithfully represented in the computer.

The latter problem is dealt with by using the computer representable real numbers, i.e., the floating point numbers, and by producing solutions in the form of sequences of intervals with floating point bounds.

The techniques of constraint programming turn out to be useful to tackle such problems. In general, given a polynomial $f(x)$, we consider a CSP with a single constraint $f(x) = 0$ where the variable x ranges over reals. Further, we assume a fixed finite set of floating point numbers augmented with $-\infty$ and ∞, and denoted by F. By an *interval CSP* we mean here a CSP with the single constraint $f(x) = 0$ and a domain expression of the form $x \in [l, r]$, where $l, r \in F$, that is a CSP of the form $\langle f(x) = 0 \; ; \; x \in [l, r] \rangle$.

The original CSP is then transformed into a disjunction of the interval CSPs the intervals of which are of sizes smaller than some fixed in advance ϵ. This disjunction is equivalent to the original CSP, in the sense that the set of solutions to the original CSP equals the union of the sets of solutions to the disjunct interval CSPs.

In the case of the above polynomial, choosing the accuracy of 16 digits after the decimal point, we get the disjunction of three interval CSPs based on the following intervals:

$$x \in [-.9243580149260359080,$$
$$-.9243580149260359031],$$

$$x \in [1.171162068483181786,$$
$$1.171162068483181791],$$

$$x \in [2.428072792707314923,$$
$$2.428072792707314924].$$

An additional argument is needed to prove that each interval contains a zero. These considerations generalise to polynomials in an arbitrary number of variables and to the constrained optimization problems on reals according to which we are asked to optimize some real-valued function subject to polynomial constraints over the reals.   □

2.4 Boolean constraint satisfaction problems

Once we identify **false** with 0 and **true** with 1, Boolean CSPs form a special case of numeric CSPs in which the variables range over the binary domain [0..1] and the constraints are expressed by means of Boolean expressions built using some basic set of connectives. From this perspective the first identified NP-complete problem, the satisfiability problem, according to which we ask whether a given Boolean expression is satisfiable, is equivalent to the question whether the corresponding Boolean CSP is consistent. In general, as we shall see in Chapter 6, the use of the constraint programming techniques does not bring any new insights into this area. However, these techniques allow us to model certain forms of reasoning in a natural way, also as programs.

Example 2.6 *The full adder circuit.*
This example deals with digital circuits built out of the AND, OR and XOR gates. These gates generate an output value given two input values.

The possible values are drawn from [0..1], so we deal here with bits or, alternatively, Boolean variables. The behaviour of these gates is defined by the following tables:

AND	0	1
0	0	0
1	0	1

OR	0	1
0	0	1
1	1	1

XOR	0	1
0	0	1
1	1	0

Alternatively, we can view these gates as connectives: the AND gate corresponds to the conjunction, the OR gate to the disjunction and the XOR gate to the exclusive disjunction. Therefore the circuits built out of these gates can be naturally represented by equations between Boolean expressions involving conjunction, written as $\wedge$, disjunction, written as $\vee$, and exclusive disjunction, written as $\oplus$. In particular, the circuit depicted in Figure 2.3 can be represented by the following two equations:

$$(i_1 \oplus i_2) \oplus i_3 = o_1, \tag{2.1}$$

$$(i_1 \wedge i_2) \vee (i_3 \wedge (i_1 \oplus i_2)) = o_2. \tag{2.2}$$

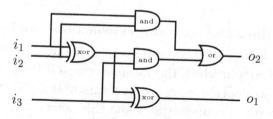

Fig. 2.3. Full adder circuit

This circuit is called **full adder** as it computes the binary sum $i_1 + i_2 + i_3$ in the binary word $o_2 o_1$. For example $1+1+0$ yields 10. To verify the correctness of this circuit it suffices to use the three tables above and to calculate using the equations (2.1) and (2.2) the outputs o_1, o_2 for all combinations of the inputs i_1, i_2, i_3.

The fact that we represent this circuit as a Boolean CSP, using relations between the Boolean variables i_1, i_2, i_3, o_1 and o_2 determined by the above equations, instead of as a function from (i_1, i_2, i_3) to (o_1, o_2), will allow us in Section 6.3 to draw in a systematic way more complex conclusions such as that $i_3 = 0$ and $o_2 = 1$ implies that $i_1 = 1, i_2 = 1$ and $o_1 = 0$. □

Example 2.7 *The n Queens Problem, again.*

When discussing in Example 2.2 the n Queens Problem we chose a representation involving n variables, each associated with one row. A different natural representation involves n^2 Boolean variables $x_{i,j}$, where $i \in [1..n]$ and $j \in [1..n]$, each of them representing one field of the chess board. The appropriate constraints can then be written as Boolean constraints represented by Boolean expressions built using the conjunction and negation (written as $\neg$) connectives.

To this end we introduce the following abbreviation. Given k Boolean expressions $s_1, \ldots, s_k$ we denote by $one(s_1, \ldots, s_k)$ the Boolean expression that states that exactly one of the expressions $s_1, \ldots, s_k$ is true. So $one(s_1, \ldots, s_k)$ is a disjunction of k expressions, each of them being a k-ary conjunction of the form $\neg s_1 \wedge \ldots \neg s_{i-1} \wedge s_i \wedge \neg s_{i+1} \ldots \wedge \neg s_k$, where $i \in [1..k]$.

The following constraints then formalise the problem:

- $one(x_{i,1}, \ldots, x_{i,n})$ for $i \in [1..n]$ (exactly one queen per row),
- $one(x_{1,i}, \ldots, x_{n,i})$ for $i \in [1..n]$ (exactly one queen per column),
- $\neg(x_{i,j} \wedge x_{k,\ell})$ for $i, j, k, \ell \in [1..n]$ such that $i \neq k$ and $|i - k| = |j - \ell|$ (at most one queen per diagonal).

The condition $i \neq k$ in the last item ensures that the fields represented by $x_{i,j}$ and $x_{k,\ell}$ are different. □

2.5 Symbolic constraint satisfaction problems

By a symbolic constraint satisfaction problem we mean a CSP the variables of which range over non-numeric domains.

Example 2.8 *The Crossword Puzzle.*

Consider the crossword grid of Figure 2.4 and suppose that we are to fill it with the words from the following list:

- HOSES, LASER, SAILS, SHEET, STEER,
- HEEL, HIKE, KEEL, KNOT, LINE,
- AFT, ALE, EEL, LEE, TIE.

This problem can be formulated as a CSP as follows. First, associate with each position $i \in [1..8]$ in this grid a variable. Then associate with each variable the domain that consists of the set of words of that can be used to fill this position. For example, position 6 needs to be filled with a

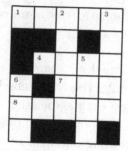

Fig. 2.4. A crossword grid

three letter word, so the domain of the variable associated with position 6 consists of the above set of five 3 letter words.

Finally, we define the constraints. They deal with the restrictions arising from the fact that the words that cross share a letter at appropriate positions. For example, the crossing of the positions 1 and 2 contributes the following constraint:

$$C_{1,2} := \{(\text{HOSES, SAILS}), (\text{HOSES, SHEET}), (\text{HOSES, STEER}),$$
$$(\text{LASER, SAILS}), (\text{LASER, SHEET}), (\text{LASER, STEER})\} \ .$$

This constraint formalises the fact that the third letter of position 1 needs to be the same as the first letter of position 2. In total there are twelve constraints. The unique solution to this CSP is depicted in Figure 2.5.

¹H	O	²S	E	³S
		A		T
	⁴H	I	⁵K	E
⁶A		⁷L	E	E
⁸L	A	S	E	R
E			L	

Fig. 2.5. The solution to the crossword puzzle

□

The next two examples deal with *qualitative reasoning*. In this form of reasoning one abstracts from the numeric quantities, such as the precise time of an event, or the location of an object in the space, and reasons instead on the level of their abstractions. Usually, these abstractions form a finite set of alternatives, as opposed to the infinite set of possibilities available at the numeric level. This allows one to carry out conclusions on an abstract level that on the numeric level would be difficult to achieve. We now discuss two examples of qualitative reasoning.

Example 2.9 *Qualitative Temporal Reasoning.*
Consider the following problem.
The meeting ran non-stop the whole day. Each person stayed at the meeting for a continuous period of time. The meeting began while Mr Jones was present and finished while Ms White was present. Ms White arrived after the meeting has began. In turn, Director Smith was also present but he arrived after Jones had left. Mr Brown talked to Ms White in presence of Smith. Could possibly Jones and White have talked during this meeting?

To properly analyse such problems we are naturally led to an abstract analysis of activities that take time, such as being present during the meeting, talking to somebody, driving to work, taking a lunch break, filling in a form, receiving a phone call, etc. In what follows we call such activities *temporal events*, or simply *events*. If we only take into account the fact that such events take a continuous but limited period of time, then we can identify them with closed non-empty intervals of the real line.

In the case of the above problem a possible scenario that matches its description is provided in Figure 2.6, where each event (like the duration of the meeting or the period during which Jones was present) is represented by a closed non-empty real interval.

Fig. 2.6. A possible scenario for the 'meeting problem'

In general, when identifying events with closed non-empty real intervals we end up with thirteen possible *temporal relations* between a pair of events. They are presented in Figure 2.7. Intuitively, these relations arise when we consider two intervals, A and B, and keep moving the interval A from left to right and record all its possible relative positions w.r.t. B, taking into account their possibly different relative sizes.

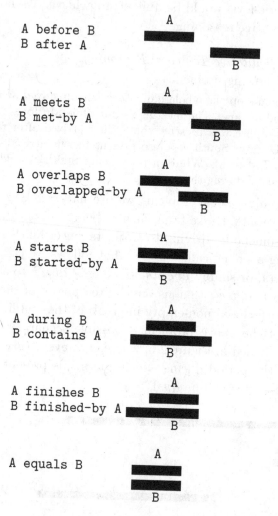

A before B
B after A

A meets B
B met-by A

A overlaps B
B overlapped-by A

A starts B
B started-by A

A during B
B contains A

A finishes B
B finished-by A

A equals B

Fig. 2.7. Thirteen temporal relations

Let *TEMP* denote the set formed by the thirteen possibilities of Figure 2.7. In what follows we provide two representations of CSPs dealing with temporal reasoning in this setting. The first one is conceptually simpler but it involves infinite domains. The second one is at first appearance more involved but has the advantage that the domains are finite and directly correspond to the set *TEMP*.

First representation.

In this representation the variables represent events. Their domains reflect the view that events are identified with closed non-empty intervals of real line. So each domain consists of the set of such intervals, that is the set

$$D := \{(a, b) \mid a, b \in \mathcal{R}, \ a < b\},$$

where $\mathcal{R}$ is the set of all reals and each pair (a, b) represents the closed interval $[a, b]$ of reals.

Next, each of the introduced thirteen temporal relations is represented as a binary constraint in the way that reflects the intended meaning. For example, the overlaps relation is represented as the following subset of $D \times D$:

$$[\![\text{overlaps}]\!] := \{((a_{begin}, a_{end}), (b_{begin}, b_{end})) \mid a_{begin} < b_{begin}, b_{begin} < a_{end},$$
$$a_{end} < b_{end}\}.$$

Finally, arbitrary constraints are set-theoretic unions of the elementary binary constraints that represent the thirteen temporal relations.

Let us illustrate now this representation by formalising as a CSP the problem we began with. First, we identify the relevant events and associate with each of them a variable. In total, we consider the following five events and variables:

event	variable
the duration of the meeting	M
the period Jones was present	J
the period Brown was present	B
the period Smith was present	S
the period White was present	W

Next, we define the appropriate constraints. The first three formalise information concerning the presence of each person during the meeting. For brevity we denote here the union of all elementary constraints excluding $[\![\text{before}]\!]$, $[\![\text{after}]\!]$, $[\![\text{meets}]\!]$ and $[\![\text{met-by}]\!]$ as $[\![\text{REAL-OVERLAP}]\!]$. Note that

$$[\![\text{REAL-OVERLAP}]\!] = \{((a_{begin}, a_{end}), (b_{begin}, b_{end})) \mid a_{begin} < b_{end},$$
$$b_{begin} < a_{end}\}.$$

These three constraints are:

$$([\![\text{overlaps}]\!] \cup [\![\text{contains}]\!] \cup [\![\text{finished-by}]\!])(J, M),$$

$$[\![\texttt{overlaps}]\!](M, W),$$

$$[\![\texttt{REAL-OVERLAP}]\!](M, S).$$

Note that the first constraint formalises the fact that

- J started strictly earlier than M started,
- M started strictly before J finished.

In turn, the second constraint formalises the fact that

- W started strictly before M finished,
- M finished strictly earlier than W finished,
- M started strictly before W started.

Finally, the constraint $[\![\texttt{REAL-OVERLAP}]\!](M, S)$ formalises the fact that M and S 'truly' overlap in time, that is, share some time interval of positive length. Note that we do not postulate any constraint on M and B, in particular not $[\![\texttt{REAL-OVERLAP}]\!](M, B)$, because from the problem formulation it is not clear whether Brown was actually present during the meeting.

Additionally, the following constraints formalise information concerning the relative presence of the persons in question:

$$[\![\texttt{before}]\!](J, S),$$

$$[\![\texttt{REAL-OVERLAP}]\!](B, S),$$

$$[\![\texttt{REAL-OVERLAP}]\!](B, W),$$

$$[\![\texttt{REAL-OVERLAP}]\!](S, W).$$

The question 'Could possibly Jones and White have talked during this meeting?' can now be formalised as a problem whether for some solution to this CSP $[\![\texttt{REAL-OVERLAP}]\!](J, W)$ holds. In other words, is it true that the above CSP augmented by the constraint $[\![\texttt{REAL-OVERLAP}]\!](J, W)$ is consistent.

Second representation.

In the first representation the domains, and thus the domain expressions, were uniquely fixed and we only had to determine the constraints all of which were binary. In the second representation we first determine the domain expressions which uniquely determine the constraints. In this representation a variable is associated with each ordered pair of events. Each domain of such a variable is a subset of the set $TEMP$. All constraints are ternary.

More specifically, consider three events, A, B and C and suppose that we know the temporal relations between the pairs A and B, and B and C. The question is what is the temporal relation between A and C. For example if A overlaps B and B is before C, then A is before C. To answer this question we have to examine 169 possibilities. They are represented in a table called *composition table*, given in Figures 2.8 and 2.9. The entry *R-OVERLAP* (an abbreviation for *REAL-OVERLAP*) which appears there three times, is a shorthand for the set of the temporal relations that express the fact that two events 'truly' overlap in time, so the set obtained from *TEMP* by excluding the relations before, after, meets and met-by:

$$REAL\text{-}OVERLAP := TEMP - \{\text{before, after, meets, met-by}\}.$$

Consider now all legally possible triples (t_1, t_2, t_3) of temporal relations such that t_1 is the temporal relation between A and B, t_2 the temporal relation between B and C and t_3 the temporal relation between A and C. The set of these triples forms a subset of $TEMP^3$. Denote it by T_3. The just mentioned table allows us to compute T_3. For example, we already noticed that (overlaps, before, before) $\in T_3$, since A overlaps B and B is before C implies that A is before C. The set T_3 has 409 elements.

By a *disjunctive temporal relation* we mean now a disjunction of temporal relations. For example before $\vee$ meets is a disjunctive temporal relation. The disjunctive temporal relations allow us to model the situations in which the temporal dependencies between the events are only partially known.

Note that each disjunctive temporal relation between the events A and B uniquely determines the disjunctive temporal relation between the event B and A. For example if the former is before $\vee$ meets, then the latter is after $\vee$ met $-$ by. So without loss of information we can confine our attention to disjunctive temporal relations associated with each ordered pair of events.

We can now define the CSPs. Assume n events $e_1, \ldots, e_n$ with $n > 2$. We consider $\frac{(n-1)n}{2}$ domain expressions, each of the form $x_{i,j} \in D_{i,j}$ where $i, j \in [1..n]$ with $i < j$ and $D_{i,j} \subseteq TEMP$. The intention is that the variable $x_{i,j}$ describes the disjunctive temporal relation associated with the events e_i and e_j.

Finally, we define the constraints. Each constraint links an ordered triple of events. So in total we have $\frac{(n-2)(n-1)n}{6}$ constraints. For $i, j, k \in [1..n]$ such that $i < j < k$ we define the constraint $C_{i,j,k}$ by setting

$$C_{i,j,k} := T_3 \cap (D_{i,j} \times D_{j,k} \times D_{i,k}).$$

So $C_{i,j,k}$ describes the possible entries in T_3 determined by the domains of the variables $x_{i,j}, x_{j,k}$ and $x_{i,k}$.

	before	after	meets	met-by	overlaps	overl.-by
before	before	TEMP	before	before meets overlaps starts during	before	before meets overlaps starts during
after	TEMP	after	during finishes after met-by overl.-by	after	during finishes after met-by overl.-by	after
meets	before	after met-by overl.-by started-by contains	before	finishes finished-by equals	before	overlaps starts during
met-by	before overlaps meets contains finished-by	after	starts started-by equals	after	during finishes overl.-by	after
overlaps	before	after met-by overl.-by started-by contains	before	overl.-by started-by contains	before meets overlaps	R-OVERLAP
overl.-by	before meets overlaps contains finished-by	after	overlaps contains finished-by	after	R-OVERLAP	after met-by overl.-by
starts	before	after	before	met-by	before meets overlaps	during finishes overl.-by
started-by	before meets overlaps contains finished-by	after	overlaps contains finished-by	met-by	overlaps contains finished-by	overl.-by
during	before	after	before	after	before meets overlaps starts during	during finishes after met-by overl.-by
contains	before meets overlaps contains finished-by	after met-by overl.-by contains started-by	overlaps contains finished-by	overl.-by started-by contains	overlaps contains finished-by	overl.-by started-by contains
finishes	before	after	meets	after	overlaps starts during	after met-by overl.-by
finished-by	before	after met-by overl.-by started-by contains	meets	overl.-by started-by contains	overlaps	overl.-by started-by contains
equals	before	after	meets	met-by	overlaps	overl.-by

Fig. 2.8. The composition table for the thirteen temporal relations, part 1

This completes the description of the CSPs. Because each constraint is determined by the corresponding triple of variable domains, each such CSP is uniquely determined by its domain expressions. Therefore when defining such CSPs it is sufficient to define the appropriate domain expressions.

Let us return now to the problem we started with. It can be formulated as a CSP as follows. We have five events, M, J, B, S, W. Here M stands for 'the duration of the meeting', J stands for 'the period Jones was present',

	starts	started-by	during	contains	finishes	finished-by	equals
before	before	before	before meets overlaps starts during	before	before meets overlaps starts during	before	before
after	during finishes after met-by overl.-by	after	during finishes after met-by overl.-by	after	after	after	after
meets	meets	meets	overlaps starts during	before	overlaps starts during	before	meets
met-by	during finishes overl.-by	after	during finishes overl.-by	after	met-by	met-by	met-by
overlaps	overlaps	overlaps contains finished-by	overlaps starts during	before meets overlaps contains finished-by	overlaps starts during	before meets overlaps	overlaps
overl.-by	during finishes overl.-by	after met-by overl.-by	during finishes overl.-by	after meets overl.-by started-by contains	overl.-by	overl.-by started-by contains	overl.-by
starts	starts	starts started-by equals	during	before meets overlaps contains finished-by	during	before meets overlaps	starts
started-by	starts started-by equals	started-by	during finishes overl.-by	contains	overl.-by	contains	started-by
during	during	during finishes after met-by overl.-by	during	*TEMP*	during	before meets overlaps starts during	during
contains	overlaps contains finished-by	contains	*R-OVERLAP*	contains	overl.-by contains started-by	contains	contains
finishes	during	after met-by overl.-by	during	after met-by overl.-by started-by contains	finishes	finishes finished-by equals	finishes
finished-by	overlaps	contains	overlaps starts during	contains	finishes finished-by equals	finished-by	finished-by
equals	starts	started-by	during	contains	finishes	finished-by	equals

Fig. 2.9. The composition table for the thirteen temporal relations, part 2

and similarly with the events S (for Smith), B (for Brown) and W (for White). Next, we order the events in some arbitrary way, say

$$J, \ M, \ B, \ S, \ W.$$

We have in total ten variables, each associated with an ordered pair of events.

Analogously as in the first representation we use the relation that two events 'truly' overlap in time. It is now represented by the already introduced set *REAL-OVERLAP* of nine temporal relations.

Then the following domain expressions deal with the presence of each person during the meeting:

$$x_{J,M} \in \{\texttt{overlaps, contains, finished-by}\},$$

$$x_{M,W} \in \{\texttt{overlaps}\},$$

$$x_{M,S} \in REAL\text{-}OVERLAP,$$

and the following domain expressions formalise information concerning the relative presence of the persons in question:

$$x_{J,S} \in \{\texttt{before}\},$$

$$x_{B,S} \in REAL\text{-}OVERLAP,$$

$$x_{B,W} \in REAL\text{-}OVERLAP,$$

$$x_{S,W} \in REAL\text{-}OVERLAP.$$

The domains of the remaining three variables, $x_{J,B}, x_{J,W}$ and $x_{M,B}$, equal to *TEMP*. The final question can then be phrased as a problem whether for some solution to this CSP we have $x_{J,W} \in REAL\text{-}OVERLAP$. In other words, is it true that the above CSP with the domain expression $x_{J,W} \in TEMP$ replaced by

$$x_{J,W} \in REAL\text{-}OVERLAP$$

is consistent.

Note that in both representations we assumed that events 'being present during the meeting' and 'talking' are of positive duration. ◻

Example 2.10 *Qualitative Spatial Reasoning.*

Consider now the following problem illustrated in Figure 2.10.

Two free standing houses are connected by a road. The first house is surrounded by its garden or is adjacent to its boundary while the second house is surrounded by its garden. The question is what can we conclude about the relation between the second garden and the road.

To analyse such problems we need to consider relative positions between contiguous objects. (We assume here for simplicity that each garden also comprises the area underneath a house.) This brings us to the eight possibilities that are summarised in Figure 2.11.

These eight relations are usually called **spatial relations** and their set,

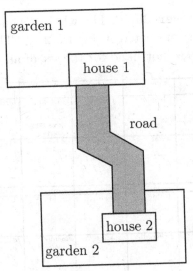

Fig. 2.10. Two houses with a garden and a road

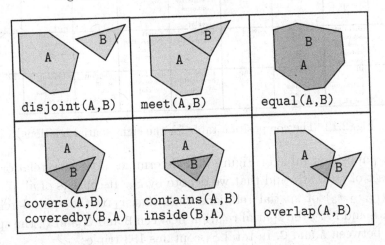

Fig. 2.11. Eight spatial relations

{disjoint,meet,equal,covers,coveredby,contains,inside,overlap},

is denoted by RCC8 (for Region Connection Calculus with 8 relations).

Consider now three contiguous objects, A,B and C and suppose that we know the spatial relations between the pairs A and B, and B and C. The question is what is the spatial relation between A and C. For example if A is inside B and B meets C, then A is disjoint from C. To answer this question we have to examine 64 possibilities. To some of them multiple answers exist. For example, if A is coveredby B and B is coveredby C, then A is either inside C or is coveredby C. The whole dependency table, called the *composition table*, is presented in Figure 2.12. The entry RCC8, which appears three times, is a shorthand for the set of all eight relations.

	disjoint	meet	equal	inside	coveredby	contains	covers	overlap
disjoint	RCC8	disjoint meet inside coveredby overlap	disjoint	disjoint meet inside coveredby overlap	disjoint meet inside coveredby overlap	disjoint	disjoint	disjoint meet inside coveredby overlap
meet	disjoint meet contains covers overlap	disjoint meet equal coveredby covers overlap	meet	inside coveredby overlap	meet inside	disjoint	disjoint meet	disjoint meet inside coveredby overlap
equal	disjoint	meet	equal	inside	coveredby	contains	covers	overlap
inside	disjoint	disjoint	inside	inside	inside	RCC8	disjoint meet inside coveredby overlap	disjoint meet inside coveredby overlap
coveredby	disjoint	disjoint meet	coveredby	inside	inside coveredby	disjoint meet contains covers overlap	disjoint meet equal coveredby covers overlap	disjoint meet overlap coveredby overlap
contains	disjoint meet contains covers overlap	contains covers overlap	contains	equal inside coveredby contains covers overlap	contains covers overlap	contains	contains	contains covers overlap
covers	disjoint meet contains covers overlap	meet contains covers overlap	covers	inside coveredby overlap	equal coveredby covers overlap	contains	contains covers	contains covers overlap
overlap	disjoint meet contains covers overlap	disjoint meet contains covers overlap	overlap	inside coveredby overlap	inside coveredby overlap	disjoint meet contains covers overlap	disjoint meet contains covers overlap	RCC8

Fig. 2.12. The composition table for the eight spatial relations

The composition table of Figure 2.12 determines a ternary relation that is a subset of $(RCC8)^3$ and that we denote by S_3. It consists of all possible triples (r_1, r_2, r_3) of spatial relations such that r_1 is the spatial relation between A and B, r_2 the spatial relation between B and C, and r_3 the spatial relation between A and C. In total S_3 contains 193 triples.

Using the set S_3 we can now formalise our problem by choosing a representation analogous to the second representation of the temporal reasoning of Example 2.9. So in this representation a variable is associated with each ordered pair of objects. The domains of these variables are subsets of the set RCC8. All constraints are ternary and are uniquely determined by the domains. More specifically, each constraint is associated with an ordered triple of objects and equals the set-theoretic intersection of S_3 with the Cartesian product of the corresponding variable domains.

In our example we have five spatial objects, H1 (for house 1), G1 (for garden 1), H2 (for house 2), G2 (for garden 2), and R (for road). We order these objects arbitrarily, for example in the way just mentioned. This leads us to an introduction of ten variables, each associated with an ordered pair of spatial objects. Given two such objects, say A and B, we denote the corresponding variable by $x_{A,B}$. Then the following domain expressions formalise the description of the problem:

- $x_{H1,G1} \in \{\text{inside},\text{coveredby}\}$,
- $x_{H2,G2} \in \{\text{inside}\}$,
- $x_{H1,H2} \in \{\text{disjoint}\}$,
- $x_{H1,R} \in \{\text{meet}\}$,
- $x_{H2,R} \in \{\text{meet}\}$,
- $x_{G1,G2} \in \{\text{disjoint},\text{meet}\}$,
- $x_{H1,G2} \in \{\text{disjoint},\text{meet}\}$,
- $x_{G1,H2} \in \{\text{disjoint},\text{meet}\}$,
- $x_{G1,R} \in \text{RCC8}$,
- $x_{G2,R} \in \text{RCC8}$.

Additionally, we have for each ordered triple A,B,C of the considered objects a constraint $C_{A,B,C}$ on the variables $x_{A,B}, x_{B,C}, x_{A,C}$ with respective domains $D_{A,B}, D_{B,C}, D_{A,C}$ defined by

$$C_{A,B,C} := S_3 \cap (D_{A,B} \times D_{B,C} \times D_{A,C}).$$

Since we have five objects, we have in total ten constraints.

This completes our description of the initial problem as a CSP. Note that in this formalisation we also captured some common sense assumptions that are implicit. For example, we assumed that both houses are disjoint even though this information is not explicitly given. Similarly, we assumed that both gardens are either disjoint or meet. In contrast, we did not assume anything about the relation between the gardens and the road. To solve the problem it suffices to determine the set of values the variable $x_{G2,R}$ can take in all solutions to this CSP. □

Example 2.11 *Analysis of Polyhedral Scenes.*

Consider now two scenes (that is, two dimensional drawings) that represent objects formed by straight edges, given in Figures 2.13 and 2.14.

It is clear that the scene given in Figure 2.13 indeed represents a cube whereas the one given in Figure 2.14 does not correspond to any possible three dimensional object. We are interested here in analysing scenes formed by straight edges and would like to know which scenes admit a three dimensional interpretation, that is correspond to a collection of possible three dimensional objects. Each such object is then a three dimensional *polyhedron*.

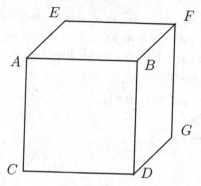

Fig. 2.13. A cube

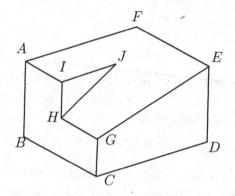

Fig. 2.14. An impossible object

Research on the computer vision carried out in the sixties and the seventies concentrated on finding the rules that could allow us to determine which scenes admit a three dimensional interpretation. This work led to an identification of four types of junctions that can arise in scenes corresponding to possible objects, in which all junctions have either two or three edges:

- the L junction, depicted by:

- the *fork* junction, depicted by:

- the *T* junction, depicted by:

- and the *arrow* junction, depicted by:

In what follows we limit our attention to the scenes that consist of such junctions. To clarify the status of the edges forming a scene, we assign to each of them a label. Each edge results from the intersection of two planes and its label provides information about the relative position of these two planes. We employ the following four labels:

- $+$, to mark the **convex** edges,
- $-$, to mark the **concave** edges,
- the arrows, $\rightarrow$ and $\leftarrow$, to mark the **boundary** edges.

We call here an edge

- **convex** if it takes 270 degrees to rotate one plane onto the other through the part of the space that contains the viewer,
- **concave** if it takes 90 degrees to rotate one plane onto the other through the part of the space that contains the viewer,
- **boundary** if it is formed by two planes one of which is hidden.

To clarify this terminology consider the figure depicted in Figure 2.15. From the point of view of the depicted person the edge at the intersection of the areas A and L is marked by $+$, since it is a convex edge. Indeed, it takes 270 degrees to rotate one area onto the other through the part of the space that contains the depicted person. For the same reason the edges at the intersection of the areas R and B, of L and U, and of R and U are marked by $+$. In contrast, the edge at the intersection of the areas L and R is marked by $-$, since it is a concave edge. Indeed, it takes 90 degrees to rotate one area onto the other through the part of the space that contains the depicted person.

Finally, the outer edges are marked by the arrows, since they are boundary edges. Here and elsewhere the direction of the arrows is chosen in such a way that when following them the scene is on the right-hand side.

In general, the edges do not have to have a unique marking assigned to

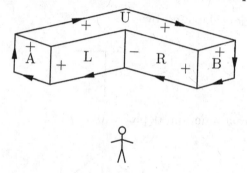

Fig. 2.15. Three types of edges

it. For example, in the scene given in Figure 2.13 the edges AC and AE can be either boundary or concave. The first possibility corresponds to the situation when the cube is 'floating' in the air.

The second possibility corresponds to the situation in which the cube is 'stuck' to a wall on the left-hand side. In this case the edge AC is at the intersection of the plane determined by the square $ABDC$ and the wall and the edge AE is at the intersection of the plane determined by the square $AEFB$ and the wall. So according to the above terminology these two edges are then concave.

Further, the edge AB can be in principle either convex or concave. Namely, if we interpret this scene as a cube then the edge AB is necessarily convex. On the other hand, if we interpret this scene as a part of a box with the bottom $ABDC$ and the sides attached to the edges AE and DG missing, at which we are looking from above, then the edge AB is concave. (Note that the second interpretation does not correspond to any possible object. For instance in this case one *fork* junction connecting C, E and G is missing.)

Clowes [1971] and Huffman [1971] independently found that a scene formed by the already mentioned four types of junctions represents a possible object exactly when its edges can be labeled in such a way that only labeled junctions listed in Figure 2.16 are used. For example, the scene given in Figure 2.13 represents a possible object, namely a cube, and four correct labelings of its edges are presented in Figure 2.17.

In turn, it is possible to check that no such labeling of the edges exists for the scene given in Figure 2.14. In what follows we provide two formalisations of the discussed problem in terms of CSPs.

First representation.

In this representation the variables represent the junctions. So we have four types of variables, depending on the type of a junction: the L variable,

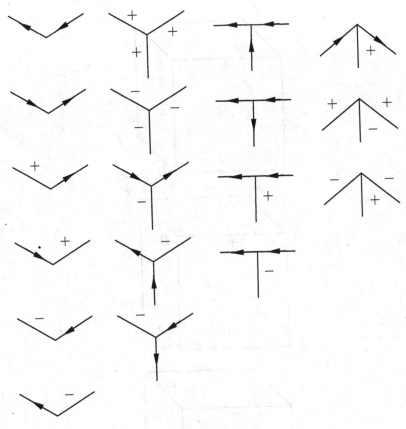

Fig. 2.16. Legal junctions

the *fork* variable, the T variable and the *arrow* variable. The domain of the L variable consists of the six labelings of the L junction given in Figure 2.16, and analogously for the other three variables. To represent these labelings in a textual form we introduce four elements, $+, -, \rightarrow, \leftarrow$, and use the the translation tables from the labeled junctions to a textual form presented in Figures 2.18, 2.19, 2.20, and 2.21.

So the domain of the L variable equals

$$\{(\rightarrow, \leftarrow), (\leftarrow, \rightarrow), (+, \rightarrow), (\leftarrow, +), (-, \leftarrow), (\rightarrow, -)\}.$$

Analogously, the domain of the *fork* variable equals

$$\{(+, +, +), (-, -, -), (\rightarrow, \leftarrow, -), (-, \rightarrow, \leftarrow), (\leftarrow, -, \rightarrow)\},$$

the domain of the T variable equals

$$\{(\rightarrow, \leftarrow, \leftarrow), (\rightarrow, \leftarrow, \rightarrow), (\rightarrow, \leftarrow, +), (\rightarrow, \leftarrow, -)\},$$

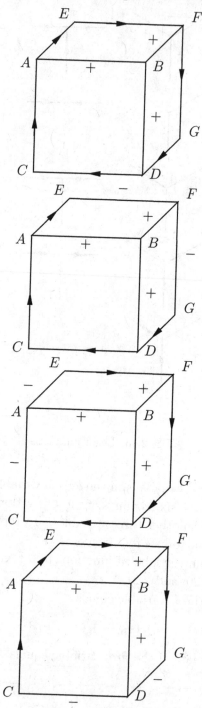

Fig. 2.17. Four correct labelings of a cube

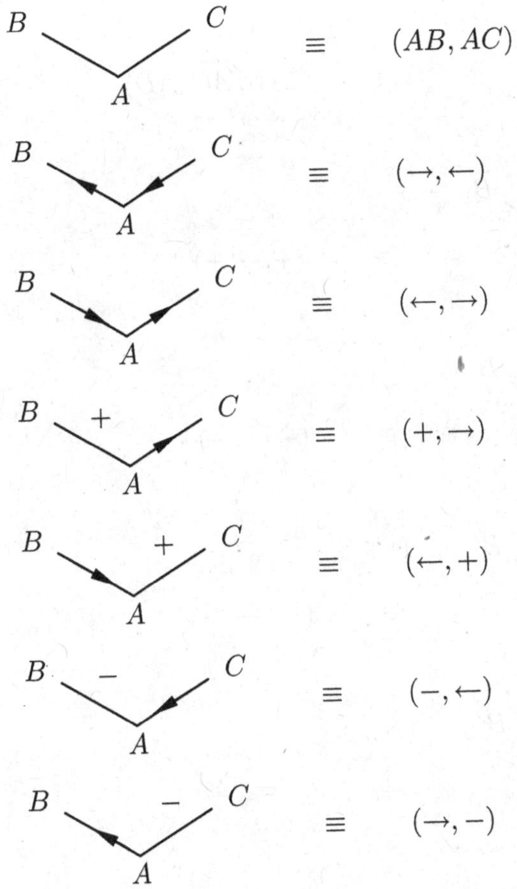

$$B \diagdown\diagup C \quad\equiv\quad (AB, AC)$$
$$A$$

$$B \diagdown\diagup C \quad\equiv\quad (\rightarrow, \leftarrow)$$
$$A$$

$$B \diagdown\diagup C \quad\equiv\quad (\leftarrow, \rightarrow)$$
$$A$$

$$B \overset{+}{\diagdown}\diagup C \quad\equiv\quad (+, \rightarrow)$$
$$A$$

$$B \diagdown\overset{+}{\diagup} C \quad\equiv\quad (\leftarrow, +)$$
$$A$$

$$B \overset{-}{\diagdown}\diagup C \quad\equiv\quad (-, \leftarrow)$$
$$A$$

$$B \diagdown\overset{-}{\diagup} C \quad\equiv\quad (\rightarrow, -)$$
$$A$$

Fig. 2.18. Translation for the L junction

and the domain of the *arrow* variable equals

$$\{(\leftarrow, \rightarrow, +), (+, +, -), (-, -, +)\}.$$

The constraints capture the information that the junctions share the edges. For example, in the scene given in Figure 2.13 the junctions A and B share the edge AB. This limits the possible values used for the junctions A and B in a similar way as the intersection of two words limited the possible values in the crossword puzzle of Example 2.8. The difference is that an intersection, here represented by an edge, is oriented.

For example, for the junction A the edge AE is used (as the second argument), while for the junction E the edge EA is used (also as the second argument). So if the edge AE of the junction A is labeled by $+$, then so is the edge EA of the junction E, and analogously for $-$. However, if the

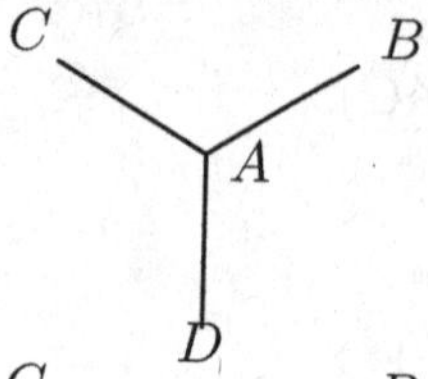

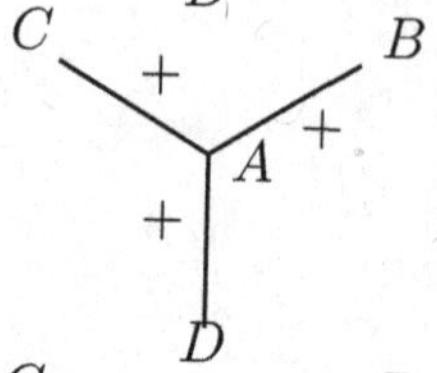

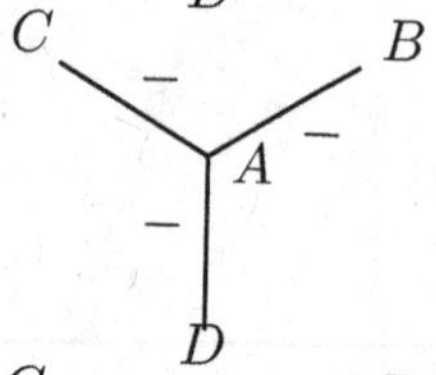

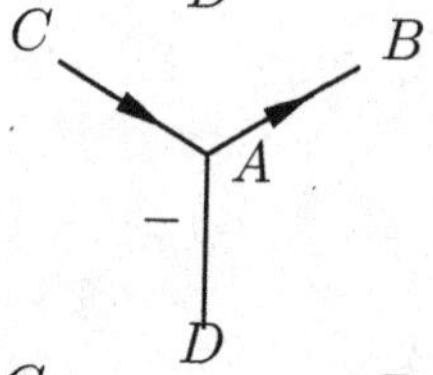

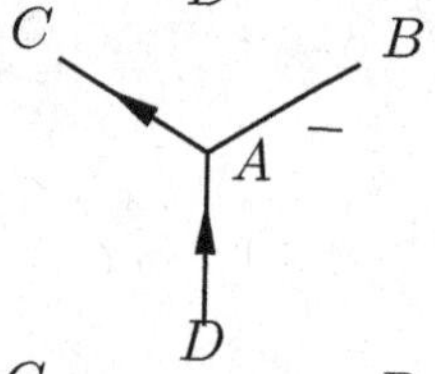

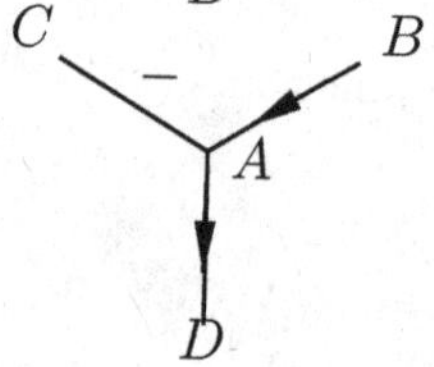

Fig. 2.19. Translation for the *fork* junction

edge AE is labeled by $\rightarrow$, then the edge EA is labeled by $\leftarrow$, and analogously for $\leftarrow$. After taking this fact into account one can easily check that the corresponding constraint C_{AE} on the junctions A and E consists of the following set of four pairs:

$$C_{AE} := \{((\leftarrow, \rightarrow, +), (\rightarrow, \leftarrow)), ((\leftarrow, \rightarrow, +), (-, \leftarrow)),$$
$$((+, +, -), (\leftarrow, +)), ((-, -, +), (\rightarrow, -))\}.$$

Each pair, for example $((\leftarrow, \rightarrow, +), (-, \leftarrow))$, represents a legal labeling

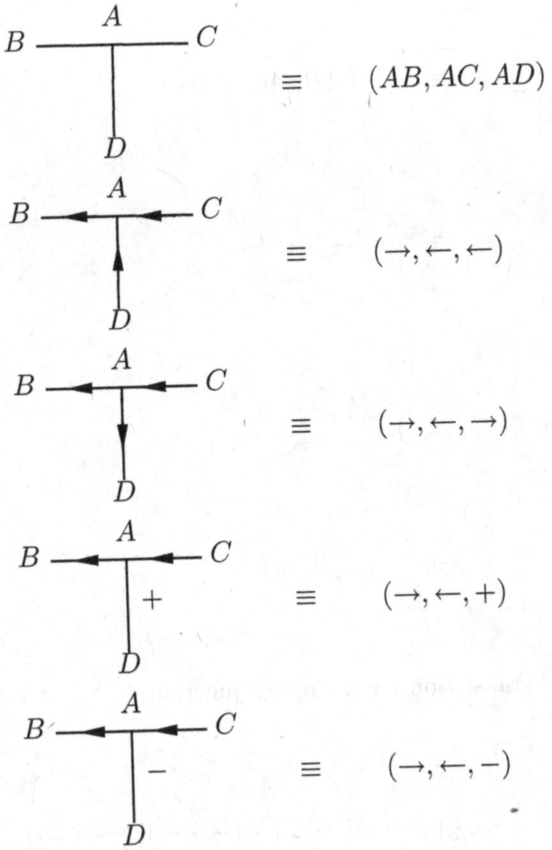

$$B \;\underset{\quad A \quad}{\rule{3cm}{0.4pt}}\; C \;\downarrow D \quad\equiv\quad (AB, AC, AD)$$

$$\equiv \quad (\rightarrow, \leftarrow, \leftarrow)$$

$$\equiv \quad (\rightarrow, \leftarrow, \rightarrow)$$

$$\equiv \quad (\rightarrow, \leftarrow, +)$$

$$\equiv \quad (\rightarrow, \leftarrow, -)$$

Fig. 2.20. Translation for the T junction

of the edges of the junctions A and E. In general, each edge contributes one, binary, constraint. So the scene given in Figure 2.13 is formalised by a CSP that consists of nine constraints, while the scene given in Figure 2.14 is formalised by a CSP that consists of thirteen constraints.

Each solution to such a CSP determines the labels assigned to each edge. The choice of the variable domains and of the constraints ensures that all junctions are labeled in a legal way, that is, they are all drawn from Figure 2.16.

Second representation.

In this representation the variables represent the edges. The domain of each variable equals $\{+, -, \rightarrow, \leftarrow\}$, the set of the used labels. In turn, the constraints represent the junctions. So we have four type of constraints: L, *fork*, T, and *arrow*, each defined by the corresponding listing in Figure 2.16.

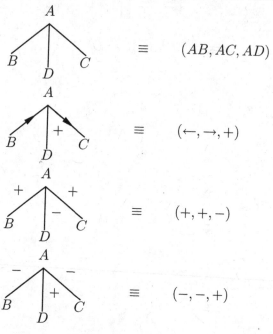

Fig. 2.21. Translation for the *arrow* junction

For instance we have

$$L := \{(\rightarrow, \leftarrow), (\leftarrow, \rightarrow), (+, \rightarrow), (\leftarrow, +), (-, \leftarrow), (\rightarrow, -)\}.$$

Each scene is formalised by means of the constraints representing its junctions. For example, the scene given in Figure 2.13 is formalised by the following seven constraints, where for each constraint we write explicitly which edges and in what order are used:

   $arrow(AC, AE, AB),$
   $fork(BA, BF, BD),$
   $L(CA, CD),$
   $arrow(DG, DC, DB),$
   $L(EF, EA),$
   $arrow(FE, FG, FB),$
   $L(GD, GF).$

So $arrow(AC, AE, AB)$ denotes the fact that we view the junction A as the *arrow* constraint over the variables AC, AE and AB, and analogously with the other six junctions. To complete the formalisation, as in the case of the first representation, we need to relate each edge with its reverse, for example in the case of Figure 2.13 the edge AE with the edge EA.

This is needed because if an edge, say AE of Figure 2.13, is labeled by $\rightarrow$, then it enters the constraint $arrow(AC, AE, AB)$ as $\rightarrow$ and the constraint $L(EF, EA)$ as $\leftarrow$ (in EA), and similarly for the labeling with $\leftarrow$. To this end we use one binary constraint, *edge*, that captures the complementary character of the values $\rightarrow$ and $\leftarrow$. It is defined by

$$edge := \{(+, +), (-, -), (\rightarrow, \leftarrow), (\leftarrow, \rightarrow)\}.$$

We now augment the representation of each scene by the *edge* constraints for all pairs of edges that are reverse of each other. In the case of the scene of Figure 2.13 we augment the already listed seven constraints by the following nine constraints:

$edge(AB, BA)$,
$edge(AC, CA)$,
$edge(CD, DC)$,
$edge(BD, DB)$,
$edge(AE, EA)$,
$edge(EF, FE)$,
$edge(BF, FB)$,
$edge(FG, GF)$,
$edge(DG, GD)$.

So in this representation both binary and ternary constraints are used. The binary constraints are the *edge* and the L constraints, while the ternary constraints are the *fork* and the *arrow* constraints. As in the first representation, each solution to the CSP that formalises a considered scene provides a consistent labeling of the scene edges, in the sense that all labeled junctions are drawn from Figure 2.16. $\square$

2.6 Constrained optimization problems

The general task of constrained optimization is to find optimal solutions to a set of constraints subject to some objective function *obj*. More precisely, consider a CSP $\mathcal{P} := \langle \mathcal{C} ; x_1 \in D_1, \ldots, x_n \in D_n \rangle$ together with a function

$$obj : Sol \rightarrow \mathcal{R}$$

from the set *Sol* of all solutions to $\mathcal{P}$ to the set $\mathcal{R}$ of real numbers. (Usually the *obj* function is defined on all sequences $d \in D_1 \times \cdots \times D_n$ but this assumption is not needed here.) We are interested in finding a solution d to $\mathcal{P}$ for which the value $obj(d)$ is optimal. Without loss of generality we assume that 'optimal' means 'maximal'. We call then the pair $(\mathcal{P}, obj)$ a *constrained optimization problem*. The area of constrained optimization is huge and several books were written on this subject. Here we limit ourselves to a presentation of three examples, the first being a classic example of an NP-complete problem.

Example 2.12 *The Knapsack Problem.*

We are given n objects, each with a volume and a value, and a knapsack of a fixed volume. The problem is to find a collection of the objects with maximal total value that fits in the knapsack. More formally, we have n objects with volumes $a_1, ..., a_n$ and values $b_1, ..., b_n$ and the knapsack volume v. Further, we have n variables, $x_1, ..., x_n$, each with the domain $\{0, 1\}$. The inclusion of the object i in a collection is modelled by setting the value of x_i to 1. The requirement that the collection fits in the knapsack translates to the constraint

$$\sum_{i=1}^{n} a_i \cdot x_i \leq v$$

on the variables $x_1, ..., x_n$. We seek a solution to this constraint for which the sum

$$\sum_{i=1}^{n} b_i \cdot x_i$$

is maximal. That is, the sum $\sum_{i=1}^{n} b_i \cdot x_i$ is the objective function.   □

Example 2.13 *A Coins Problem.*

Consider the following problem.

What is the minimum number of coins that allows one to pay *exactly* any amount smaller than one euro? Recall that there are six different euro cent coins, of denomination 1, 2, 5, 10, 20, 50.

We formulate it as a constrained optimization problem. To this end we first determine the variables and their domains. Since the question refers to the number of coins, it is natural to adopt the variables that represent the selected amounts of each coin. This brings us to six variables that we denote by $x_1, x_2, x_5, x_{10}, x_{20}, x_{50}$. The idea is that each variable x_i denotes the selected amount of coins of denomination i. Since we need to be able to pay exactly any amount up to and including 99 euro cents, we end up with the following domain expressions:

$$x_1 \in [0..99], x_2 \in [0..49], x_5 \in [0..19], x_{10} \in [0..9], x_{20} \in [0..4], x_{50} \in [0..1].$$

Next, we state the appropriate constraints. Given $i \in [1..99]$ we formulate a constraint stating that the amount of i euro cents can be paid exactly using the selected coins. To this end we use existentially quantified variables that range over integer intervals:

$$\exists i_1 \in [0..x_1] \; \exists i_2 \in [0..x_2] \; \exists i_5 \in [0..x_5] \; \exists i_{10} \in [0..x_{10}]$$

$$\exists i_{20} \in [0..x_{20}] \; \exists i_{50} \in [0..x_{50}] \; i_1 + 2i_2 + 5i_5 + 10i_{10} + 20i_{20} + 50i_{50} = i.$$

So we use in total 99 constraints. Clearly, for each solution to the just formulated CSP the sum

$$x_1 + x_2 + x_5 + x_{10} + x_{20} + x_{50}$$

represents the total amount of coins that we would like to minimise. Since in our setup we seek solutions with a maximal value of the objective function, we use

$$-(x_1 + x_2 + x_5 + x_{10} + x_{20} + x_{50})$$

as the objective function.

A drawback of the proposed representation of the problem is that the constraints involve existentially quantified variables. Such constraints are difficult to manipulate and to reason about. So we now provide a different representation that involves simpler constraints.

In addition to the already considered variables $x_1, x_2, x_5, x_{10}, x_{20}, x_{50}$ we introduce for each $i \in [1..99]$ six variables $x_1^i, x_2^i, x_5^i, x_{10}^i, x_{20}^i, x_{50}^i$ with respectively the same domains as $x_1, x_2, x_5, x_{10}, x_{20}$ and x_{50}. So we now have 600 variables instead of six. However, the constraints become considerably simpler. Namely, for each $i \in [1..99]$ we use the following constraint:

$$x_1^i + 2x_2^i + 5x_5^i + 10x_{10}^i + 20x_{20}^i + 50x_{50}^i = i$$

that states that the amount of i euro cents can be paid using x_1^i coins of 1 euro cent, x_2^i coins of 2 euro cents, x_5^i coins of 5 euro cents, x_{10}^i coins of 10 euro cents, x_{20}^i coins of 20 euro cents and x_{50}^i coins of 50 euro cents.

Additionally, we add the constraints stating that for each $i \in [1..99]$ the amounts x_j^i are respectively smaller than x_j. More precisely, for each $i, \in [1..99]$ and $j \in \{1, 2, 5, 10, 20, 50\}$ we use the following constraint:

$$x_j^i \le x_j.$$

These 594 inequality constraints ensure that each amount of i euro cents can also be paid using the collection represented by the x_j variables. Finally, we use the same objective function as in the previous representation.

For the interested reader: the answer is eight coins and the respective amounts of coins of denomination 1, 2, 5, 10, 20, 50 in such a combination are 1, 2, 1, 1, 2, 1.   □

Example 2.14 *Golomb Ruler.*

A **Golomb ruler with m marks** is an ordered sequence of m natural numbers such that the distance between any two elements in this sequence is unique. The largest element of a Golomb ruler is called its **length**. An **optimum Golomb ruler with m marks** is a Golomb ruler with m marks with a minimal length. For example

$$0, 1, 4, 9, 11$$

is a Golomb ruler with 5 marks. Indeed, the distances between the elements in this sequences are:

- for the elements one apart: 1, 3, 5, 2,
- for the elements two apart: 4, 8, 7,
- for the elements three apart: 9, 10,
- for the elements four apart: 11,

and all these values are different. One can show that 0,1,4,9,11 is in fact an optimum Golomb ruler with 5 marks with another one being 0,3,4,9,11.

To represent the problem of finding an optimum Golomb ruler with m marks as a constrained optimization problem we use the following terminology. We call two numbers i, j such that $1 \leq i < j \leq m$ a *pair*. We say that the pairs i, j and k, l are *different* if $i \neq k$ or $j \neq l$ and *disjoint* if $i \neq k$ and $j \neq l$.

We then use m variables, $x_1, \ldots, x_m$, each with the domain $\mathcal{N}$, and adopt the following constraints:

- $x_i < x_{i+1}$ for $i \in [1..m-1]$,
- $x_j - x_i \neq x_l - x_k$ for all different pairs i, j and k, l.

As the objective function we choose simply $-x_m$. Then the task of maximising $-x_m$ is equivalent to the task of of minimising x_m.

A better representation is obtained by noting that for $i, k < j$ if $x_i \neq x_k$, then $x_j - x_i \neq x_j - x_k$, and for $i < j, l$ if $x_j \neq x_l$, then $x_j - x_i \neq x_l - x_i$. This observation allows us to replace the second set of constraints by a smaller one:

- $x_j - x_i \neq x_l - x_k$ for all disjoint pairs i, j and k, l.

Yet another representation is obtained by introducing auxiliary variables that represent the differences between the elements in the sequence $x_1, \ldots, x_m$ and by using disequality constraints between these auxiliary variables. So for each pair i, j we introduce a variable $z_{i,j}$ ranging over positive natural numbers and adopt the following constraints:

- $z_{i,j} = x_j - x_i$ for each pair i, j,
- $z_{i,j} \neq z_{k,l}$ for all different pairs i, j and k, l.

As above we can safely replace here 'different' by 'disjoint'. Also we can replace the disequality constraints by a single **all_different** constraint on the variables $z_{i,j}$.

Golomb rulers play an important role in radio communication, x-ray crystallography, coding theory, radio astronomy and optical communication. The largest known optimum Golomb ruler has 21 marks and is of length 333. □

2.7 Summary

The aim of this chapter was to discuss various examples of constraint satisfaction problems (CSPs). First we defined precisely the notions of a constraint and of a CSP. Then we presented examples of CSPs classified according to the domains used. We discussed in turn problems that can be formalised as CSPs with variables ranging over

- integers,
- reals,
- the interval $[0..1]$ representing the Boolean values **false, true,**
- symbolic domains, i.e., non-numeric domains.

We also considered constrained optimization problems in which we are interested in finding an optimal solution to a CSP according to some criterion.

Several examples discussed here are most useful in explaining the techniques of constraint programming. More specifically, using the *SEND + MORE = MONEY* puzzle of Example 2.1 we can clarify in a natural way the effect of constraint propagation. We shall return to it in Chapter 6. In turn, the n Queens Problem of Example 2.2 is an excellent vehicle to explain various forms of search. We shall return to it in Chapter 8. Finally, the Zebra puzzle of Example 2.3 will allow us to discuss in Chapter 9 the impact of various ways of modeling a problem.

Next, the problem of finding zeros of polynomials discussed in Example 2.5 is a typical problem dealt with by techniques considered at the end of Chapter 6. The crossword puzzle of Example 2.8 will allow us in Chapter 5 to illustrate the notion of arc consistency. Finally, Golomb rulers discussed in Example 2.14 show how a simple problem can admit several natural formulations as a CSP.

When presenting these examples we stressed the fact that each problem can be formalised as a CSP in a number of different ways. In general, it is difficult to find which representation is better and good insights into the principles of constraint programming are of help. We shall return to this matter in Chapter 9. When discussing various alternative representations of a problem as a CSP we focused here on simple examples. Less contrived examples will be mentioned at the end of the book, in Chapter 9.

2.8 Exercises

Exercise 2.1 Consider the following multiplication problem:

```
    P P P
      P P
  ---------
    P P P P
  P P P P
  ---------
  P P P P P
```

where each P stands for a (possibly different) prime digit (so 2, 3, 5 or 7). Formulate this problem as a CSP.

For your information: this problem has a unique solution, namely:

```
    7 7 5
      3 3
  ---------
    2 3 2 5
  2 3 2 5
  ---------
  2 5 5 7 5
```

Exercise 2.2 Consider the following puzzle.

Ten cells numbered 0,..,9 inscribe a 10-digit number such that each cell, say i, indicates the total number of occurrences of the digit i in this number. Find this number.

For your information: the answer is 6210001000. Indeed, cell 0 is filled with 6 and there are 6 zeros in this number, etc.

Formulate this problem as a CSP problem.

Exercise 2.3 *Magic Squares.*

A **magic square of order** n is defined to be an $n \times n$ matrix made out of the integers from $[1..n^2]$ arranged in such a way that the sum of every row, column, and the two main diagonals is the same. For example

```
 1 15 24  8 17
23  7 16  5 14
20  4 13 22  6
12 21 10 19  3
 9 18  2 11 25
```

is a magic square of order 5, because each row, column and main diagonal sums up to 65. Formulate the problem of finding a magic square of order n as a task of finding a solution to a CSP.

Exercise 2.4 *Latin Squares.*

A **Latin square of order** n is defined to be an $n \times n$ matrix made out of the integers in $[1..n]$ with the property that each of the these n integers occurs exactly once in each row and exactly once in each column of the array. For example

```
1 2 3 4 5
2 3 4 5 1
3 4 5 1 2
4 5 1 2 3
5 1 2 3 4
```

is a Latin square of order 5. Formulate the problem of finding a Latin square of order n as a CSP.

Exercise 2.5 *The Graph Colouring Problem.*

Consider the task of assigning to each node of a finite graph a colour in such a way that no two adjacent nodes have the same colour. Such an assignment is called a **colouring** of the graph. A colouring of the graph involving the minimal number of colours is called the **chromatic number** of the graph. The problem of finding the chromatic number of a graph has several applications, in particular in the fields of scheduling and compiler optimization.

Formulate this problem as a constrained optimization problem.

Exercise 2.6 *The Frequency Assignment Problem.*

Given is a set of n **cells**, $C := \{c_1, c_2, \ldots, c_n\}$ and a set of m **frequencies** (or **channels**) $F := \{f_1, f_2, \ldots, f_m\}$. An **assignment** is a function which associates with each cell c_i a frequency $x_i \in F$. The problem consists in finding an assignment that satisfies the following constraints:

Separations: Given h and k we call the value $d(f_h, f_k) = |h - k|$ the **distance** between two channels f_h and f_k. (The assumption is that consecutive frequencies lie one unit apart.) Given is an $n \times n$ non-negative integer symmetric matrix S, called a **separation matrix**, such that each s_{ij} represents the minimum distance between the frequencies assigned to the cells c_i and c_j. That is, for all $i \in [1..n]$ and $j \in [1..n]$ it holds that $d(x_i, x_j) \geq s_{ij}$.

Illegal channels: Given is an $n \times m$ Boolean matrix F such that if $F_{ij} = true$, then the frequency f_j cannot be assigned to the cell i, i.e., $x_i \neq f_j$.

Separation constraints prevent interference between cells that are located geographically close and that broadcast in each other's area of service. Illegal channels account for channels reserved for external uses (e.g., for military bases). Formalise this problem as a CSP.

Exercise 2.7 Consider the following variant of the Eight Queens Problem. One is asked for a given integer k to place on the (8×8) chess board a maximum number of queens so that each of them attacks exactly k other queens. Formulate this problem as a constrained optimization problem. *Hint.* See the alternative formalisation of the n Queens Problem given in Example 2.7.

Exercise 2.8 *Peaceable Coexisting Armies of Queens.*

Two armies of queens (black and white) peacefully coexist on a chessboard when they are placed upon the board in such a way that no two queens from opposing armies can attack each other. The problem is to find the maximum two equal-sized armies. Formulate this problem as a constrained optimization problem.

Exercise 2.9 Formulate the following problem as a constrained optimization problem:

Place a minimum number of queens on the chess board so that each unoccupied field comes under attack.

2.9 Bibliographic remarks

Most of the CSPs discussed in this chapter are classics in the field. In particular, the representation of the *SEND + MORE = MONEY* and the *Zebra* puzzles and of the eight queens problem as a CSP is discussed in Van Hentenryck [1989]. The *SEND + MORE = MONEY* puzzle is due to H.E. Dudeney and appeared in England, in the July 1924 issue of Strand Magazine. Other well-known examples of alphametic problems with unique solutions include *GERALD + DONALD = ROBERT*, in French *LIONNE + TIGRE = TIGRON*, and in German *WEIN + WEIB = LIEBE*. The website http://users.aol.com/s6sj7gt/mikealp.htm created by Mike Keith includes several jewels of alphametic problems with unique solutions, of his creation, such as *ATTRACTIONS + INTENTIONS = REGENERATION*. Several other alphametic problems with unique solutions, created by Jorge A.C.B. Soares, can be found at his website http://www.geocities.com/Athens/Agora/2160/puzzles.html#ALPHAMET.

According to Russell and Norvig [2003] the eight queens problem was originally published anonymously in the German chess magazine *Schach* in 1848 and its generalisation to the n queens problem in Netto [1901]. Falkowski and Schmitz [1986] show how to construct a solution to this problem for arbitrary $n > 3$. The website http://www.wi.leidenuniv.nl/~kosters/nqueens.html created by Walter Kosters contains a bibliography related to the n Queens Problem.

The representation of spreadsheets as CSPs is taken from Winston [1992] and the crossword puzzle discussed in Example 2.8 is from Mackworth [1992]. The thirteen temporal relations presented in Figure 2.7 and the ensuing temporal CSPs were introduced in Allen [1983]. In this paper the first representation discussed in Example 2.9 is used, while the second one is used in van Beek [1992]. Allen [1983] is one of the most often cited papers in computer science. It stimulated a huge amount of research on qualitative temporal reasoning. For a survey of this subject from the point of view of constraint satisfaction see Schwalb and Vila [1998].

The eight spatial relations presented in Figure 2.11 and the composition table given in Figure 2.12 were introduced in Egenhofer [1991] and, independently, in Randell, Cohn and Cui [1992]. In Egenhofer [1994a] these relations were systematically derived and in Egenhofer [1994b] a connection with the CSPs was made explicit. For a recent survey of qualitative spatial reasoning see Cohn and Hazarika [2001].

Waltz [1975] was the first to realize that an analysis of the polyhedral scenes can be formalised as the task of solving CSPs. Winston [1992] provides a readable account and outlines a proof that the eighteen labelings of the junctions listed in Figure 2.16 are the only possible ones. Figures 2.14, 2.15 and 2.16 are taken from this book.

The second representation used in Example 2.11 is based on By [1997] who noted the need for the *edge* constraints. Golomb rulers discussed in Example 2.14 are named after Solomon W. Golomb. An interested reader can consult Dollas, Rankin and McCracken [1998] for more detailed information about their history, applications and for a presentation of algorithms used to generate Golomb rulers and verify their optimum. An account of various representations of Golomb rulers as CSPs is from Smith, Stergiou and Walsh [2000] where also encodings of the problem using binary constraints are studied. Bacchus and van Beek [1998] discuss the tradeoffs involved in the conversion of arbitrary CSPs to CSPs with unary and binary constraints only and provide pointers to the earlier literature on this subject.

The puzzle from Exercise 2.2 is taken from Gardner [1979]. The Frequency Assignment problem from Exercise 2.6 is from Hale [1980]. The variant of the Eight Queens Problem from Exercise 2.7 is due to Scott Kim and is discussed in Gardner [1997,pages 275-282]. The problem of the peaceable coexisting armies of queens discussed in Exercise 2.8 is from Bosch [1999]. We learned of it from Smith, Petrie and Gent [2002]. The Coins Problem from Example 2.13 is discussed and solved in Wallace, Novello and Schimpf [1997].

2.10 References

J. F. ALLEN
   [1983]   Maintaining knowledge about temporal intervals, *Communications of ACM*, 26, pp. 832–843.

F. BACCHUS AND P. VAN BEEK
   [1998]   On the conversion between non-binary and binary constraint satisfaction problems, in: *AAAI-98: Proceedings of the 15th National Conference on Artificial Intelligence*, AAAI Press, Menlo Park.

R. BOSCH
   [1999]   Peaceably coexisting armies of queens, *OPTIMA (Newsletter of the Mathematical Programming Society)*, 62, pp. 6–9.

T. BY
   [1997]   *Line Labelling by Meta-programming*, Tech. Rep. CS-97-07, University of Sheffield.

M. B. CLOWES
   [1971]   On seeing things, *Artificial Intelligence*, 2, pp. 79–116.

A. G. COHN AND S. M. HAZARIKA
   [2001]   Qualitative spatial representation and reasoning: an overview, *Fundamenta Informaticae*, 46, pp. 1–29.

A. DOLLAS, W. T. RANKIN, AND D. MCCRACKEN
   [1998]   A new algorithm for Golomb ruler derivation and proof of the 19 mark rule, *IEEE Transactions on Information Theory*, pp. 379–382.

M. EGENHOFER
  [1991] Reasoning about binary topological relations, in: *Proceedings of the 2nd International Symposium on Large Spatial Databases (SSD)*, O. Günther and H.-J. Schek, eds., vol. 525 of Lecture Notes in Computer Science, Springer-Verlag, pp. 143–160.
  [1994a] Deriving the composition of binary topological relations, *Journal of Visual Languages and Computing*, 5, pp. 133–149.
  [1994b] Pre-processing queries with spatial constraints, *Photogrammetric Engineering & Remote Sensing*, 60, pp. 783–790.

B.-J. FALKOWSKI AND L. SCHMITZ
  [1986] A note on the queens' problem, *Information Processing Letters*, 23, pp. 39–46.

M. GARDNER
  [1979] *Mathematical Circus*, Knopf.
  [1997] *The Last Recreations: Hydras, Eggs, and Other Mathematical Mystifications*, Copernicus Books.

W. K. HALE
  [1980] Frequency assignment: theory and applications, in: *Proceedings of the IEEE Transactions on Vehicular Technology*, vol. 68, pp. 1497–1514.

D. HUFFMAN
  [1971] Impossible objects as nonsense sentences, in: *Machine Intelligence 6*, B. Meltzer and D. Mitchie, eds., pp. 295–323.

A. MACKWORTH
  [1992] Constraint satisfaction, in: *Encyclopedia of Artificial Intelligence*, S. C. Shapiro, ed., John Wiley and Sons, pp. 285–293. Volume 1.

E. NETTO
  [1901] *Lehrbuch der Combinatorik*, Teubner, Stuttgart.

D. A. RANDELL, A. G. COHN, AND Z. CUI
  [1992] Computing transitivity tables: A challenge for automated theorem provers, in: *Proceedings CADE 11*, Springer, Berlin.

S. RUSSELL AND P. NORVIG
  [2003] *Artifical Intelligence: A Modern Approach*, Prentice-Hall, Englewood Cliffs, NJ, second ed.

E. SCHWALB AND L. VILA
  [1998] Temporal constraints: a survey, *Constraints*, 3, pp. 129–149.

B. M. SMITH, K. E. PETRIE, AND I. P. GENT
  [2002] Models and symmetry breaking. presented at the ECAI 2002 workshop W9 Modelling and Solving Problems with Constraints. available via http://4c.ucc.ie/~tw/ecai02/smith.ps.

B. M. SMITH, K. STERGIOU, AND T. WALSH
  [2000] Using auxiliary variables and implied constraints to model non-binary problems, in: *AAAI-00: Proceedings National Conference on Artificial Intelligence*, pp. 182–187.

P. VAN BEEK
  [1992] Reasoning about qualitative temporal information, *Artificial Intelligence*, 58, pp. 297–326.

P. VAN HENTENRYCK
  [1989] *Constraint Satisfaction in Logic Programming*, The MIT Press.

M. WALLACE, S. NOVELLO, AND J. SCHIMPF
  [1997] *ECL^{i}PS^e: A Platform for Constraint Logic Programming*, tech. rep., IC-Parc, Imperial College, London. Available via http://www.icparc.ic.ac.uk/eclipse/reports/index.html.

D. L. WALTZ
  [1975] Generating semantic descriptions from drawings of scenes with shadows, in: *The Psychology of Computer Vision*, P. H. Winston, ed., McGraw Hill, pp. 19–91.

P. H. WINSTON
  [1992] *Artificial Intelligence*, Addison-Wesley, third ed.

3

Constraint programming in a nutshell

A T THIS STAGE it is useful to get a better feeling of what constraint programming is about. Recall that we stated in Chapter 1 that in constraint programming the programming process is limited to a generation of constraints and a solution of these constraints by means of domain specific or general methods. The aim of this chapter is to provide an intuitive introduction to these methods. In the subsequent chapters we shall discuss them in a more detailed and precise way.

To discuss these techniques it is useful to formalise appropriate notions of equivalence between CSPs. We do this in Section 3.1. Then we describe in Section 3.2 a general framework which allows us to explain the basics of constraints programming. It involves various procedures that capture specific aspects of constraint programming. Subsequently we illustrate these procedures by means of two extended examples. In Section 3.3 we consider the Boolean CSPs and in Section 3.4 constrained optimization problems involving the polynomial constraints on integer intervals.

3.1 Equivalence of CSPs

We mentioned already in Chapter 1 that we view constraint programming as a process of transforming the CSPs. To describe this process closer it is useful to formalise a number of notions concerning CSPs.

First, recall that a constraint C on a sequence of variables $y_1, \ldots, y_k$ with respective domains $D_1, \ldots, D_k$ associated with them is a subset of $D_1 \times \cdots \times D_k$. If C equals $D_1 \times \cdots \times D_k$ and is non-empty, then we say that C is **solved**. We assumed in these definitions that $k > 0$. In the boundary case when $k = 0$ we admit two constraints, denoted by $\top$ and $\bot$, that respectively stand for the **true constraint** (for example $0 = 0$) and the **false constraint** (for example $0 = 1$).

We call a CSP **solved** if all its constraints are solved and no domain of it is empty, and **failed** if it either contains the false constraint $\bot$ or some of its domains or constraints is empty. Clearly, each solved CSP is consistent and each failed CSP is inconsistent. It is useful to note that given a CSP

$$\langle \mathcal{C} \; ; \; x_1 \in D_1, \ldots, x_n \in D_n \rangle$$

each solution $(d_1, \ldots, d_n)$ to it corresponds to a unique solved CSP. This solved CSP is of the form

$$\langle \mathcal{C}' \; ; \; x_1 \in \{d_1\}, \ldots, x_n \in \{d_n\} \rangle,$$

where $\mathcal{C}' = \{C' \mid C \in \mathcal{C}\}$ and where for each constraint C in $\mathcal{C}$ on a subsequence $x_{i_1}, \ldots, x_{i_m}$ of $x_1, \ldots, x_n$ the constraint C' is defined by $C' := \{(d_{i_1}, \ldots, d_{i_m})\}$. So each constraint in $\mathcal{C}'$ is a singleton set.

To solve CSPs one often transforms them in a specific way until a solution, respectively all solutions, have been found or it is clear that no solution exists. The 'final' CSPs generated in this process are then either solved or failed. If a final CSP is solved, it yields one solution in case all domains are singleton sets, or more solutions in case some domain has more than one element. If a final CSP is failed, it yields no solution. The transformations of CSPs need to be such that their equivalence in an appropriate sense is preserved. This brings us to the notion of an equivalence of CSPs. We define it first for a special case.

Consider two CSPs $\mathcal{P}_1$ and $\mathcal{P}_2$ with the same sequence of variables. We say that $\mathcal{P}_1$ and $\mathcal{P}_2$ are **equivalent** if they have the same set of solutions. For example, the CSPs

$$\langle 3x - 5y = 4 \; ; \; x \in [0..9], y \in [1..8] \rangle$$

and

$$\langle 3x - 5y = 4 \; ; \; x \in [3..8], y \in [1..4] \rangle$$

are equivalent, since both of them have $x = 3, y = 1$ and $x = 8, y = 4$ as the only solutions.

In general, since we use some language to describe the constraints, it may be difficult to establish that two CSPs are equivalent. For example, it is not easy to see that the CSP

$$\langle x^4 - 10x^3 + 35x^2 - 50x + 24 = 0 \; ; \; x \in \mathcal{R} \rangle$$

is equivalent to the CSP

$$\langle \; ; \; x \in \{1, 2, 3, 4\} \rangle$$

in which no constraints are present and the domain of x consists of just four values. Fortunately, we shall use the above notion in much more elementary situations in which it will be straightforward to check that the considered CSPs are equivalent.

The above definition is rather limited as it cannot be used to compare CSPs with different sequences of variables. Such situations often arise, for example when new variables are introduced or some variables are eliminated. Consider for instance the problem of solving the equation

$$2x^5 - 5x^4 + 5 = 0 \tag{3.1}$$

over the reals. One way to proceed is by introducing a new variable y and transforming (3.1) to the following two equations:

$$2x^5 - y + 5 = 0, \tag{3.2}$$

$$y = 5x^4, \tag{3.3}$$

so that in each equation every variable occurs at most once.

Now, the CSP formed by the equations (3.2) and (3.3) has one variable more than the one formed by (3.1), so we cannot claim that these two CSPs are equivalent in the sense of the definition just introduced. To deal with such situations we introduce a more general notion of equivalence.

Definition 3.1 Consider two CSPs $\mathcal{P}_1$ and $\mathcal{P}_2$ and a sequence X of their common variables (that is, X is a subsequence of both X_1 and X_2, where X_1 and X_2 are respectively the sequences of the variables of $\mathcal{P}_1$ and $\mathcal{P}_2$). We say that $\mathcal{P}_1$ and $\mathcal{P}_2$ are *equivalent w.r.t.* X if

- for every solution d to $\mathcal{P}_1$ a solution to $\mathcal{P}_2$ exists that coincides with d on the variables in X,
- for every solution e to $\mathcal{P}_2$ a solution to $\mathcal{P}_1$ exists that coincides with e on the variables in X. $\square$

For a further discussion it is useful to introduce the following simple notion.

Definition 3.2 Consider a sequence of variables $X := x_1, \ldots, x_n$ with the corresponding sequence of domains $D_1, \ldots, D_n$. Take an element $d := (d_1, \ldots, d_n)$ of $D_1 \times \cdots \times D_n$ and a subsequence $Y := x_{i_1}, \ldots, x_{i_\ell}$ of X. Then we denote the sequence $(d_{i_1}, \ldots, d_{i_\ell})$ by $d[Y]$ and call it the ***projection*** of d on Y. In particular for $d \in D_1 \times \cdots \times D_n$ $d[x_i]$ denotes the ith element of d. $\square$

Using the notion of a projection we can define the notion of a solution to a CSP in a succinct way. Namely, given a CSP $\mathcal{P} := \langle \mathcal{C} \; ; \; x_1 \in D_1, \ldots, x_n \in D_n \rangle$ an n-tuple $(d_1, \ldots, d_n) \in D_1 \times \cdots \times D_n$ is a solution to $\mathcal{P}$ iff for every constraint C of $\mathcal{P}$ on a sequence of variables Y we have $d[Y] \in C$.

Using the notion of projection we can also define the notion of equivalence in a more succinct way. Namely, the CSPs $\mathcal{P}_1$ and $\mathcal{P}_2$ are equivalent w.r.t. X iff

$$\{d[X] \mid d \text{ is a solution to } \mathcal{P}_1\} = \{d[X] \mid d \text{ is a solution to } \mathcal{P}_2\}.$$

Clearly, two CSPs with the same sequence of variables X are equivalent iff they are equivalent w.r.t. X, so the newly introduced notion of equivalence is a generalisation of the former one. When transforming CSPs one often tries to maintain equivalence w.r.t. the initial sequence of variables. Note for example that the CSP formed by the equation (3.1) and the one formed by the equations (3.2) and (3.3) are equivalent w.r.t. x.

In general, a reduction of a CSP to another one that is equivalent does not suffice to solve it. Therefore we also allow a split of a given CSP into two or more CSPs. To reason about such a split we need to formalise another concept of an equivalence.

Definition 3.3 Consider CSPs $\mathcal{P}_0, \ldots, \mathcal{P}_m$, where $m \geq 1$, and a sequence X of their common variables (that is, X is a subsequence of each of the sequences of the variables of $\mathcal{P}_0, \ldots, \mathcal{P}_m$). We say that the ***union of*** $\mathcal{P}_1, \ldots, \mathcal{P}_m$ ***is equivalent w.r.t.*** X ***to*** $\mathcal{P}_0$ if

- for every solution d to some $\mathcal{P}_i$, where $i \geq 1$, a solution to $\mathcal{P}_0$ exists that coincides with d on the variables in X,

- for every solution e to $\mathcal{P}_0$ a solution to some $\mathcal{P}_i$, where $i \geq 1$, exists that coincides with e on the variables in X. □

Again, using the notion of a projection we can define this notion more succinctly as follows. The union of $\mathcal{P}_1, \ldots, \mathcal{P}_m$ is equivalent w.r.t. X to $\mathcal{P}_0$ if

$$\{d[X] \mid d \text{ is a solution to } \mathcal{P}_0\} = \bigcup_{i=1}^{m} \{d[X] \mid d \text{ is a solution to } \mathcal{P}_i\}.$$

If $m = 1$, this definition coincides with the earlier introduced notion of equivalence of two CSPs , here $\mathcal{P}_1$ and $\mathcal{P}_0$, w.r.t. a sequence of variables X.

Below we represent the transformations of the CSPs in an informal way, by means of proof rules. This approach will be made more precise in Section 4.1. Here it suffices to remember that a rule of the form

$$\frac{\phi}{\psi}$$

represents a transformation of the CSP ϕ to the CSP ψ and a rule of the form

$$\frac{\phi}{\psi_1 \mid \ldots \mid \psi_n}$$

represents a transformation of the CSP ϕ to the CSPs $\psi_1, \ldots, \psi_n$.

Suppose that X is the sequence of the variables present in ϕ. The discussed rules preserve equivalence in the sense that, in the first rule ϕ and ψ are equivalent w.r.t. X, and in the second rule the union of $\psi_1, \ldots, \psi_n$ is equivalent to ϕ w.r.t. X. When the context CSP is irrelevant, we omit it and mention in the rule only the part that is changed.

3.2 Basic framework for constraint programming

We can now formulate a basic framework for constraint programming that we shall use in this book to explain its specific aspects. First, we formulate our initial problem as a CSP. As we saw in Chapter 2 this in itself can be a non-trivial problem. In particular, at this stage we have to take decisions concerning the choice of variables, domains and constraints. As already mentioned in Chapter 1 this phase of constraint programming is called *modeling* and in contrast to programming in other programming styles is more time consuming and more involved. Modeling is more an art than science and a number of rules of thumb and various heuristics are useful at this stage.

Subsequently, we apply to the formulated CSP the generic procedure

SOLVE defined in Figure 3.1. It is parametrised by the subsidiary procedures PREPROCESS, CONSTRAINT PROPAGATION, HAPPY, ATOMIC, SPLIT, and PROCEED BY CASES. The PROCEED BY CASES procedure leads to a recursive invocation of SOLVE for each newly formed CSP. The Boolean variable CONTINUE is local to SOLVE so it is declared anew each time SOLVE is invoked recursively.

SOLVE:

```
VAR CONTINUE: BOOLEAN;
CONTINUE:= TRUE;
WHILE CONTINUE AND NOT HAPPY DO
    PREPROCESS;
    CONSTRAINT PROPAGATION;
    IF NOT HAPPY
    THEN
        IF ATOMIC
        THEN
            CONTINUE:= FALSE
        ELSE
            SPLIT;
            PROCEED BY CASES
        END
    END
END
```

Fig. 3.1. Generic procedure SOLVE

The SOLVE procedure represents the basic loop of constraint programming. In what follows we explain, in an informal way, the meaning of all the procedures used in SOLVE. As the notion of constraint propagation is central to constraint programming we defer its discussion to the end of the section. At this stage it suffices to know that constraint propagation transforms a given CSP into another one that is equivalent to it, possibly w.r.t. a sequence of the initial variables.

3.2.1 PREPROCESS

The aim of this procedure is to bring the considered CSP into a desired syntactic form. The resulting CSP should be equivalent to the original one w.r.t. the initial sequence of variables. To illustrate it we consider two simple examples.

First, consider Boolean constraints as discussed in Section 2.4. Most of the procedures that deal with them assume that these constraints are in a specific syntactic form. A well-known example is the **conjunctive normal form** according to which the Boolean constraint is a conjunction of clauses. A **clause** is a disjunction of literals, where in turn a **literal** is a Boolean variable or its negation. For example, the Boolean constraint

$$(x \lor y) \land (\neg x \lor y \lor z) \land (\neg x \lor \neg z)$$

is in conjunctive normal form, since each conjunct of it is a clause. In this case the preprocessing consists of the rules that transform an arbitrary Boolean expression to an equivalent one that is in conjunctive normal form.

As a second example consider constraints on reals as discussed in Section 2.3. Often, specific procedures that deal with such constraints assume that in each constraint each variable appears at most once. In this case the preprocessing consists of transforming each constraint into such a form by introducing auxiliary variables. For instance, given an equation

$$ax^7 + bx^5 y + cy^{10} = 0$$

we employ an auxiliary variable z and replace it by two equations,

$$ax^7 + z + cy^{10} = 0$$

and

$$bx^5 y = z.$$

Usually, the PREPROCESS procedure is applied only once, at the top level of the SOLVE procedure. To deal with arbitrary situations we put it inside the SOLVE procedure, so that it is also called each time after the SPLIT procedure is invoked. It can for example happen that SPLIT generates constraints that have to be preprocessed before being passed to the CONSTRAINT PROPAGATION procedure.

3.2.2 HAPPY

Informally, HAPPY means that the goal set for the initial CSP has been achieved. What goal it is depends of course on the applications. The following contingencies are most common:

- a solution has been found,
- all solutions have been found,

- a 'solved form' has been reached from which it is straightforward to generate all solutions;

This contingency is useful to deal with situations when several, possibly infinitely many, solutions exist,

- an inconsistency was detected,
- an optimal solution w.r.t. some objective function was found,
- all optimal solutions w.r.t. some objective function were found,
- (in the case of constraints on reals) all interval domains are reduced to sizes smaller than some fixed in advance ϵ.

In general, HAPPY can be viewed as a test applied to the current CSP in which some additional parameters can be taken into account in case we look for an optimal, respectively all optimal, solutions w.r.t. some objective function.

3.2.3 ATOMIC

Before we split a CSP we need to check whether it is amenable for splitting. This is done using as a test the ATOMIC procedure. Usually, we stipulate that a CSP satisfies this test if its domains are singleton sets or empty. But a CSP $\mathcal{P}$ can be also viewed atomic if further search 'under' it is not anymore needed. This can be for example the case, when $\mathcal{P}$ is solved or, in case we look for an optimal solution, an optimal solution for $\mathcal{P}$ can be computed directly.

3.2.4 SPLIT

If after termination of the constraint propagation we did not reach the original goal, that is the test HAPPY fails, and the current CSP $\mathcal{P}$ is not atomic, that is NOT ATOMIC holds, $\mathcal{P}$ is split into two or more CSPs, the union of which is equivalent to $\mathcal{P}$. Such a split is obtained either by splitting a domain or by splitting a constraint. It leads to a replacement of the current CSP by two or more CSPs that differ from the current one in that the split domain, respectively the split constraint, is replaced by one of the constituents. Additionally, in case a domain is split, each constraint is restricted to the new domains.

In the following three examples a split of a domain is represented by a rule that transforms a domain expression into two or more domain expressions separated by means of the '|' symbol.

- **Enumeration**.

   Assume that the domain D is finite and contains at least two elements. The following rule can then be used:

$$\frac{x \in D}{x \in \{a\} \mid x \in D - \{a\}}$$

where $a \in D$.

   This rule corresponds to a reasoning by cases. In the first case we assume that x is instantiated to (or substituted by) the value a. In the second case we consider a modified domain from which the element a is removed. So this rule leads to the replacement of a CSP

$$\langle \mathcal{C} \; ; \; \mathcal{DE}, x \in D \rangle$$

by two CSPs,

$$\langle \mathcal{C}_1 \; ; \; \mathcal{DE}, x \in \{a\} \rangle$$

and

$$\langle \mathcal{C}_2 \; ; \; \mathcal{DE}, x \in D - \{a\} \rangle,$$

where $\mathcal{C}_1$ consists of the restrictions of the constraints in $\mathcal{C}$ to the new domains (with the domain of x being now the singleton set $\{a\}$), and similarly with $\mathcal{C}_2$. So a repeated use of this rule leads to a consideration of binary trees.

- **Labeling**.

   Alternatively, we can use the following rule which corresponds to a reasoning with k cases:

$$\frac{x \in \{a_1, \ldots, a_k\}}{x \in \{a_1\} \mid \ldots \mid x \in \{a_k\}}$$

Each application of this rule leads to a replacement of a CSP by k CSPs, where k equals the current size of the domain of the selected variable. So this rule is parametrised by k and its repeated use leads to a consideration of arbitrary finitely branching trees.

- **Bisection**.

   Assume that the domain is a non-empty real interval, written as $[a, b]$. We can then employ the following rule:

$$\frac{x \in [a, b]}{x \in [a, \frac{a+b}{2}] \mid x \in [\frac{a+b}{2}, b]}$$

that maintains the property that the domains are non-empty at the cost of making the split domains overlapping. Clearly, the same rule can be applied to non-empty integer intervals.

In turn, the following two examples, also written as rules, illustrate a split of a constraint.

- Disjunctive constraints.

Suppose that the constraint is a Boolean disjunction. The constituents of this disjunction can be arbitrary constraints. Such constraints are called **disjunctive constraints**. An example is the following constraint

$$\texttt{Start}[\texttt{task}_1] + \texttt{Duration}[\texttt{task}_1] \leq \texttt{Start}[\texttt{task}_2] \ \lor$$
$$\texttt{Start}[\texttt{task}_2] + \texttt{Duration}[\texttt{task}_2] \leq \texttt{Start}[\texttt{task}_1]$$

that typically occurs in scheduling problems. It states that either $\texttt{task}_1$ is scheduled before $\texttt{task}_2$ or vice versa. To process it we can apply the following rule:

$$\frac{C_1 \lor C_2}{C_1 \mid C_2}$$

This corresponds to reasoning in which we deal with each disjunct *separately*, in the presence of other, unchanged constraints.

- Constraints in 'compound' form.

The idea is that such constraints are split into syntactically simpler constraints that can be dealt with directly. Consider for example the constraint $|p(\bar{x})| = a$, where $p(\bar{x})$ a polynomial over reals and a is a non-negative real.

It can be dealt with using the following rule:

$$\frac{|p(\bar{x})| = a}{p(\bar{x}) = a \mid p(\bar{x}) = -a}$$

Applying it amounts to rewriting the original constraint as a disjunctive constraint

$$p(\bar{x}) = a \lor p(\bar{x}) = -a$$

and using the above rule for disjunctive constraints.

It is useful to mention that constraints that can be rewritten as disjunctions do not need to be processed as disjunctive constraints. For example, a constraint of the form $|x - y| = a$ could be also processed by transforming it to the linear constraint $x - y = z$, where z is a new variable with the domain $\{-a, a\}$. In general, the use of the disjunctive constraints with the corresponding rule leads to a combinatorial explosion that, if possible, should be avoided.

In general, the SPLIT procedure also determines which split operation is to be applied next. In general, several alternatives arise. For example, even if we limit our attention to the enumeration procedure, we still face the choice which variable x is to be selected and which value a from its domain is to be used. In other words, the rule dealing with the enumeration is parametrised by the variable x and the value a and the SPLIT procedure determines which instance of this rule is to be used next.

This leads us to the issue of heuristics that are used when solving CSPs. Informally, a **heuristic** is a rule that tells us how to choose out of many alternatives. Here we need to determine

- which variable to select,
- which value to select, or
- which constraint to split.

A number of heuristics exist. Let us just mention two examples to illustrate their flavour:

- select a variable that appears in the largest number of constraints; such a variable is called the **most constrained variable**,
- for a domain being an integer interval: select the middle value.

3.2.5 PROCEED BY CASES

The SPLIT procedure yields two or more new CSPs. They are then dealt with by means of the PROCEED BY CASES procedure.

The order in which these new CSPs are considered depends on the adopted **search technique**. In general, due to the repeated use of the SPLIT procedure a tree of CSPs is generated. The purpose of the PROCEED BY CASES procedure is to traverse this search tree in a specific order and, if needed, to update the relevant variables with some newly gathered information (in the case of search for the optimal solution). Two most known of these techniques are backtracking and, when searching for the optimal solution, branch and bound.

Informally, given a finite tree, the **backtracking search** starts at the root of the tree and proceeds by descending to its first descendant. This process continues as long as a node is not a leaf. If a leaf is encountered the search proceeds by moving back to the parent node of the leaf. Then the next descendant, if any, of this parent node is selected. This process continues until the control is back at the root node and all of its descendants have been visited. In Figure 3.2 we depict the backtracking search on a simple tree, where the arrows indicate the order in which the nodes are visited.

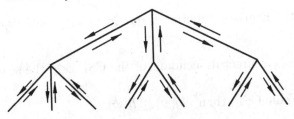

Fig. 3.2. Backtracking search

An important aspect of the search here considered is that the search tree to be traversed is not given in advance: it is generated 'on the fly'. Further, in our case the nodes of the search tree are CSPs and the leaves are CSPs that are either solved or failed. Usually, all domains of a leaf that is a solved CSP will be singleton sets which means that such a solved CSP yields one solution. Leaves that are solved CSPs with non-singleton set domain typically arise when we reduce a given CSP to a 'solved form', a contingency mentioned when discussing the HAPPY procedure in Subsection 3.2.2.

If we are interested in finding just one solution, the backtracking search stops as soon as a leaf is generated that is a solved CSP. If we wish to find all solutions, the search continues until all leaves have been generated. If we are interested in detecting inconsistency, the search stops as soon as a leaf being a solved CSP is generated and otherwise it continues until all leaves have been generated.

The **branch and bound search** is a modification of the backtracking search that takes into account the value of the objective function. Informally, it can be explained as follows. Suppose that we are interested in finding a solution with the maximal value of the objective function. During the search one maintains the **currently best value** of the objective function in a variable bound. This variable is initialised to $-\infty$ and is updated each time a solution with a larger value is generated. This solution is then recorded.

The objective function is usually used in combination with a **heuristic function** that assigns a real value to each considered CSP. To deal with the situations when no useful information is provided by the heuristic function one can extend the set of values it can take by ∞. We already noted in Section 3.1 that each solution to a given CSP corresponds to a unique solved CSP with singleton set domains. So we may assume that to each such solved CSP $\mathcal{P}$ the objective function *obj* assigns a real value. More generally, we may assume that the objective function *obj* assigns a real value $obj(\mathcal{P})$ to each atomic CSP $\mathcal{P}$, that is, to each CSP that satisfies the ATOMIC test. The correct use of the heuristic function h requires that it satisfies the following two properties:

- If the CSP ψ is a direct descendant of the CSP ϕ in the search tree, then $h(\psi) \leq h(\phi)$.
- If ψ is an atomic CSP, then $obj(\psi) \leq h(\psi)$.

The first condition states that the heuristic function gets 'more precise' once one descends down the search tree. The second condition states that the heuristic function overestimates the objective function.

The heuristic function is then used together with the currently best value **bound** to identify nodes under which no solution with a maximum value of the objective function can lie. These are nodes ϕ for which during the search process we have $h(\phi) < \textbf{bound}$. Indeed, by the above two assumptions for all solved ψ lying under ϕ we have $obj(\psi) < \textbf{bound}$. So the heuristic function allows us to ignore some parts of the tree during the search process.

In Figure 3.3 we depict a possible branch and bound search on the tree already considered in Figure 3.2. The parts of the tree that are ignored during the search are represented using the dotted lines.

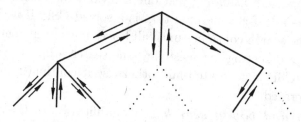

Fig. 3.3. Branch and bound search

Backtracking and branch and bound, when combined with appropriate instances of the CONSTRAINT PROPAGATION procedure lead to more complex forms of search methods that are specific for constraint programming. Let us just mention here that one also studies ways of faster backtracking, which allow us in case a failed CSP is generated to jump further back in the tree than just to the parent node. These techniques are usually called *intelligent backtracking*.

3.2.6 CONSTRAINT PROPAGATION

At this stage let us return to the CONSTRAINT PROPAGATION procedure. In general, this procedure replaces a given CSP by a 'simpler' one, yet equivalent. The idea is that such a replacement, if efficient, is profitable, since the

subsequent search resulting from the repeated calls of the SPLIT and PRO-
CEED BY CASES procedures is then performed on a (usually substantially)
smaller search space. What 'simpler' means depends on the applications.
Typically, it refers to the fact that the domains and/or constraints become
smaller. The constraint propagation is performed by repeatedly reducing
domains and/or reducing constraints while maintaining equivalence.

Let us consider some examples. In each of them we stress the benefit
accrued by repeated reduction. We again use here proof rules but now they
represent a replacement of a (fragment of a) CSP by another one. The first
two examples deal with the domain reduction.

- Arbitrary CSPs.

  Consider a constraint C. Choose a variable x of it and perform the
  following operation on its domain D:

  remove from D all values for x that do not participate in a solution to C.

  The idea is that the removed values cannot be present in any solution
  to the considered CSP. We call this operation ***projection of C on x***.

  As an example, consider the crossword puzzle discussed in Example 2.8.
  If we apply the above rule to the constraint $C_{1,2}$ on the variables x_1 and
  x_2 and to the variable x_1, then we reduce the domain of x_1 to the set
  {HOSES, LASER}. Indeed, only these two five letter words can be used
  for position 1 in combination with a five letter word for position 2; both
  of them can be combined with the word SAILS for position 2.

  This reduction process can be continued. For example, we can now
  apply the above rule to the constraint $C_{1,3}$ on the variables x_1 and x_3, and
  the variable x_3. This way we reduce the domain of x_3 to the set {SAILS,
  SHEET, STEER}.

- Linear inequalities on integers.

  Assume that the domains are non-empty intervals of integers, written
  as $[a..b]$, and the constraints are linear inequalities of the form $x < y$.
  Then we can apply the following rule:

$$\frac{\langle x < y \; ; \; x \in [l_x..h_x], y \in [l_y..h_y] \rangle}{\langle x < y \; ; \; x \in [l_x..min(h_x, h_y - 1)], y \in [max(l_y, l_x + 1)..h_y] \rangle}$$

that allows us to transform both considered intervals to smaller ones.

To see that this rule preserves equivalence, it suffices to show that any
solution to the CSP in the premise is also a solution to the CSP in the
conclusion. So take a pair (a, b) that is a solution to the CSP in the
premise, i.e., such that $a \in [l_x..h_x]$, $b \in [l_y..h_y]$ and $a < b$. Then since
$b \le h_y$ we get $a \le h_y - 1$ and since $l_x \le a$ we get $l_x + 1 \le b$. So

$a \leq min(h_x, h_y - 1)$ and $max(l_y, l_x + 1) \leq b$, which means that the pair (a, b) is also a solution to the CSP in the conclusion.

This rule can be applied several times in succession. Consider for example the CSP

$$\langle x < y, y < z \; ; \; x \in [50..200], y \in [0..100], z \in [0..100] \rangle.$$

Applying this rule to the constraint $x < y$ we transform this CSP into

$$\langle x < y, y < z \; ; \; x \in [50..99], y \in [51..100], z \in [0..100] \rangle.$$

Another application of this rule, this time to the constraint $y < z$, yields

$$\langle x < y, y < z \; ; \; x \in [50..99], y \in [51..99], z \in [52..100] \rangle.$$

Applying this rule third time, again to the constraint $x < y$, yields

$$\langle x < y, y < z \; ; \; x \in [50..98], y \in [51..99], z \in [52..100] \rangle.$$

So we could reduce all three variable domains. It is easy to see that further applications of this rule yield no change.

Next, consider the reduction of constraints. We illustrate it by means of two examples. In each of them a new constraint is introduced. Such a new constraint is called in this context an **implied constraint** or a **derived constraint**. (Sometimes a rather misleading terminology of *redundant constraints* is used.)

Such an addition of a new constraint can be viewed as a reduction of a constraint. Namely, an introduction of a new constraint, say on the variables X, augments the set of used constraints on X. As each constraint is a set, we can identify this set of constraints on X with their intersection, without affecting the set of solutions. Under this identification the new set of constraints on X, viewed as a single constraint, is a subset of the old one.

- Linear inequalities.

    Consider the following rules that invoke the transitivity and the antisymmetry of the $<$ relation on some numeric domain:

$$\frac{\langle x < y, y < z \; ; \; \mathcal{DE} \rangle}{\langle x < y, y < z, x < z \; ; \; \mathcal{DE} \rangle}$$

$$\frac{\langle x < y, y < x \; ; \; \mathcal{DE} \rangle}{\langle x < y, y < x, \bot \; ; \; \mathcal{DE} \rangle}$$

The first rule introduces a new constraint $x < z$ and the second rule introduces the false constraint $\bot$. As an example of their use consider the obviously inconsistent CSP

$$\langle x < y, y < z, z < x \; ; \; \mathcal{DE} \rangle.$$

Using the first rule we get then

$$\langle x < y, y < z, x < z, z < x \; ; \; \mathcal{DE} \rangle.$$

Applying now the second rule to the constraints $x < z, z < x$ we get the failed CSP

$$\langle x < y, y < z, x < z, z < x, \bot \; ; \; \mathcal{DE} \rangle.$$

- Resolution method.

This rule deals with clauses, that is, disjunctions of literals. (Recall from Subsection 3.2.1 that a literal is a Boolean variable or its negation.) Let C_1 and C_2 be clauses, L a literal and $\bar{L}$ the literal opposite to L, that is $\overline{\neg x} = x$ and $\bar{x} = \neg x$. To abstract from the order of the disjuncts in a clause and to automatically dispense of repeated literals we write each clause as a set of literals. Then the following rule, called the **resolution rule**:

$$\frac{\langle C_1 \cup \{L\}, C_2 \cup \{\bar{L}\} \; ; \; \mathcal{DE} \rangle}{\langle C_1 \cup \{L\}, C_2 \cup \{\bar{L}\}, C_1 \cup C_2 \; ; \; \mathcal{DE} \rangle}$$

introduces a new constraint, the clause $C_1 \cup C_2$. This rule is a cornerstone of the automated theorem proving.

To illustrate its use consider the Boolean CSP

$$\langle x \vee y, \neg x \vee y \vee z, \neg x \vee \neg z \; ; \; \mathcal{DE} \rangle$$

that involves the Boolean constraint mentioned earlier in Subsection 3.2.1. Applying the resolution rule to the first two clauses we get, with $L \equiv x$,

$$\langle x \vee y, \neg x \vee y \vee z, \neg x \vee \neg z, y \vee z \; ; \; \mathcal{DE} \rangle.$$

Now applying this rule to the clauses $\neg x \vee \neg z$ and $y \vee z$ we get, with $L \equiv z$,

$$\langle x \vee y, \neg x \vee y \vee z, \neg x \vee \neg z, y \vee z, \neg x \vee y \; ; \; \mathcal{DE} \rangle.$$

Another application of the resolution rule, this time to the clauses $x \vee y$ and $\neg x \vee y$, again with $L \equiv x$, leads to the addition of the constraint y to the last CSP.

So using the resolution rule we could deduce from the original Boolean CSP that y is true.

It should be stressed here that not all implied constraints are useful. For example, returning to the above example of linear inequalities, the rule

$$\frac{\langle x < y \; ; \; \mathcal{DE} \rangle}{\langle x < y, x < y + 1 \; ; \; \mathcal{DE} \rangle}$$

introduces an implied constraint that is certainly worthless. Usually, the challenge is to find *useful* implied constraints the use of which leads to an effective progress in solving the considered CSP.

In general, various general techniques drawn from the fields of linear algebra, linear programming, integer programming, and automated theorem proving can be explained as a reduction of constraints: the resolution rule is just one example. More examples will be given in Chapter 4.

3.2.7 Constraint propagation algorithms

The above examples dealt with the atomic reduction steps in which either a domain or a constraint was reduced. The **constraint propagation algorithms** deal with the scheduling of such atomic reduction steps. They attempt to avoid useless applications of the atomic reduction steps. Upon termination these algorithms achieve a property called a **local consistency notion**.

The concept of local consistency is crucial for the theory of constraint programming. In the literature a plethora of such notions have been introduced. To illustrate them let us clarify what local consistency notion corresponds to the first domain reduction rule presented above. It is defined as follows:

for every constraint C and every variable x of it each value in the domain of x participates in an element of C.

This property is called **hyper-arc consistency**. In the case of binary constraints it is called **arc consistency** and is perhaps the most popular local consistency notion.

As an example of an arc consistent CSP take

$$\langle x < y, y < z, x < z \; ; \; x \in [0..5], y \in [1..7], z \in [3..8] \rangle.$$

It is straightforward to check that it is arc consistent: for each constraint and each variable of it every value in the domain of this variable belongs to a pair that satisfies the selected constraint. For example, if we choose the constraint $x < y$, the variable y and the value 1 in the domain of y, then it belongs to the pair $(0, 1)$ that satisfies this constraint $x < y$ on the assumed domains.

In contrast, the CSP

$$\langle x < y, y < z, x < z \ ; \ x \in [0..5], y \in [0..7], z \in [3..8]\rangle$$

is not arc consistent, since for the value 0 for y no value for x in $[0..5]$ exists such that $x < y$.

It is important to realise that in general a locally consistent CSP does not need to be consistent. For example, the CSP

$$\langle x \neq y, y \neq z, z \neq x \ ; \ x \in [1..2], y \in [1..2], z \in [1..2]\rangle,$$

depicted in Figure 3.4, is easily seen to be arc consistent but it is not consistent.

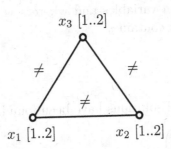

Fig. 3.4. An arc consistent but inconsistent CSP

To summarise, each constraint propagation algorithm reduces a given CSP to an equivalent one that satisfies some local consistency notion. Which local consistency notion is reached depends on the type of the CSPs considered and on the form of rules used.

3.3 Example: Boolean constraints

Let us illustrate now the above discussion by means of two examples. They will clarify what choices one needs to make when solving specific CSPs. These choices will be reflected in specific decisions concerning the subsidiary procedures of the generic SOLVE procedure of Figure 3.1. As the first example we choose Boolean constraints. A more detailed account of constraint propagation for these constraints will be given in Section 6.3.

Suppose that we wish to find all solutions to a given Boolean constraint satisfaction problem. Then we could consider the following selection of the procedures discussed above.

PREPROCESS

We wish to bring each Boolean constraint to one of the following forms:

- $x = y$,
- $\neg x = y$,
- $x \wedge y = z$,
- $x \vee y = z$,

where x, y, z are different variables.

Consequently, for PREPROCESS we choose transformation rules that transform each Boolean constraint into a set of constraints in the above form. An example of such a transformation rule is

$$\frac{x \wedge s = z}{x \wedge y = z, s = y}$$

where x, y, z are Boolean variables and where s is a non-variable Boolean expression that does not contain y.

HAPPY

We choose the test:

all solutions have been found.

ATOMIC

We postulate that a CSP is atomic if no domain of it contains more than one element.

SPLIT

We use the labeling rule discussed in Subsection 3.2.4. In our case it boils down to the following rule:

$$\frac{x \in \{0, 1\}}{x \in \{0\} \mid x \in \{1\}}$$

As already noted there this rule is parametrised by a variable, the choice of which is of relevance here, and by a value, the choice of which is of no relevance here. We use this rule in combination with the heuristic according to which the most constrained variable, i.e., the variable that occurs in the largest number of constraints, is chosen first.

CONSTRAINT PROPAGATION

Next, we determine the actions of the constraint propagation algorithm. We do this by choosing specific domain reduction steps. They are based on the simple observation that for the Boolean constraints in one of the forms considered in the definition of the PREPROCESS procedure, if the values of some variables are determined, then values of some other variables can be determined. For example, for the constraint $x \wedge y = z$, if we know that z is 1 (which is identified with **true**), then we can conclude that both x and y are 1. This is expressed by means of the following rule:

$$\frac{\langle x \wedge y = z \; ; \; x \in D_x, y \in D_y, z \in \{1\} \rangle}{\langle \; ; \; x \in D_x \cap \{1\}, y \in D_y \cap \{1\}, z \in \{1\} \rangle}$$

where the absence of the constraint $x \wedge y = z$ in the conclusion indicates that this constraint is solved. We can abbreviate it to a more suggestive form, namely

$$x \wedge y = z, z = 1 \rightarrow x = 1, y = 1.$$

It is useful to understand why we do not adopt the following rule instead:

$$\frac{\langle x \wedge y = z \; ; \; x \in D_x, y \in D_y, z \in \{1\} \rangle}{\langle \; ; \; x \in \{1\}, y \in \{1\}, z \in \{1\} \rangle}$$

If we did, then with $D_x = \{0\}$ we would get different outcomes. Indeed, using the adopted rule we would generate the empty domain for x. This is conforming to the observation that $x \wedge y = z$ combined with z and $\neg x$ yields inconsistency. The analogous observation holds for the domain D_y. In contrast, with the rule that we did not adopt we would not discover inconsistency and instead wrongly deduce that $(1, 1, 1)$ is a solution to the CSP in the rule premise.

In total we have the following six rules for the constraint $x \wedge y = z$:

CONJUNCTION

$$x \wedge y = z, x = 1, y = 1 \rightarrow z = 1,$$

$$x \wedge y = z, x = 1, z = 0 \rightarrow y = 0,$$

$$x \wedge y = z, y = 1, z = 0 \rightarrow x = 0,$$

$$x \wedge y = z, x = 0 \rightarrow z = 0,$$

$$x \wedge y = z, y = 0 \rightarrow z = 0,$$

$$x \wedge y = z, z = 1 \rightarrow x = 1, y = 1.$$

We adopt similar rules for the other three constraints considered in the definition of the PREPROCESS procedure. They are discussed in detail in Section 6.3.

PROCEED BY CASES

As we want to find all solutions we choose here the backtracking search.

This completes the description of a sample procedure using which we can find all solutions to a Boolean constraint satisfaction problem. It can be easily implemented and it yields a reasonable approach to solving such constraints.

3.4 Example: polynomial constraints on integer intervals

As the second example of an instantiation of the framework of Section 3.2 consider the problem of finding optimal solutions to polynomial constraints on integer intervals subject to a polynomial objective function. So we deal here with constrained optimization problems. A more detailed account of constraint propagation for such constraints is given in Section 6.5. As an example of a problem we are interested in consider the task of finding a solution to the constraint

$$x^3 + y^2 - z^3 = 0$$

in the integer interval [1..1000] for which the value of

$$2x \cdot y - z$$

is maximal. (For the interested reader: the answer is $x = 112$, $y = 832$ and $z = 128$, for which the value of $2x \cdot y - z$ is 186240.)

Let us be more precise about the constraints and the objective functions we are interested in. By a *polynomial constraint* we mean here an expression of the form

$$s = 0,$$

where s is a polynomial (in possibly several variables) with integer coefficients. For example

$$2x^5 \cdot y^2 \cdot z^4 + 3x \cdot y^3 \cdot z^5 - 4x^4 \cdot y^6 \cdot z^2 + 10 = 0$$

is a polynomial constraint.

We also assume that the objective function is a polynomial with integer coefficients.

PREPROCESS

We deal with these constraints by reducing them first to one of the following syntactic forms:

- $\sum_{i=1}^{n} a_i x_i = b$, where $n > 0$, $a_1, \ldots, a_n$ are non-zero integers, $x_1, \ldots, x_n$ are different variables, and b is an integer,
- $x \cdot y = z$, where x, y, z are different variables.

So for the PREPROCESS procedure we adopt appropriate transformation rules that transform each polynomial constraint into a set of constraints in one of the above two forms. An example of such a transformation rule is

$$\frac{\langle \sum_{i=1}^{n} m_i = 0 \; ; \; \mathcal{DE} \rangle}{\langle \sum_{i=1}^{n} v_i = 0, \; m_1 = v_1, \ldots, \; m_n = v_n \; ; \; \mathcal{DE}, v_1 \in \mathcal{Z}, \ldots, v_n \in \mathcal{Z} \rangle}$$

where some m_i is not of the form $a x_i$ and where $v_1, \ldots, v_n$ are variables that do not appear in $\mathcal{DE}$. It simplifies a complex sum by introducing a constraint in the first syntactic form listed above and a sequence of constraints of lower syntactic complexity.

Another transformation rule is the following one:

$$\frac{\langle s \cdot t = v \; ; \; \mathcal{DE} \rangle}{\langle x \cdot y = z, \; s = x, \; t = y, \; v = z \; ; \; \mathcal{DE}, x \in \mathcal{Z}, y \in \mathcal{Z}, z \in \mathcal{Z} \rangle}$$

where x, y, z do not appear in $\mathcal{DE}$.

Since we do not want to apply this rule to the constraints of the form $x \cdot y = z$, $a \cdot y = z$ or $x \cdot a = z$, where x, y, z are different variables and a an integer, which are already in a desired syntactic form, we stipulate that none of the following contingency holds:

- s, t, v are different variables,
- s is an integer and t and v variables,
- t is an integer and s and v variables.

Both rules introduce variables that range over the set of all integers $\mathcal{Z}$. But, as we shall see at the end of this section, if the domains of the original variables are intervals of integers, then we can ensure that the domains of the auxiliary variables are intervals of integers, as well.

HAPPY

We are interested in finding an optimal solution, so we choose the test:

an optimal solution w.r.t. the objective function was found.

ATOMIC

As in the previous example we postulate that a CSP is atomic if no domain of it contains more than one element.

CONSTRAINT PROPAGATION

Next, we consider the crucial issue of constraint propagation. We take care of it by proposing rules for the $\sum_{i=1}^{n} a_i x_i = b$ and $x \cdot y = z$ constraints. This is done by introducing first an ***interval arithmetic*** on integers.

It involves a generalisation of the arithmetic operations to the sets of integers. For X, Y sets of integers we define the following operations:

- addition:

$$X + Y := \{x + y \mid x \in X, y \in Y\},$$

- subtraction:

$$X - Y := \{x - y \mid x \in X, y \in Y\},$$

- multiplication:

$$X \cdot Y := \{x \cdot y \mid x \in X, y \in Y\},$$

- division:

$$X/Y := \{u \in \mathcal{Z} \mid \exists x \in X \exists y \in Y \; u \cdot y = x\}.$$

For an integer a and $op \in \{+, -, \cdot, /\}$ we identify $a \, op \, X$ with $\{a\} \, op \, X$ and $X \, op \, a$ with $X \, op \, \{a\}$.

Without entering into details let us mention that there are some subtleties concerned the above definition of the division. An interested reader will find more details in Section 6.5. Note that this operation is defined for all sets of integers, including $Y = \emptyset$ and $Y = \{0\}$.

When limiting our attention to intervals of integers the following observation is then of importance.

Note For X, Y integer intervals and a an integer the following holds:

- $X \cap Y, X + Y, X - Y$ are integer intervals.
- $X/\{a\}$ is an integer interval.
- $X \cdot Y$ does not have to be an integer interval, even if $X = \{a\}$ or $Y = \{a\}$.
- X/Y does not have to be an integer interval. $\square$

For example we have

$$[2..4] + [3..8] = [5..12],$$

$$[3..7] - [1..8] = [-5..6],$$

$$[3..3] \cdot [1..2] = \{3, 6\},$$

$$[3..5]/[-1..2] = \{-5, -4, -3, 2, 3, 4, 5\},$$

and

$$[-3..5]/[-1..2] = \mathcal{Z}.$$

To deal with the problem that non-interval domains can be produced by the interval multiplication and division we introduce the following operation on the subsets of the set of the integers $\mathcal{Z}$:

$$int(X) := \begin{cases} \text{smallest integer interval containing } X & \text{if } X \text{ is finite,} \\ \mathcal{Z} & \text{otherwise.} \end{cases}$$

For example $int([3..3] \cdot [1..2]) = [3..6]$, $int([3..5]/[-1..2]) = [-5..5]$ and $int([-3..5]/[-1..2]) = \mathcal{Z}$.

We are now ready to introduce the appropriate rules that deal with the $\sum_{i=1}^{n} a_i x_i = b$ and $x \cdot y = z$ constraints. For the first constraint note that

$$\sum_{i=1}^{n} a_i x_i = b$$

implies that for $j \in [1..n]$ we have

$$x_j = \frac{b - \sum_{i \in [1..n] - \{j\}} a_i x_i}{a_j}$$

This suggests the following rule:

LINEAR EQUALITY

$$\frac{\langle \sum_{i=1}^{n} a_i x_i = b \; ; \; x_1 \in D_1, \ldots, x_n \in D_n \rangle}{\langle \sum_{i=1}^{n} a_i x_i = b \; ; \; x_1 \in D'_1, \ldots, x_n \in D'_n \rangle}$$

where

- for $i \neq j$

$$D'_i := D_i,$$

-

$$D'_j := D_j \cap \frac{b - \sum_{i \in [1..n] - \{j\}} int(a_i \cdot D_i)}{a_j}.$$

So this rule is parametrised by j and it allows us to reduce the domain of the x_j variable. Note the use of the int function to convert $a_i \cdot D_i$ to an integer interval. Thanks to the above Note the new domain of x_j remains an interval. Note that after this rule is applied the inclusion

$$D_j \subseteq \frac{b - \sum_{i \in [1..n] - \{j\}} int(a_i \cdot D_i)}{a_j}$$

holds.

To deal with the $x \cdot y = z$ constraint we introduce three rules that aim at similar inclusions between the variable domains. To maintain the property that the domains remain intervals we use in each of them the int function:

MULTIPLICATION 1

$$\frac{\langle x \cdot y = z \; ; \; x \in D_x, y \in D_y, z \in D_z \rangle}{\langle x \cdot y = z \; ; \; x \in D_x, y \in D_y, z \in D_z \cap int(D_x \cdot D_y) \rangle}$$

MULTIPLICATION 2

$$\frac{\langle x \cdot y = z \; ; \; x \in D_x, y \in D_y, z \in D_z \rangle}{\langle x \cdot y = z \; ; \; x \in D_x \cap int(D_z/D_y), y \in D_y, z \in D_z \rangle}$$

MULTIPLICATION 3

$$\frac{\langle x \cdot y = z \; ; \; x \in D_x, y \in D_y, z \in D_z \rangle}{\langle x \cdot y = z \; ; \; x \in D_x, y \in D_y \cap int(D_z/D_x), z \in D_z \rangle}$$

Each of the *MULTIPLICATION* rules allows us to reduce one variable domain. Note that after the first rule is applied the inclusion $D_z \subseteq int(D_x \cdot D_y)$ holds, after the second rule is applied, the inclusion $D_x \subseteq int(D_z/D_y)$ holds, and after the third rule is applied, the inclusion $D_y \subseteq int(D_z/D_x)$ holds.

These three rules, when combined together, allow us to carry out important domain reductions. Consider for example the CSP

$$\langle x \cdot y = z \; ; \; x \in [1..20], y \in [9..11], z \in [155..161] \rangle.$$

One can check that using all three *MULTIPLICATION* rules we can transform it to

$$\langle x \cdot y = z \; ; \; x \in [16..16], y \in [10..10], z \in [160..160] \rangle.$$

So using these rules we can find here a unique solution, $x = 16, y = 10$ and $z = 160$, to the original CSP.

SPLIT

We apply the following bisection rule:

$$\frac{x \in [a..b]}{x \in [a..\lfloor \frac{a+b}{2} \rfloor] \mid x \in [\lfloor \frac{a+b}{2} \rfloor + 1..b]}$$

where a, b are integers such that $a < b$. We combine it with the following heuristic:

choose the variable with the smallest interval domain.

PROCEED BY CASES

We are interested in finding a solution with a maximal value of the objective function, so we choose here the branch and bound method. To be able to prune the search tree we need an appropriate heuristic function. To this end we employ the interval arithmetic on integers. Using it we can extend the objective function to a function from the integer intervals to finite sets of integers. The heuristic function will then be the maximum this extension can achieve on the current intervals.

More precisely, given an objective function obj that is a polynomial with the variables $x_1, \ldots, x_n$, we denote by $obj(a_1, \ldots, a_n)$ the result of evaluating obj when each variable x_i is replaced by a_i. For example, for

$$obj(x, y) := x^2 \cdot y - 3x \cdot y^2 + 5$$

we have $obj(2, 3) = 2^2 \cdot 3 - 3 \cdot 2 \cdot 3^2 + 5$, i.e., $obj(2, 3) = -37$.

Further, we define the extension obj^+ of obj to a function from the sets of integers to the sets of integers by interpreting exponentiation as a repeated multiplication and using the provided above definition of the interval arithmetic. For example, for $obj(x, y)$ defined as above, we have for X, Y sets of integers

$$obj^+(X, Y) = X \cdot X \cdot Y - 3 \cdot X \cdot Y \cdot Y + 5,$$

where we interpreted x^2 as $x \cdot x$ and y^2 as $y \cdot y$.

In general, since the multiplication operation does not map integer intervals to integer intervals, the extension obj^+ of obj, when applied to integer intervals, does not need to produce an integer interval. Still the following holds.

Lemma Consider a function obj that is a polynomial with the variables $x_1, \ldots, x_n$. Let $X_1, \ldots, X_n$ be intervals of integers. Then

(i) $obj^+(X_1, \ldots, X_n)$ is a finite set of integers.

(ii) For any sequence of integers $a_1, \ldots, a_n$ such that $a_i \in X_i$ for $i \in [1..n]$

$$obj(a_1, \ldots, a_n) \in obj^+(X_1, \ldots, X_n).$$

(iii) For any sequence of intervals of integers $Y_1, \ldots, Y_n$ such that $Y_i \subseteq X_i$ for $i \in [1..n]$

$$obj^+(Y_1, \ldots, Y_n) \subseteq obj^+(X_1, \ldots, X_n).$$

$\square$

The first statement holds since the addition, subtraction and multiplication operations map finite sets of integers to finite sets of integers. The second and third statements can be proved by induction on the structure of obj. The third statement states that the obj^+ function is monotonic w.r.t. the set inclusion.

This brings us to the definition of the heuristic function h. Take a CSP $\mathcal{P} := \langle \mathcal{C} \; ; \; x_1 \in D_1, \ldots, x_n \in D_n \rangle$ with $D_1, \ldots, D_n$ integer intervals and a function obj that is a polynomial with the variables $x_1, \ldots, x_n$. We define

$$h(\mathcal{P}) := max(obj^+(D_1, \ldots, D_n)).$$

Then by the above Lemma and the fact that we use the bisection rule as the SPLIT procedure, the function h satisfies the two properties we stipulated in Subsection 3.2.5 for the heuristic function.

Let us return now to the problem that in the PREPROCESS procedure we introduced the variables with the domains that are not intervals. Note that each time we introduce such a variable x, it is equated with a polynomial, say s. On the account of the first item of the above Lemma the function s^+, when applied to the domains of the variables present in s, yields a finite set of integers D. We can then use $int(D)$ as the domain of the variable x instead of $\mathcal{Z}$.

This completes the presentation of a specific approach for dealing with constrained optimization problems concerning polynomial constraints on the integer intervals.

3.5 Summary

The aim of this chapter was to introduce informally the main concepts of constraint programming. To this end we provided a simple general framework and discussed its main components. In particular, we clarified the following aspects of constraint programming:

- preprocessing,
- search, and
- constraint propagation.

We also introduced two standard search methods:

- backtracking, and
- branch and bound,

and mentioned the role of

- heuristics

in the search process. Finally, we illustrated these concepts on two examples:

- Boolean constraints, and
- polynomial constraints on integer intervals.

Many elements of constraint programming have been by necessity omitted in this informal presentation. For example, we devoted to the constraint propagation algorithms just one paragraph, mentioned just one local consistency notion, and did not discuss any algorithms for backtracking and the branch and bound method.

Still, this brief introduction to the specifics of constraint programming sheds some light on the subject and provides some insights into the choices that need to be made when trying to solve a problem by means of constraint programming techniques.

3.6 Bibliographic remarks

All bibliographic references to the methods and approaches mentioned here will be found in the later chapters. In particular, in Chapter 5 we provide a detailed account of several notions of local consistency and in Chapter 7 we study the constraint propagation algorithms. Finally, the search methods are explained in Chapter 8.

4

Some complete constraint solvers

B Y A *constraint solver* we mean any procedure that transforms a CSP into an equivalent one. In practice we are interested in efficient constraint solvers. In this book we distinguish between complete and incomplete constraint solvers. [3]

Intuitively, a *complete constraint solver* transforms the initial CSP $\mathcal{P}$ to one from which it is straightforward to generate all solutions to $\mathcal{P}$ or to determine that no solution exists. Admittedly, this statement is imprecise. In the case of the solvers discussed in this chapter we shall make it precise by employing the notion of a solved form. Its definition depends on the type of constraints used.

We call a constraint solver that is not complete an *incomplete constraint solver*. Intuitively, such a constraint solver transforms the initial CSP into a simpler one, all solutions to which can be eventually found by a, possibly repeated, case analysis modeled by splitting. As such a repeated case analysis results in general in an exponential running time, we do not allow it to be a part of the constraint solvers.

For the incomplete solvers a natural question arises what they actually

---

[3] The reader familiar with the basics of mathematical logic should be warned that this terminology has no relation to the concepts of complete and incomplete theories.

achieve. To clarify this issue we introduce various notions of local consistency. This explains the order of the chapters that follow. In this one we focus on some complete constraint solvers, in the next one on various notions of local consistency and in Chapter 6 we study a number of incomplete constraint solvers.

For a number of domains and constraints complete constraint solvers were developed. The aim of this chapter is to illustrate such solvers by means of three well-known examples. They are described in a uniform way using a simple proof theoretic framework involving rules that transform CSPs while maintaining equivalence. The executions of a constraint solver correspond then to specific derivations in the considered proof system. The so presented complete constraint solvers resemble the original formulations of the considered algorithms. This framework will also be used in the next two chapters, to characterise the notions of local consistency and to define various incomplete constraint solvers.

This chapter is organised as follows. First, in Section 4.1, we introduce the already mentioned proof theoretic framework. Then, in Section 4.2 we consider finite sets of term equations. The problem of solving them is known as the unification problem. To solve it we introduce the MARTELLI–MONTANARI algorithm.

Next, in Section 4.3 we study the problem of solving finite sets of linear equations over reals. We present two classic algorithms that allow us to solve them: the GAUSS–JORDAN ELIMINATION algorithm and the GAUSSIAN ELIMINATION algorithm. Finally, in Section 4.4 we study a related problem of solving finite sets of linear inequalities over reals. To this end we discuss the FOURIER–MOTZKIN ELIMINATION algorithm.

4.1 A proof theoretical framework

We begin by introducing a simple formal framework that we shall use for a number of purposes, namely

- to define in this chapter three complete constraint solvers,
- to characterise in Chapter 5 various notions of local consistency, and
- to define in Chapter 6 a number of incomplete constraint solvers.

In this framework we introduce proof rules and derivations.

4.1.1 Proof rules

The proof rules are used to express transformations of CSPs. So they are of the form

$$\frac{\phi}{\psi}$$

where ϕ and ψ are CSPs. In these rules, just as in the definition of CSPs, the order of the constraints in the premise and in the conclusion is irrelevant.

Our intention is to use the proof rules to reduce one CSP to another CSP in such a way that the equivalence (usually w.r.t. to the initial sequence of the variables) is maintained. This motivates the following definition.

Definition 4.1 A proof rule

$$\frac{\phi}{\psi}$$

is called **equivalence preserving** (respectively, **equivalence preserving** w.r.t. a sequence of the variables X) if ϕ and ψ are equivalent (respectively, equivalent w.r.t. X).

If X is the empty sequence, we say that the proof rule is **consistency preserving**.

□

As in the case of the equivalence notion introduced in Section 3.1, it is in general not easy to determine whether a rule is equivalence preserving. Fortunately, the rules that we shall consider will be very simple and from the way we introduce them it will be clear that they are all equivalence preserving. If the sets of variables of the premise CSP and conclusion CSP differ, then the rule under consideration will be equivalence preserving w.r.t. the sequence of the common variables.

The consistency preserving rules will be of interest only in Section 4.4. Note that a proof rule

$$\frac{\phi}{\psi}$$

is consistency preserving if the following equivalence holds:

ϕ is consistent iff ψ is consistent.

So consistency preserving is a weaker property than equivalence preserving.

In general, constraint solvers aim at either reducing the domains of the considered variables or at reducing the considered constraints, while maintaining equivalence. This translates into two types of equivalence preserving rules. Assume that

$$\phi := \langle \mathcal{C} \; ; \; \mathcal{DE} \rangle$$

and

$$\psi := \langle \mathcal{C}' \; ; \; \mathcal{DE}' \rangle.$$

Domain reduction rules These are rules in which the new domains are respective subsets of the old domains and the new constraints are respective restrictions of the old constraints to the new domains. So here

- $\mathcal{DE} := x_1 \in D_1, \ldots, x_n \in D_n,$
- $\mathcal{DE}' := x_1 \in D_1', \ldots, x_n \in D_n',$
- for $i \in [1..n]$ we have $D_i' \subseteq D_i,$
- $\mathcal{C}'$ is the result of restricting each constraint in $\mathcal{C}$ to the corresponding subsequence of the domains $D_1', \ldots, D_n'.$

Here a failure is reached only when a domain of one or more variables gets reduced to the empty set.

A typical example of a domain reduction rule is the following rule from Subsection 3.2.6 that deals with linear inequalities over integer intervals:

$$\frac{\langle x < y \; ; \; x \in [l_x..h_x], y \in [l_y..h_y] \rangle}{\langle x < y \; ; \; x \in [l_x..min(h_x, h_y - 1)], y \in [max(l_y, l_x + 1)..h_y] \rangle}$$

Two other examples are the following rules that deal with, respectively, equality and disequality constraints. Here and elsewhere we delete from the conclusion all solved constraints (but keep all the domain expressions). Also, we abbreviate the domain expression $x \in \{a\}$ to $x = a$.

EQUALITY

$$\frac{\langle x = y \; ; \; x \in D_x, y \in D_y \rangle}{\langle x = y \; ; \; x \in D_x \cap D_y, y \in D_x \cap D_y \rangle}$$

Note that this rule yields a failure when $D_x \cap D_y = \emptyset$. In case $D_x \cap D_y$ is a singleton set the constraint $x = y$ becomes solved and is then deleted.

DISEQUALITY

$$\frac{\langle x \neq y \; ; \; x \in D, y = a \rangle}{\langle \; ; \; x \in D - \{a\}, y = a \rangle}$$

where $a \in D$, and similarly with $x \neq y$ replaced by $y \neq x$.

Following the just introduced convention we dropped the constraint from the conclusion of this rule. This explains its format. Note that this rule yields a failure when $D - \{a\} = \emptyset$.

Transformation rules These rules are not domain reduction rules and are such that $C' \neq \emptyset$ and $\mathcal{DE}'$ extends $\mathcal{DE}$ by domain expressions referring to non-empty domains.

The fact that $\mathcal{DE}'$ extends $\mathcal{DE}$ means that the domains of common variables are identical and that possibly new domain expressions have been added to $\mathcal{DE}$. Such new domain expressions deal with new variables on which some constraints have been introduced. These variables range over non-empty domains. Here a failure is reached only when the false constraint $\perp$ is generated.

An example of a transformation rule is the following rule that simplifies the disequality constraint for integer variables:

$$\textit{DISEQUALITY TRANSFORMATION}$$

$$\frac{\langle s \neq t \; ; \; \mathcal{DE} \rangle}{\langle x \neq t, \; x = s \; ; \; \mathcal{DE}, x \in \mathcal{Z} \rangle}$$

where

- s is not a variable,
- $\mathcal{DE}$ is a sequence of the domain expressions involving the variables present in s and t,
- x is a variable that does not appear in $\mathcal{DE}$.

Another example is the following rule that substitutes a variable by a value, in case the domain of this variable is a singleton set:

$$\textit{VARIABLE ELIMINATION}$$

$$\frac{\langle C \; ; \; \mathcal{DE}, x = a \rangle}{\langle C\{x/\bar{a}\} \; ; \; \mathcal{DE}, x = a \rangle}$$

where x occurs in C.

We assume here that the constraints in C are written in some further unspecified language. Here $\bar{a}$ stands for the constant that denotes in this language the value a and $C\{x/\bar{a}\}$ denotes the set of constraints obtained from C by substituting in each of them every occurrence of x by $\bar{a}$. So x does not occur in $C\{x/\bar{a}\}$.

To further clarify this rule consider the following instance of it:

$$\frac{\langle 3xy^2 + 5xy - 5yz \leq 6 \; ; \; x \in [0..100], y = 2, z \in [0..100] \rangle}{\langle 22x - 10z \leq 6 \; ; \; x \in [0..100], y = 2, z \in [0..100] \rangle}$$

It transforms a non-linear constraint to a linear one.

Typical examples of transformation rules are

Introduction rules. These rules are of the form

$$\frac{\langle \mathcal{C} \; ; \; \mathcal{DE} \rangle}{\langle \mathcal{C}, C \; ; \; \mathcal{DE} \rangle}$$

in which a new constraint, C, was introduced in the conclusion.

If such a rule does not depend on $\mathcal{DE}$, then we abbreviate it to

$$\frac{\mathcal{C}}{\mathcal{C}, C}$$

and similarly with other transformation rules.

As an example of an introduction rule recall the already mentioned in Subsection 3.2.6 resolution rule:

$$RESOLUTION$$

$$\frac{C_1 \vee L, C_2 \vee \bar{L}}{C_1 \vee L, C_2 \vee \bar{L}, C_1 \vee C_2}$$

We assume here that C_1 and C_2 are clauses, L is a literal, $\bar{L}$ the literal opposite to L and that all variables range over the $\{0, 1\}$ domain.

4.1.2 Derivations

Now that we have defined the proof rules, we define the result of applying a proof rule to a CSP. Intuitively, a rule application leads to a replacement in the given CSP of the part that coincides with the premise by the conclusion and the restriction of the 'old' constraints to the new domains in case this is a domain reduction rule. Because of possible variable clashes we need to be more precise. So assume a CSP of the form $\langle \mathcal{C} \cup \mathcal{C}_1 \; ; \; \mathcal{DE}, \mathcal{DE}_1 \rangle$, where $\mathcal{C}$ and $\mathcal{C}_1$ are disjoint, and consider a rule of the form

$$\frac{\langle \mathcal{C}_1 \; ; \; \mathcal{DE}_1 \rangle}{\langle \mathcal{C}_2 \; ; \; \mathcal{DE}_2 \rangle} \tag{4.1}$$

Call a variable that appears in the conclusion but not in the premise an ***introduced variable*** of the rule. The application of the rule (4.1) to the CSP $\langle \mathcal{C} \cup \mathcal{C}_1 \; ; \; \mathcal{DE}, \mathcal{DE}_1 \rangle$ is performed by carrying out the following steps:

- ***rename*** the introduced variables of (4.1) so that they do not appear in $\langle \mathcal{C} \; ; \; \mathcal{DE} \rangle$,
- ***replace*** the $\langle \mathcal{C}_1 \; ; \; \mathcal{DE}_1 \rangle$ part by $\langle \mathcal{C}_2 \; ; \; \mathcal{DE}_2 \rangle$,
- ***restrict*** the constraints of $\mathcal{C}$ to the domains of $\mathcal{DE}, \mathcal{DE}_2$. Denote the resulting set of constraints by $\mathcal{C}'$.

We say then that rule (4.1) *can be applied* to $\langle \mathcal{C} \cup \mathcal{C}_1 \; ; \; \mathcal{DE}, \mathcal{DE}_1 \rangle$ and call

$$\langle \mathcal{C}' \cup \mathcal{C}_2 \; ; \; \mathcal{DE}, \mathcal{DE}_2 \rangle$$

the *result of applying rule* (4.1) *to* $\langle \mathcal{C} \cup \mathcal{C}_1 \; ; \; \mathcal{DE}, \mathcal{DE}_1 \rangle$.

The following lemma explains why the equivalence preserving rules are important.

Lemma 4.2 (Equivalence) *Suppose that the CSP ψ is the result of applying an equivalence preserving rule to the CSP ϕ. Then ϕ and ψ are equivalent.*

Proof   The proof is left as Exercise 4.1.   □

To discuss the effect of an application of a proof rule to a CSP we introduce the following notions.

Definition 4.3   Consider two CSPs ϕ and ψ and a rule R.

- Suppose that ψ is the result of applying the rule R to the CSP ϕ. If ψ differs from ϕ, then we call this a **relevant application** of R to ϕ.
- Suppose that the rule R cannot be applied to ϕ or no application of it to ϕ is relevant. Then we say that ϕ is **closed under the applications of** R.   □

When the constraints are represented in some language, it is in general not easy to determine whether a rule application is relevant, or whether a CSP is closed under the applications of the considered rules. Fortunately, we shall use both concepts only in concrete situations in which it will be easy to check them.

When introducing proof rules our intention is to obtain CSPs that are closed under the applications of these rules. So the last notion is crucial for our considerations. To understand it better consider the following examples.

Example 4.4

(i) Consider the following domain reduction rule already discussed in Subsection 3.2.6:

$$\frac{\langle x < y \; ; \; x \in [l_x..h_x], y \in [l_y..h_y] \rangle}{\langle x < y \; ; \; x \in [l_x..min(h_x, h_y - 1)], y \in [max(l_y, l_x + 1)..h_y] \rangle}$$

It is easy to check that the CSP considered there

$$\langle x < y, y < z \; ; \; x \in [50..98], y \in [51..99], z \in [52..100] \rangle$$

is closed under the applications of this rule.

(ii) Assume for a moment the expected interpretation of propositional formulas. As a more subtle example consider now the CSP

$$\phi := \langle x \wedge y = z \ ; \ x \in \{0, 1\}, y = 0, z = 0 \rangle.$$

Here $y = 0$ is an abbreviation for the domain expression $y \in \{0\}$ and similarly for $z = 0$.

This CSP is closed under the applications of the transformation rule

$$\frac{\langle x \wedge y = z \ ; \ x = 1, y \in D_y, z \in D_z \rangle}{\langle y = z \ ; \ x = 1, y \in D_y, z \in D_z \rangle}$$

since this rule cannot be applied to ϕ.

(iii) In contrast, the CSP $\phi := \langle x \wedge y = z \ ; \ x = 1, y \in \{0, 1\}, z \in \{0, 1\} \rangle$ is not closed under the applications of the above rule because this rule can be applied to ϕ and the outcome, $\langle y = z \ ; \ x = 1, y \in \{0, 1\}, z \in \{0, 1\} \rangle$, differs from ϕ. □

By iterating rule applications we obtain derivations. Intuitively, the derivations correspond to the computation process started with the initial CSP. In practice, all the used proof rules will be equivalence preserving. So, ideally, we would like to reach using derivations either a solved or a failed CSP, because this way we could either generate all solutions to the initial CSP or show that no solution exists. Unfortunately, in general this is not possible. Therefore we strive at a less ambitious goal, namely reducing the original CSP to one that is closed under the applications of the considered rules. This brings us to the following notions that are of interest to us.

Definition 4.5 Assume a finite set of proof rules.

- By a **derivation** we mean a sequence of CSPs such that each of them is obtained from the previous one by an application of a proof rule.
- A finite derivation is called
  - **successful** if its last element is a first solved CSP in this derivation,
  - **failed** if its last element is a first failed CSP in this derivation,
  - **stabilising** if its last element is a first CSP in this derivation that is closed under the applications of the considered proof rules. □

The following examples illustrate these notions.

Example 4.6 Take the *EQUALITY* and *DISEQUALITY* rules introduced earlier in this section.

(i) First consider the CSP

$$\langle x = y, y \neq z, u \neq z \; ; \; x \in \{a, b, c\}, y \in \{a, b, d\}, z \in \{a, b\}, u = b \rangle$$

depicted in Figure 4.1.

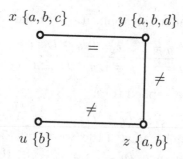

Fig. 4.1. A CSP consisting of equality and disequality constraints

Applying the *EQUALITY* rule to the $x = y$ constraint we obtain the CSP

$$\langle x = y, y \neq z, u \neq z \; ; \; x \in \{a, b\}, y \in \{a, b\}, z \in \{a, b\}, u = b \rangle.$$

Then applying the *DISEQUALITY* rule to the $u \neq z$ constraint we obtain

$$\langle x = y, y \neq z \; ; \; x \in \{a, b\}, y \in \{a, b\}, z = a, u = b \rangle.$$

Another application of the *DISEQUALITY* rule, this time to the $y \neq z$ constraint, yields

$$\langle x = y \; ; \; x \in \{a, b\}, y = b, z = a, u = b \rangle.$$

Finally, by the second application of the *EQUALITY* rule to the $x = y$ constraint we obtain the solved CSP

$$\langle \; ; \; x = b, y = b, z = a, u = b \rangle.$$

So we exhibited a successful derivation. This shows that using the *EQUA-LITY* and *DISEQUALITY* rules we could find a unique solution to the original CSP, namely (b, b, a, b).

(ii) Next, consider the CSP

$$\langle x = y, y \neq z, x \neq z \; ; \; x \in \{a, c\}, y \in \{b, c, d\}, z = c \rangle$$

depicted in Figure 4.2.

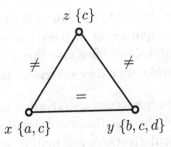

Fig. 4.2. An inconsistent CSP consisting of equality and disequality constraints

Applying the *EQUALITY* rule we obtain here

$$\langle y \neq z, x \neq z \; ; \; x = c, y = c, z = c \rangle.$$

Now applying the *DISEQUALITY* rule to the $y \neq z$ constraint we get the failed CSP

$$\langle x \neq z \; ; \; x = c, y \in \emptyset, z = c \rangle.$$

So we exhibited a failed derivation. Note that the last CSP is not closed under the applications of the *DISEQUALITY* rule so this derivation is not stabilising.

(iii) Finally, consider the CSP

$$\langle x = y, y \neq z, x \neq z \; ; \; x \in \{a, b, c\}, y \in \{a, b, d\}, z = c \rangle$$

depicted in Figure 4.3.

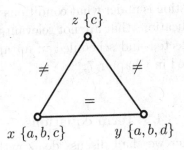

Fig. 4.3. A consistent CSP consisting of equality and disequality constraints

Applying the *EQUALITY* rule we obtain now

$$\langle x = y, y \neq z, x \neq z \; ; \; x \in \{a, b\}, y \in \{a, b\}, z = c \rangle.$$

The *EQUALITY* can be again applied to this CSP but its application is not relevant. Further, the *DISEQUALITY* rule cannot be applied here. So this CSP is closed under the applications of these two rules. Consequently, this one step derivation is stabilising. Note also that this CSP is neither solved nor failed. So this derivation is neither successful nor failed.   □

It is easy to see that every successful derivation is stabilising. Further, as we have just seen, it is not the case that every failed derivation is stabilising.

Usually, the stabilising derivations are neither successful nor failed. In fact, many constraint solvers yield CSPs that are neither solved nor failed: their aim is to bring the initial CSP to some specific, simpler form that usually satisfies some specific local consistency notion.

By definition the derivations can be either finite or infinite. Of course, in practice we would like to avoid infinite derivations. One possibility is to ensure that each infinite derivation has a prefix that is a stabilising (which subsumes successful) or a failed derivation. Then we can prevent a generation of the infinite derivations once we can test that a CSP is failed or closed under the applications of the considered proof rules.

A natural question then arises how to generate failed or stabilising derivations. Of course, in general, such derivations may not exist. However, when all rules are domain reduction rules and the initial CSP has finite domains, then it is easy to generate such derivations. Indeed, it suffices then to limit one's attention to relevant rule applications, i.e., only consider derivations in which each rule application is relevant. Alternatively, one can schedule the rules in an appropriate way. This way we can reach a CSP that is closed under the applications of the considered rules. These issues are further elaborated in Exercise 4.2.

Another natural question is under what conditions the final CSP is unique. Also, to avoid rule applications that are not relevant, in any implementation the rules should be selected and scheduled in an appropriate way. These matters will be discussed in Chapter 7.

4.2 Term equations

The first complete solver we shall discuss deals with solving finite sets of term equations. It is known as the unification problem and is of paramount importance for automated theorem proving and for logic programming.

To properly define it we introduce in the subsequent subsections a language of terms, the notion of a substitution and of a most general unifier. Then we show how the unification problem can be formulated as the task of solving certain type of CSPs. To solve the unification problem we introduce a set of rules in the sense of the proof theoretic framework of the previous section and formulate the appropriate algorithm using these rules.

4.2.1 Terms

We begin by introducing the notion of an alphabet. An **alphabet** consists of the following disjoint classes of symbols:

- *variables*,
- *function symbols*,
- *parentheses*, which are: '(' and ')',
- *comma*, that is: ',' .

We assume that the set of variables is infinite and fixed. We denote the variables by x, y, z, u. In contrast, the set of function symbols may vary and in particular may be empty. Each function symbol has a fixed **arity**, that is the number of arguments associated with it. 0-ary function symbols are called

- *constants*, and are denoted by a, b, c, d.

We denote function symbols of positive arity by f, g, h, k.
   Terms are defined inductively as follows:

- a variable is a term,
- if f is an n-ary function symbol and $t_1, \ldots, t_n$ are terms, then $f(t_1, \ldots, t_n)$ is a term.

In particular every constant is a term. Terms are denoted by s, t, v.

Example 4.7 Consider an alphabet with two constants, a and b, one unary function symbol, f, and one binary function symbol, g. Then the following are examples of terms in this alphabet (separated by ';'):

$$f(a); \ g(x, a); \ g(f(a), f(b)); \ f(g(a, y)).$$

In contrast, none of these strings of symbols is a term:

$$f(x, a); \ g(b); \ f(g(x)); \ g(a, f(a, b)).$$

□

The set of terms is thus determined by the set of the function symbols of the considered alphabet. In what follows we denote by $Var(s)$ the set of variables occurring in s. Given two terms s and t we write $s \equiv t$ to denote that s and t are identical. The often used for this purpose equality symbol '=' is reserved for writing term equations. Also we write $s \not\equiv t$ to denote that s and t differ.

4.2.2 Substitutions

Consider now a fixed alphabet and consequently a fixed set of terms. A *substitution* is a finite mapping from variables to terms which assigns to each variable x in its domain a term t different from x. We write it as

$$\{x_1/t_1, \ldots, x_n/t_n\}$$

where

- $x_1, \ldots, x_n$ are different variables,
- $t_1, \ldots, t_n$ are terms,
- for $i \in [1..n]$, $x_i \not\equiv t_i$.

Informally, it is to be read: the variables $x_1, \ldots, x_n$ are *simultaneously replaced by* $t_1, \ldots, t_n$, respectively. A pair x_i/t_i is called a **binding**. When $n = 0$, the mapping becomes the empty mapping. The resulting substitution is then called the **empty substitution** and is denoted by ε.

Further, given a substitution $\theta := \{x_1/t_1, \ldots, x_n/t_n\}$ we denote

- by $Dom(\theta)$, the set of variables $\{x_1, \ldots, x_n\}$, and
- by $Range(\theta)$, the set of terms $\{t_1, \ldots, t_n\}$.

We now define the result of **applying a substitution θ to a term s**, written as $s\theta$, as the result of the simultaneous replacement of each occurrence in s of a variable from $Dom(\theta)$ by the corresponding term in $Range(\theta)$. We call then $s\theta$ an **instance of** s. Further, for two substitutions θ and η we write $\theta = \eta$ if for all variables x we have $x\theta \equiv x\eta$.

Example 4.8 Consider a language allowing us to build arithmetic expressions in prefix form. It contains two binary function symbols, '+' and '·' and infinitely many constants: 0, 1, ... Then $s := +(\cdot(x, 7), \cdot(4, y))$ is a term and for the substitution $\theta := \{x/0, y/ + (z, 2)\}$ we have

$$s\theta \equiv +(\cdot(0, 7), \cdot(4, +(z, 2))).$$

$\square$

Next, we define the composition of two substitutions.

Definition 4.9 Let θ and γ be substitutions. Their composition is defined as follows. We define first a mapping η from the variables to terms by putting for a variable x

$$\eta(x) := (x\theta)\gamma.$$

In other words, η assigns to a variable x the term obtained by applying the substitution γ to the term $x\theta$. Clearly, for $x \notin Dom(\theta) \cup Dom(\gamma)$ we have $\eta(x) \equiv x$, so η is not an identity only on finitely many variables. Hence η uniquely identifies a substitution that we denote by $\theta\gamma$ and call the *composition* of θ and γ.   □

For example, for $\theta = \{u/z, x/a, y/f(x,b)\}$ and $\gamma = \{x/c, z/u\}$ we can check that $\theta\gamma = \{x/a, y/f(c,b), z/u\}$.

Next, we introduce the following notion.

Definition 4.10 Let θ and η be substitutions. We say that θ is *more general than* η if for some substitution γ we have $\eta = \theta\gamma$.   □

For example, $\{x/y\}$ is more general than $\{x/a, y/a\}$ since $\{x/y\}\{y/a\} = \{x/a, y/a\}$. The notion of 'more general than' is pretty subtle. Note for example that the substitution $\{x/y\}$ is not more general than $\{x/a\}$. Indeed, if we had $\{x/y\}\gamma = \{x/a\}$ for some substitution γ, then the binding y/a would belong to γ and thus also to $\{x/y\}\gamma$. An analogous argument shows that $\{x/y\}$ is not more general than the empty substitution ε either.

Thus θ is more general than η if η can be obtained from θ by applying to it some substitution γ. Since γ can be chosen to be the empty substitution ε, we conclude that every substitution is more general than itself.

4.2.3 Unifiers and mgus

As stated at the beginning of this section we are interested in solving finite sets of term equations. To define precisely the considered problem we need to introduce a couple of notions.

Definition 4.11 Consider a finite set of term equations (or, simply, equations) $\{s_1 = t_1, \ldots, s_n = t_n\}$.

- We define the result of *applying a substitution* θ to such a set of equations by

$$\{s_1 = t_1, \ldots, s_n = t_n\}\theta := \{s_1\theta = t_1\theta, \ldots, s_n\theta = t_n\theta\}.$$

- θ is called a **unifier** of $\{s_1 = t_1, \ldots, s_n = t_n\}$ if

$$s_1\theta \equiv t_1\theta, \ldots, s_n\theta \equiv t_n\theta.$$

  If a unifier θ of a singleton set $\{s = t\}$ exists, then we say that θ is a **unifier** of $s = t$. We also say that s and t are **unifiable** and call such a θ a **unifier** of s and t.

- A unifier θ of a finite set of equations E is called a **most general unifier** (in short **mgu**) of E if it is more general than all unifiers of E.

$\square$

Intuitively, an mgu is a substitution which makes in each equation both terms identical but which does it in a 'most general way', without unnecessary bindings. Note that if a finite set of term equations has a unifier, then it has an infinite number of unifiers. Indeed, if θ is a unifier of such a set E, then so is $\theta\gamma$ for any substitution γ. However, this infinite set admits a finite representation. This is the essence of the definition of a most general unifier and of the final theorem of this section.

Let us consider an example.

Example 4.12

(i) Consider $E := \{f(g(x, a), z) = f(y, b)\}$. Then $\{x/c, y/g(c, a), z/b\}$ is one of the unifiers of E and so is $\{y/g(x, a), z/b\}$ which is more general than $\{x/c, y/g(c, a), z/b\}$ since

$$\{x/c, y/g(c, a), z/b\} = \{y/g(x, a), z/b\}\{x/c\}.$$

Actually, one can show that $\{y/g(x, a), z/b\}$ is an mgu of E.

(ii) Next, consider $\{f(g(a, y), z) = f(h(x, b), b)\}$. It has no unifier as for no substitution θ we have $g(a, y)\theta \equiv h(x, b)\theta$.

(iii) Finally, consider $\{g(x, a) = g(f(x), a)\}$. It has no unifier either because $f(x)\theta \equiv f(x\theta)$ and hence for any substitution θ the term $x\theta$ is a proper substring of $f(x)\theta$ and thus differs from $f(x)\theta$.

$\square$

The problem of deciding whether a finite set of term equations has a unifier is called the **unification problem**. It is solved by providing an algorithm that terminates with failure if the set has no unifier and otherwise produces a most general unifier of it.

In general, a unifier may not exist for two reasons. The first one is exemplified in item (ii) above which shows that two terms starting with a different function symbol cannot unify. The second one is exemplified in item (iii) above which shows that x and $f(x)$ (or more generally, x and a term different from x but in which x occurs) cannot unify. As we saw, each possibility can occur at an 'inner level' of the considered two terms. These two possibilities can be found back in the discussed unification algorithm. In the correctness proof of this algorithm we shall rely on the following notion.

Definition 4.13 Given a set of equations E we say that an equation from E is in **solved form** if it is of the form $x = t$, where $x \notin Var(t)$ and x does not occur elsewhere in E. If each equation in E is in solved form, we say that E is **in solved form**. □

So a finite set of equations is in solved form if it is of the form

$$\{x_1 = t_1, \ldots, x_n = t_n\},$$

where the x_is are distinct variables and none of them occurs in a term t_j.

Example 4.14
(i) The set of equations $\{z = h(g(a)), x = g(a), y = b\}$ is in solved form, because the variables z, x and y occur in it only once.

(ii) In contrast, the set of equations $\{z = h(g(z)), x = g(a), y = b\}$ is not in solved form, because z appears in $h(g(z))$. □

The interest in finite sets of equations in solved form is revealed by the following lemma. The reference to a strong mgu will be helpful in the correctness proof of the unification algorithm.

Lemma 4.15 (Solved Form) *Call an mgu θ of a set of equations E **strong** if for every unifier η of E we have $\eta = \theta\eta$. If $E := \{x_1 = t_1, \ldots, x_n = t_n\}$ is in solved form, then the substitution $\theta := \{x_1/t_1, \ldots, x_n/t_n\}$ is a strong mgu of E.*

Proof First note that θ is a unifier of E. Indeed, for $i \in [1, n]$ we have $x_i\theta \equiv t_i$ and moreover $t_i\theta \equiv t_i$, since by assumption no x_j occurs in t_i.
Next, suppose η is a unifier of E. Then for $i \in [1, n]$ we have $x_i\eta \equiv t_i\eta \equiv x_i\theta\eta$ because $t_i \equiv x_i\theta$ and for $x \notin \{x_1, \ldots, x_n\}$ we have $x\eta \equiv x\theta\eta$ because $x \equiv x\theta$. So we showed that for all variables x we have $x\eta \equiv x\theta\eta$. Thus by definition $\eta = \theta\eta$, that is, θ is a strong mgu. □

We say then that E **determines** θ. For example, the already mentioned set of equations

$$\{z = h(g(a)), x = g(a), y = b\}$$

determines the substitution

$$\{z/h(g(a)), x/g(a), y/b\}.$$

4.2.4 Unification problem and solving of CSPs

True to the spirit of this book we deal with the unification problem by formulating it as a task of solving a CSP. So we first represent it as a CSP and then solve it by repeatedly transforming it until we reach a failed CSP or a CSP from which it is straightforward to generate all solutions.

We now explain how we view finite sets of term equations as a CSP. Fix an alphabet. We assume that the variables range over the same domain, the set of all terms, denoted by $\mathcal{T}$.

Next, we interpret term equations as constraints. Consider an equation $s = t$ with the variables $x_1, \ldots, x_n$ occurring in it. We interpret $s = t$ as the following subset of the Cartesian product $\mathcal{T}^n$:

$$\{(x_1\eta, \ldots, x_n\eta) \mid \eta \text{ is a unifier of } s \text{ and } t\}.$$

Example 4.16

(i) Consider the equation $x = f(y)$. We interpret it as the following subset of $\mathcal{T}^2$:

$$\{(x\eta, y\eta) \mid \eta \text{ is a unifier of } x \text{ and } f(y)\}.$$

One can show that η is a unifier of x and $f(y)$ iff it is of the form $\{x/f(y)\}\gamma$, where γ is an arbitrary substitution. So the above set equals

$$\{(f(y)\gamma, y\gamma) \mid \gamma \text{ is a substitution}\}.$$

Alternatively, we can write this set as

$$\{(f(t), t) \mid t \text{ is a term}\}.$$

$\square$

This leads to a unique interpretation of a finite set of term equations E as a CSP. The following simple observation then links the notions of a solution to a CSP and of a unifier. For a CSP $\mathcal{P}$ we write here $Sol(\mathcal{P})$ to denote the set of all solutions to $\mathcal{P}$.

Note 4.17 (Unification) *Consider a finite set of term equations E with the variables $x_1, \ldots, x_n$. Then*

$$Sol(\langle E \ ; \ x_1 \in \mathcal{T}, \ldots, x_n \in \mathcal{T} \rangle) = \{(x_1\eta, \ldots, x_n\eta) \mid \eta \text{ is a unifier of } E\}.$$

Proof It is a direct consequence of the way we interpret the equations as constraints. □

This observation allows us to reduce the problem of finding a unifier to the problem of solving a CSP.

4.2.5 The *UNIF* proof system

To solve the unification problem we now introduce six transformation rules. These rules do not depend on the domain expressions, so they refer only to the constraints, i.e., to the equations. These rules amount to some syntactic manipulations of the constraints, so they are actually applied to the syntactic representations of the considered constraints.

$$DECOMPOSITION$$

$$\frac{f(s_1, \ldots, s_n) = f(t_1, \ldots, t_n)}{s_1 = t_1, \ldots, s_n = t_n}$$

$$FAILURE \ 1$$

$$\frac{f(s_1, \ldots, s_n) = g(t_1, \ldots, t_m)}{\perp}$$

where $f \not\equiv g$,

$$DELETION$$

$$x = x$$

$$TRANSPOSITION$$

$$\frac{t = x}{x = t}$$

where t is not a variable,

$$SUBSTITUTION$$

$$\frac{x = t, \; E}{x = t, \; E\{x/t\}}$$

where $x \notin Var(t)$ and $x \in var(E)$,

$$FAILURE \; 2$$

$$\frac{x = t}{\perp}$$

where $x \in Var(t)$ and $x \not\equiv t$.

Recall that the ordering of the constraints in the rules is irrelevant so in the *SUBSTITUTION* rule the order of the considered equations is immaterial. Denote the set of the above six rules by *UNIF*. To illustrate the use of these rules consider an example. As the variable domains are always equal to the set of all terms, $\mathcal{T}$, we drop the references to the domain expressions and just consider sets of equations. The selected equations are underlined.

Example 4.18
(i) Consider the set of equations

$$\{k(z, f(x, b, z)) = k(h(x), f(g(a), y, z))\}.$$

Using the *DECOMPOSITION* rule we get

$$\{z = h(x), \underline{f(x, b, z) = f(g(a), y, z)}\}.$$

Using the *DECOMPOSITION* rule again we get

$$\{z = h(x), x = g(a), b = y, \underline{z = z}\}.$$

Using the *DELETION* rule we can get rid of the last equation. This yields

$$\{z = h(x), x = g(a), \underline{b = y}\}.$$

By the *TRANSPOSITION* rule we get

$$\{z = h(x), \underline{x = g(a)}, y = b\}.$$

Using the *SUBSTITUTION* rule with $x = g(a)$ as the isolated equation we get

$$\{z = h(g(a)), x = g(a), y = b\}.$$

At this stage no rule applies so we reached a CSP closed under the applications of the rules of *UNIF*.

(ii) Consider now the set of equations

$$\{k(z, f(x, b, z)) = k(h(x), f(g(z), y, z))\}.$$

The only difference between this set and the one considered in (i) is that instead of the subterm $g(a)$ here the subterm $g(z)$ occurs. Let us try to repeat the choices made in (i). By the *DECOMPOSITION* rule we get

$$\{z = h(x), \underline{f(x, b, z) = f(g(z), y, z)}\}.$$

By another application of the *DECOMPOSITION* rule we get

$$\{z = h(x), x = g(z), b = y, \underline{z = z}\}.$$

Using the *DELETION* rule we can get rid of the last equation. This yields

$$\{z = h(x), x = g(z), \underline{b = y}\}.$$

By the *TRANSPOSITION* rule we now get

$$\{z = h(x), \underline{x = g(z)}, y = b\}.$$

Next, by the *SUBSTITUTION* rule with $x = g(z)$ as the isolated equation we get

$$\{\underline{z = h(g(z))}, x = g(z), y = b\}.$$

Now, however, the *FAILURE 2* rule applies and we get the set

$$\{\bot, x = g(z), y = b\}$$

that contains the false constraint $\bot$. By definition, no rule can be applied to a failed CSP, so the last set closed under the applications of the rules of *UNIF*. $\qquad\square$

Unfortunately, if we use as the algorithm the rules of *UNIF* applied in an arbitrary fashion, this algorithm can diverge, as the following example shows. As before the selected equations are underlined.

Example 4.19 Consider the set of equations

$$\{\underline{x = f(y)}, y = g(x), \underline{x = a}\}.$$

Using the *SUBSTITUTION* rule with $x = f(y)$ as the isolated equation we get

$$\{x = f(y), \underline{y = g(x), f(y) = a}\}.$$

Again using the *SUBSTITUTION* rule, this time with $y = g(x)$ as the isolated equation, we get

$$\{x = f(y), y = g(x), \underline{f(g(x)) = a}\}.$$

Iterating this process we get an infinite derivation. Note also that the third equation repeatedly changes so each rule application is relevant and consequently no prefix of this infinite derivation is a stabilising derivation. $\quad\square$

So the *SUBSTITUTION* rule as it stands causes problems. Before we consider a possible remedy let us prove that in absence of divergence the *UNIF* system allows us to solve the original set of term equations. We need first the following lemma.

Lemma 4.20 (*UNIF*) *Each rule of UNIF is equivalence preserving w.r.t. the sequence of the variables present in the rule premise.*

Proof   On the account of the Unification Note 4.17 it suffices to prove that for each rule the sets of equations considered in the premise and in the conclusion have the same set of unifiers.

This claim holds for the *DECOMPOSITION* rule because for all θ we have $f(s_1, \ldots, s_n)\theta \equiv f(t_1, \ldots, t_n)\theta$ iff for $i \in [1, n]$ it holds that $s_i\theta \equiv t_i\theta$. For the *DELETION* and *TRANSPOSITION* rules the claim is obvious.

For the *SUBSTITUTION* rule consider two sets of equations $\{x = t\} \cup E$ and $\{x = t\} \cup E\{x/t\}$ and assume that $x \notin Var(t)$.
Then

$$\theta \text{ is a unifier of } \{x = t\} \cup E$$
$$\text{iff}\quad \theta \text{ is a unifier of } x = t \text{ and } \theta \text{ is a unifier of } E$$
$$\text{iff}\quad \{\text{Solved Form Lemma 4.15}\}$$
$$\theta \text{ is a unifier of } x = t \text{ and } \{x/t\}\theta \text{ is a unifier of } E$$
$$\text{iff}\quad \theta \text{ is a unifier of } x = t \text{ and } \theta \text{ is a unifier of } E\{x/t\}$$
$$\text{iff}\quad \theta \text{ is a unifier of } \{x = t\} \cup E\{x/t\}.$$

Finally, for the *FAILURE 1* and *FAILURE 2* rules the claim holds since in each case no unifier exists for the equation in the rule premise. $\quad\square$

We can now establish the relevant result.

Theorem 4.21 (*UNIF*) *Consider a failed or a stabilising derivation in the proof system UNIF starting with a finite set of equations E and terminating* *with a set of constraints F. If E has a unifier, then F is in solved form that determines an mgu of E and otherwise F contains the false constraint $\perp$.*

Proof If F does not contain $\perp$, the final set of constraints F is closed under the applications of all the rules of *UNIF*. Then on the account of the *DECOMPOSITION, FAILURE 1* and *TRANSPOSITION* rules the left-hand side of every equation in F is a variable. Further, on the account of the *DELETION, SUBSTITUTION* and *FAILURE 2* rules these variables are distinct and none of them occurs in the right-hand side of an equation in F. This implies that F is in solved form. By the Unification Note 4.17 and the *UNIF* Lemma 4.20 F has the same set of unifiers as the original set E. So, on the account of the Solved Form Lemma 4.15, F determines an mgu of E.

If the final set of constraints F contains $\perp$, then the last selected equation is either $f(s_1, \ldots, s_n) = g(t_1, \ldots, t_m)$ with $f \not\equiv g$, or $x = t$ with $x \in Var(t)$ and $x \not\equiv t$. In both cases the selected equation has no unifier. By the the Unification Note 4.17 and the *UNIF* Lemma 4.20 E has no unifier.

This implies the claim. $\qquad\square$

4.2.6 The MARTELLI–MONTANARI algorithm

To ensure termination we introduce the following concept, where we refer to the arbitrary rules as considered in Section 4.1.

Definition 4.22 Consider a CSP $\mathcal{P} := \langle \mathcal{C} \; ; \; \mathcal{DE} \rangle$ and a rule

$$\frac{\langle \mathcal{C} \; ; \; \mathcal{DE} \rangle}{\langle \mathcal{C}' \; ; \; \mathcal{DE}' \rangle}$$

Then $\langle \mathcal{C}' \; ; \; \mathcal{DE}' \rangle$ is the result of applying this rule to $\mathcal{P}$. We call this rule application **global**. $\qquad\square$

So in the global rule application *all* constraints and domain expressions present in the considered CSP are used in the rule premise.

Example 4.23 Reconsider the set of equations

$$\{x = f(y), y = g(x), x = a\}$$

of Example 4.19. We begin with

$$\{\underline{x = f(y)}, y = g(x), x = a\},$$

where $x = f(y)$ is the isolated equation. Using the *SUBSTITUTION* rule we get

$$\{x = f(y), \underline{y = g(f(y))}, f(y) = a\}.$$

Now, using the *FAILURE 2* rule we get

$$\{x = f(y), \perp, f(y) = a\}$$

and the derivation terminates with a failed CSP. □

Note that the considered application of the *SUBSTITUTION* rule was global. In contrast, the applications of the *SUBSTITUTION* rule considered in Example 4.19 were not global: each time one equation was 'left out'. Note also the applications of the *SUBSTITUTION* rule considered in Example 4.18 were not global either. However, they amounted to global applications since each time the substituted variable occurred only in one other equation. In contrast, the applications of the *SUBSTITUTION* rule considered in Example 4.19 do not correspond to the global applications since each time the substituted variables occurred in two other equations.

So the use of global applications of the *SUBSTITUTION* rule can make a difference. In fact, if we limit ourselves to such applications of this rule, all derivations are finite. More specifically, the following lemma holds.

Lemma 4.24 (Termination) *Every derivation in UNIF in which all the applications of the SUBSTITUTION rule are global is finite.*

Proof   The proof is rather subtle because the *DECOMPOSITION* and *SUBSTITUTION* rules seem to be 'in conflict' with each other. The first one makes the equations structurally simpler while the second rule can make the individual equations more complex.

A solution is to order in an appropriate way the relevant quantities that are supposed to decrease. To this end we use the following relation $\prec_3$ defined on triples of natural numbers:

$$(a_1, a_2, a_3) \prec_3 (b_1, b_2, b_3)$$

iff

$$a_1 < b_1$$
$$\text{or} \quad a_1 = b_1 \text{ and } a_2 < b_2$$
$$\text{or} \quad a_1 = b_1 \text{ and } a_2 = b_2 \text{ and } a_3 < b_3.$$

For example, we have $(1, 15, 10000) \prec_3 (2, 1, 1)$, $(1, 15, 10000) \prec_3 (1, 16, 1)$ and $(1, 16, 1) \prec_3 (1, 16, 10000)$.

This relation, called a **lexicographic ordering** (here on the triples of natural numbers), is **well-founded** which means that no infinite $\prec_3$-descending sequence of triples of natural numbers exists.

Given a set of equations E, we call a variable x **solved in** E if for some term t we have $x = t \in E$ and this is the only occurrence of x in E, that is, if the equation $x = t$ is in solved form. We call a variable **unsolved in** E if it is not solved.

For example for $E := \{x = f(y), y = g(b), a = z\}$ the variable x is solved in E while the variables y and z are unsolved.

With each set of equations E we now associate the following three functions:

$uns(E)$ — the number of variables in E that are unsolved,

$lfun(E)$ — the total number of occurrences of function symbols on the left-hand side of an equation in E,

$card(E)$ — the number of equations in E.

We claim that each rule application to a set of equations E reduces the triple of natural numbers

$$(uns(E), lfun(E), card(E))$$

in the lexicographic ordering $\prec_3$. In the case of the *SUBSTITUTION* rule we assume that we are dealing with a global application.

Indeed, no rule application turns a solved variable into an unsolved one, so $uns(E)$ never increases. Further, each application of the *DECOMPOSITION* and *TRANSPOSITION* rule decreases $lfun(E)$ by at least 1. In turn, each application of the *FAILURE 1*, *DELETION* and *FAILURE 2* rules does not change or reduces $lfun(E)$ and decreases $card(E)$ by 1.

Finally, each global application of the *SUBSTITUTION* rule reduces $uns(E)$ by 1. Indeed, 'global' means that at the moment of the rule application $\{x = t\} \cup E$ is the set of all equations. So such an application of the *SUBSTITUTION* rule turns x from an unsolved variable to a solved one. (Note that an arbitrary application of the *SUBSTITUTION* rule does not need to reduce $uns(E)$; see for instance the applications of this rule in Example 4.19.)

The termination is now the consequence of the well-foundedness of $\prec_3$. □

We can now present the desired algorithm. Consider the six rules of the *UNIF* system but limit the use of the *SUBSTITUTION* rule to the global applications. As explained in Section 4.1 these rules determine a constraint solver, in this case a unification algorithm. So the unification algorithm consists of the above six rules together with a scheduler that repeatedly applies them until a failed CSP or a CSP closed under the applications of these rules is reached. In the case of the *SUBSTITUTION* rule only the global applications are performed.

This algorithm is called the MARTELLI–MONTANARI algorithm. Once we view the applications of the *SUBSTITUTION* rule as global applications, the derivations presented in Example 4.18 are example executions of this algorithm. The following result establishes its correctness.

Theorem 4.25 (MARTELLI–MONTANARI **Algorithm**) *The* MARTELLI–MONTANARI *algorithm always terminates. If the original finite set of equations E has a unifier, then each execution of the algorithm terminates with a set of equations in solved form that determines an mgu of E and otherwise each execution terminates with a set containing the false constraint $\perp$.*

Proof It is a direct consequence of the *TERMINATION* Lemma 4.24 and the *UNIF* Theorem 4.21.

$\square$

Let us clarify now why the MARTELLI–MONTANARI algorithm can be viewed as a complete constraint solver. In Subsection 4.2.4 we explained how each set of term equations E with the variables $x_1, \ldots, x_n$ corresponds to a unique CSP $\langle E \, ; \, x_1 \in \mathcal{T}, \ldots, x_n \in \mathcal{T} \rangle$ and summarised this relationship by the Unification Note 4.17.

In particular, for each finite set of equations $E := \{x_1 = t_1, \ldots, x_n = t_n\}$ in solved form we have

$$Sol(\langle E \, ; \, x_1 \in \mathcal{T}, \ldots, x_n \in \mathcal{T} \rangle) = \{(t_1\eta, \ldots, t_n\eta) \mid \eta \text{ is a substitution}\},$$

since by the Solved Form Lemma 4.15 any unifier of E is of the form $\{x_1/t_1, \ldots, x_n/t_n\}\eta$ for an arbitrary substitution η. So it is straightforward to generate all solutions to $\langle E \, ; \, x_1 \in \mathcal{T}, \ldots, x_n \in \mathcal{T} \rangle$ if E is in solved form.

Now, in view of the above theorem, the MARTELLI–MONTANARI algorithm transforms a given finite set of term equations into an equivalent set of equations that is either in solved form or contains the false constraint $\perp$. In the terminology adopted at the beginning of this chapter it means that this algorithm is a complete constraint solver.

It is useful to point out that the MARTELLI–MONTANARI algorithm is inefficient, as for some inputs it can take an exponential time to compute an mgu. A standard example is the following pair of two terms, where $n > 0$:

$$f(x_1, \ldots, x_n) \text{ and } f(g(x_0, x_0), \ldots, g(x_{n-1}, x_{n-1})).$$

Define now inductively a sequence of terms $t_1, \ldots, t_n$ as follows:

$$t_1 := g(x_0, x_0),$$

$$t_{i+1} := g(t_i, t_i).$$

It is easy to check that $\{x_1/t_1, \ldots, x_n/t_n\}$ is then a mgu of the terms $f(x_1, \ldots, x_n)$ and $f(g(x_0, x_0), \ldots, g(x_{n-1}, x_{n-1}))$.

For example, for $n = 2$ the discussed pair of terms is

$$f(x_1, x_2) \text{ and } f(g(x_0, x_0), g(x_1, x_1))$$

and the mentioned mgu is

$$\{x_1/g(x_0, x_0), x_2/g(g(x_0, x_0), g(x_0, x_0))\}.$$

Now, a simple proof by induction shows that each t_i has more than 2^i symbols. This shows that the total number of symbols in any mgu of the above two terms is exponential in their size. So as long as in the MARTELLI–MONTANARI algorithm terms are represented as strings this algorithm runs in exponential time.

Finally, note that the mgu of the above two terms can be computed using n rule applications of the MARTELLI–MONTANARI algorithm. This shows that the number of rule applications used in an execution of the MARTELLI–MONTANARI algorithm is not the right measure of the time complexity of this algorithm. More efficient unification algorithms avoid explicit presentations of the most general unifiers and rely on different internal representation of terms than strings.

4.3 Linear equations over reals

In this section we present two complete constraint solvers that deal with linear equations over reals. To discuss them we define in the next subsection the syntax and relate the linear equations over reals to CSPs. Then we introduce a set of rules in the sense of Section 4.1 and discuss two algorithms for solving finite sets of linear equations in terms of these rules: the GAUSS–JORDAN ELIMINATION algorithm and the GAUSSIAN ELIMINATION algorithm.

4.3.1 Linear expressions and linear equations

Consider an alphabet such that

- each real number is a constant,

- for each real number r a single unary function symbol '$r\cdot$' (standing for the multiplication by r) exists,
- a single binary function symbol '$+$', written in the infix notation, is present.

By a *linear expression over reals* we mean a term formed in this alphabet and by a *linear equation over reals* an equation of the form

$$s = t,$$

where s and t are linear expressions. From now on we omit the qualification 'over reals'.

To facilitate the reading of linear expressions and equations we introduce a number of syntactic conventions. We abbreviate $-1 \cdot (s)$ to $-(s)$, drop the references to $1\cdot$, and abbreviate $r \cdot (x)$ to rx, where r is different than 1 and -1 and x is a variable. We also write $s + (t + v)$ and $(s + t) + v$ as $s + t + v$ and abbreviate $s + (-t)$ to $s - t$. In the presence of these conventions both $4x + 3.5y$ and $3x - 1.2 \cdot (2 + 2.5y) - 2x + 5$ are linear expressions and

$$4x + 3.5y = 3x - 1.2 \cdot (2 + 2.5y) - 2x + 5$$

is a linear equation. Note that terms of the form $s \cdot (t)$, now abbreviated to $s\,t$, are allowed only if s is a constant. Consequently, terms of the form $x\,y$ are not allowed.

We are interested in linear expressions and equations in specific forms.

Definition 4.26 Assume a predetermined ordering $\prec$ on the variables.

- We say that a linear expression is in *normal form* if it is of the form

$$\Sigma_{i=1}^{n} a_i x_i + r, \tag{4.2}$$

where $n \geq 0$, each a_i is a non-zero real number, r is a real number, and the variables $x_1, \ldots, x_n$ are ordered w.r.t. $\prec$.
- We say that a linear equation is in *normal form* if it is of the form

$$\Sigma_{i=1}^{n} a_i x_i = r, \tag{4.3}$$

where $n \geq 0$, each a_i is a non-zero real number, r is a real number, and the variables $x_1, \ldots, x_n$ are ordered w.r.t. $\prec$.
- We say that a linear equation

$$x = t$$

is in *pivot form* if $x \notin Var(t)$ and t is in normal form. $\qquad\square$

Using appropriate transformation rules each linear expression s can be rewritten to a unique linear expression (4.2) in normal form. We then call (4.2) the **normal form of** s and denote it by $norm(s)$. Similarly, using appropriate transformation rules each linear equation $s = t$ can be rewritten to a unique equivalent linear equation (4.3) in normal form. (We shall explain the meaning of the qualification 'equivalent' in Subsection 4.3.3.) We then call (4.3) **the normal form of** $s = t$ and say that $s = t$ **normalises to** (4.3).

In all subsequent examples we assume that x precedes y. So for example, the already mentioned linear expression $3x - 1.2 \cdot (2 + 2.5y) - 2x + 5$ can be rewritten to the linear expression $x - 3y + 2.6$ in normal form. Further, the already considered linear equation $4x + 3.5y = 3x - 1.2 \cdot (2 + 2.5y) - 2x + 5$ normalises to the linear equation $3x + 6.5y = 2.6$.

Depending on the value of n and r in (4.3) we distinguish three types of normal forms:

- $0 = 0$, when both $n = 0$ and $r = 0$,
- $0 = r$, when $n = 0$ and r is a non-zero real,
- $\sum_{i=1}^{n} a_i x_i = r$, when $n > 0$.

The linear expressions s and $norm(s)$ are equivalent in the sense that the normal form of the linear equation $s = norm(s)$ is $0 = 0$.

With the last type of a normal form we associate n linear equations in pivot form:

$$x_j = \Sigma_{i \in [1..j-1] \cup [j+1..n]} - \frac{a_i}{a_j} x_i + \frac{r}{a_j}, \qquad (4.4)$$

where $j \in [1..n]$.

Given a linear equation e in pivot form, we stipulate that e is its only pivot form. Further, given a linear equation e not in pivot form, with the normal form (4.3), where $n > 0$, we call each equation of the form (4.4) a **pivot form** of e. Finally, we stipulate that an equation with the normal form $0 = r$, where r is a real has no pivot form.

For example, the linear equation

$$z = 2x + 3y + 4$$

is its only pivot form. Further, the already considered linear equation

$$4x + 3.5y = 3x - 1.2 \cdot (2 + 2.5y) - 2x + 5$$

is not in pivot form and it normalises to $3x + 6.5y = 2.6$, so it has two pivot forms: $x = -\frac{6.5}{3}y + \frac{2.6}{3}$ and $y = -\frac{3}{6.5}x + \frac{2.6}{3}$. Finally, the equation

$x+1+y = x+y+1$ is not in pivot form and it normalises to $0 = 0$, so it has no pivot form.

4.3.2 Substitutions, unifiers and mgus

In the remainder of the exposition we need to slightly adjust the notions introduced in Section 4.2. The following definition summarises the differences.

Definition 4.27

- By a **substitution** we mean a finite mapping from variables to linear expressions in normal form which assigns to each variable x in its domain a linear expression t different from x.

  We write the substitutions in the same way as in the previous section and define the result of applying a substitution to a term (now a linear expression) or to a set of linear equations as before.

- Let θ and γ be substitutions. Their **composition**, written as $\theta\gamma$, is the substitution uniquely identified by the following mapping η from the variables to linear expressions in normal form

$$\eta(x) := norm((x\theta)\gamma).$$

- θ is called a **unifier** of a set of linear equations E if each equation in $E\theta$ normalises to the equation $0 = 0$. If $E = \{e\}$, we say that θ is a **unifier** of e. $\square$

For example, if $\theta := \{x/2y + 1\}$ and $\eta := \{y/2z + 1\}$, then their composition $\theta\eta$ equals $\{x/4z + 3, y/2z + 1\}$. Also, the substitution $\theta := \{x_1/x + 1, x_2/y, x_3/x+y+1\}$ is a unifier of $x_1 + x_2 = x_3$ because $(x_1+x_2)\theta \equiv x+1+y$, $x_3\theta \equiv x+y+1$, and the equation $x+1+y = x+y+1$ normalises to $0 = 0$.

Also, the following concept is a counterpart of the notion of a set of equations in solved form introduced in Definition 4.13.

Definition 4.28 Given a set of linear equations E we say that an equation from E is in **solved form** if it is in the pivot form $x = t$ and x does not occur elsewhere in E. If each equation in E is in solved form, we say that E is **in solved form**. $\square$

So a finite set of linear equations is in solved form if it is of the form $\{x_1 = t_1, \ldots, x_n = t_n\}$, where the x_is are distinct variables, none of them occurs in a term t_j, and the t_is are linear expressions in normal form. We have then the following counterpart of the Solved Form Lemma 4.15.

Lemma 4.29 (Solved Form) *Call an mgu θ of a set of linear equations E **strong** if for every unifier η of E we have $\eta = \theta\eta$. If the set of linear equations $E := \{x_1 = t_1, \ldots, x_n = t_n\}$ is in solved form, then the substitution $\theta := \{x_1/t_1, \ldots, x_n/t_n\}$ is a strong mgu of E.*

Proof First note that θ is a unifier of E. Indeed, for $i \in [1, n]$ we have $x_i\theta \equiv t_i$ and moreover $t_i\theta \equiv t_i$, since by assumption no x_j occurs in t_i. So for $i \in [1..n]$ we have $x_i\theta \equiv t_i\theta$. So the equation $x_i\theta = t_i\theta$ is identical to $t_i = t_i$ and consequently it normalises to $0 = 0$.

Next, suppose η is a unifier of E. This means that for $i \in [1, n]$ the equation $x_i\eta = t_i\eta$ normalises to $0 = 0$. But $t_i \equiv x_i\theta$, so this means that $x_i\eta = x_i\theta\eta$ normalises to $0 = 0$, as well. Further, for $x \notin \{x_1, \ldots, x_n\}$ we have $x\eta \equiv x\theta$. A fortiori, $x\eta = x\theta\eta$ normalises to $0 = 0$.

So we showed that for all variables x the equation $x\eta = x\theta\eta$ normalises to $0 = 0$. But $x\eta$ and $x\theta\eta$ are both linear expressions in normal form, so $x\eta \equiv x\theta\eta$. In other words, $\eta = \theta\eta$, that is, θ is a strong mgu. $\square$

As in the previous section we say then that E **determines** θ.

4.3.3 Linear equations and CSPs

Let us now relate linear equations to constraints. One natural choice for the variable domains is the set of all reals. We pursue here a more general possibility according to which each variable domain consists of the set of linear expressions in normal form, that we denote by $\mathcal{NF}$.

Then we interpret each linear equation as a constraint as follows. With a linear equation e with the variables $x_1, \ldots, x_n$ we associate the following subset of the Cartesian product $\mathcal{NF}^n$:

$$\{(t_1, \ldots, t_n) \mid \text{the equation } e\{x_1/t_1, \ldots, x_n/t_n\} \text{ normalises to } 0 = 0\}.$$

For example, the interpretation of the equation $x_1 + x_2 = x_3$ as a constraint contains as typical elements the triples $(1, 1, 2), (x, y, x+y), (x, y+1, x+y+1)$ and $(x + 1, y, x + y + 1)$. Another way to write the above set is

$$\{(t_1, \ldots, t_n) \mid \{x_1/t_1, \ldots, x_n/t_n\} \text{ is a unifier of } e\}.$$

The resulting interpretation of a set of linear equations as a CSP allows us to talk about solutions to such sets and about equivalence between linear equations. We say that two linear equations e_1 and e_2 with the same sequence of variables $x_1, \ldots, x_n$ are **equivalent** if the corresponding CSPs

$\langle e_1 ; x_1 \in \mathcal{NF}, \ldots, x_n \in \mathcal{NF} \rangle$ and $\langle e_2 ; x_1 \in \mathcal{NF}, \ldots, x_n \in \mathcal{NF} \rangle$ are equivalent, that is, if they have the same set of solutions.

Further, we say that two linear equations e_1 and e_2 with a sequence X of common variables are **equivalent w.r.t.** X if the corresponding CSPs determined by these two equations are equivalent w.r.t. X. Then according to this definition each linear equation e and its normal form are equivalent w.r.t. the sequence of the variables of e.

The following counterpart of the Unification Note 4.17 holds. As in the previous section we denote here by $Sol(\mathcal{P})$ the set of all solutions to a CSP $\mathcal{P}$.

Note 4.30 (Solution) *Consider a finite set of linear equations E with the variables $x_1, \ldots, x_n$. Then*

$$Sol(\langle E ; x_1 \in \mathcal{NF}, \ldots, x_n \in \mathcal{NF} \rangle) = \{(x_1\eta, \ldots, x_n\eta) \mid \eta \text{ is a unifier of } E\}.$$

$\square$

This observation allows us to relate solutions to finite sets of linear equations and unifiers.

4.3.4 The *LIN* proof system

As a final preparation step to present the proof rules we introduce the following notation. Given a linear equation $s = t$ we denote by $stand(s = t)$ the equation $norm(s) = norm(t)$. We call then $stand(s = t)$ the **standard form** of $s = t$ and say that $s = t$ **standardises to** $norm(s) = norm(t)$. We extend the *stand* operation elementwise to sets of linear equations.

For example, the standard form of the equation $x - 2y + y = 4$ is $x - y = 4$, while the standard form of the equation $x = 2y - y + 4$ is $x = y + 4$. So a standard form does not need to be in normal form.

In the algorithms discussed below we repeatedly transform linear equations to a pivot form, perform an appropriate substitution in some other equations and apply to these equations the *stand* operation.

The three possible forms of the normal form naturally induce the following three proof rules.

DELETION

$$\frac{s = v}{}$$

if $s = v$ normalises to $0 = 0$,

FAILURE

$$\frac{s = v}{\bot}$$

if $s = v$ normalises to $0 = r$, where r is a non-zero real,

SUBSTITUTION

$$\frac{s = v,\ E}{x = t,\ stand(E\{x/t\})}$$

where $x = t$ is a pivot form of $s = v$.

Denote the set of these three rules by *LIN*. The *SUBSTITUTION* rule can be applied if the selected linear equation $s = v$ has a pivot form. If $s = v$ has no pivot form, then it normalises to $0 = r$, where r is a real. Then either the *DELETION* or the *FAILURE* rule can be applied. Consequently, to each linear equation exactly one rule can be applied.

If in the *SUBSTITUTION* rule the selected equation $s = v$ is in pivot form, then it is not modified, since $x = t$ is then identical to $s = v$. Otherwise $s = v$ is transformed into one of its pivot forms $x = t$. Note that we do not specify which pivot form we choose and do not insist that $x \in Var(E)$. The substitution $\{x/t\}$ is performed on the equations in E and is followed by the application of the *stand* operation. The set E can be empty.

Using the rules of *LIN* we can solve finite sets of linear equations. These rules can be seen as transformation rules in the sense of Section 4.1, where the sequences of the domain expressions are omitted. Let us consider an example. The selected equations are underlined.

Example 4.31 Consider the following set of linear equations in normal form:

$$\{x - y = 1, -x + y = 1, \underline{x = 0}\}.$$

We apply to it the *SUBSTITUTION* rule with $x = 0$ as the isolated equation. The pivot form of $x = 0$ is $x = 0$, so after performing the substitution and standardisation we get

$$\{\underline{-y = 1}, -x + y = 1, x = 0\}.$$

Using the *SUBSTITUTION* rule again, this time with $-x + y = 1$ as the isolated equation and with its pivot form $y = x + 1$, we get

$$\{\underline{x = -2}, y = x + 1, \underline{x = 0}\}.$$

Using the *SUBSTITUTION* rule again with $x = 0$ as the isolated equation we get after performing the substitution and standardisation

$$\{\underline{0 = -2}, y = x + 1, x = 0\}.$$

Applying now the *FAILURE* rule we reach the set

$$\{\perp, y = x + 1, x = 0\}.$$

So this derivation ends in a failure. Note that after two applications of the *SUBSTITUTION* rule we transformed all equations into a pivot form.

$\square$

Unfortunately, an arbitrary use of the *SUBSTITUTION* rule causes complications, even if we insist that x occurs in the set of equations E. Namely, similarly to the case of the *UNIF* system we can generate infinite derivations. An example is provided in Exercise 4.7. Before we discuss possible remedies let us prove that in absence of divergence the *LIN* system allows us to solve the original set of linear equations. We need first the following lemma.

Lemma 4.32 (*LIN*) *Each rule of LIN is equivalence preserving w.r.t. the sequence of the variables present in the rule premise.*

Proof On the account of the Solution Note 4.30 it suffices to prove that for each rule the sets of equations considered in the premise and in the conclusion have the same set of unifiers.

For the *DELETION* rule and the *FAILURE* rule the claim is an immediate consequence of the fact that each linear equation is equivalent to its normal form.

For the *SUBSTITUTION* we proceed as in the *UNIF* Lemma 4.20. Consider two sets of equations $\{s = v\} \cup E$ and $\{x = t\} \cup stand(E\{x/t\})$ where $x = t$ is a pivot form of $s = v$. Then

$\qquad\qquad \theta$ is a unifier of $\{s = v\} \cup E$

iff $\qquad$ {each equation and its pivot form have the same unifiers}

$\qquad\qquad \theta$ is a unifier of $\{x = t\} \cup E$

iff $\quad \theta$ is a unifier of $x = t$ and θ is a unifier of E

iff $\qquad$ {Solved Form Lemma 4.29}

$\qquad\qquad \theta$ is a unifier of $x = t$ and $\{x/t\}\theta$ is a unifier of E

iff $\quad \theta$ is a unifier of $x = t$ and θ is a unifier of $E\{x/t\}$

iff θ is a unifier of $\{x = t\} \cup E\{x/t\}$

iff $\{E\{x/t\}$ and $stand(E\{x/t\})$ have the same unifiers$\}$

     θ is a unifier of $\{x = t\} \cup stand(E\{x/t\})$.

            □

We can now establish the desired theorem. Its formulation and proof are similar to that of the *UNIF* Theorem 4.21.

Theorem 4.33 (LIN) *Consider a failed or a stabilising derivation in the proof system LIN starting with a finite set of linear equations E and terminating with a set of constraints F. If E has a solution, then F is in solved form that determines an mgu of E and otherwise F contains the false constraint $\perp$.*

Proof   If F does not contain $\perp$, the final set of constraints F is closed under the applications of all the rules of *LIN*. Then on the account of the considered rules each equation in F is in pivot form $x = t$ where x does not occur elsewhere. In other words, F is in solved form. By the Solution Note 4.30 and the *LIN* Lemma 4.32 F has the same set of unifiers as the original set E. So, on the account of the Solved Form Lemma 4.29, F determines an mgu of E.

If the final set of constraints F contains $\perp$, then the last selected equation has the normal form $0 = r$, where r is a non-zero real and hence it has no solution. By the Solution Note 4.30 and the *LIN* Lemma 4.32 E has no solution. This implies the claim.   □

To ensure termination a number of possibilities exist. The most obvious one is to limit attention, as in the previous section, to the global applications of the *SUBSTITUTION* rule and to add the condition $x \in Var(E)$. There also exists a less drastic alternative. Let us discuss these options in turn. In both algorithms we assume for simplicity that the initial linear equations are all in normal form.

4.3.5 The Gauss–Jordan Elimination algorithm

The first algorithm consists of the *LIN* system together with a scheduler that repeatedly applies them until a failed CSP or a CSP closed under the applications of these rules is reached. In the case of the *SUBSTITUTION* rule only the global applications are performed and it is assumed that the condition $x \in Var(E)$ holds. This algorithm is called the Gauss–Jordan

ELIMINATION algorithm, though we present it in a slightly different form. The following example illustrates its operation.

Example 4.34 Take the following set of linear equations:

$$
\begin{aligned}
-x_1 + x_2 + x_3 + 2\,x_4 - x_5 &= 4 \\
x_1 + x_2 - x_3 - 4\,x_4 + 3\,x_5 &= 0 \\
x_1 - x_2 + x_3 - 3\,x_5 &= 2
\end{aligned}
$$

We select the first equation and rewrite it into the following pivot form:

$$x_1 = x_2 + x_3 + 2x_4 - x_5 - 4.$$

Using the *SUBSTITUTION* rule with the other two equations as E we transform the above set, after performing the substitution and standardisation, into the following set:

$$
\begin{aligned}
x_1 &= x_2 + x_3 + 2\,x_4 - x_5 - 4 \\
& 2x_2 - 2\,x_4 + 2\,x_5 = 4 \\
& 2\,x_3 + 2\,x_4 - 4\,x_5 = 6
\end{aligned}
$$

The second equation can be rewritten into the following pivot form:

$$x_2 = x_4 - x_5 + 2.$$

Using the *SUBSTITUTION* rule with the other two equations as E we transform the last set, after performing the substitution and standardisation, into

$$
\begin{aligned}
x_1 &= x_3 + 3\,x_4 - 2\,x_5 - 2 \\
x_2 &= x_4 - x_5 + 2 \\
& 2\,x_3 + 2\,x_4 - 4\,x_5 = 6
\end{aligned}
$$

Selecting now the last equation we can rewrite it into the following pivot form:

$$x_3 = -x_4 + 2x_5 + 3.$$

Using the *SUBSTITUTION* rule third time, with the first two equations as E, we transform the last set into

$$
\begin{aligned}
x_1 &= 2\,x_4 + 1 \\
x_2 &= x_4 - x_5 + 2 \\
x_3 &= -x_4 + 2\,x_5 + 3
\end{aligned}
$$

At this moment no rule of *LIN* applies so the the exhibited derivation is stabilising.   □

The following result establishes correctness of the GAUSS–JORDAN ELIM-INATION algorithm. Both its formulation and the proof are similar to that of the MARTELLI–MONTANARI Algorithm Theorem 4.25.

Theorem 4.35 (GAUSS–JORDAN ELIMINATION) *The* GAUSS–JORDAN ELI-MINATION *algorithm always terminates. If the original finite set of linear equations E has a solution, then each execution of the algorithm terminates with a set of linear equations in a solved form that determines an mgu of E and otherwise each execution terminates with a set containing the false constraint* ⊥.

Proof   Given a set of equations E, we call a variable x **solved in** E if for some term t in normal form $x = t \in E$ and this is the only occurrence of x in E, that is, if the equation $x = t$ is in solved form. We call a variable **unsolved in** E if it is not solved.

To prove termination we associate with each set of linear equations E the following two functions:

$uns(E)$ – the number of variables in E that are unsolved,
$card(E)$ – the number of equations in E.

We now show that each rule application to a set of equations E reduces natural number

$$uns(E) + card(E).$$

In the case of the *SUBSTITUTION* rule we assume that we are dealing with a global application and that $x \in Var(E)$.

For the *DELETION* rule and the *FAILURE* rule note that each rule application does not increase $uns(E)$ and decreases $card(E)$ by 1. In turn, each global application of the *SUBSTITUTION* rule with $x \in Var(E)$ reduces $uns(E)$ by 1 and does not change $card(E)$. Indeed, on the account of globality each such application of the *SUBSTITUTION* rule turns x from an unsolved variable to a solved one.

This implies termination. The other claim follows from the *LIN* Theorem 4.33, since each execution of the GAUSS–JORDAN ELIMINATION algorithm corresponds to a failed or stabilising derivation.   □

Just like in the case of the MARTELLI–MONTANARI algorithm we can argue that the GAUSS–JORDAN ELIMINATION algorithm can be viewed as a complete constraint solver. To see this let us return to the Solution Note 4.30 that summarised the relationship between sets of linear equations and

CSPs. In conjunction with the Solved Form Lemma 4.29 it implies that for a set of linear equations $E := \{x_1 = t_1, \ldots, x_n = t_n\}$ in solved form we have

$$Sol(\langle E \; ; \; x_1 \in \mathcal{NF}, \ldots, x_n \in \mathcal{NF} \rangle) =$$
$$\{(norm(t_1\eta), \ldots, norm(t_n\eta)) \mid \eta \text{ is a substitution}\}.$$

So for a finite set of linear equations in solved form it is straightforward to generate all solutions to the corresponding CSP $\langle E \; ; \; x_1 \in \mathcal{NF}, \ldots, x_n \in \mathcal{NF} \rangle$. Now, in view of the above theorem, the GAUSS–JORDAN ELIMI-NATION algorithm transforms a given finite set of linear equations into an equivalent set of equations that is either in solved form or contains the false constraint $\perp$. So in the terminology of this chapter this algorithm can indeed be viewed as a complete constraint solver.

4.3.6 The GAUSSIAN ELIMINATION algorithm

In the second algorithm we use specific applications of the *SUBSTITUTION* rule that are not necessarily global. The algorithm has two phases. Assume that the equations are ordered in an arbitrary way.

In the first phase, called the **forward substitution phase**, we repeatedly take the first not yet considered equation from the *left*. If the *DELETION* rule is applicable, the equation is deleted and the next equation is considered. If the *FAILURE* rule is applicable, a failure is reached and the execution terminates. If the *SUBSTITUTION* rule is applicable, we apply it taking as E the set of equations lying *to the right* of the selected equation.

In the second phase, called the **backward substitution phase**, we repeatedly take the first not yet considered equation from the *right* and apply the *SUBSTITUTION* rule by taking as E the set of equations lying *to the left* of the selected equation.

This algorithm is called the GAUSSIAN ELIMINATION algorithm. In contrast to the other algorithms here considered it is deterministic. The following example illustrates its operation.

Example 4.36 Take again the set of linear equations considered in Example 4.34, i.e.,

$$
\begin{array}{rrrrrrl}
-x_1 & + & x_2 & + & x_3 & + & 2\,x_4 & - & x_5 & = & 4 \\
x_1 & + & x_2 & - & x_3 & - & 4\,x_4 & + & 3\,x_5 & = & 0 \\
x_1 & - & x_2 & + & x_3 & & & - & 3\,x_5 & = & 2
\end{array}
$$

We start with the forward substitution phase. As before we select the first equation, rewrite it into the following pivot form:

$$x_1 = x_2 + x_3 + 2x_4 - x_5 - 4$$

and use the *SUBSTITUTION* rule with the other two equations as E. This yields the following set:

$$
\begin{array}{rcrcrcrcrcr}
x_1 & = & x_2 & + & x_3 & + & 2\,x_4 & - & x_5 & - & 4 \\
    &   & 2x_2 &   &   & - & 2\,x_4 & + & 2\,x_5 & = & 4 \\
    &   &   &   & 2\,x_3 & + & 2\,x_4 & - & 4\,x_5 & = & 6
\end{array}
$$

Selecting now the second equation we can rewrite it into the following pivot form:

$$x_2 = x_4 - x_5 + 2.$$

Now, however, in contrast to Example 4.34, we use the *SUBSTITUTION* rule with the third equation only as E. The variable x_2 does not occur in this equation, so we get the following set of equations:

$$
\begin{array}{rcrcrcrcrcr}
x_1 & = & x_2 & + & x_3 & + & 2\,x_4 & - & x_5 & - & 4 \\
    &   & x_2 & = &   &   & x_4 & - & x_5 & + & 2 \\
    &   &   &   & 2\,x_3 & + & 2\,x_4 & - & 4\,x_5 & = & 6
\end{array}
$$

Selecting now the last equation we can rewrite it into the following pivot form:

$$x_3 = -x_4 + 2x_5 + 3.$$

and apply *SUBSTITUTION* rule with the empty set of equations as E. This yields the following set:

$$
\begin{array}{rcrcrcrcrcr}
x_1 & = & x_2 & + & x_3 & + & 2\,x_4 & - & x_5 & - & 4 \\
    &   & x_2 & = &   &   & x_4 & - & x_5 & + & 2 \\
    &   &   &   & x_3 & = & -\,x_4 & + & 2\,x_5 & + & 3
\end{array}
$$

We are now ready with the forward substitution phase of the algorithm and proceed with the backward substitution phase.

Using the *SUBSTITUTION* rule with the last equation as the selected one and the other two equations as E we transform the above set into

$$
\begin{array}{rcrcrcrcr}
x_1 & = & x_2 &   & + & x_4 & + & x_5 & - & 1 \\
    &   & x_2 & = &   & x_4 & - & x_5 & + & 2 \\
    &   &   & x_3 & = & -\,x_4 & + & 2\,x_5 & + & 3
\end{array}
$$

Using now the *SUBSTITUTION* rule with the second equation as the selected one and the first one as E we transform the above set into

$$
\begin{aligned}
x_1 &= & 2\,x_4 & & &+ & 1 \\
x_2 &= & x_4 &- & x_5 &+ & 2 \\
x_3 &= & -\,x_4 &+ & 2\,x_5 &+ & 3
\end{aligned}
$$

At this moment no application of a rule of *LIN* is relevant and the derivation terminates with the last set of equations. So we reached the same outcome as in Example 4.34.

□

In general, the GAUSSIAN ELIMINATION algorithm is more efficient than the GAUSS–JORDAN ELIMINATION algorithm since it leads to a smaller number of substitutions. The following result establishes correctness of the GAUSSIAN ELIMINATION algorithm.

Theorem 4.37 (GAUSSIAN ELIMINATION) *The* GAUSSIAN ELIMINATION *algorithm always terminates. If the original finite sequence of linear equations E has a solution, then the algorithm terminates with a set of linear equations in a solved form that determines an mgu of E and otherwise it terminates with a set containing the false constraint* ⊥*.*

Proof The termination is a direct consequence of the way the algorithm is defined. In fact, the algorithm terminates after at most $2n - 1$ rule applications, where n is the number of equations.

However, in contrast to the GAUSS–JORDAN ELIMINATION algorithm, it is not clear now that each execution of the algorithm is a failed or stabilising derivation. To prove it we need to distinguish two cases. If the final set of constraints contains ⊥, the corresponding execution is clearly a failed derivation.

Otherwise the final set of constraints does not contain ⊥, which means that the algorithm terminates after a successful execution of both the forward substitution and the backward substitution phase. Upon termination of the forward substitution phase we reach the set of equations

$$
\{x_1 = t_1, \ldots, x_n = t_n\},
$$

where each equation $x_i = t_i$ is in pivot form and where for $i \in [1..n]$ we have

$$
Var(t_i) \cap \{x_1, \ldots, x_i\} = \emptyset. \tag{4.5}
$$

So upon termination of the backward substitution phase we reach the set of equations

$$
\{x_1 = s_1, \ldots, x_n = s_n\}, \tag{4.6}
$$

where

$$s_n := t_n$$

and, by proceeding backwards,

$$s_i := (t_i[x_n/s_n])\ldots[x_{i+1}/s_{i+1}],$$

where $i \in [1..n]$ and $s[x/t] \equiv norm(s\{x/t\})$. That is, $s[x/t]$ is the outcome of normalising the linear expression $s\{x/t\}$. So s_i is the outcome of an appropriate alternation of normalisation and substitution starting with the linear expression t_i.

On the account of (4.5) we have

$$Var(s_n) \cap \{x_1, \ldots, x_n\} = \emptyset.$$

Proceeding backwards from n down to 1 assume by induction that for $j \in [i+1..n]$

$$Var(s_j) \cap \{x_1, \ldots, x_n\} = \emptyset.$$

Then, again on the account of (4.5), we have

$$Var(t_i\{x_n/s_n\}\ldots\{x_{i+1}/s_{i+1}\}) \cap \{x_1, \ldots, x_n\} = \emptyset,$$

which implies that $Var(s_i) \cap \{x_1, \ldots, x_n\} = \emptyset$.

By definition each s_i is in normal form. So the set of equations (4.6) is in solved form and consequently it is closed under the applications of all the rules of *LIN*. So the considered execution of the algorithm is a stabilising derivation.

The second claim now follows from the *LIN* Theorem 4.33.   □

This concludes our discussion of complete solvers for linear equations over reals. In Section 6.7 we shall return to the rules of the proof system *LIN* when discussing an incomplete constraint solver for non-linear equations over reals.

4.4 Linear inequalities over reals

4.4.1 Syntax

After having dealt with the linear equations over reals we now discuss the problem of solving finite sets of linear inequalities over reals. As in the previous section we consider linear expressions over reals and assume the same syntactic conventions. By a *linear inequality over reals* we mean a constraint of the form

$$s \leq t,$$

where s and t are linear expressions. As before we omit the qualification 'over reals'. For example,

$$4x - 3.5y - 1.2z \leq 3x - 1.2 \cdot (2 + 2.5y + z) - 2x + 5$$

is a linear inequality.

When solving finite sets of linear inequalities we shall repeatedly eliminate variables present in them. This will be done by transforming first each linear inequality to a normal form in which a selected variable will be isolated. This brings us to the normal forms we shall be interested in.

Definition 4.38 Assume a predetermined ordering $\prec$ on the variables. Fix a variable x.

We say that a linear inequality is in an *x-normal form* if it is in one of the following forms, where $x \notin Var(t)$ and t is a linear expression in normal form:

- the $\leq x$-**normal form**: $t \leq x$,
- the $x^{\leq}$-**normal form**: $x \leq t$,
- the $\bar{x}$-**normal form**: $t \leq 0$.   □

So the variable x does not appear in the $\bar{x}$-normal form. Using appropriate transformation rules, given a variable x, each linear inequality $s \leq t$ can be rewritten to a unique equivalent linear inequality in an x-normal form. We say that $s \leq t$ *normalises to* its normal form. Here is an example. We assume here and elsewhere an ordering $\prec$ such that $x \prec y \prec z$.

Example 4.39 Reconsider the linear inequality

$$4x - 3.5y - 1.2z \leq 3x - 1.2 \cdot (2 + 2.5y + z) - 2x + 5.$$

It normalises to the $x^{\leq}$-normal form $x \leq \frac{0.5}{3}y + \frac{2.6}{3}$ and to the $\leq y$-normal form $6x - 5.2 \leq y$. In contrast, its z-normal form is $6x - y - 5.2 \leq 0$, which is a $\bar{z}$-normal form, without an occurrence of z.   □

4.4.2 Linear inequalities and CSPs

We interpret linear inequalities as constraints analogously as the linear equations. So, as in the previous section, we assume that each variable domain consists of the set of linear expressions in normal form, that we denoted by $\mathcal{NF}$. Then with a linear inequality li with the variables $x_1, \ldots, x_n$ we associate the following subset of the Cartesian product $\mathcal{NF}^n$:

$\{(t_1, \ldots, t_n) \mid$ the inequality $li\{x_1/t_1, \ldots, x_n/t_n\}$ normalises to $r \leq 0$, where r is a strictly negative real or $0\}$.

For example, the interpretation of the inequality $x_1 + x_2 \leq x_3$ as a constraint contains as typical elements the triples $(1, 1, 3), (x + 1, 1, x + 3)$, $(x, y, x + y), (x, y, x + y + 2), (x, y + 1, x + y + 2)$ and $(x + 1, y, x + y + 1)$. For instance, $x + y \leq x + y + 2$ normalises to $-2 \leq 0$ and similarly for the other triples.

The resulting interpretation of a set of linear inequalities as a CSP allows us to talk about solutions to such sets and about equivalence between linear inequalities. We say that two linear inequalities li_1 and li_2 with the same sequence of variables $x_1, \ldots, x_n$ are **equivalent** if the CSPs $\langle li_1 \; ; \; x_1 \in \mathcal{NF}, \ldots, x_n \in \mathcal{NF} \rangle$ and $\langle li_2 \; ; \; x_1 \in \mathcal{NF}, \ldots, x_n \in \mathcal{NF} \rangle$ are equivalent.

Further, we say that two linear inequalities li_1 and li_2 with a sequence X of common variables are **equivalent w.r.t.** X if the corresponding CSPs determined by these two inequalities are equivalent w.r.t. X. Then according to this definition each linear inequality li and its normal form are equivalent w.r.t. the sequence of the variables of li. In particular, the already discussed inequality

$$4x - 3.5y - 1.2z \leq 3x - 1.2 \cdot (2 + 2.5y + z) - 2x + 5$$

and each of its normal forms, so $x \leq \frac{0.5}{3}y + \frac{2.6}{3}$, $6x - 5.2 \leq y$, and $6x - y - 5.2 \leq 0$ are equivalent w.r.t. x, y.

4.4.3 The *INEQ* proof system

To reason about finite sets of linear inequalities we introduce now three proof rules. To present them we need the following notation.

Definition 4.40 Given a variable x and a set of linear inequalities LI we introduce the following three sets of linear inequalities derived from it:

- $\leq x(LI) := \{li \mid li$ is the $\leq x$-normal form of an inequality from $LI\}$,
- $x\leq(LI) := \{li \mid li$ is the $x\leq$-normal form of an inequality from $LI\}$,
- $\bar{x}(LI) := \{li \mid li$ is the $\bar{x}$-normal form of an inequality from $LI\}$.

We also introduce the following operation on sets of linear inequalities:

$$E \cdot F := \{s \leq v \mid s \leq t \in E, \; t \leq v \in F\}.$$

So if either E or F is empty, then so is $E \cdot F$. $\qquad\square$

The idea behind the algorithm that we are going to discuss is very simple. We repeatedly select a variable, say x, and perform the following two steps:

- we normalise all inequalities in the current set LI to the x-normal form,
- we eliminate all occurrences of x by replacing the sets $^\leq x(LI)$ and $x^\leq(LI)$ by their 'composition' $^\leq x(LI) \cdot x^\leq(LI)$.

Note that in the case one of these sets is empty, it amounts to deleting all inequalities in the other set.

This procedure can be described using the following proof rule:

$$x\text{-}ELIMINATION$$

$$\frac{LI}{^\leq x(LI) \cdot x^\leq(LI),\ \bar{x}(LI)}$$

Additionally, we introduce the following two rules that deal with specific $\bar{x}$-normal forms:

$$DELETION$$

$$\underline{s \leq t}$$

if $s \leq t$ normalises to $r \leq 0$, where r is a strictly negative real or 0,

$$FAILURE$$

$$\frac{s \leq t}{\perp}$$

if $s \leq t$ normalises to $r \leq 0$, where r is a strictly positive real.

Denote the set of these three rules by $INEQ$.

4.4.4 The Fourier–Motzkin Elimination algorithm

We can now introduce the desired algorithm. It consists of the above three rules together with a scheduler that repeatedly applies them until a failed CSP or a CSP closed under the applications of these rules is reached. In the case of the x-$ELIMINATION$ rule each of its applications is global and refers to a different variable. This algorithm is called the Fourier–Motzkin Elimination algorithm. The following example illustrates its operation.

Example 4.41

(i) Consider the following set of linear inequalities:

$$
\begin{aligned}
0 &\leq x \\
-x - y &\leq 2 \\
-x + y &\leq 3 \\
x + 2y &\leq 6 \\
0 &\leq y \\
-x - y + 2 &\leq z
\end{aligned}
\qquad (4.7)
$$

Transforming each of them to the x-normal form yields the following set:

$$
\begin{aligned}
0 &\leq x \\
-y - 2 &\leq x \\
y - 3 &\leq x \\
x &\leq -2y + 6 \\
-y &\leq 0 \\
-y - z + 2 &\leq x
\end{aligned}
$$

Hence using the x-*ELIMINATION* rule we obtain the following set of inequalities in which x does not appear:

$$
\begin{aligned}
0 &\leq -2y + 6 \\
-y - 2 &\leq -2y + 6 \\
y - 3 &\leq -2y + 6 \\
-y &\leq 0 \\
-y - z + 2 &\leq -2y + 6
\end{aligned}
$$

Transforming each of these five inequalities to the y-normal form we now obtain the following set:

$$
\begin{aligned}
y &\leq 3 \\
y &\leq 8 \\
y &\leq 3 \\
0 &\leq y \\
y &\leq z + 4
\end{aligned}
\qquad (4.8)
$$

Eliminating now y using the y-*ELIMINATION* rule we obtain the following set of three inequalities:

$$
\begin{array}{rcl}
0 & \leq & 3 \\
0 & \leq & 8 \\
0 & \leq & z + 4
\end{array}
$$

We can now delete the first two inequalities using the *DELETION* rule and we end up with a single inequality the z-normal form of which is:

$$
-4 \leq z.
$$

At this moment we apply the z-*ELIMINATION* rule. No inequality is in the $z^{\leq}$-normal form or the $\bar{z}$-normal form, so this rule application amounts to a deletion of the above inequality and we end up with the empty set. This, as we shall see, implies that the original set of inequalities (4.7) is consistent.

(ii) Consider now the following set of linear inequalities:

$$
\begin{array}{rcl}
x + z & \leq & x + z + 1 \\
y + 3z + 6 & \leq & x + y \\
-y + 2z + 6 & \leq & x - y \\
x + y & \leq & -2y + 2 \\
x + z & \leq & 2y + z + 3 \\
x + 2y & \leq & x + z + 1 \\
x + y & \leq & x + z + 1
\end{array}
$$

The first inequality normalises to $-1 \leq 0$, so using the *DELETION* rule we can delete it. Transforming each of the remaining six inequalities to the x-normal form yields the following set:

$$
\begin{array}{rcl}
3z + 6 & \leq & x \\
2z + 6 & \leq & x \\
x & \leq & -3y + 2 \\
x & \leq & 2y + 3 \\
2y - z - 1 & \leq & 0 \\
y - z - 1 & \leq & 0
\end{array}
$$

So the first two inequalities are in the $^{\leq}x$-normal form, the next two in the $x^{\leq}$-normal form and the last two in the $\bar{x}$-normal form. Hence using the x-*ELIMINATION* rule we obtain the following set of inequalities in which x does not appear:

$$
\begin{array}{rcl}
3z + 6 & \leq & -3y + 2 \\
3z + 6 & \leq & 2y + 3 \\
2z + 6 & \leq & -3y + 2 \\
2z + 6 & \leq & 2y + 3 \\
2y - z - 1 & \leq & 0 \\
y - z - 1 & \leq & 0
\end{array}
$$

Transforming each of these six inequalities to the y-normal form we obtain the following set:

$$
\begin{array}{rcl}
y & \leq & -z - \frac{4}{3} \\
\frac{3}{2}z + \frac{3}{2} & \leq & y \\
y & \leq & -\frac{2}{3}z - \frac{4}{3} \\
z + \frac{3}{2} & \leq & y \\
y & \leq & \frac{1}{2}z + \frac{1}{2} \\
y & \leq & z + 1
\end{array}
$$

So using the y-*ELIMINATION* rule we obtain a set of eight inequalities. One of them, resulting from the inequalities $z + \frac{3}{2} \leq y$ and $y \leq z + 1$ is $z + \frac{3}{2} \leq z + 1$ that normalises to $\frac{1}{2} \leq 0$. So applying the *FAILURE* rule we introduce the false constraint $\bot$ which yields a failed derivation. This means, as we shall see at the end of this section, that the original set of inequalities is inconsistent. $\square$

In the remainder of this section we clarify the status of the Fourier–Motzkin Elimination algorithm. To this end let us return to the x-*ELIMINATION* rule. Because the conclusion of this rule does not refer to x, this rule is not equivalence preserving. The reason is that the conclusion does not put any conditions on the variable x, while the premise does. Take for example the equations $y \leq x$ and $x \leq z$. Then after an application of the x-*ELIMINATION* rule we obtain the inequality $y \leq z$ that is satisfied by any triple x, y, z such that $y \leq z$ holds, so with an arbitrary x. However, this rule does enjoy a weaker property.

Lemma 4.42 (*INEQ*)

   (i) *The rules DELETION and FAILURE are equivalence preserving.*

   (ii) *Each global application of the x-ELIMINATION rule is equivalence preserving w.r.t. the sequence of the variables present in the rule conclusion. Consequently, this rule is consistency preserving.*

Proof (i) The claim is immediate.

(*ii*) First, we note that the rule

$$\frac{LI}{\leq x(LI),\ x^{\leq}(LI),\ \bar{x}(LI)}$$

is equivalence preserving since every linear inequality li is equivalent to its normal form w.r.t. to the sequence of the variables of li. So it suffices to prove that the rule

$$\frac{\leq x(LI),\ x^{\leq}(LI),\ \bar{x}(LI)}{\leq x(LI) \cdot x^{\leq}(LI),\ \bar{x}(LI)}$$

is equivalence preserving w.r.t. the sequence of the variables present in the rule conclusion, that is w.r.t. to the sequence of the variables in

$$Var(^{\leq}x(LI),\ x^{\leq}(LI),\ \bar{x}(LI)) - \{x\}.$$

So consider a solution d to the premise of this rule. It satisfies each inequality $s \leq x$ in $^{\leq}x(LI)$ and each inequality $x \leq t$ in $x^{\leq}(LI)$, so by the transitivity of $\leq$ it satisfies each inequality $s \leq t$ in $^{\leq}x(LI) \cdot x^{\leq}(LI)$. Hence d is a solution to the conclusion of this rule.

Conversely, consider a solution d to the conclusion of this rule. We need to extend it, by assigning a value to x, to a solution to the premise of the rule. We can assume that either $^{\leq}x(LI)$ or $x^{\leq}(LI)$ is non-empty, since otherwise the premise and conclusion of the above rule coincide. Three cases arise.

Case 1. $^{\leq}x(LI)$ is non-empty and $x^{\leq}(LI)$ is empty.

Then the above rule reduces to

$$\frac{\leq x(LI),\ \bar{x}(LI)}{\bar{x}(LI)}$$

Extend d in an arbitrary way to the variables in $Var(^{\leq}x(LI)) - \{x\}$. Let

$$s_0 := max(t \mid t \leq x \in {}^{\leq}x(LI)).$$

Now assign to x the value of s_0 determined by the above extension of the solution d. This final extension of d satisfies all the inequalities in $^{\leq}x(LI)$.

Case 2. $^{\leq}x(LI)$ is empty and $x^{\leq}(LI)$ is non-empty.

Then the above rule reduces to

$$\frac{x^{\leq}(LI),\ \bar{x}(LI)}{\bar{x}(LI)}$$

Extend d in an arbitrary way to the variables in $Var(x^{\leq}(LI)) - \{x\}$. Let

$$t_0 := min(s \mid x \leq s \in x^{\leq}(LI)).$$

Now assign to x the value of t_0 determined by the above extension of the solution d. This final extension of d satisfies all the inequalities in $x^{\leq}(LI)$.

Case 3. Both $^{\leq}x(LI)$ and $x^{\leq}(LI)$ are non-empty.

d assigns a value to all the variables in $^{\leq}x(LI) \cdot x^{\leq}(LI)$, so it assigns unique values to the terms s_0 from Case 1 and t_0 from Case 2. These values correspond to linear expressions s_1 and t_1 in normal form such that $s_1 \leq x \in {}^{\leq}x(LI)$ and $x \leq t_1 \in x^{\leq}(LI)$. So $s_1 \leq t_1 \in {}^{\leq}x(LI) \cdot x^{\leq}(LI)$. Hence d is a solution to $s_1 \leq t_1$.

As in Case 1 extend d by setting to x the value of s_0, i.e., the value of s_1. As in Case 1 the resulting extension e of d satisfies all the inequalities in $^{\leq}x(LI)$. Since e satisfies then the inequality $x \leq t_1$, it also satisfies all the inequalities in $x^{\leq}(LI)$. (Alternatively, we can extend d by setting to x the value of t_0.)

This proof also shows that the x-*ELIMINATION* rule is consistency preserving. Indeed, we showed that if the rule premise has a solution, then it is also a solution of the rule conclusion, and conversely, if the rule conclusion has a solution, then it can be extended to a solution of the rule premise. $\square$

This brings us to the following conclusion.

Theorem 4.43 (*INEQ*) *The* FOURIER–MOTZKIN ELIMINATION *algorithm always terminates. If the original finite set of linear inequalities is consistent, then each execution of the algorithm terminates with the empty set of constraints and otherwise each execution terminates with a set containing the false constraint* $\bot$.

Proof   The termination is an immediate consequence of the fact that there are finitely many variables in the original finite set LI of inequalities.

By the form of the rules of the *INEQ* system the final set of constraints F is either empty or it contains the false constraint $\bot$. By the *INEQ* Lemma 4.42 the CSPs forming the considered derivation are either all inconsistent or all consistent. So if the original set of linear inequalities is consistent, then the final set of constraints is also consistent, so it is empty. And if the original set of linear inequalities is inconsistent, then the final set of constraints is also inconsistent, so it contains $\bot$. $\square$

Thus the FOURIER–MOTZKIN ELIMINATION algorithm allows us to determine consistency of a finite set of linear inequalities. So, according to our terminology, this algorithm is not a complete constraint solver. However, one can modify this algorithm to one that allows us to reduce the original set of inequalities to an equivalent set in an appropriately defined solved form. To this end, we employ the terms s_0 and t_0 defined in the proof of the *INEQ* Lemma 4.42 and add to the conclusion of x-*ELIMINATION* rule none, one or both inequalities $s_0 \leq x$, $x \leq t_0$ depending on the case analysis provided in the proof of the *INEQ* Lemma 4.42. Note that the terms s_0 and t_0 are defined in an extension of the considered language obtained by adding the functions *min* and *max* in each arity. Then the resulting algorithm terminates either with the set of such added inequalities, that we view as a solved form, or with a set containing the false constraint $\perp$. From this solved form we can generate all solutions to the original set of inequalities.

The FOURIER–MOTZKIN ELIMINATION algorithm also allows us to find optimal solutions to a finite set of linear inequalities subject to a linear objective function. To see how consider as an example the problem of finding a solution to the following set of inequalities:

$$
\begin{array}{rcl}
0 & \leq & x \\
-x - y & \leq & 2 \\
-x + y & \leq & 3 \\
x + 2y & \leq & 6 \\
0 & \leq & y
\end{array}
$$

for which the value of the objective function $-2x - y + 2$ is minimal.

To solve it we introduce a new variable, z, and add the following inequality to the above ones:

$$-2x - y + 2 \leq z.$$

This becomes then the set of inequalities considered in Example 4.41(i). We reduced there this set of inequalities to the single inequality $-4 \leq z$. So the minimal possible value for z is -4. By proceeding backwards we can now find the values for x and y for which $z = -4$. Namely, we substitute z by -4 in the equations of (4.8), so in $y \leq z + 4$. This, together with the inequality $0 \leq y$ of (4.8), yields $y = 0$. Now substituting y by 0 and z by -4 in the original set of inequalities (4.7) yields in particular $-x \leq -6$ and $x \leq 6$ from which we conclude that $x = 6$.

Unfortunately, the FOURIER–MOTZKIN ELIMINATION algorithm is not efficient. To see this let us have a closer look at the x-*ELIMINATION* rule. Each global application of this rule eliminates from the current set of inequalities all the inequalities containing x. However, this happens at the cost of introducing a possibly large set of inequalities that do not contain x. Indeed, the cardinality of the set $^{\leq}x(LI) \cdot x^{\leq}(LI)$ is the product of the cardinalities of the sets $^{\le}x(LI)$ and $x^{\le}(LI)$. The accumulated increase of the number of inequalities can lead in the worst case to a doubly exponential number of inequalities.

A more practical approach is provided by the SIMPLEX algorithm. This algorithm allows us to compute optimal solutions to a finite set of linear inequalities subject to a linear objective function by repeatedly transforming a solution to the considered set of linear inequalities to one with a better value of the objective function. On certain problem sets this algorithm runs in exponential time. However, in practice it is remarkably efficient. Consequently, it is used in several linear programming packages and constraint programming systems. A discussion of the SIMPLEX algorithm would take us too far afield. An interested reader can consult any book on linear programming, e.g., Papadimitriou and Steiglitz [1982].

4.5 Summary

In this chapter we discussed three complete constraint solvers. They dealt with:

- term equations,
- linear equations over reals, and
- linear inequalities over reals.

In our presentation we aimed at a uniform presentation of these solvers. Consequently, we discussed them using a simple proof theoretic framework. This presentation allowed us to clarify the similarities between these solvers.

4.6 Exercises

Exercise 4.1 Prove the Equivalence Lemma 4.2.

Exercise 4.2 Call a derivation *maximal* if it is finite and cannot be extended to a longer derivation or it is infinite. Call a derivation *fair* if it is infinite and every rule is applied in it infinitely often or it is finite.

Consider a CSP $\mathcal{P}$ with finite domains and a finite set of domain reduction rules.

- Prove that every derivation starting in $\mathcal{P}$, in which each rule application is relevant, is finite. Conclude that every maximal derivation of this type is stabilising.

- Prove that every maximal and fair derivation has a prefix that is a stabilising derivation.

Exercise 4.3 Give an example of a CSP $\mathcal{P}$ with finite domains and of equivalence preserving proof rules such that infinite and fair derivations exist starting from $\mathcal{P}$ in which each rule application is relevant.
Hint. Note that by Exercise 4.2 some of these rules have to be transformation rules.

Exercise 4.4 Call a substitution θ ***idempotent*** if $\theta = \theta\theta$. Denote by $Ran(\theta)$ the set of variables that occur in a term from $Range(\theta)$. Prove that θ is idempotent iff $Dom(\theta) \cap Ran(\theta) = \emptyset$. Conclude that the mgus produced by the Martelli–Montanari algorithm are idempotent.

Exercise 4.5 Prove that the composition of the substitutions is associative, also in the case of the substitutions for linear expressions, as defined in Definition 4.27.

Exercise 4.6 Propose appropriate transformation rules using which each linear equation over reals can be rewritten to an equivalent one in normal form.

Exercise 4.7 Exhibit an infinite derivation in the proof system *LIN* in which each rule application is relevant.
Hint. Consider the set of linear equations introduced in Example 4.31.

Exercise 4.8 Propose appropriate transformation rules using which, given a variable x, each linear inequality over reals can be rewritten to an equivalent one in x-normal form.

4.7 Bibliographic remarks

The proof theoretic framework of Section 4.1 is adopted from Apt [1998]. The unification problem was introduced and solved by Robinson [1965] who recognised its importance for automated theorem proving. The unification problem also appeared implicitly in the PhD thesis of Herbrand in 1930 Herbrand [1971,page 148]) in the context of solving term equations, but in an informal way and without proofs. The Martelli–Montanari Unification algorithm was published in Martelli and Montanari [1982]. It is similar to Herbrand's original algorithm. Efficient unification algorithms are presented in Paterson and Wegman [1978] and Martelli and Montanari [1982]. For a survey on various variants of the unification problem see Baader and Siekmann [1994]. In Robinson [1992] an interesting account of the history of the unification algorithms is provided.

The GAUSS–JORDAN and the GAUSSIAN ELIMINATION algorithms are usually presented in terms of operations on matrices. Our presentation is inspired by the presentation of the GAUSS–JORDAN algorithm in Marriott and Stuckey [1998]. The more traditional presentation of these algorithms and a discussion of their complexity and of various improvements can be found for example in Press et al. [1992].

The FOURIER–MOTZKIN ELIMINATION algorithm goes back to Fourier [1827]. It was later reintroduced in Motzkin [1936]. Various historical comments and related references can be found in Schrijver [1986]. Some improvements of this algorithm are discussed in Jaffar et al. [1993] and Imbert [1995].

4.8 References

K. R. APT
[1998] A proof theoretic view of constraint programming, *Fundamenta Informaticae*, 33, pp. 263–293. Available via http://arXiv.org/archive/cs/.

F. BAADER AND J. H. SIEKMANN
[1994] Unification theory, in: *Handbook of Logic in Artificial Intelligence and Logic Programming Vol. 2, Deduction Methodologies*, D. M. Gabbay, C. J. Hogger, and J. A. Robinson, eds., Oxford University Press, pp. 41–125.

J. FOURIER
[1827] Analyse des travaux de l'Académie Royale des Sciences pendant l'année 1824, partie mathématique, *Histoire de l'Académie Royale des Sciences de l'Institut de France*, 7. English Translation (partially) in: D .A. Kohler, Translation of a report by Fourier on his work on linear inequalities, *Opsearch*, 10, 1973, pp. 38-42.

J. HERBRAND
[1971] *Logical Writings*, Reidel. W. D. Goldfarb, ed.

J.-L. IMBERT
[1995] Fourier Elimination: which to choose, in: *Principles and Practice of Constraint Programming*, P. Van Hentenryck and V. Saraswat, eds., MIT Press, pp. 245–268.

J. JAFFAR, M. J. MAHER, P. J. STUCKEY, AND R. H. C. YAP
[1993] Projecting CLP($\mathcal{R}$) constraints, *New Generation Computing*, 11, pp. 449–469.

K. MARRIOTT AND P. J. STUCKEY
[1998] *Programming With Constraints: An Introduction*, The MIT Press.

A. MARTELLI AND U. MONTANARI
[1982] An efficient unification algorithm, *ACM Transactions on Programming Languages and Systems*, 4, pp. 258–282.

T. S. MOTZKIN
[1936] *Beiträge zur Theorie der linearen Ungleichungen*, PhD thesis, University of Zurich.

C. H. PAPADIMITRIOU AND K. STEIGLITZ
[1982] *Combinatorial Optimization: Algorithms and Complexity*, Prentice-Hall.

M. S. PATERSON AND M. N. WEGMAN
[1978] Linear unification, *J. Comput. System Sci.*, 16, pp. 158–167.

W. H. Press, B. P. Flannery, S. A. Teukolsky, and W. T. Vetterling
   [1992]   *Numerical Recipes in C : The Art of Scientific Computing,* Cambridge University Press, 2nd ed.

J. A. Robinson
   [1965]   A machine-oriented logic based on the resolution principle, *J. ACM,* 12, pp. 23–41.
   [1992]   Logic and logic programming, *Communications of ACM,* 35, pp. 40–65.

A. Schrijver
   [1986]   *Theory of Linear and Integer Programming,* John Wiley and Sons.

5

Local consistency notions

I DEALLY, WE WOULD like to solve CSPs directly, by means of some efficient algorithm. But the definition of a CSP is extremely general, so, as already mentioned in Chapter 1, no universal efficient methods for solving them exist. Various general techniques were developed to solve CSPs and in the absence of efficient algorithms a combination of these techniques is a natural way to proceed.

In Chapter 3 we explained that the main idea is to reduce a given CSP to another one that is equivalent but easier to solve. This process is called constraint propagation and the algorithms that achieve this reduction are called constraint propagation algorithms. They are discussed in Chapter 7. These algorithms usually aim at reaching some form of 'local consistency'. Several forms of local consistency have been defined but it is not clear how to provide a satisfactory formalisation of this notion. So we rather confine ourselves to a review of the most common types of local consistency. Informally, local consistency means that some subparts of the considered CSP are in a 'desired form', for example consistent.

To achieve a smooth transition between this chapter and Chapter 7, each time we introduce a notion of local consistency we also provide its characterisation. These characterisations are then used in Chapter 7 to generate the appropriate constraint propagation algorithms. They are based on the proof theoretic framework introduced in Section 4.1.

This chapter is organised as follows. We begin by presenting in Section 5.1 node consistency that deals with unary constraints. In Section 5.2 we study the most popular notion of local consistency, the arc consistency, that deals with the binary constraints. Then, in Section 5.3, we discuss its natural generalisation to arbitrary constraints, called the hyper-arc consistency (occasionally called generalised arc consistency (GAC)). Next, in Section 5.4, we study another modification of the arc consistency, called the directional arc consistency, that takes into account a linear ordering on the considered variables. All three notions deal with each constraint separately.

Another class of local consistency notions deals with more than one constraint at a time. The first two examples are discussed in Sections 5.5 and Section 5.6. These are the notions of the path consistency and the directional path consistency. Next, we discuss two other forms of local consistency that generalise both the arc and the path consistency, by focusing on the notion of a consistent instantiation. The first notion, discussed in Section 5.7, is called k-consistency. Its 'accumulated' form, called strong k-consistency, is considered in Section 5.8. We conclude this presentation of the local consistency notions by discussing in Section 5.9 a powerful notion of local consistency, called relational (i, m)-consistency.

In general, local consistency neither implies nor is implied by consistency (sometimes called global consistency). However, in the presence of some additional information about the considered CSP, local consistency can imply global consistency. In Section 5.10 we provide an example of such a result. It involves the notion of a graph associated with a CSP and is concerned with the notion of strong k-consistency. By specialising this result for $k = 2$ and $k = 3$ we obtain results that clarify for which CSPs directional arc consistency, respectively directional path consistency, entails consistency.

5.1 Node consistency

We begin our review of the most common notions of local consistency by considering the node consistency. It deals with the unary constraints.

Definition 5.1 We call a CSP **node consistent** if for every variable x every unary constraint on x coincides with the domain of x. □

In particular, a CSP with no unary constraints is vacuously node consistent. Let us consider two simple examples.

Example 5.2
(i) Consider a CSP of the form

$$\langle \mathcal{C}, x_1 \geq 0, \ldots, x_n \geq 0 \; ; \; x_1 \in \mathcal{N}, \ldots, x_n \in \mathcal{N} \rangle,$$

where $\mathcal{C}$ does not contain unary constraints. Recall that $\mathcal{N}$ denotes the set of natural numbers. Then this CSP is node consistent, since for each variable its unique unary constraint is satisfied by all the values in the variable domain.

(ii) Consider now a CSP of the form

$$\langle \mathcal{C}, x_1 \geq 0, \ldots, x_n \geq 0 \; ; \; x_1 \in \mathcal{N}, \ldots, x_{n-1} \in \mathcal{N}, x_n \in \mathcal{Z} \rangle,$$

where $\mathcal{C}$ does not contain unary constraints and $\mathcal{Z}$ denotes the set of all integers. Then this CSP is not node consistent, since for the variable x_n the constraint $x_n \geq 0$ is not satisfied by the negative integers from its domain. □

Clearly, node consistency neither implies nor is implied by consistency. Indeed, node consistency imposes no condition on non-unary constraints, which can be the source of inconsistency. Also, the CSP $\langle x = 0, y = 0 \; ; \; x \in \mathcal{N}, y \in \mathcal{N} \rangle$ is clearly consistent but not node consistent.

To derive an algorithm that transforms an arbitrary CSP into one that satisfies node consistency we characterise this notion in terms of proof rules. To this end we introduce the following domain reduction rule, where C is a unary constraint on a variable x:

NODE CONSISTENCY

$$\frac{\langle C \; ; \; x \in D \rangle}{\langle C \; ; \; x \in C \cap D \rangle}$$

So this rule is parametrised by a variable x and a unary constraint C on it. It is clear that this rule is equivalence preserving. Indeed, any solution to the CSP in the rule premise consists of an element d such that both $d \in C$ and $d \in D$ holds. So d is a solution of the CSP in the conclusion of the rule.

The following simple result characterises node consistency in terms of the above rule.

Note 5.3 (Node Consistency) *A CSP is node consistent iff it is closed under the applications of the NODE CONSISTENCY rule.*

Proof It suffices to note that a CSP $\mathcal{P}$ is node consistent iff for each variable x with the domain D and each unary constraint C on x we have $C = D$. But each unary constraint is a subset of the variable domain, so the latter holds iff for each such C we have $D \subseteq C$, i.e., $C \cap D = D$, which holds iff $\mathcal{P}$ is closed under the applications of the *NODE CONSISTENCY* rule. $\square$

So to transform a CSP $\mathcal{P}$ to one that is node consistent it suffices to repeatedly apply the *NODE CONSISTENCY* rule for all unary constraints, starting with $\mathcal{P}$. In fact, as we shall explain in Section 7.3, it is enough to apply this rule for each unary constraint once. This yields a straightforward algorithm that imposes node consistency, that is, an algorithm that transforms a CSP to an equivalent one that is node consistent.

5.2 Arc consistency

We begin now our review of the most common notions of local consistency. The first notion we introduce is arc consistency. Informally, a binary constraint is arc consistent if every value in each domain participates in a solution. And a CSP is arc consistent if all its binary constraints are. Here is the precise definition.

Definition 5.4

- Consider a binary constraint C on the variables x, y with the domains D_x and D_y, that is $C \subseteq D_x \times D_y$. We call C **arc consistent** if
  - $\forall a \in D_x \exists b \in D_y \ (a, b) \in C$,
  - $\forall b \in D_y \exists a \in D_x \ (a, b) \in C$.
- We call a CSP **arc consistent** if all its binary constraints are arc consistent. $\square$

So a binary constraint is arc consistent if every value in each domain has a **support** in the other domain, where we call b a support for a if the pair (a, b) (or, depending on the ordering of the variables, (b, a)) belongs to the constraint.

Note that a CSP with no binary constraints is vacuously arc consistent. That is, the property of arc consistency automatically holds in absence of binary constraints. Among the notions of local consistency arc consistency is the most popular. The following three examples illustrate this notion.

Example 5.5

(i) Consider the CSP which consists of only one constraint, $x < y$ interpreted over the domains $D_x = [5..10]$ of x and $D_y = [3..7]$ of y. It is visualised in Figure 5.1.

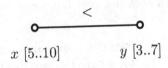

$$x\ [5..10] \qquad\qquad y\ [3..7]$$

Fig. 5.1. A CSP that is not arc consistent

This CSP is not arc consistent. Indeed, take for instance the value 8 in the domain $[5..10]$ of x. Then there is no b in $[3..7]$ such that $8 < b$.

(ii) Next, consider the CSP of Example 2.2 that formalises the n Queens Problem where $n \geq 3$. It is easy to see that this CSP is arc consistent. Formally, we need to analyse each constraint separately. Consider for instance the constraint $x_i - x_j \neq i - j$ with $1 \leq i < j \leq n$ and take $a \in [1..n]$. Then there exists $b \in [1..n]$ such that $a - b \neq i - j$: just take $b \in [1..n]$ that is different from $a - i + j$.

(iii) Finally, consider the CSP of Example 2.8 that deals with the crossword puzzle. This CSP is not arc consistent. Indeed, take for instance the already discussed constraint

$$C_{1,2} = \{(\text{HOSES, SAILS}), (\text{HOSES, SHEET}), (\text{HOSES, STEER}),$$
$$(\text{LASER, SAILS}), (\text{LASER, SHEET}), (\text{LASER, STEER})\} \ .$$

on the variables associated with the positions 1 and 2. Both positions need to be filled by five letter words, so both domains equal {HOSES, LASER, SAILS, SHEET, STEER}.

Now, no word in this set begins with the letter I, so for the value SAILS for the first variable no value for the second variable exists such that the resulting pair satisfies the considered constraint.   □

Let us discuss now closer the status of the arc consistency. First, note that arc consistency does not imply consistency. For example, returning to item (ii) in the above example we noted that the 3 Queens Problem is arc consistent, even though obviously it has no solution. Actually, the simplest illustration of this phenomenon is the CSP $\langle x = y, x \neq y \ ; \ x \in \{a, b\}, y \in \{a, b\}\rangle$ visualised in Figure 5.2. It is obviously arc consistent and also inconsistent.

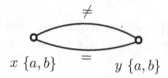

$$x \; \{a, b\} \qquad y \; \{a, b\}$$

Fig. 5.2. An arc consistent but inconsistent CSP

Next, note that consistency does not imply arc consistency either. Indeed, take the CSP $\langle x = y \; ; \; x \in \{a, b\}, y \in \{a\} \rangle$ visualised in Figure 5.3. It is ob-

$$x \; \{a, b\} \qquad y \; \{a\}$$

Fig. 5.3. A consistent but not arc consistent CSP

viously consistent yet not arc consistent. So both notions are incomparable.

However, as we shall see at the end of this section and also in Section 5.10 for certain CSPs arc consistency does imply consistency. So it is of interest to transform a CSP into an equivalent one that is arc consistent. As we shall see in Chapter 7, this can be done in an efficient way.

As a preparation to obtain such an algorithm we characterise the notion of arc consistency in terms of proof rules. To this end we introduce the following two rules, where C is a constraint on the variables x and y:

ARC CONSISTENCY 1

$$\frac{\langle C \; ; \; x \in D_x, y \in D_y \rangle}{\langle C \; ; \; x \in D'_x, y \in D_y \rangle}$$

where $D'_x := \{a \in D_x \mid \exists \, b \in D_y \, (a, b) \in C\}$,

ARC CONSISTENCY 2

$$\frac{\langle C \; ; \; x \in D_x, y \in D_y \rangle}{\langle C \; ; \; x \in D_x, y \in D'_y \rangle}$$

where $D'_y := \{b \in D_y \mid \exists \, a \in D_x \, (a, b) \in C\}$.

In other words, the *ARC CONSISTENCY* rules *1* and *2* deal with projections, respectively on the first or the second domain. Note that in the case of the *ARC CONSISTENCY* rule *1* we have $C \subseteq D'_x \times D_y$ and in the case of the *ARC CONSISTENCY* rule *2* we have $C \subseteq D_x \times D'_y$. So in both rules we use CSPs in the conclusions as required by the definition of a proof rule.

It is straightforward to see that these two rules are equivalence preserving. Take for instance the *ARC CONSISTENCY 1* rule. Consider a pair (d_1, d_2) that is a solution of the CSP in the premise of the rule. So $(d_1, d_2) \in C$ and $(d_1, d_2) \in D_x \times D_y$. Hence $d_1 \in \{a \in D_x \mid \exists b \in D_y \ (a, b) \in C\}$, i.e., $d_1 \in D'_x$ and consequently (d_1, d_2) is a solution of the CSP in the conclusion of the rule.

Intuitively, the *ARC CONSISTENCY* rules remove from the domain of x, respectively the domain of y, the values that do not participate in a solution to the constraint C. The domains used in these rules can be visualised by means of Figure 5.4.

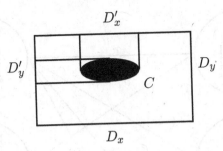

Fig. 5.4. Old and new domains in the *ARC CONSISTENCY* rules

The following simple result provides a characterisation of arc consistency in terms of the above two rules.

Note 5.6 (Arc Consistency) *A CSP is arc consistent iff it is closed under the applications of the ARC CONSISTENCY rules 1 and 2.*

Proof It suffices to note that a constraint C on the variables x and y with the respective domains D_x and D_y is arc consistent iff $D'_x = D_x$ and $D'_y = D_y$, where D'_x and D'_y are defined as in the *ARC CONSISTENCY* rules *1* and *2*. $\qquad\square$

To understand better the use of the *ARC CONSISTENCY* rules let us return now to the CSP of Example 2.8 that represents a crossword puzzle. In Example 5.5(iii) above we noted that this CSP is not arc consistent. Assume now the *ARC CONSISTENCY* rules *1* and *2* and consider a derivation that starts with this CSP to see its outcome.

Let, as in Example 2.8, $C_{i,j}$ with $i, j \in [1..8]$ denote the constraint that represents the crossing of the positions i and j. Suppose now that we apply in an alternating fashion the *ARC CONSISTENCY* rules *1* and *2* to the following sequence of ten constraints labeled by the letters $a–j$:

$$a : C_{1,2}, \ b : C_{1,3}, \ c : C_{4,2}, \ d : C_{4,5}, \ e : C_{4,2},$$

$$f : C_{7,2}, \ g : C_{7,5}, \ h : C_{8,2}, \ i : C_{8,6}, \ j : C_{8,3}.$$

The constraints are labeled in the order they are used in the derivation. For example, $C_{1,3}$ is the second constraint used and is labeled by the letter b. The $C_{4,2}$ constraint is used more than once in the derivation and is labeled by the letters c and e.

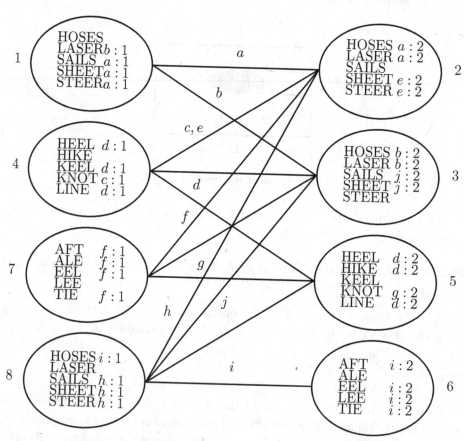

Fig. 5.5. A representation of a derivation

The resulting derivation is depicted by Figure 5.5. It consists of twenty steps. In this figure the circles correspond to the variable domains and the lines to the constraints. In turn, the letters $(a\text{–}j)$ and the numbers (1 or 2) attached to the domain elements. that is, to the elements inside the circles, explain by means of which constraint in this derivation and by means of which rule applied to it (1 or 2) the element is removed.

For example, the entry SHEET j:2 within the circle numbered by 3 means that the element SHEET is removed from the domain of the variable associated with the position 3 at the moment the *ARC CONSISTENCY* rule *2* is applied to the constraint j, that is, to the constraint $C_{8,3}$.

Note that in Figure 5.5 the numberings c:2, e:1, f:2, g:1, h:2 and j:1 are not used. This reflects the fact that the corresponding rule applications do not cause any change, that is, are not relevant. For example, at the moment the *ARC CONSISTENCY* rule *2* is applied to constraint h, so to $C_{8,2}$, this application is not relevant.

In the final CSP each variable domain is reduced to a singleton set and consequently this CSP is solved and the exhibited derivation is successful. This final CSP is depicted in Figure 2.5 of Chapter 2. Because the *ARC CONSISTENCY* rules *1* and *2* are equivalence preserving, by virtue of the Equivalence Lemma 4.2 the resulting CSP is equivalent to the original one and consequently the original CSP has a unique solution. So in this example we could solve the original CSP by transforming it to an arc consistent one by repeatedly using the *ARC CONSISTENCY* rules *1* and *2*. In general, such a transformation is not sufficient, as the example of the n Queens Problem discussed in Example 5.5(ii) shows.

5.3 Hyper-arc consistency

The notion of arc consistency generalises in a natural way to arbitrary constraints.

Definition 5.7

- Consider a constraint C on the variables $x_1, \ldots, x_k$ with the respective domains $D_1, \ldots, D_k$, that is $C \subseteq D_1 \times \cdots \times D_k$. We call C **hyper-arc consistent** if for every $i \in [1..k]$ and $a \in D_i$ there exists $d \in C$ such that $a = d[x_i]$. (Recall from Definition 3.2 that $d[x_i]$ denotes the ith element of d.)
- We call a CSP **hyper-arc consistent** if all its constraints are hyper-arc consistent. $\qquad\square$

Intuitively, a constraint C is hyper-arc consistent if for every involved domain each element of it participates in a solution to C. Note that for a binary constraint hyper-arc consistency coincides with arc consistency. The following two examples of Boolean constraints illustrate this notion for ternary constraints.

Example 5.8

(i) Consider the following CSP already mentioned in Subsection 4.1.1:

$$\langle x \wedge y = z \; ; \; x = 1, y \in \{0,1\}, z \in \{0,1\} \rangle.$$

It is easily seen to be hyper-arc consistent. Indeed, each element of every domain participates in a solution. For example, the value 0 of the domain of z participates in the solution $(1,0,0)$.

(ii) In contrast, the CSP

$$\langle x \wedge y = z \; ; \; x \in \{0,1\}, y \in \{0,1\}, z = 1 \rangle$$

is not hyper-arc consistent. Indeed, the value 0 of the domain of x does not participate in any solution.

$\square$

In the previous section we characterised arc consistency by means of the domain reduction rules. We can easily modify this characterisation to the case of hyper-arc consistency. To this end we introduce the following proof rule parametrised by a constraint C on the variables $x_1, \ldots, x_k$ and $i \in [1..k]$:

HYPER-ARC CONSISTENCY

$$\frac{\langle C \; ; \; x_1 \in D_1, \ldots, x_k \in D_k \rangle}{\langle C \; ; \; x_1 \in D_1, \ldots, x_{i-1} \in D_{i-1}, x_i \in D_i', x_{i+1} \in D_{i+1}, \ldots, x_k \in D_k \rangle}$$

where

$$D_i' := \{a \in D_i \mid \exists d \in C \; a = d[x_i]\}.$$

The following analogue of the Arc Consistency Note 5.6 then holds.

Note 5.9 (Hyper-arc Consistency) *A CSP is hyper-arc consistent iff it is closed under the applications of the HYPER-ARC CONSISTENCY rule.*

Proof Again, it suffices to note that a constraint C on the variables $x_1, \ldots, x_k$ with respective domains $D_1, \ldots, D_k$ is hyper-arc consistent iff for every $i \in [1..k]$ we have $D_i' = D_i$, where D_i' is defined as in the *HYPER-ARC CONSISTENCY* rule.

$\square$

5.4 Directional arc consistency

The notion of arc consistency can be modified taking into account some linear ordering $\prec$ on the considered variables. The idea is that we require the existence of supports only 'in one direction'. This yields directional arc consistency defined as follows.

Definition 5.10 Assume a linear ordering $\prec$ on the considered variables.

- Consider a binary constraint C on the variables x, y with the domains D_x and D_y. We call C **directionally arc consistent w.r.t.** $\prec$ if
  - $\forall a \in D_x \exists b \in D_y \ (a, b) \in C$ provided $x \prec y$,
  - $\forall b \in D_y \exists a \in D_x \ (a, b) \in C$ provided $y \prec x$.

  So out of these two conditions on C exactly one needs to be checked.
- We call a CSP **directionally arc consistent w.r.t.** $\prec$ if all its binary constraints are directionally arc consistent w.r.t. $\prec$. □

To see the difference between the notions of arc consistency and directional arc consistency consider the following examples.

Example 5.11
(i) The CSP

$$\langle x < y \ ; \ x \in [5..10], y \in [3..7] \rangle$$

already considered in Example 5.5(i) and visualised in Figure 5.1 is not directionally arc consistent w.r.t. any linear ordering $\prec$. Indeed, if $x \prec y$, then, as already noted, for $x = 8$ no $y \in [3..7]$ exists such that $8 < y$. And if $y \prec x$, then for $y = 4$ no $x \in [5..10]$ exists such that $x < 4$.

(ii) In contrast, the CSP

$$\langle x < y \ ; \ x \in [2..10], y \in [3..7] \rangle$$

visualised in Figure 5.6 is not arc consistent but it is directionally arc consistent w.r.t. the ordering $\prec$ such that $y \prec x$. Namely, for each $b \in [3..7]$ a value $a \in [2..10]$ exists such that $a < b$, namely $a = 2$.

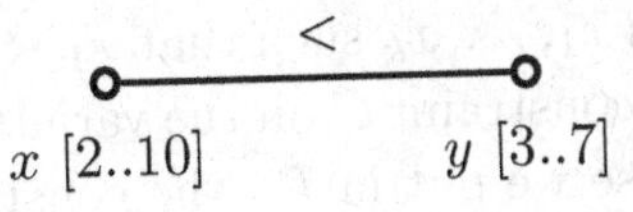

$$\overset{<}{\underset{x \ [2..10] \qquad\qquad y \ [3..7]}{\circ\!\!-\!\!-\!\!-\!\!-\!\!-\!\!-\!\!-\!\!-\!\!-\!\!-\!\!\circ}}$$

Fig. 5.6. A directionally arc consistent CSP w.r.t. $y \prec x$

(iii) Finally, reconsider the CSP of Example 2.8 that deals with the crossword puzzle. In Example 5.5(iii) we noted that it is not arc consistent. In fact, this CSP is not directionally arc consistent w.r.t. any linear ordering $\prec$ on its variables. For example, the constraint $C_{1,2}$ is not directionally arc consistent no matter what ordering we choose on its variables. Indeed, as already noted, no word in the set {HOSES, LASER, SAILS, SHEET, STEER} begins with the letter I, so the value SAILS for the first variable has no support in the second domain. Moreover, no word in this set has L as the third letter, so the value LASER for the second variable has no support in the first domain.

□

As in the case of arc and hyper-arc consistency a simple characterisation of directional arc consistency can be given in terms of rules. To this end it is useful to think in terms of graphs.

Recall that a **graph** is a pair (N, A) where N is a finite non-empty set and A is a binary relation on N, that is a subset of the Cartesian product $N \times N$. We call the elements of N **nodes** and the elements of A **arcs**.

Definition 5.12 Take a CSP $\mathcal{P}$. Consider a graph defined as follows. Its nodes are all the variables of $\mathcal{P}$ and two variables are connected by an arc if there is a binary constraint that involves them. We say then that this graph is **associated with the binary constraints of** $\mathcal{P}$.

□

In the above-defined graph each arc is associated with one or more binary constraints. In the case of arc consistency for each binary constraint we postulate the existence of the supports for both directions of each arc. In contrast, in the case of directional arc consistency we postulate the existence of the supports only in one direction, the one induced by the variable ordering. This amounts to considering directed graphs. In a **directed graph**, in contrast to a usual (undirected) graph, each arc has a direction.

Consider now a CSP $\mathcal{P}$ and a linear ordering $\prec$ on its variables. This linear ordering $\prec$ turns each arc of the graph associated with the binary constraints of $\mathcal{P}$ into a directed arc and consequently turns this graph into a directed graph.

In what follows it is more convenient to deal with the CSP $\mathcal{P}_\prec$ obtained from $\mathcal{P}$ by reordering its variables along $\prec$ so that each constraint in $\mathcal{P}_\prec$ is on a sequence of variables $x_1, \ldots, x_k$ such that $x_1 \prec x_2 \prec \cdots \prec x_k$. So, given a CSP $\mathcal{P}$, for each binary constraint C on the variables x, y, if $x \prec y$, then we put C in $\mathcal{P}_\prec$ and otherwise we put in $\mathcal{P}_\prec$ the constraint $\{(b, a) \mid (a, b) \in C\}$ on y, x. The precise definition of $\mathcal{P}_\prec$ is left as Exercise 5.1.

As an illustration, consider the CSP

$$\mathcal{P} := \langle x < y, y \neq z \; ; \; x \in [2..10], y \in [3..7], z \in [3..6] \rangle$$

with $y \prec x \prec z$. Then

$$\mathcal{P}_\prec := \langle y > x, y \neq z \; ; \; y \in [3..7], x \in [2..10], z \in [3..6] \rangle.$$

We have then the following simple result the proof of which we leave as Exercise 5.2.

Note 5.13 (Directional Arc Consistency) *A CSP $\mathcal{P}$ is directionally arc consistent w.r.t. $\prec$ iff the CSP $\mathcal{P}_\prec$ is closed under the applications of the ARC CONSISTENCY rule 1.* □

Proof The proof is left as Exercise 5.2.

5.5 Path consistency

The notions of local consistency introduced so far dealt with each constraint separately. This can lead to a very inefficient form of reasoning. Consider for example the CSP

$$\langle x < y, y < z, z < x \; ; \; x \in \{1..100000\}, y \in \{1..100000\}, z \in \{1..100000\}\rangle.$$

We would like to prove that it is inconsistent. We can use for this purpose the ARC CONSISTENCY rules *1* and *2*. For example, applying the first rule to the constraint $x < y$ we obtain the CSP

$$\langle x < y, y < z, z < x \; ; \; x \in \{1..99999\}, y \in \{1..100000\}, z \in \{1..100000\}\rangle.$$

Next, applying the ARC CONSISTENCY 1 rule to the constraint $z < x$ we obtain the CSP

$$\langle x < y, y < z, z < x \; ; \; x \in \{1..99999\}, y \in \{1..100000\}, z \in \{1..99998\}\rangle.$$

Iterating this process we obtain a derivation that ends in a failed CSP. So, by the fact that these two rules are equivalence preserving, we conclude that the original CSP is inconsistent. But this reasoning results in a huge number of steps. Moreover, the length of the derivation depends on the size of the domains.

On the other hand, another, trivial, reasoning yields the same conclusion. Namely, by the transitivity of $<$ from $x < y$ and $y < z$ we conclude $x < z$, which together with $z < x$ yields a contradiction. Path consistency is a local consistency notion that generalises this form of reasoning to arbitrary binary constrains. So path consistency involves two constraints considered together.

In the remaining part of this chapter, to keep things notationally simple, we shall limit our attention to successively more specific types of CSPs. We shall introduce all three types now.

Definition 5.14
- We call a CSP $\mathcal{P}$ *normalised* if for each subsequence x, y of its variables at most one constraint on x, y exists in $\mathcal{P}$.
  Given a normalised CSP and a subsequence x, y of its variables we

denote by $C_{x,y}$ the unique constraint on x, y if it exists and otherwise the 'universal' relation on x, y that equals the Cartesian product of the domains of the variables x and y. Note that these universal relations $C_{x,y}$ are not constraints of the normalised CSP.

- We call a CSP $\mathcal{P}$ **standardised** if for each pair x, y of variables a unique constraint on x, y exists.
- We call a CSP $\mathcal{P}$ **regular** if for each sequence X of its variables a unique constraint on X exists. Given a regular CSP and a subsequence X of its variables we denote by C_X the unique constraint on X. $\square$

Example 5.15 Consider the following CSP

$$\langle x + y < 5, x + y \neq 2, x < z, y = z, x + y = z \ ;$$
$$x \in [0..4], y \in [1..5], z \in [6..10]\rangle.$$

It is not normalised since two constraints on the subsequence x, y exist in it. Also it is not standardised and not regular. If we replace the constraints $x + y < 5, x + y \neq 2$ by one, written as $x + y < 5 \wedge x + y \neq 2$, and consider the resulting CSP, so

$$\langle x + y < 5 \wedge x + y \neq 2, x < z, y = z, x + y = z \ ;$$
$$x \in [0..4], y \in [1..5], z \in [6..10]\rangle,$$

then this CSP is normalised. Even more, this CSP is standardised, since for each subsequence of two variables, so for x, y, for x, z and for y, z, precisely one constraint on the subsequence exists. However, this CSP is not regular, since no unary constraint is present in it. $\square$

The following simple observation holds.

Note 5.16 (Equivalence)
 (i) *Every CSP is equivalent to a normalised CSP.*
 (ii) *Every CSP is equivalent to a standardised CSP.*
 (iii) *Every CSP is equivalent to a regular CSP.* $\square$

Proof (i) For each subsequence x, y of the variables such that a constraint on x, y exists, replace the set of all constraints on x, y by their intersection. The resulting CSP is equivalent to the original one and is normalised.

(ii) First add for each subsequence x, y for which no constraint on x, y exists a constraint on x, y that equals the Cartesian product of the domains of the variables x and y. Then transform the resulting CSP to a normalised one, as above.

(iii) Perform the procedure described in (ii) and (i) above for each subsequence X of the variables instead of for each subsequence x, y of the variables. □

Even though the proof of the above result is straightforward, it has subtle consequences. Namely, the transformation of a CSP into the one that is normalised, respectively standardised or regular, can affect the local consistency notion such a CSP satisfies.

As an example consider the 3 Queens Problem formalised as a CSP in Example 2.2. We noted already in Example 5.5(ii) that this CSP is arc consistent. However, if we transform it into one that is normalised, the resulting CSP is not anymore arc consistent. Indeed, the resulting single constraint on the variables x_1 and x_2 is then not arc consistent: the value 2 in the domain of x_2 has no support in the domain of x_1. More intuitively, if we place the second queen in the center of the 3×3 chess board, we cannot place anymore the first queen in such a way that these two queens do not attack each other. So the above transformations of CSPs maintain equivalence but not necessarily specific local consistency notions.

Next, we introduce two simple operations on binary relations.

Definition 5.17 Given two binary relations R and S we define

- the **transposition** of R by

$$R^T := \{(b, a) \mid (a, b) \in R\},$$

- the **composition** of R and S by

$$R \cdot S := \{(a, b) \mid \exists c \, ((a, c) \in R, (c, b) \in S)\}.$$

□

Note that if R_1 is a constraint on the variables x, y and R_2 a constraint on the variables y, z, then $R_1 \cdot R_2$ is a constraint on the variables x, z.

Given a subsequence x, y of the variables of a normalised CSP we now introduce a 'supplementary' relation $C_{y,x}$ defined by

$$C_{y,x} := C_{x,y}^T.$$

The supplementary relations are not parts of the considered CSP as none of them is defined on a subsequence of its variables, but they allow us a more compact presentation. Finally, we introduce the central notion of this section. We define it for normalised CSPs.

Definition 5.18 We call a normalised CSP *path consistent* if for each subset $\{x, y, z\}$ of its variables we have

$$C_{x,z} \subseteq C_{x,y} \cdot C_{y,z}.$$

                                                                               □

In other words, a normalised CSP is path consistent if for each subset $\{x, y, z\}$ of its variables the following holds:

if $(a, c) \in C_{x,z}$, then there exists b such that $(a, b) \in C_{x,y}$ and $(b, c) \in C_{y,z}$.

So a CSP with non-empty domains and with no binary constraints is trivially path consistent. That is, for such CSPs the property of path consistency holds automatically.

Since the subset $\{x, y, z\}$ is arbitrary and the order of the elements in a set is irrelevant, the condition $C_{x,z} \subseteq C_{x,y} \cdot C_{y,z}$ is a shorthand for the following six conditions, in which we now refer to an arbitrary *subsequence* x, y, z of the considered variables:

$$C_{x,y} \subseteq C_{x,z} \cdot C_{z,y}, \quad C_{x,z} \subseteq C_{x,y} \cdot C_{y,z}, \quad C_{y,z} \subseteq C_{y,x} \cdot C_{x,z},$$

$$C_{y,x} \subseteq C_{y,z} \cdot C_{z,x}, \quad C_{z,x} \subseteq C_{z,y} \cdot C_{y,x}, \quad C_{z,y} \subseteq C_{z,x} \cdot C_{x,y}.$$

The latter three inclusions are easily seen to be equivalent to the first three, since for binary relations R, S we have $R \subseteq S$ iff $R^T \subseteq S^T$ and $(R \cdot S)^T = S^T \cdot R^T$. Further, using the transposition operation '$.^T$' the first three inclusions can be rewritten so that only the constraints of the considered CSP and the universal relations are involved.

This is the contents of the following observation that will be useful later in this section. Recall that for a subsequence x, y, z of the variables the relations $C_{x,y}, C_{x,z}$ and $C_{y,z}$ denote either the constraints of the considered normalised CSP or the universal binary relations on the domains of the corresponding variables.

Note 5.19 (Alternative Path Consistency) *A normalised CSP is path consistent iff for each subsequence x, y, z of its variables we have*

$$C_{x,y} \subseteq C_{x,z} \cdot C_{y,z}^T,$$

$$C_{x,z} \subseteq C_{x,y} \cdot C_{y,z},$$

$$C_{y,z} \subseteq C_{x,y}^T \cdot C_{x,z}.$$

                                                                               □

Figure 5.7 illustrates this observation. For instance, an indirect path from x to y via z goes through the arc (x, z) followed by the reversal of the arc (y, z). This translates to the first formula.

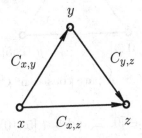

Fig. 5.7. Three relations on three variables

To further clarify this notion consider the following two examples.

Example 5.20
(i) Consider the following normalised CSP

$$\langle x < y, y < z, x < z \; ; \; x \in [0..4], y \in [1..5], z \in [6..10]\rangle,$$

visualised in Figure 5.8. This CSP is path consistent. Indeed, we have

$$C_{x,y} = \{(a, b) \mid a < b, a \in [0..4], b \in [1..5]\},$$

$$C_{x,z} = \{(a, c) \mid a < c, a \in [0..4], c \in [6..10]\},$$

$$C_{y,z} = \{(b, c) \mid b < c, b \in [1..5], c \in [6..10]\}.$$

It is straightforward to check that these three constraints satisfy the conditions of the Alternative Path Consistency Note 5.19. For example, for every pair $(a, c) \in C_{x,z}$ there exists $b \in [1..5]$ such that $a < b$ and $b < c$. Namely, we can always take $b = 5$.

(ii) Take now the following normalised CSP

$$\langle x < y, y < z, x < z \; ; \; x \in [0..4], y \in [1..5], z \in [5..10]\rangle$$

depicted in Figure 5.9. It differs from the previous one, depicted in Figure 5.8, only in the domain for z. Then this CSP is not path consistent. Indeed, in this CSP we have

$$C_{x,z} = \{(a, c) \mid a < c, a \in [0..4], c \in [5..10]\}$$

Local consistency notions

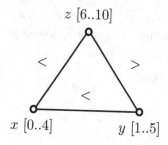

Fig. 5.8. A path consistent CSP

and for the pair of values $4 \in [0..4]$ and $5 \in [5..10]$ no value $b \in [1..5]$ exists such that $4 < b$ and $b < 5$.

□

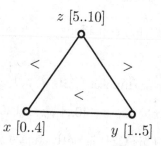

Fig. 5.9. A CSP that is not path consistent

To characterise the notion of path consistency we introduce three transformation rules that correspond to the Alternative Path Consistency Note 5.19. In these rules, following the convention introduced in Subsection 4.1.1, we omit the domain expressions. We assume here that x, y, z is a subsequence of the variables of the considered CSP.

PATH CONSISTENCY 1

$$\frac{C_{x,y},\, C_{x,z},\, C_{y,z}}{C'_{x,y},\, C_{x,z},\, C_{y,z}}$$

where the constraint $C'_{x,y}$ on the variables x, y is defined by $C'_{x,y} := C_{x,y} \cap C_{x,z} \cdot C^T_{y,z}$,

PATH CONSISTENCY 2

$$\frac{C_{x,y},\, C_{x,z},\, C_{y,z}}{C_{x,y},\, C'_{x,z},\, C_{y,z}}$$

where the constraint $C'_{x,z}$ on the variables x, z is defined by $C'_{x,z} := C_{x,z} \cap C_{x,y} \cdot C_{y,z}$,

$$PATH\ CONSISTENCY\ 3$$

$$\frac{C_{x,y}, C_{x,z}, C_{y,z}}{C_{x,y}, C_{x,z}, C'_{y,z}}$$

where the constraint $C'_{y,z}$ on the variables y, z is defined by $C'_{y,z} := C_{y,z} \cap C^T_{x,y} \cdot C_{x,z}$.

As already stated such rules are actually abbreviations in the sense that the corresponding domain expressions are omitted in them. So for example the *PATH CONSISTENCY 1* rule actually stands for

$$\frac{\langle C_{x,y}, C_{x,z}, C_{y,z} \ ; \ x \in D_x, y \in D_y, z \in D_z \rangle}{\langle C'_{x,y}, C_{x,z}, C_{y,z} \ ; \ x \in D_x, y \in D_y, z \in D_z \rangle}$$

where $C'_{x,y} := C_{x,y} \cap C_{x,z} \cdot C^T_{y,z}$.

To see that it is equivalence preserving consider a triple (a, b, c) that is a solution to the CSP in the premise of the rule. Then $(a, b) \in C_{x,y}, (a, c) \in C_{x,z}$ and $(b, c) \in C_{y,z}$. So by definition $(a, b) \in C_{x,z} \cdot C^T_{y,z}$ and consequently $(a, b) \in C'_{x,y}$. The proof that the other two rules are equivalence preserving is equally straightforward.

The following observation provides the corresponding characterisation result.

Note 5.21 (Path Consistency) *A normalised CSP is path consistent iff it is closed under the applications of the PATH CONSISTENCY rules 1, 2 and 3.*

Proof Using the Alternative Path Consistency Note 5.19 it is straightforward to see that a normalised CSP is closed under the applications of the *PATH CONSISTENCY* rules *1, 2* and *3* iff for each subsequence x, y, z of its variables we have

- $C'_{x,y} = C_{x,y}$, where $C'_{x,y}$ is defined as in the *PATH CONSISTENCY 1* rule,
- $C'_{x,z} = C_{x,z}$, where $C'_{x,z}$ is defined as in the *PATH CONSISTENCY 2* rule,
- $C'_{y,z} = C_{y,z}$, where $C'_{y,z}$ is defined as in the *PATH CONSISTENCY 3* rule.

Now $C'_{x,y} = C_{x,y}$ iff $C_{x,y} \subseteq C_{x,z} \cdot C^T_{y,z}$ and similarly for the other two equalities. $\square$

The notion of path consistency involves two relations in the sense that each relation $C_{x,z}$ is defined in terms of two other relations, $C_{x,y}$ and $C_{y,z}$. It can be easily generalised to involve m relations.

Definition 5.22 We call a normalised CSP m-**path consistent**, where $m \geq 2$, if for each subset $\{x_1, \ldots, x_{m+1}\}$ of its variables we have

$$C_{x_1,x_{m+1}} \subseteq C_{x_1,x_2} \cdot C_{x_2,x_3} \cdot \ldots \cdot C_{x_m,x_{m+1}}.$$

□

In other words, a normalised CSP is m-path consistent if for each subset $\{x_1, \ldots, x_{m+1}\}$ of its variables the following holds:

if $(a_1, a_{m+1}) \in C_{x_1,x_{m+1}}$, then there exists a sequence of values $a_2, \ldots, a_m$ such that for all $i \in [1..m]$ we have $(a_i, a_{i+1}) \in C_{x_i,x_{i+1}}$.

This sequence $a_2, \ldots, a_m$ can be viewed as a path connecting a_1 and a_{m+1}. This explains the name 'path consistency' that was originally defined as m-path consistency. The existence of such a 'path' is depicted in Figure 5.10, where we illustrate the fact that $(a_1, a_{m+1}) \in C_{x_1,x_{m+1}}$ implies that for some $a_2, \ldots, a_m$ we have $(a_i, a_{i+1}) \in C_{x_i,x_{i+1}}$ for $i \in [1..m]$.

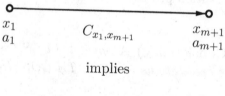

implies

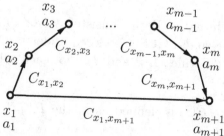

Fig. 5.10. m-path consistency: existence of a 'path' connecting a_1 and a_{m+1}

Clearly 2-path consistency is identical to path consistency. The following theorem shows that for other values of m the equivalence holds, as well.

Theorem 5.23 (Path Consistency) *Consider a normalised CSP that is path consistent. Then it is m-path consistent for each $m \geq 2$.*

Proof　We proceed by induction. As already noticed, the claim holds for

$m = 2$. Assume the claim holds for some $m \geq 2$. Consider now a subset $\{x_1, \ldots, x_{m+2}\}$ of the variables of this CSP. By virtue of path consistency applied to the set $\{x_1, x_{m+1}, x_{m+2}\}$ we have

$$C_{x_1, x_{m+2}} \subseteq C_{x_1, x_{m+1}} \cdot C_{x_{m+1}, x_{m+2}}.$$

By induction the considered CSP is m-path consistent. By m-path consistency applied to the set $\{x_1, \ldots, x_{m+1}\}$ we have

$$C_{x_1, x_{m+1}} \subseteq C_{x_1, x_2} \cdot C_{x_2, x_3} \cdot \ldots \cdot C_{x_m, x_{m+1}}.$$

Consequently,

$$C_{x_1, x_{m+2}} \subseteq C_{x_1, x_2} \cdot C_{x_2, x_3} \cdot \ldots \cdot C_{x_{m+1}, x_{m+2}}.$$

This concludes the proof of the inductive step and hence the proof of the claim. $\square$

So this generalisation of the path consistency does not bring anything new.

5.6 Directional path consistency

This is not the case for another modification of the path consistency that takes into account a linear ordering $\prec$ on the considered variables. Then, just as in the case of the arc consistency, we obtain a new notion of local consistency. It is defined as follows.

Definition 5.24 Assume a linear ordering $\prec$ on the considered variables. We call a normalised CSP **directionally path consistent w.r.t.** $\prec$ if for each subset $\{x, y, z\}$ of its variables we have

$$C_{x,z} \subseteq C_{x,y} \cdot C_{y,z} \text{ provided } x, z \prec y.$$

$\square$

This definition relies on the supplementary relations because the ordering $\prec$ may differ from the original ordering of the variables. For example, in the original ordering z can precede x. In this case $C_{z,x}$ and not $C_{x,z}$ is a constraint of the CSP under consideration. But just as in the case of path consistency we can rewrite this definition using the original constraints only. In fact, we have the following analogue of the Alternative Path Consistency Note 5.19.

Note 5.25 (Alternative Directional Path Consistency) *A normalised CSP is directionally path consistent w.r.t. $\prec$ iff for each subsequence x, y, z of its variables we have*

$$C_{x,y} \subseteq C_{x,z} \cdot C_{y,z}^T \ provided \ x, y \prec z,$$

$$C_{x,z} \subseteq C_{x,y} \cdot C_{y,z} \ provided \ x, z \prec y,$$

$$C_{y,z} \subseteq C_{x,y}^T \cdot C_{x,z} \ provided \ y, z \prec x.$$

Proof   The proof is left as Exercise 5.3.   □

Thus out of the above three inclusions precisely one needs to be checked. To see the difference between the notions of path consistency and directional path consistency consider the following example.

Example 5.26   Reconsider the CSP

$$\langle x < y, y < z, x < z \ ; \ x \in [0..4], y \in [1..5], z \in [5..10] \rangle$$

of Example 5.20(ii). We already noted that it is not path consistent. The argument given there also shows that it is not directionally path consistent w.r.t. the ordering $\prec$ in which $x, z \prec y$.

In contrast, it is easy to see that this CSP is directionally path consistent w.r.t. the ordering $\prec$ in which $x, y \prec z$. Indeed, for every pair $(a, b) \in C_{x,y}$ there exists $c \in [5..10]$ such that $a < c$ and $b < c$. Namely, we can always take $c = 6$.

Similarly, this CSP is also directionally path consistent w.r.t. the ordering $\prec$ in which $y, z \prec x$, as for every pair $(b, c) \in C_{y,z}$ there exists $a \in [0..4]$ such that $a < b$ and $a < c$, namely $a = 0$.   □

To characterise the notion of directional path consistency we proceed as in Section 5.4 and reason in terms of the CSP $\mathcal{P}_\prec$. We have the following characterisation result.

Note 5.27 (Directional Path Consistency) *A normalised CSP $\mathcal{P}$ is directionally path consistent w.r.t. $\prec$ iff $\mathcal{P}_\prec$ is closed under the applications of the PATH CONSISTENCY rule 1.*

Proof   The proof is left as Exercise 5.4.   □

5.7 k-consistency

The notion of path consistency can be also generalised in a different way. For further discussion we need to be more precise about the way values are assigned to variables. To this end we introduce the following notions.

Definition 5.28 Consider a CSP $\mathcal{P}$.

- By an *instantiation* we mean a function defined on a subset of the variables of $\mathcal{P}$ which assigns to each variable a value from its domain. We represent instantiations as sets of the form

$$\{(x_1, d_1), \ldots, (x_k, d_k)\}.$$

This notation assumes that $x_1, \ldots, x_k$ are distinct variables and that for $i \in [1..k]$ d_i is an element from the domain of x_i.

- Consider a subsequence $x_{i_1}, \ldots, x_{i_m}$ of the sequence $x_1, \ldots, x_k$. We say that an instantiation $\{(x_1, d_1), \ldots, (x_k, d_k)\}$ *satisfies* a constraint C on $x_{i_1}, \ldots, x_{i_m}$ if $(d_{i_1}, \ldots, d_{i_m}) \in C$, that is, if $(d_1, \ldots, d_k)$ satisfies C in the sense of Section 2.1.

- We call an instantiation I with the domain X *consistent* if it satisfies all constraints of $\mathcal{P}$ on the subsequences of the variables from X.

- We call a consistent instantiation k-*consistent* if its domain consists of k variables.

- We call an instantiation a *solution* to $\mathcal{P}$ if it is consistent and defined on all variables of $\mathcal{P}$.

- Consider an instantiation I with a domain X and a subset Y of X. We denote by $I \mid Y$ the instantiation obtained by restricting I to the elements of Y and call it the *restriction of I to Y*. ▫

So an instantiation is a solution to a CSP if it is k-consistent, where k is the number of its variables. Let us illustrate the introduced notions by an example.

Example 5.29 Take the following CSP already considered in Example 5.20(ii) and depicted in Figure 5.9:

$$\langle x < y, y < z, x < z \; ; \; x \in [0..4], y \in [1..5], z \in [5..10] \rangle.$$

Consider the instantiation $I := \{(x, 0), (y, 5), (z, 6)\}$. It clearly satisfies the first constraint $x < y$, since $0 < 5$. It also satisfies the second constraint $x < z$, since $0 < 6$ and the third constraint $y < z$ since $5 < 6$. So I is a consistent (or, equivalently, 3-consistent) instantiation which is a solution to this CSP.

Further, note that the restrictions of I to two element subsets of its domain are:

$$I \mid \{x, y\} := \{(x, 0), (y, 5)\},$$

$$I \mid \{x, z\} := \{(x, 0), (z, 6)\},$$

and

$$I \mid \{y, z\} := \{(y, 5), (z, 6)\}.$$

□

Next, we introduce some properties of CSP the study of which is the topic of this section.

Definition 5.30

- We call a CSP 1-*consistent* if it is node consistent.
- We call a CSP k-*consistent*, where $k > 1$, if for every $(k - 1)$-consistent instantiation and for every variable x not in its domain there exists a value in the domain of x such that the resulting instantiation is k-consistent.

□

So, a CSP is k-consistent where $k > 1$, if every $(k - 1)$-consistent instantiation can be extended to a k-consistent instantiation *no matter* what new variable is selected. In the case no $(k - 1)$-consistent instantiation exists, the CSP is vacuously k-consistent.

The following example clarifies this definition.

Example 5.31 Consider the CSP

$$\langle x \neq y, x + y = z \; ; \; x \in [1..2], y \in [1..2], z \in [2..4] \rangle.$$

Since no unary constraints are present, this CSP is vacuously 1-consistent, i.e., node consistent.

Further, any instantiation with the singleton domain can be extended to a 2-consistent instantiation no matter what new variable we choose. For example, the instantiation $\{(x, 1)\}$ can be extended to the consistent instantiation $\{(x, 1), (y, 2)\}$ with the domain $\{x, y\}$. So this CSP is 2-consistent.

The 2-consistent instantiation $\{(x, 1), (y, 2)\}$ can be extended to a 3-consistent instantiation, namely $\{(x, 1), (y, 2), (z, 3)\}$. However, this is not sufficient to show 3-consistency, since we need to consider *all* 2-consistent instantiations and all 'new' variables. In fact, the 2-consistent instantiation

$\{(x,1),(z,4)\}$ cannot be extended to a 3-consistent instantiation, so this CSP is not 3-consistent.   □

The following observation shows that the notion of k-consistency generalises both arc consistency and path consistency. By a **binary constraint satisfaction problem**, in short **binary CSP**, we mean here a CSP all constraints of which are unary or binary.

Note 5.32 (Characterisation)

   (i) *A node consistent normalised CSP that does not contain the false constraint* $\perp$ *is arc consistent iff it is 2-consistent.*

   (ii) *A node consistent normalised binary CSP that does not contain the false constraint* $\perp$ *is path consistent iff it is 3-consistent.*

Proof   The proof is left as Exercise 5.5.   □

It is useful to notice that in general there is no relation between the notions of consistency, k-consistency and l-consistency for $k \neq l$.

Example 5.33

(i) First notice that for every $k > 1$ there exists an inconsistent CSP on k variables that is $(k-1)$-consistent but not k-consistent.

   Indeed, consider a domain $D := [1..k-1]$, a sequence of k variables $x_1, \ldots, x_k$, each with the domain D, and assume the constraints $x_i \neq x_j$ for $i \in [1..k-1]$ and $j \in [i+1..k]$. These constraints just state that all variables are different. For $k = 3$ this CSP is depicted in Figure 5.11. It is easy to see that the resulting CSP is $(k-1)$-consistent because every $(k-2)$-consistent instantiation 'uses' $k-2$ values out of $[1..k-1]$ so it can be extended to a $(k-1)$-consistent instantiation by assigning the 'remaining' value to the newly selected variable. However, this CSP is not k-consistent as there is no solution to it.

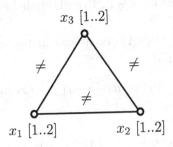

Fig. 5.11. A 2-consistent but 3-inconsistent CSP

(ii) Next, note that for every $k > 2$ there exists a consistent CSP on k variables that is not $(k-1)$-consistent but is k-consistent.

Indeed, take a sequence of k variables $x_1, \ldots, x_k$, with the domain $\{a, b\}$ for the variable x_1 and with the singleton domain $\{a\}$ for each of the variables $x_2, \ldots, x_k$. Now assume the constraints $x_1 \neq x_2$ and $x_1 \neq x_3$. The resulting CSP is depicted in Figure 5.12.

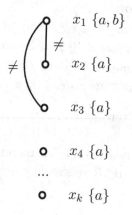

$x_1 \ \{a, b\}$

$\neq$

$x_2 \ \{a\}$

$\neq$

$x_3 \ \{a\}$

$x_4 \ \{a\}$

$\ldots$

$x_k \ \{a\}$

Fig. 5.12. A k-consistent but not $(k-1)$-consistent CSP

Consider now the instantiation the domain of which consists of the variables x_l for $l \neq 2, 3$ and which assigns to each of these variables, in particular to x_1, the value a. This instantiation is vacuously $(k-2)$-consistent. It can be extended to an instantiation of $k-1$ variables in two ways: by either adding the pair (x_2, a) or the pair (x_3, a). In each case the resulting instantiation is not $(k-1)$-consistent. So this CSP is not $(k-1)$-consistent.

However, this CSP is k-consistent. Indeed, if an instantiation I with $k-1$ variables in its domain cannot be extended to a k-consistent instantiation, then the pair (x_1, a) occurs in I. But I has $k-1$ variables in its domain, so also either the pair (x_2, a) occurs in I or the pair (x_3, a) occurs in I. So I is then not consistent.

In other words, every $(k-1)$-consistent instantiation is a restriction of the consistent instantiation

$$\{(x_1, b), (x_2, a), (x_3, a), \ldots, (x_k, a)\}.$$

(iii) Next, note that for every $k > 2$ there exists an inconsistent CSP on k variables that is k-consistent.

Indeed, consider a domain $D := [1..k-2]$, a sequence of k variables $x_1, \ldots, x_k$, each with the domain D, and assume the constraints $x_i \neq x_j$ for $i \in [1..k-1]$ and $j \in [i+1..k]$. The only difference between this CSP and the one considered in (i) is that the domains now equal $[1..k-2]$ instead of $[1..k-1]$. For $k=3$ this CSP is depicted in Figure 5.13. As a consequence no $(k-1)$-consistent instantiation exists. So this CSP is vacuously k-consistent.

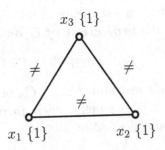

Fig. 5.13. A 3-consistent but inconsistent CSP

(iv) Finally, note that for every $k > 2$ there exists a consistent CSP on k variables that is not k-consistent.

Indeed, consider a sequence of k variables $x_1, \ldots, x_k$. Take for x_1 the domain $\{1\}$ and for the variables $x_2, \ldots, x_k$ the domain $D := [1..k]$. As in (i) and (iii) assume the constraints $x_i \neq x_j$ for $i \in [1..k-1]$ and $j \in [i+1..k]$. For $k=3$ this CSP is depicted in Figure 5.14.

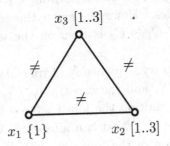

Fig. 5.14. A consistent but 3-inconsistent CSP

As the instantiation $\{(x_1, 1), (x_2, 2), \ldots, (x_k, k)\}$ shows, this CSP is clearly consistent. However, this CSP is not k-consistent, since the $(k-1)$-consistent instantiation $\{(x_2, 1), (x_3, 2), \ldots, (x_k, k-1)\}$ cannot be extended to a k-consistent instantiation. □

As in the case of the previously considered notions of local consistency, we now characterise the notion of k-consistency by means of rules. To this end we confine our attention to regular CSPs that were introduced in Definition 5.14, i.e., the ones in which for each sequence X of its variables a unique constraint on X exists, denoted by C_X.

We now need to introduce some notation.

Definition 5.34

- Given a constraint C on a sequence of variables X and a subsequence Y of X we define the **projection of C on Y** by

$$\Pi_Y(C) := \{d[Y] \mid d \in C\}.$$

- Given a sequence of constraints $C_1, \ldots, C_m$ on, respectively, sequences of variables $X_1, \ldots, X_m$ we define their **join**, written as $C_1 \bowtie \cdots \bowtie C_m$, as the constraint defined by

$$C_1 \bowtie \cdots \bowtie C_m := \{d \mid d[X_i] \in C_i \text{ for } i \in [1..m]\}.$$

- Given a sequence X of variables we define

$$\overline{C_X} := \bowtie \{C_Y \mid Y \text{ is a subsequence of } X\}.$$

□

We should still clarify on what sequence of variables is the above-defined constraint $C_1 \bowtie \cdots \bowtie C_m$. In general, it depends on the assumed sequence of variables. For example, given the sequence x_1, x_2, x_3, x_4 and two constraints, C_1 on x_1, x_2 and C_2 on x_1, x_3, the constraint $C_1 \bowtie C_2$ is on the sequence x_1, x_2, x_3 of the variables. However, given the sequence x_1, x_3, x_2 of the variables the constraint $C_1 \bowtie C_2$ is then on the sequence x_1, x_3, x_2 of the variables.

Consider now an arbitrary sequence X of variables such that for $i \in [1..m]$ X_i is a subsequence of X, and the constraints $C_1, \ldots, C_m$ on, respectively, $X_1, \ldots, X_m$. Then by definition the join $C_1 \bowtie \cdots \bowtie C_m$ is a constraint on the shortest subsequence of X that contains each X_i as a subsequence.

Note that the definition of the join does not depend on the ordering of the constraints. This justifies the definition of $\overline{C_X}$. Also note that by the definition of the join d is a solution to $\langle C_1, \ldots, C_m ; \mathcal{DE} \rangle$ iff $d \in C_1 \bowtie \cdots \bowtie C_m$. So the join operation $\bowtie$ provides us with a compact way of representing all solutions to a CSP.

We can now introduce the desired proof rule. It is parameterised by a sequence of variables X of length $k-1$ and a variable y that does not occur in X. For simplicity, we write X, y to denote the subsequence of the variables of the given CSP that consists of the variables present in X and y.

$$k\text{-}CONSISTENCY$$

$$\frac{C_X}{C_X \cap \Pi_X(\overline{C_{X,y}})}$$

To understand better this rule note that for each subsequence Y of the variables $d \in \overline{C_Y}$ iff the corresponding instantiation with the domain Y is consistent. Consequently, $d \in \Pi_X(\overline{C_{X,y}})$ iff the corresponding instantiation with the domain (formed by the elements of) X can be extended to a consistent instantiation with the domain X, y.

To illustrate how this rule is applied consider an example.

Example 5.35 Consider now the regular CSP corresponding to the CSP

$$\langle x \neq y, x + y = z \; ; \; x \in [1..2], y \in [1..2], z \in [2..4]\rangle.$$

from Example 5.31.

Let us apply to it the k-$CONSISTENCY$ rule with X equal to $\{x, y\}$ and y equal to z. Then C_X is the constraint $x \neq y$ which denotes the set $\{(1, 2), (2, 1)\}$. In turn, $C_{X,y}$ denotes the constraint $x + y = z$, i.e, the set $\{(1, 1, 2), (1, 2, 3), (2, 1, 3), (2, 2, 4)\}$. There are two 'non-trivial' constraints in this CSP, so $\overline{C_{X,y}}$ equals $(x \neq y) \bowtie (x + y = z)$ which denotes the set $\{(1, 2, 3), (2, 1, 3)\}$. Consequently, $\Pi_X(\overline{C_{X,y}}) = \{(1, 2), (2, 1)\}$ and this application of the k-$CONSISTENCY$ rule is not relevant.

Let us apply now to this CSP the k-$CONSISTENCY$ rule with X equal to $\{x, z\}$. The constraint C_X on X is the Cartesian product $[1..2] \times [2..4]$, and, as before, $C_{X,y}$ denotes the constraint $x + y = z$, i.e, the set

$$\{(1, 1, 2), (1, 2, 3), (2, 1, 3), (2, 2, 4)\}.$$

Also, as before $\overline{C_{X,y}}$ equals $(x \neq y) \bowtie (x + y = z)$ and denotes the set $\{(1, 2, 3), (2, 1, 3)\}$. So now $\Pi_X(\overline{C_{X,y}}) = \{(1, 3), (2, 3)\}$. So this application of the k-$CONSISTENCY$ rule transforms the universal constraint C_X on x, z to the constraint $\{(1, 3), (2, 3)\}$, which amounts syntactically to adding the constraint $(x = 1 \wedge z = 3) \vee (x = 2 \wedge z = 3)$ on x, z. This constraint has an indirect effect of removing the value 4 from the domain of z.   □

The following result clarifies the status of the k-$CONSISTENCY$ rule.

Note 5.36 (k-**Consistency**) *Fix $k \geq 1$. If a regular CSP is closed under the applications of the k-$CONSISTENCY$ rule for all subsequences X of $k - 1$ variables and all variables y not in X, then it is k-consistent.*

Proof Call the considered CSP $\mathcal{P}$. Take a subsequence X of $k-1$ variables and a variable y of $\mathcal{P}$ not in X. Suppose $\mathcal{P}$ is closed under the applications of the k-*CONSISTENCY* rule for each such X and y. Then $C_X \subseteq \Pi_X(\overline{C_{X,y}})$. But by definition $\overline{C_X} \subseteq C_X$, so $\overline{C_X} \subseteq \Pi_X(\overline{C_{X,y}})$. This means that every $(k-1)$-consistent instantiation with the domain X is a restriction of a consistent instantiation with the domain X, y. In other words, every $(k-1)$-consistent instantiation with the domain X can be extended to a k-consistent instantiation with the domain X, y. $\qquad\qquad\square$

Note that in contrast to the previous characterisations of the local consistency notions by means of the proof rules we only have here an implication. This implication cannot be reversed. Indeed, take the CSP of Example 5.33(ii) depicted in Figure 5.12, that is,

$$\langle x_1 \neq x_2, x_1 \neq x_3 \; ; \; x_1 \in \{a, b\}, x_2 \in \{a\}, \ldots, x_k \in \{a\}\rangle,$$

where $k > 2$, which, as we showed, is k-consistent. Transform it to a regular CSP by adding to it the universal constraints for all sequences of variables different from x_1, x_2 and x_1, x_3. It is easy to see that the resulting CSP is still k-consistent. Consider now the instantiation $I := \{(x_1, a), \ldots, (x_{k-1}, a)\}$. Then I does not satisfy the constraint $x_1 \neq x_2$. So for

$$d := (\underbrace{a, \ldots, a}_{k-1 \text{ times}})$$

and $X := x_1, \ldots, x_{k-1}$ we have $d \in C_X$, since C_X is a universal constraint, and $d \notin \Pi_X(\overline{C_{X,x_k}})$, since

$$\overline{C_{X,x_k}} = \{(b, \underbrace{a, \ldots, a}_{k-1 \text{ times}})\}.$$

So this regular CSP is not closed under the applications of the k-*CONSISTENCY* rule for X and $y := x_k$.

However, the fact that in the above Note we only have an implication is of no consequence for us. Indeed, this result provides us with a method of transforming a regular CSP into a k-consistent one: by means of a repeated application of the k-*CONSISTENCY* rule for all subsequences of variables X of length $k-1$ and all variables y not in X.

5.8 Strong k-consistency

A natural question arises what is the use of k-consistency. After all, Example 5.33 shows that k-consistency, even for a large, relative to the number of variables, k does not guarantee yet that the CSP is consistent. This seems to indicate that in general there is no relation between k-consistency and consistency. This, however, is not completely true. The discussed examples only show that the notion of k-consistency is of limited value when considered in isolation. What we need is an accumulated effect of the k-consistency notions. This brings us to the following definition.

Definition 5.37 We call a CSP *strongly k-consistent*, where $k \geq 1$, if it is i-consistent for every $i \in [1..k]$.   □

Now, the following simple result relates strong consistency and consistency.

Theorem 5.38 (Consistency 1) *Consider a CSP that does not contain the false constraint $\perp$, with k variables where $k \geq 1$, and such that*

- *at least one domain is non-empty,*
- *it is strongly k-consistent.*

Then this CSP is consistent.

Proof   We construct a solution to the considered CSP by induction. More precisely, we prove that

(i) there exists a 1-consistent instantiation,
(ii) for every $i \in [2..k]$ each $(i - 1)$-consistent instantiation can be extended to an i-consistent instantiation.

Rearrange the variables in question in a sequence $x_1, \ldots, x_k$ such that the domain D_1 of x_1 is non-empty. Since the considered CSP is 1-consistent and the domain D_1 is non-empty, there exists d_1 such that $\{(x_1, d_1)\}$ is 1-consistent. This proves (i).

Now (ii) is simply a consequence of the fact that the CSP is i-consistent for every $i \in [2..k]$.   □

Note that the assumption that at least one domain is non-empty is essential. Indeed, every CSP with all domains empty is trivially i-consistent for every $i \in [1..k]$, where k is the number of variables. Yet it has no solution. Note also that the implication in the Consistency 1 Theorem 5.38 cannot be reversed. Indeed, consider the CSP discussed in Example 5.33(ii). It is consistent but not $(k - 1)$-consistent, so a fortiori not strongly k-consistent.

In general, a CSP can involve a large number of variables, so to use the above theorem one either needs to check strong k-consistency or to reduce the given CSP to a strong k-consistent one, in both cases for a large k. We shall see in Section 5.10 that in many cases we can use a much smaller k.

We conclude this section by noting the following immediate consequence of the k-Consistency Note 5.36.

Note 5.39 (Strong k-Consistency) *Fix $l \geq 1$. If a regular CSP is closed under the applications of the k-CONSISTENCY rule for all subsequences of variables X of length $k \in [1..l-1]$ and all variables y not in X, then it is strongly l-consistent.*

$\square$

5.9 Relational consistency

We considered by now several notions of local consistency. Some of them, like the hyper-arc consistency, dealt with each constraint separately and focused on the variable domains. Other notions, like the path consistency dealt with two binary constraints at a time. We saw also that m-path consistency, the extension of the path consistency that dealt with m binary constraints at a time, was equivalent to path consistency.

One can, however, modify the notion of m-path consistency and consider arbitrary sequences of m not necessarily binary constraints. At the same time one can consider an arbitrary number of variables present in these constraints. This yields perhaps the ultimate notion of local consistency, called relational consistency. To illustrate the use of such a notion consider the following CSP:

$\langle$ all_different(x, y, z), $x + y + z = u$;
$$x \in [1..3], y \in [1..3], z \in [1..3], u \in [3..5]\rangle,$$

where the all_different constraint was defined in Section 2.2. This CSP is clearly inconsistent since when x, y and z are all different, their sum is at least 6. However, this CSP is easily seen to be hyper-arc consistent. Also, it is vacuously node consistent, arc consistent and path consistent, since no unary or binary constraints are present. A fortiori, it is directionally arc consistent and directionally path consistent, w.r.t. all variable orderings. So none of these local consistency notions can be directly used to detect inconsistency.

Thanks to the Consistency 1 Theorem 5.38 we know that for some k this CSP is not k-consistent. In fact, this CSP is not 4-consistent, since the 3-consistent instantiation $\{(x, 1), (y, 2), (z, 3)\}$ cannot be extended to a 4-consistent instantiation. However, this reasoning does not capture the original intuition for inconsistency, namely that the two considered constraints cannot be considered jointly. The relational consistency notion, that we are about to define, does allow us to capture this intuition.

Given a sequence of constraints $C_1, \ldots, C_m$ we denote by $Var(C_1, \ldots, C_m)$ the set of variables that are used in them.

Definition 5.40

- Consider a CSP $\mathcal{P}$ with a subsequence $\mathcal{C}$ of its constraints. Denote by $\mathcal{P} \mid \mathcal{C}$ the CSP obtained from $\mathcal{P}$ by removing all constraints not in $\mathcal{C}$ and by deleting all domain expressions involving variables not present in any constraint in $\mathcal{C}$.
- We call a CSP $\mathcal{P}$ *relationally* (i, m)-*consistent* if for every sequence $\mathcal{C}$ of its constraints of length m and a subset X of $Var(\mathcal{C})$ of size i the following holds:
  every consistent (relative to $\mathcal{P}$) instantiation with the domain X can be extended to a solution to $\mathcal{P} \mid \mathcal{C}$. $\qquad \square$

In other words, to verify that a CSP is relationally (i, m)-consistent, we need to check that for every sequence of m constraints and for every set X of i variables, each present in one of these m constraints, any consistent instantiation with the domain X can be extended to a solution to all these m constraints.

Returning now to the CSP considered above we note that it is not $(1,2)$-relationally consistent. Indeed, no instantiation with the domain $\{u\}$ can be extended to an instantiation that satisfies both considered constraints. Also, this CSP is not $(3,2)$-relationally consistent since no consistent instantiation with the domain $\{x, y, z\}$ can be extended to an instantiation that satisfies both constraints. So, in contrast to the notion of 4-consistency, we could focus our reasoning either on the 'offensive' variable $\{u\}$ or on the other three variables.

The following observation clarifies the relationship between the relational (i, m)-consistency and other notions of local consistency considered in this chapter. It shows that relational consistency generalises various local consistency notions and can be also used to characterise the consistency property. By a *strictly binary* CSP we mean here a CSPs with exclusively binary constraints.

Note 5.41 (Relational Consistency 1)

- *A node consistent binary CSP is arc consistent iff it is relationally $(1, 1)$-consistent.*
- *A node consistent CSP that does not contain the false constraint $\perp$ is hyper-arc consistent iff it is relationally $(1, 1)$-consistent.*

- *Every node consistent normalised relationally $(2,3)$-consistent CSP is path consistent.*

- *Every strictly binary relationally $(k-1, k)$-consistent CSP is k-consistent.*

- *A CSP with m constraints is consistent iff it is relationally $(0, m)$-consistent.*

Proof   The proof is left as Exercise 5.6. $\square$

As usual, we conclude the section by characterising the discussed notion of local consistency by means of the proof rules. The rule we are going to introduce uses the join operation $\bowtie$ introduced in Definition 5.34 in Section 5.7. This operation allows us to combine several constraints present in the original CSP into a 'compound' constraint. The compound constraint can be viewed as an outcome of a deduction step applied to the original constraints, much like in the case of path consistency $x < z$ could be seen as an outcome of a deduction step applied to the constraints $x < y$ and $y < z$. The difference is that now several constraints, of arbitrary arities, can be combined.

We confine our attention to regular CSPs introduced in Definition 5.14. Given a regular CSP we introduce the following rule parameterised by a sequence of constraints $C_1, \ldots, C_m$ and a subsequence X of $Var(C_1, \ldots, C_m)$ of length i:

$$RELATIONAL \ (i, m)\text{-}CONSISTENCY$$

$$\frac{C_X}{C_X \cap \Pi_X(C_1 \bowtie \cdots \bowtie C_m)}$$

To see the use of this rule consider an example.

Example 5.42

(i) Consider the CSP

$$\langle \texttt{all\_different}(x, y, z), \ x + y + z = u \ ; $$
$$x \in [1..3], y \in [1..3], z \in [1..3], u \in [3..10] \rangle,$$

(or more precisely, the regular CSP that corresponds to it). Then the `all_different`(x, y, z) constraint denotes the set of triples

$$(1, 2, 3), \ (1, 3, 2), \ (2, 1, 3), \ (2, 3, 1), \ (3, 1, 2), (3, 2, 1)$$

and the $x + y + z = u$ constraint denotes the set of 27 tuples $(i, k, l, i+k+l)$

such that $i, j, k \in [1..3]$. So $\texttt{all\_different}(x, y, z) \bowtie (x + y + z = u)$ denotes the following set of 4-tuples:

$$(1, 2, 3, 6), \ (1, 3, 2, 6), \ (2, 1, 3, 6), \ (2, 3, 1, 6), \ (3, 1, 2, 6), \ (3, 2, 1, 6).$$

Consequently, $\Pi_{\{u\}}(\texttt{all\_different}(x, y, z) \bowtie x + y + z = u)$ represents the unary constraint $\{6\}$ on u. So using the *RELATIONAL* $(1, 2)$-*CONSISTENCY* rule we can reduce the domain of u to $\{6\}$.

(ii) Let us return now to the CSP

$$\langle \texttt{all\_different}(x, y, z), \ x + y + z = u \ ;$$
$$x \in [1..3], y \in [1..3], z \in [1..3], u \in [3..5] \rangle,$$

already considered earlier in this section and in which the domain of u is now $[3..5]$. In contrast to (i) $x + y + z = u$ corresponds now to the following set of 10 tuples:

$$(1, 1, 1, 3), \ (1, 1, 2, 4), \ (1, 2, 1, 4), \ (2, 1, 1, 4), \ (1, 2, 2, 5),$$

$$(2, 1, 2, 5), \ (2, 2, 1, 5), \ (1, 1, 3, 5), \ (1, 3, 1, 5), \ (3, 1, 1, 5).$$

So now $\texttt{all\_different}(x, y, z) \bowtie (x + y + z = u)$ is the empty set and consequently so is the set $\Pi_{\{u\}}(\texttt{all\_different}(x, y, z) \bowtie x + y + z = u)$. So applying the *RELATIONAL* $(1, 2)$-*CONSISTENCY* rule we get the empty constraint on u and consequently reduce the considered CSP to a failed CSP. Thus the above rule allowed us to discover that the original CSP is inconsistent. $\square$

We now get the following characterisation of the notion of relational (i, m)-consistency in terms of the proof rules.

Note 5.43 (Relational Consistency 2) *Fix $i, m \geq 0$. If a regular CSP is closed under the applications of the RELATIONAL (i, m)-CONSISTENCY rule for each subsequence of constraints $C_1, \ldots, C_m$ and each subsequence X of $Var(C_1, \ldots, C_m)$ of length i, then this CSP is relationally (i, m)-consistent.*

Proof Call the considered CSP $\mathcal{P}$. Take a subsequence of constraints $C_1, \ldots, C_m$ and a subsequence X of $Var(C_1, \ldots, C_m)$ of length i. Suppose $\mathcal{P}$ is closed under the applications of the *RELATIONAL* (i, m)-*CONSISTEN-CY* rule for each such subsequence of the constraints $C_1, \ldots, C_m$ and a subsequence of the variables X. Then $C_X \subseteq \Pi_X(C_1 \bowtie \cdots \bowtie C_m)$. But by definition $\overline{C_X} \subseteq C_X$, so

$$\overline{C_X} \subseteq \Pi_X(C_1 \bowtie \cdots \bowtie C_m).$$

This means that every i-consistent instantiation with the domain X can be extended to a solution to $\mathcal{P} \mid (C_1, \ldots, C_m)$. $\qquad\square$

So similarly as in the k-Consistency Note 5.36 we have here only an implication. To see that the reverse implication does not hold take the CSP that we used for an analogous purpose after the proof of the k-Consistency Note 5.36, so the transformation of the CSP

$$\langle x_1 \neq x_2, x_1 \neq x_3 \; ; \; x_1 \in \{a, b\}, x_2 \in \{a\}, \ldots, x_k \in \{a\}\rangle,$$

into a regular CSP obtained by adding to it the universal constraints for all sequences of variables different from x_1, x_2 and x_1, x_3. As already noted in Example 5.33(ii) every $(k-1)$-consistent instantiation is a restriction of the consistent instantiation $\{(x_1, b), (x_2, a), (x_3, a), \ldots, (x_k, a)\}$. This implies that for any m this regular CSP is $(k-1, m)$ consistent. Yet it is not closed under the applications of the *RELATIONAL* $(k-1, m)$-*CONSISTENCY* rule. Indeed, take $X := x_1, \ldots, x_{k-1}$ and the constraints $x_1 \neq x_2$ and C_{X, x_k}. Then for

$$d := (\; \underbrace{a, \ldots, a}_{k-1 \text{ times}} \;)$$

we have $d \in C_X$ and $d \notin \Pi_X((x_1 \neq x_2) \bowtie C_{X, x_k})$, since

$$(x_1 \neq x_2) \bowtie C_{X, x_k} = \{(b, \; \underbrace{a, \ldots, a}_{k-1 \text{ times}} \;)\}.$$

5.10 Graphs and CSPs

In this section we show how a graph-theoretic analysis leads to an improvement of the Consistency 1 Theorem 5.38 of Section 5.8. First, we associate with each CSP graphs that are more general than those considered in Section 5.4. The reason is that we now wish to take into account arbitrary constraints, not only binary ones.

Definition 5.44 Take a CSP $\mathcal{P}$. Consider a graph defined as follows. Its nodes are all the variables of $\mathcal{P}$ and two variables are connected by an arc if there is a constraint that involves them. We say then that this graph is *associated with* $\mathcal{P}$. $\qquad\square$

Let us consider some examples.

Example 5.45

(i) Consider the $SEND + MORE = MONEY$ puzzle discussed in Example 2.1. The graph associated with the first CSP presented there has eight nodes, namely the variables S, E, N, D, M, O, R, Y and is complete, that is every two nodes are connected by an arc. This holds already even if we disregard all disequality constraints: the only equality constraint already involves all eight variables.

(ii) The graph associated with a CSP with two constraints, $x + y = z$ and $x + u = v$ is depicted in Figure 5.15.

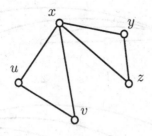

Fig. 5.15. The graph associated with the CSP $\langle x + y = z, x + u = v \; ; \; \mathcal{DE} \rangle$

(iii) Finally, the graph associated with a CSP with four constraints, $x < z$, $x < y, y < u, y < v$ is depicted in Figure 5.16.   □

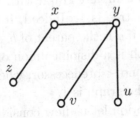

Fig. 5.16. The graph associated with the CSP $\langle x < z, x < y, y < u, y < v \; ; \; \mathcal{DE} \rangle$

Next, we associate with each graph a numeric value.

Definition 5.46 Consider a finite graph G. Assume a linear ordering $\prec$ on its nodes.

- The $\prec$-**width** of a node of G is the number of arcs in G that connect it to $\prec$-smaller nodes.
- The $\prec$-**width** of G is the maximum of the $\prec$-widths of its nodes.

- The **width** of G is the minimum of its $\prec$-widths for all linear orderings $\prec$ on its nodes.

☐

To illustrate the notion of the $\prec$-width of a node consider the graph discussed in Example 5.45(ii) and depicted in Figure 5.15 and two linear orderings on its nodes, $x \prec y \prec z \prec v \prec u$ and $u \prec v \prec z \prec y \prec x$. In Figure 5.17 for each of them we list under each node its $\prec$-width. For example, the width of x in the second ordering is 4, since there are 4 arcs that connect x with an $\prec$-smaller node. So for the first ordering the $\prec$-width of this graph is 2 while for the second it is 4.

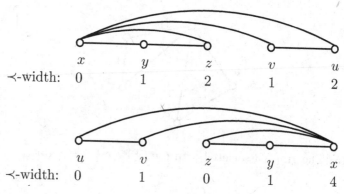

Fig. 5.17. Two examples of the $\prec$-widths of the nodes of the graph from Figure 5.15

Note that the width of a complete graph with n nodes is $n - 1$. Also, the width of a graph that is a tree is 1. Indeed, it suffices to take the linear ordering $\prec$ such that $a \prec b$ if a is the parent of b. Conversely, if the width of a graph is 1, then the graph is a disjoint union of trees. The roots of these trees are the elements with no $\prec$-predecessor, where $\prec$ is the linear ordering for which the $\prec$-width of the graph is 1.

To further clarify this notion let us now consider the graphs discussed in Example 5.45.

Example 5.47

(i) The graph from Example 5.45(i) is a complete graph with 8 nodes, so its width is 7.

(ii) Next, the width of the graph discussed in Example 5.45(ii) and depicted in Figure 5.15 is 2. Indeed, consider any ordering $\prec$ of the variables in which x is the first variable, for example the first one used in Figure 5.17. Then the $\prec$-width of this graph is 2. Further, the width of this graph is at least 2 since it contains a complete subgraph with 3 nodes.

(iii) Finally, the width of the graph discussed in Example 5.45(iii) and depicted in Figure 5.16 is 1, since it is a tree. □

We now prove the following result that greatly improves upon the Consistency 1 Theorem 5.38.

Theorem 5.48 (Consistency 2) *Consider a CSP such that*

- *all its domains are non-empty,*
- *it is strongly k-consistent,*
- *the graph associated with it has width $k - 1$.*

Then this CSP is consistent.

Proof Let $\prec$ be a linear ordering on the variables of this CSP such that the $\prec$-width of the graph associated with this CSP is $k-1$. Let $x_1, \ldots, x_n$ be the sequence of the variables of this CSP linearly ordered by $\prec$ and $D_1, \ldots, D_n$ the corresponding domains.

We now prove that

(i) there exists a consistent instantiation with the domain $\{x_1\}$,
(ii) for every $j \in [1..n-1]$ each consistent instantiation with the domain $\{x_1, \ldots, x_j\}$ can be extended to a consistent instantiation with the domain $\{x_1, \ldots, x_{j+1}\}$.

Since the considered CSP is 1-consistent and the domain D_1 is non-empty, there exists d_1 such that $\{(x_1, d_1)\}$ is consistent. This proves (i).

To prove (ii) let Y be the set of variables in $\{x_1, \ldots, x_j\}$ that are connected by an arc with x_{j+1}. By the definition of the width of a graph the set Y has at most $k - 1$ elements. Let now I be a consistent instantiation with the domain $\{x_1, \ldots, x_j\}$. Consider its restriction $I \mid Y$ to Y. By the definition of strong k-consistency for some d_{j+1} the instantiation $I \mid Y \cup \{(x_{j+1}, d_{j+1})\}$ is consistent.

Now, by the definition of Y, each constraint on a sequence of variables from $\{x_1, \ldots, x_{j+1}\}$ is either on a sequence of variables from $\{x_1, \ldots, x_j\}$ or from $Y \cup \{x_{j+1}\}$. In both cases the corresponding restriction of $I \cup \{(x_{j+1}, d_{j+1})\}$ is consistent. So the instantiation $I \cup \{(x_{j+1}, d_{j+1})\}$ itself is consistent.

We can now construct a solution to $\mathcal{P}$ proceeding by induction using (i) and (ii). □

The above theorem is indeed an improvement over the Consistency 1 Theorem 5.38 because it rarely happens that for a CSP the width of its graph equals the number of its variables minus one which is the case is when the graph associated with a CSP is complete.

To understand better the use of this theorem consider under its assumptions the situation when $k = 2$. In this case the graph associated with the considered CSP has width 1, so it is a disjoint union of trees. By virtue of the Characterisation Note 5.32(i) we can conclude that under the assumption that all the domains of this CSP are non-empty, node and arc consistency imply consistency. In fact, we can slightly improve this observation as follows.

Theorem 5.49 (Directional Arc Consistency) *Consider a CSP and a linear ordering $\prec$ on its variables such that*

- *all its domains are non-empty,*
- *it is node consistent and directionally arc consistent w.r.t. $\prec$,*
- *the $\prec$-width of the graph associated with it is 1, (i.e., this graph is a disjoint union of trees).*

Then this CSP is consistent.

Proof It is a straightforward specialisation of the proof of the Consistency 2 Theorem 5.48 for $k = 2$. In this case the set Y considered in its proof is either empty or a singleton set. □

An analogous result holds when $k = 3$.

Theorem 5.50 (Directional Path Consistency) *Consider a normalised binary CSP and a linear ordering $\prec$ on its variables such that*

- *all its domains are non-empty,*
- *it is node consistent,*
- *it is directionally arc consistent and directionally path consistent, both w.r.t. $\prec$,*
- *the $\prec$-width of the graph associated with it is 2.*

Then this CSP is consistent.

Proof The result follows by a specialisation of the proof of the Consistency 2 Theorem 5.48 for $k = 3$. In this case the set Y considered in this proof has $0, 1$ or 2 elements. We then rely on, respectively, node, directional arc, or directional path consistency, to show that the instantiation $I \mid Y \cup \{(x_{j+1}, d_{j+1})\}$ is consistent. □

5.11 Summary

The aim of this chapter was to introduce various local consistency notions. Informally, local consistency means that some subparts of the considered CSP are in a 'desired form', for example consistent. We discussed in turn:

- node consistency,
- arc consistency,
- hyper-arc consistency,
- directional arc consistency,
- path consistency,
- directional path consistency,
- k-consistency,
- strong k-consistency,
- relational (i, m)-consistency.

In preparation of the presentation of the constraint propagation algorithms that enforce these notions of local consistency we characterised each of them by means of the proof rules.

As already mentioned earlier, local consistency neither implies nor is implied by consistency. This means that to solve a CSP it is in general not sufficient to reduce it to an equivalent one that is locally consistent. On the other hand, in the presence of some additional information, it is possible to prove that local consistency implies consistency. In that case search is not needed. An example of such a result was given in Section 5.10. It relied on the notion of a graph associated with a CSP. In general, however, a reduction of a CSP to a locally consistent one has to be combined with search, a topic to which Chapter 8 is devoted.

5.12 Exercises

Exercise 5.1 Consider a $\mathcal{P}$ and a linear ordering $\prec$ on its variables. Define precisely $\mathcal{P}_{\prec}$ and extend the notion of the equivalence of CSPs in such a way that $\mathcal{P}$ and $\mathcal{P}_{\prec}$ are equivalent.

Exercise 5.2 Prove the Directional Arc Consistency Note 5.13.

Exercise 5.3 Prove the Alternative Directional Path Consistency 5.25.

Exercise 5.4 Prove the Directional Path Consistency Note 5.27.

Exercise 5.5 Prove the Characterisation Note 5.32.

Exercise 5.6 Prove the Relational Consistency 1 Note 5.41.

5.13 Bibliographic remarks

The notions of node consistency and arc consistency were introduced in Mackworth [1977]. The example of a derivation presented by means of Figure 5.5 at the end of Section 5.2 is modeled after Mackworth [1992].

The notions of directional arc consistency and directional path consistency are due to Dechter and Pearl [1988], where also the Directional Arc Consistency Theorem 5.49 and the Directional Path Consistency Theorem 5.50 were established. In turn, the notion of hyper-arc consistency is from Mohr and Masini [1988], where it is called arc consistency. This notion also appears implicitly in Davis [1987] and the adopted terminology follows Marriott and Stuckey [1998].

Further, the notions of path consistency and m-path consistency are due to Montanari [1974] where the Path Consistency Theorem 5.23 was proved. In turn, the notion of k-consistency is from Freuder [1978], while the Characterisation Note 5.32, the notion of strong k-consistency, and the Consistency 2 Theorem 5.48 are from Freuder [1982].

The 'directional' variant of the k-consistency notion, called the **adaptive consistency**, was studied in Dechter and Pearl [1988]. Finally, the notion of the relational (i, m)-consistency was introduced in Dechter and van Beek [1997] where also a 'directional' variant of this notion is discussed. In Walsh [2001] an extensive study this notion is provided.

Finally, the proof theoretic approach used to specify the local consistency notions is closely related to the one proposed in Castro [1998]. In his approach the proof rules are represented as rewrite rules in the programming language ELAN of Borovansky et al. [1998]. This approach was also used to show how various search algorithms (discussed in Chapter 8) can be expressed in the form of rules.

5.14 References

P. Borovansky, C. Kirchner, H. Kirchner, P.-E. Moreau, and C. Ringeissen
  [1998]   An Overview of ELAN, in: *Proceedings of the Second International Workshop on Rewriting Logic and its Applications*, C. Kirchner and H. Kirchner, eds., vol. 15 of Electronic Notes in Theoretical Computer Science, Elsevier, Pont-à-Mousson (France), September.

C. Castro
  [1998]   Building constraint satisfaction problem solvers using rewrite rules and strategies, *Fundamenta Informaticae*, 33, pp. 263–293.

E. DAVIS
  [1987]   Constraint propagation with interval labels, *Artificial Intelligence*, 32, pp. 281–331.

R. DECHTER AND P. VAN BEEK
  [1997]   Local and global relational consistency, *Theoretical Computer Science*, 173, pp. 283–308.

R. DECHTER AND J. PEARL
  [1988]   Network-based heuristics for constraint-satisfaction problems, *Artificial Intelligence*, 34, pp. 1–38.

E. C. FREUDER
  [1978]   Synthesizing constraint expressions, *Communications of the ACM*, 21, pp. 958–966.
  [1982]   A sufficient condition for backtrack-free search, *Journal of the ACM*, 29, pp. 24–32.

A. MACKWORTH
  [1977]   Consistency in networks of relations, *Artificial Intelligence*, 8, pp. 99–118.
  [1992]   Constraint satisfaction, in: *Encyclopedia of Artificial Intelligence*, S. C. Shapiro, ed., John Wiley and Sons, pp. 285–293. Volume 1.

K. MARRIOTT AND P. J. STUCKEY
  [1998]   *Programming With Constraints: An Introduction*, The MIT Press.

R. MOHR AND G. MASINI
  [1988]   Good old discrete relaxation, in: *Proceedings of the 8th European Conference on Artificial Intelligence (ECAI)*, Y. Kodratoff, ed., Pitman Publishers, pp. 651–656.

U. MONTANARI
  [1974]   Networks of constraints: fundamental properties and applications to picture processing, *Information Science*, 7, pp. 95–132. Also Technical Report, Carnegie Mellon University, 1971.

T. WALSH
  [2001]   *Relational Consistencies*, Tech. Rep. APES-28-2001, APES Research Group, January. Available from http://www.dcs.st-and.ac.uk/ apes/apesreports.html.

6

Some incomplete constraint solvers

F OR SOME SPECIFIC domains and constraints for which no efficient solving methods exist or are known to exist specialised techniques have been developed. The aim of this chapter is to illustrate such techniques on a number of examples. In each case they amount to reducing a given CSP to a simpler one that is equivalent to the original one. Because in general from the resulting CSP one cannot immediately generate solutions to it, these methods amount in the terminology of Chapter 4 to incomplete constraint solvers. We define these incomplete constraint solvers using the proof theoretic framework introduced in Section 4.1, so by means of the proof rules that work on CSPs.

Ideally, we would like to use the general rules defined in Chapter 5. Unfortunately, this is easier said than done. Consider for example the *HYPER-ARC CONSISTENCY* rule of Section 5.3 that is clearly of interest, since given a constraint C on the variables $x_1, \ldots, x_k$, it allows us to remove all 'unneeded' elements from the domains of the variables $x_1, \ldots, x_k$. When the constraints are defined using a specific language, it is not clear how to compute the new variable domains that appear in the rule conclusion. So for each specific language we rather provide rules that are defined syntactically and consequently can be readily implemented. In other words, we 'customise' the general framework to a specific language in which constraints are defined and to specific domains that are used.

In what follows we present six examples of such a customisation, for

- the equality and disequality constraints,
- the Boolean constraints,
- the linear constraints over integer intervals and over finite integer domains,
- the arithmetic constraints over integer intervals and over finite integer domains,
- the arithmetic constraints over specific subsets of reals that we call extended intervals; they include all real intervals and the set of all reals,
- the arithmetic equations over reals.

The following table summarises the syntax of the constraints and the domains involved:

Syntax	Domain	Discussed in
equalities and disequalities	arbitrary	Section 6.2
Boolean constraints	subsets of $\{0, 1\}$	Section 6.3
linear constraints	integer intervals and finite integer domains	Section 6.4
arithmetic constraints	integer intervals and finite integer domains	Section 6.5
arithmetic constraints	extended intervals of reals	Section 6.6
arithmetic equations	the set of reals	Section 6.7

In each case we illustrate the use of the introduced techniques by means of examples. Then we relate the introduced proof rules to a notion of local consistency. This clarifies what form of local consistency is actually achieved and allows us to view these specialised techniques as methods of enforcing specific forms of local consistency. In a number of these characterisation results the mentioned above notion of hyper-arc consistency will play an important role.

In any implementation, to avoid possible redundancies, the rules introduced in this chapter should be selected and scheduled in an appropriate way. This matter will be discussed in detail in Chapter 7.

6.1 A useful lemma

Many constraint solvers considered in this chapter consist exclusively of domain reduction rules. These rules are either applied to the original constraints or to certain 'atomic' constraints to which each discussed constraint is reduced. When considering such sets of rules it is useful to know what is the optimal domain reduction they could achieve. This question is answered in the following lemma that clarifies the importance of the notion of hyper-arc consistency. This lemma will allow us to establish optimality of a couple of constraint solvers here considered.

Lemma 6.1 (Hyper-arc Consistency) *Consider a hyper-arc consistent CSP $\mathcal{P}$. Then $\mathcal{P}$ is closed under the applications of every domain reduction rule which is*

- *equivalence preserving, and*
- *has only one constraint in its premise.*

Proof   Such a domain reduction rule R is of the form

$$\frac{\mathcal{P}_1}{\mathcal{P}_2}$$

where $\mathcal{P}_1$ and $\mathcal{P}_2$ are equivalent,

$$\mathcal{P}_1 := \langle C \ ; \ x_1 \in D_1, \ldots, x_n \in D_n \rangle,$$

$$\mathcal{P}_2 := \langle C' \ ; \ x_1 \in D'_1, \ldots, x_n \in D'_n \rangle,$$

and

- for $i \in [1..n]$ we have $D'_i \subseteq D_i$,
- C' is the result of restricting C to the domains $D'_1, \ldots, D'_n$.

Suppose that R can be applied to $\mathcal{P}$. Choose now a variable x_i. If x_i is not present in the constraint C involved in this application of R, then, since that $\mathcal{P}_1$ and $\mathcal{P}_2$ are equivalent, we have $D'_i = D_i$.

If x_i is present in the constraint C, take an element $a \in D_i$. The constraint C is hyper-arc consistent so the element a participates in a sequence that satisfies C. Extend it to a solution d to $\mathcal{P}_1$ by choosing arbitrary values for the variables not present in C. Due to the equivalence of $\mathcal{P}_1$ and $\mathcal{P}_2$ the sequence d is also a solution to $\mathcal{P}_2$. Thus $a \in D'_i$. So $D'_i = D_i$. This proves the claim.

$\square$

This lemma states that hyper-arc consistency is the best one can hope to achieve when using a constraint solver that consists exclusively of equivalence preserving domain reduction rules, each involving a single constraint. That is, if such a constraint solver imposes hyper-arc consistency, then it achieves the optimal domain reduction.

Recall that by the Hyper-arc Consistency Note 5.9 of Section 5.3 the hyper-arc consistency is achieved by the *HYPER-ARC CONSISTENCY* rule. So the above lemma states that among the equivalence preserving domain reduction rules with one constraint in the premise the *HYPER-ARC CONSISTENCY* rule is the strongest.

Note that the above lemma does not hold if the rule in question deals with more than one constraint. To see it take the arc consistent CSP

$$\mathcal{P} := \langle x = y, x \neq y \; ; \; x \in \{a, b\}, y \in \{a, b\}\rangle$$

and consider the domain reduction rule

$$R := \frac{\langle x = y, x \neq y \; ; \; x \in \{a, b\}, y \in \{a, b\}\rangle}{\langle x = y, x \neq y \; ; \; x \in \emptyset, y \in \{a, b\}\rangle}$$

that is clearly equivalence preserving. Since the conclusion of this rule differs $\mathcal{P}$, we conclude that $\mathcal{P}$ is not closed under the applications R.

6.2 Equality and disequality constraints

As a first example of an incomplete constraint solver consider the equality and disequality constraints. Of course, these constraints alone are insufficient to formalise any interesting problems. But they are often used in combination with other constraints so it is of interest to have at one's disposal some means to deal with them. We do this by adopting the following domain reduction rules.

EQUALITY 1

$$\frac{\langle x = x \; ; \; x \in D\rangle}{\langle \; ; \; x \in D\rangle}$$

EQUALITY 2

$$\frac{\langle x = y \; ; \; x \in D_x, y \in D_y\rangle}{\langle x = y \; ; \; x \in D_x \cap D_y, y \in D_x \cap D_y\rangle}$$

$$\text{\textit{DISEQUALITY 1}}$$

$$\frac{\langle x \neq x \; ; \; x \in D \rangle}{\langle \; ; \; x \in \emptyset \rangle}$$

$$\text{\textit{DISEQUALITY 2}}$$

$$\frac{\langle x \neq y \; ; \; x \in D_x, y \in D_y \rangle}{\langle \; ; \; x \in D_x, y \in D_y \rangle}$$

where $D_x \cap D_y = \emptyset$,

$$\text{\textit{DISEQUALITY 3}}$$

$$\frac{\langle x \neq y \; ; \; x \in D, y = a \rangle}{\langle \; ; \; x \in D - \{a\}, y = a \rangle}$$

where $a \in D$,

$$\text{\textit{DISEQUALITY 4}}$$

$$\frac{\langle x \neq y \; ; \; x = a, y \in D \rangle}{\langle \; ; \; x = a, y \in D - \{a\} \rangle}$$

where $a \in D$.

Recall that in this context $y = a$, respectively $x = a$, is here a shorthand for the domain expression $y \in \{a\}$, respectively $x \in \{a\}$. Denote the set of these rules by EQU. Note that the inconsistent CSP

$$\langle x = y, x \neq y \; ; \; x \in \{0,1\}, y \in \{0,1\} \rangle$$

is closed under the applications of the rules of EQU. Also, recall that in Example 4.6 we presented three examples of a derivation in this proof system. The $EQUALITY\ 2$ rule was referred there as the $EQUALITY$ rule and the $DISEQUALITY$ rule represented the $DISEQUALITY\ 3$ and 4 rules.

In particular, one of these derivations started with the CSP

$$\langle x = y, y \neq z, z \neq u \; ; \; x \in \{a,b,c\}, y \in \{a,b,d\}, z \in \{a,b\}, u = b \rangle$$

and led to a solved CSP. In view of these examples it would help to clarify the status of the rules of EQU. The following simple characterisation result does it.

Theorem 6.2 (EQU) *A CSP that consists exclusively of equality and disequality constraints is hyper-arc consistent iff it is closed under the applications of the rules of the proof system EQU.*

That is, a CSP with only equality and disequality constraints is hyper-arc consistent iff it is a final CSP in a stabilising derivation for the proof system *EQU*.

Proof   ($\Rightarrow$) This is a direct consequence of the Hyper-arc Consistency Lemma 6.1 and the fact that the proof rules of the proof system *EQU* are equivalence preserving domain reduction rules.

($\Leftarrow$) Let ϕ be the CSP under consideration. Since each constraint of ϕ is either unary or binary, the hyper-arc consistency is equivalent to node and arc consistency.

Since ϕ is closed under the applications of the *EQUALITY 1* and *DISEQUALITY 1* rules, the constraints $x = x$ and $x \neq x$ do not belong to ϕ. So ϕ is vacuously node consistent.

Consider now an equality constraint $x = y$ of ϕ on the variables x, y with respective domains D_x and D_y. Since ϕ is closed under the applications of the *EQUALITY 2* rule, $D_x = D_y$. So $x = y$ is arc consistent.

Next, consider a disequality constraint $x \neq y$ of ϕ on the variables x, y with respective domains D_x and D_y. Suppose by contradiction that $x \neq y$ is not arc consistent. Then either D_x or D_y is non-empty. Suppose it is D_x. Take $a \in D_x$. So for no $b \in D_y$ the pair (a, b) belongs to the disequality constraint. This means that either $D_y = \emptyset$ or $D_y = \{a\}$. If $D_y = \emptyset$, then ϕ is not closed under the applications of the *DISEQUALITY 2* rule and if $D_y = \{a\}$, then ϕ is not closed under the applications of the *DISEQUALITY 3* rule. This contradicts the assumption. A symmetric argument holds for the domain D_y of the variable y. This shows that $x \neq y$ is arc consistent. Consequently ϕ is arc consistent.

This means that ϕ is hyper-arc consistent. $\square$

The above result shows that in the case of the equality and disequality constraints we succeeded to represent node and arc consistency by means of specific elementary rules. We already noticed that the inconsistent CSP $\langle x = y, x \neq y \; ; \; x \in \{0, 1\}, y \in \{0, 1\} \rangle$ is closed under the applications of the rules of *EQU*. This means that using only these rules we cannot reduce this CSP to a failed one. In other words, these rules alone are insufficient to detect the inconsistency of this CSP. So the constraint solver determined by *EQU* is incomplete.

On the other hand the rules of *EQU* boil down to very simple operations on the variable domains —setting it to the empty set, intersecting two domains, and removing an element from a domain— and consequently they are easy to implement.

6.3 Boolean constraints

Boolean constraint satisfaction problems deal with Boolean variables and constraints on them defined by means of Boolean connectives and equality. We already referred to these CSPs at various places. Let us define them now formally for the purpose of the analysis that follows.

By a **Boolean variable** we mean a variable which ranges over the domain that consists of two values: 0 denoting **false** and 1 denoting **true**. By a **Boolean domain expression** we mean an expression of the form $x \in D$ where $D \subseteq \{0, 1\}$. In what follows we write the Boolean domain expression $x \in \{1\}$ as $x = 1$ and $x \in \{0\}$ as $x = 0$. By a **Boolean expression** we mean an expression built out of the Boolean variables using three connectives: $\neg$ (**negation**), $\wedge$ (**conjunction**) and $\vee$ (**disjunction**). The connectives are just function symbols written in the case of $\wedge$ and $\vee$ in the infix form, i.e., between the arguments. Also, $\neg$, when applied to a variable is written without the brackets.

The only relation symbol in the language is the equality symbol $=$. Next, by a **Boolean constraint** we mean a formula of the form $s = t$, where s, t are Boolean expressions. In the presence of Boolean domain expressions each such formula uniquely determines a subset of the Cartesian product of the variable domains (so a constraint in the sense used so far). For example, in the presence of the domain expressions $x \in \{0\}, y \in \{0, 1\}, z \in \{0, 1\}$, the formula $\neg x \wedge y = z$ determines the subset $\{(0, 0, 0), (0, 1, 1)\}$. So from now on we identify each Boolean constraint with the constraint determined by it. Finally, by a **Boolean constraint satisfaction problem**, in short a **Boolean CSP**, we mean a CSP with Boolean domain expressions and all constraints of which are Boolean constraints.

Note that in our framework the Boolean constants, **true** and **false**, are absent. They can be easily modeled by using two predefined variables, say x_T and x_F, with fixed Boolean domain expressions $x_T = 1$ and $x_F = 0$. Boolean expressions are more often known under the name of **propositional formulas**. By studying Boolean CSPs instead of propositional formulas we do not lose any expressiveness since each Boolean expression s can be modelled by a CSP

$$\psi_s := \langle s = x_T \ ; \ x_1 \in \{0, 1\}, \dots, x_n \in \{0, 1\}, x_T = 1 \rangle$$

where $x_1, \dots, x_n$ are the variables of s. Then s is satisfiable (i.e., becomes true for some assignment of truth values to its variables) iff ψ_s has a solution.

There are many ways to deal with Boolean constraints. The one we discuss here separates them into two classes: those that are in a 'simple' form and those that are in a 'compound' form. Those in a simple form will be dealt with directly; the latter ones will be reduced to the former ones.

In the sequel x, y, z denote different Boolean variables. We call a Boolean constraint **simple** if it is in one of the following form:

- $x = y$; we call it the **equality constraint**,
- $\neg x = y$; we call it the **NOT constraint**,
- $x \wedge y = z$; we call it the **AND constraint**,
- $x \vee y = z$; we call it the **OR constraint**.

6.3.1 Transformation rules

By introducing auxiliary variables it is straightforward to transform each Boolean CSP into an equivalent one all constraints of which are simple. This process, as already discussed in Chapter 3, can be viewed as a preprocessing stage, or the PREPROCESS procedure of the SOLVE procedure of Figure 3.1 from Section 3.2.

More precisely, we adopt the following two transformation rules for negation:

$$\frac{\langle \neg s = t \; ; \; \mathcal{DE} \rangle}{\langle \neg x = t, \; s = x \; ; \; \mathcal{DE}, x \in \{0,1\} \rangle}$$

where s is not a variable and where x does not appear in $\mathcal{DE}$ (in short, x is a fresh variable),

$$\frac{\langle \neg s = t \; ; \; \mathcal{DE} \rangle}{\langle \neg s = y, \; t = y \; ; \; \mathcal{DE}, y \in \{0,1\} \rangle}$$

where t is not a variable and where y is a fresh variable.

The following transformation rules for the binary connectives are equally straightforward. Here op stands for $\wedge$ or for $\vee$.

$$\frac{\langle s \; op \; t = u \; ; \; \mathcal{DE} \rangle}{\langle s \; op \; t = z, \; u = z \; ; \; \mathcal{DE}, z \in \{0,1\} \rangle}$$

where u is not a variable or is a variable identical to s or t, and where z is a fresh variable,

$$\frac{\langle s \; op \; t = u \; ; \; \mathcal{DE} \rangle}{\langle x \; op \; t = u, \; s = x \; ; \; \mathcal{DE}, x \in \{0,1\} \rangle}$$

where s is not a variable or is a variable identical to t or u, and where x is a fresh variable,

$$\frac{\langle s \; op \; t = u \; ; \; \mathcal{DE} \rangle}{\langle s \; op \; y = u, \; t = y \; ; \; \mathcal{DE}, y \in \{0,1\} \rangle}$$

where t is not a variable or is a variable identical to s or u, and where y is a fresh variable.

It is straightforward to prove that each of these rules is equivalence preserving w.r.t. to the sequence of the variables of the premise (see Exercise 6.1) and that every derivation obtained by means of these transformation rules is finite (see Exercise 6.2).

6.3.2 Domain reduction rules

We now introduce domain reduction rules that deal with the simple Boolean constraints. We write these rules in a simplified form already suggested in Subsection 3.2.6 that we illustrate by means of three representative examples.

We write the rule

$$\frac{\langle \neg x = y \; ; \; x \in D_x, y = 0 \rangle}{\langle \; ; \; x \in D_x \cap \{1\}, y = 0 \rangle}$$

as

$$\neg x = y, y = 0 \rightarrow x = 1,$$

the already mentioned in Section 3.2.6 transformation rule

$$\frac{\langle x \wedge y = z \; ; \; x = 1, y \in D_y, z \in D_z \rangle}{\langle y = z \; ; \; x = 1, y \in D_y, z \in D_z \rangle}$$

as

$$x \wedge y = z, x = 1 \rightarrow y = z,$$

and the rule

$$\frac{\langle x \vee y = z \; ; \; x = 0, y \in D_y, z = 1 \rangle}{\langle \; ; \; x = 0, y \in D_y \cap \{1\}, z = 1 \rangle}$$

as

$$x \vee y = z, x = 0, z = 1 \rightarrow y = 1.$$

Using this convention we now introduce twenty rules presented in Table 6.1. We call the resulting proof system *BOOL*. To read properly such formulas it helps to remember that 0 and 1 are domain elements, so atomic formulas of the form $x = 0$ and $x = 1$ are domain expressions while all other atomic formulas are constraints. Intuitively, the *AND 1* rule should be interpreted as: $x \wedge y = z, x = 1$ and $y = 1$ imply that z *becomes* 1. Additionally, as a side effect of applying such a rule, the constraint —here

$$
\begin{array}{lll}
EQU\ 1 & x = y, x = 1 \rightarrow y = 1 \\
EQU\ 2 & x = y, y = 1 \rightarrow x = 1 \\
EQU\ 3 & x = y, x = 0 \rightarrow y = 0 \\
EQU\ 4 & x = y, y = 0 \rightarrow x = 0 \\
\\
NOT\ 1 & \neg x = y, x = 1 \rightarrow y = 0 \\
NOT\ 2 & \neg x = y, x = 0 \rightarrow y = 1 \\
NOT\ 3 & \neg x = y, y = 1 \rightarrow x = 0 \\
NOT\ 4 & \neg x = y, y = 0 \rightarrow x = 1 \\
\\
AND\ 1 & x \wedge y = z, x = 1, y = 1 \rightarrow z = 1 \\
AND\ 2 & x \wedge y = z, x = 1, z = 0 \rightarrow y = 0 \\
AND\ 3 & x \wedge y = z, y = 1, z = 0 \rightarrow x = 0 \\
AND\ 4 & x \wedge y = z, x = 0 \rightarrow z = 0 \\
AND\ 5 & x \wedge y = z, y = 0 \rightarrow z = 0 \\
AND\ 6 & x \wedge y = z, z = 1 \rightarrow x = 1, y = 1 \\
\\
OR\ 1 & x \vee y = z, x = 1 \rightarrow z = 1 \\
OR\ 2 & x \vee y = z, x = 0, y = 0 \rightarrow z = 0 \\
OR\ 3 & x \vee y = z, x = 0, z = 1 \rightarrow y = 1 \\
OR\ 4 & x \vee y = z, y = 0, z = 1 \rightarrow x = 1 \\
OR\ 5 & x \vee y = z, y = 1 \rightarrow z = 1 \\
OR\ 6 & x \vee y = z, z = 0 \rightarrow x = 0, y = 0 \\
\end{array}
$$

Table 6.1. *Proof system BOOL*

$x \wedge y = z$— is deleted since it becomes solved. And analogously with the other rules.

Note also that each of these rules can yield a failed CSP —take for instance the *NOT 2* rule. When applied to the CSP $\langle \neg x = y \ ; \ x = 0, y = 0 \rangle$ it yields $\langle \ ; \ x = 0, y \in \emptyset \rangle$. The point is that the CSP to which the rule is applied, here $\langle \neg x = y \ ; \ x = 0, y = 0 \rangle$, can be inconsistent though not failed and the outcome of this application, here $\langle \ ; \ x = 0, y \in \emptyset \rangle$, can be a failed CSP.

Further, observe that no rule is introduced for $x \wedge y = z$ when $z = 0$. In this case either $x = 0$ or $y = 0$, but $x = 0 \vee y = 0$ is not a legal Boolean domain expression. Alternatively, either $x = z$ or $y = z$ holds, but rewriting $x \wedge y = z$ into $x = z \vee y = z$ is not a legal step, since the latter is not a simple Boolean constraint. The same considerations apply to $x \vee y = z$ when $z = 1$.

Finally, note that some Boolean CSPs that are closed under these rules are neither failed nor solved even if some of the domains are singleton sets. Take for instance the CSP $\langle x \wedge y = z \; ; \; x \in \{0,1\}, y \in \{0,1\}, z = 0 \rangle$ to which no rule applies. In Subsection 6.3.4 we shall provide a characterisation of the Boolean CSPs that are closed under the rules of the system *BOOL*.

6.3.3 Example: full adder circuit

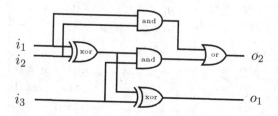

Fig. 6.1. Full adder circuit

We now show how we can reason using the proof rules for Boolean CSPs about the full adder circuit originally introduced in Example 2.6 and depicted, again, in Figure 6.1. Recall that this circuit computes the binary sum $i_1 + i_2 + i_3$ in the binary word $o_2 o_1$. For example $1 + 1 + 0$ yields 10.

First, we need to enrich the language by the exclusive disjunction symbol $\oplus$ and adopt some rules that deal with $\oplus$. For the purpose of the example here discussed we just need two rules that are presented in Table 6.2 and that we add to the system *BOOL*.

XOR 1	$x \oplus y = z, x = 1, y = 1 \rightarrow z = 0$
XOR 2	$x \oplus y = z, x = 0, y = 0 \rightarrow z = 0$

Table 6.2. *Two proof rules for XOR*

We now show how in the case of the Boolean constraints

$$(i_1 \oplus i_2) \oplus i_3 = o_1,$$

$$(i_1 \wedge i_2) \vee (i_3 \wedge (i_1 \oplus i_2)) = o_2$$

representing this circuit we can conclude that $i_1 = 1, i_2 = 1$ and $o_1 = 0$ follows from the assumption that $i_3 = 0$ and $o_2 = 1$.

As a first step, we transform the above two constraints using the transformation rules into the following five simple Boolean constraints:

$$i_1 \oplus i_2 = x_1,$$

$$i_1 \wedge i_2 = y_1,$$

$$x_1 \oplus i_3 = o_1,$$

$$i_3 \wedge x_1 = y_2,$$

$$y_1 \vee y_2 = o_2,$$

where we used an informal optimization and used only one variable, x_1, to represent the Boolean expression $i_1 \oplus i_2$.

We can now derive the desired conclusion by means of the following successful derivation consisting of five steps. The selected constraints are underlined. The original CSP, so

$$\langle i_1 \oplus i_2 = x_1, i_1 \wedge i_2 = y_1, x_1 \oplus i_3 = o_1, \underline{i_3 \wedge x_1 = y_2}, y_1 \vee y_2 = o_2 ;$$
$$i_3 = 0, o_2 = 1 \rangle$$

gets transformed by the *AND 4* rule into

$$\langle i_1 \oplus i_2 = x_1, i_1 \wedge i_2 = y_1, x_1 \oplus i_3 = o_1, \underline{y_1 \vee y_2 = o_2} ;$$
$$i_3 = 0, o_2 = 1, y_2 = 0 \rangle.$$

By the *OR 4* rule we now get

$$\langle i_1 \oplus i_2 = x_1, \underline{i_1 \wedge i_2 = y_1}, x_1 \oplus i_3 = o_1 ; i_3 = 0, o_2 = 1, y_2 = 0, y_1 = 1 \rangle.$$

Next, applying the *AND 6* rule we get

$$\langle \underline{i_1 \oplus i_2 = x_1}, x_1 \oplus i_3 = o_1 ; i_3 = 0, o_2 = 1, y_2 = 0, y_1 = 1, i_1 = 1, i_2 = 1 \rangle.$$

Using the *XOR 1* rule we now obtain

$$\langle \underline{x_1 \oplus i_3 = o_1} ; i_3 = 0, o_2 = 1, y_2 = 0, y_1 = 1, i_1 = 1, i_2 = 1, x_1 = 0 \rangle.$$

Finally, by the *XOR 2* rule we conclude

$$\langle \; ; i_3 = 0, o_2 = 1, y_2 = 0, y_1 = 1, i_1 = 1, i_2 = 1, x_1 = 0, o_1 = 0 \rangle.$$

Because at each step the equivalence is maintained, we conclude that for every solution to the original CSP we have $i_1 = 1, i_2 = 1$ and $o_1 = 0$.

In Figure 6.2 this derivation is represented by means of a sequence of five copies of the circuit in which the successive instantiations of the variables are recorded. In each copy of the circuit the gate 'responsible' for the propagation of a value is shaded.

Some incomplete constraint solvers

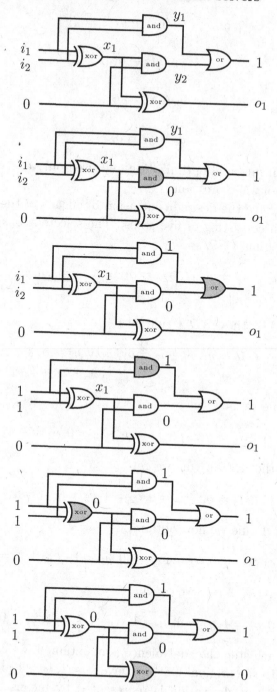

Fig. 6.2. Constraint propagation in the full adder circuit

6.3.4 A characterisation of the system *BOOL*

It is natural to ask in what sense the proof rules of the system *BOOL* are complete. After all, perhaps some obvious rule is missing and its absence does not allow us to draw some specific conclusion. To provide an answer to this question we establish the following result that uses the notion of hyper-arc consistency.

Theorem 6.3 (*BOOL*) *A non-failed Boolean CSP is hyper-arc consistent iff it is closed under the applications of the rules of the proof system BOOL.*

That is, a non-failed Boolean CSP is hyper-arc consistent iff it is a final CSP in a stabilising derivation for the proof system *BOOL*.

Proof ($\Rightarrow$) This implication follows directly on the account of the Hyper-arc Consistency Lemma 6.1 as the proof rules of the proof system *BOOL* are equivalence preserving domain reduction rules.

($\Leftarrow$) In the proof we limit our attention to the *AND* constraint. The reasoning for the other three simple Boolean constraints is analogous and omitted. Suppose that $C := x \wedge y = z$ is some *AND* constraint belonging to the considered CSP. So C is the constraint on the variables x, y, z with the respective domains D_x, D_y and D_z defined by

$$C := \{(1,1,1), (1,0,0), (0,1,0), (0,0,0)\} \cap D_x \times D_y \times D_z.$$

We have to show that each element in each domain participates in a solution to the constraint C. We do this by considering each possible value in each variable domain. By assumption all three domains are non-empty, so we need to consider the following six cases.

Case 1. Suppose $1 \in D_x$.
  Assume that neither $(1,1) \in D_y \times D_z$ nor $(0,0) \in D_y \times D_z$. Then either $D_y = \{1\}$ and $D_z = \{0\}$ or $D_y = \{0\}$ and $D_z = \{1\}$. Suppose the former holds. The considered CSP is closed under the applications of the *AND 3* rule (in short, by the *AND 3* rule) so we get $D_x = \{0\}$ which is a contradiction. If the latter holds, then by the *AND 5* rule we get $D_z = \{0\}$ which is a contradiction.
  We conclude that for some d we have $(1, d, d) \in C$.

Case 2. Suppose $0 \in D_x$.
  Assume that $0 \notin D_z$. Then $D_z = \{1\}$, so by the *AND 6* rule we get $D_x = \{1\}$ which is a contradiction. Hence $0 \in D_z$. Let now d be some element of D_y. We then have $(0, d, 0) \in C$.

Case 3. Suppose $1 \in D_y$.

This case is symmetric to Case 1.

Case 4. Suppose $0 \in D_y$.

This case is symmetric to Case 2.

Case 5. Suppose $1 \in D_z$.

Assume that $(1,1) \notin D_x \times D_y$. Then either $D_x = \{0\}$ or $D_y = \{0\}$. If the former holds, then by the *AND 4* rule we conclude that $D_z = \{0\}$. If the latter holds, then by the *AND 5* rule we conclude that $D_z = \{0\}$. For both possibilities we reached a contradiction. So both $1 \in D_x$ and $1 \in D_y$ and consequently $(1,1,1) \in C$.

Case 6. Suppose $0 \in D_z$.

Assume that both $D_x = \{1\}$ and $D_y = \{1\}$. By the *AND 1* rule we conclude that $D_z = \{1\}$ which is a contradiction. So either $0 \in D_x$ or $0 \in D_y$ and consequently for some d either $(0,d,0) \in C$ or $(d,0,0) \in C$.

So we proved that the constraint C is hyper-arc consistent. $\qquad\square$

Note that the restriction to non-failed CSPs is necessary here. For example, the failed CSP

$$\langle x \wedge y = z \; ; \; x \in \emptyset, y \in \{0,1\}, z \in \{0,1\} \rangle$$

is not hyper-arc consistent but it is closed under the applications of the proof rules of *BOOL*.

It is also easy to check that all the proof rules of the *BOOL* system are needed, that is, the above result does not hold when any of these 20 rules is omitted. For example, if the rule *AND 4* is left out, then the CSP $\langle x \wedge y = z \; ; \; x = 0, y \in \{0,1\}, z \in \{0,1\} \rangle$ is closed under the applications of all remaining rules but is not hyper-arc consistent.

The above theorem shows that in order to reduce a Boolean CSP to an equivalent one that is either failed or hyper-arc consistent it suffices to close it under the applications of the rules of the *BOOL* system.

6.4 Linear constraints on integer intervals

As an example of another incomplete constraint solver we now consider linear constraints over domains that consist of integer intervals. Using this constraint solver we shall analyse the *SEND + MORE = MONEY* puzzle discussed in Example 2.1 of Chapter 2. First, let us introduce the relevant notions. We are interested in linear expressions over integers. We define them in such a way that the underlying alphabet is finite.

By a *linear expression* we mean a term formed in the alphabet that contains

- two constants, 0 and 1,
- the unary minus function symbol '$-$',
- and two binary function symbols, '$+$' and '$-$', both written in the infix notation.

For $n \geq 0$ we abbreviate terms of the form

$$\underbrace{1 + \cdots + 1}_{n \text{ times}}$$

to n, terms of the form

$$\underbrace{x + \cdots + x}_{n \text{ times}}$$

to nx and analogously with -1 and $-x$ used instead of 1 and x. For example, $4x + 3y - x + 7$ is a linear expression. Below we use the customary terminology and for $n \geq 0$ call a term of the form n or $-n$ an *integer*, for $n > 0$ a term of the form n a *positive integer*, and for $n \neq 0$ a term of the form n a *non-zero integer*.

In what follows we assume implicitly appropriate transformation rules that allow us to rewrite each linear expression to an expression in the form

$$\Sigma_{i=1}^{n} a_i x_i + b,$$

where $n \geq 0$, $a_1, \ldots, a_n$ are non-zero integers, $x_1, \ldots, x_n$ are different variables, and b is an integer.

By a *linear constraint* we mean a formula of the form

$$s \, op \, t,$$

where s and t are linear expressions and $op \in \{<, \leq, =, \neq, \geq, >\}$. For example

$$4x + 3y - x \leq 5z + 7 - y \tag{6.1}$$

is a linear constraint.

In what follows we drop the qualification 'linear' when discussing linear expressions and linear constraints.

Further, we call

- $s < t$ and $s > t$ *strict inequality constraints*,

- $s \leq t$ and $s \geq t$ *inequality constraints*,
- $s = t$ an *equality constraint*, or an *equation*,
- $s \neq t$ a *disequality constraint*,
- $x \neq y$, for variables x, y, a *simple disequality constraint*.

By an *integer interval*, or an *interval* in short, we mean an expression of the form

$$[a..b]$$

where a and b are integers; $[a..b]$ denotes the set of all integers between a and b, including a and b. If $a > b$, we call $[a..b]$ the *empty interval*.

Finally, by a *range* we mean a domain expression of the form

$$x \in I$$

where x is a variable and I is an interval. We abbreviate $x \in [a..b]$ to $x = a$ if $a = b$ and write $x \in \emptyset$ if $a > b$.

In what follows we discuss various rules that allow us to manipulate linear constraints over interval domains. These rules then determine a constraint solver. To avoid consideration of some uninteresting cases we assume that all considered linear constraints have at least one variable.

6.4.1 Domain reduction rules for inequality constraints

We divide the rules according to the type of the constraint they involve. We begin with the inequality constraints. As the heavy notation can blur a simple idea behind it consider first an illustrative special case. The appropriate rule uses the $\lceil \ \rceil$ and $\lfloor \ \rfloor$ functions on reals that for a real r yield, respectively, the smallest integer larger or equal than r and the largest integer smaller or equal than r.

Take the constraint

$$3x + 4y - 5z \leq 7$$

with the domain expressions $x \in [l_x..h_x], y \in [l_y..h_y], z \in [l_z..h_z]$. We can rewrite it as

$$x \leq \frac{7 - 4y + 5z}{3}$$

Any value of x that satisfies this constraint also satisfies the inequality

$$x \leq \frac{7 - 4l_y + 5h_z}{3}$$

where we maximised the value of the right-hand side by minimising y and maximising z w.r.t. their domains.

Because we seek integer solutions, we can in fact write

$$x \leq \left\lfloor \frac{7 - 4l_y + 5h_z}{3} \right\rfloor$$

So we can reduce the interval $[l_x..h_x]$ to $[l_x..min(\left\lfloor \frac{7-4l_y+5h_z}{3} \right\rfloor, h_x)]$ without losing any solution. A similar procedure can be applied to the variables y and z, though in the case of z we should remember that a division by a negative number leads to the change of $\leq$ to $\geq$.

After this example consider now a general case. Using appropriate transformation rules each inequality constraint can be rewritten in the form

$$\sum_{i \in POS} a_i x_i - \sum_{i \in NEG} a_i x_i \leq b \qquad (6.2)$$

where

- a_i is a positive integer for $i \in POS \cup NEG$,
- x_i and x_j are different variables for $i, j \in POS \cup NEG$, where $i \neq j$,
- b is an integer.

Below we refer to these rules as **normalisation rules**.

For example, (6.1) can be equivalently written as $3x + 4y - 5z \leq 7$. Further, assume the ranges

$$x_i \in [l_i..h_i]$$

for $i \in POS \cup NEG$.

Choose now some $j \in POS$ and let us rewrite (6.2) as

$$x_j \leq \frac{b - \sum_{i \in POS-\{j\}} a_i x_i + \sum_{i \in NEG} a_i x_i}{a_j}$$

Computing the maximum of the expression on the right-hand side w.r.t. the ranges of the involved variables we get

$$x_j \leq \alpha_j$$

where

$$\alpha_j := \frac{b - \sum_{i \in POS-\{j\}} a_i l_i + \sum_{i \in NEG} a_i h_i}{a_j}$$

so, since the variables assume integer values,

$$x_j \leq \lfloor \alpha_j \rfloor.$$

We conclude that

$$x_j \in [l_j..min(h_j, \lfloor \alpha_j \rfloor)].$$

By analogous calculations we conclude for $j \in NEG$

$$x_j \geq \lceil \beta_j \rceil$$

where

$$\beta_j := \frac{-b + \sum_{i \in POS} a_i l_i - \sum_{i \in NEG - \{j\}} a_i h_i}{a_j}$$

In this case we conclude that

$$x_j \in [max(l_j, \lceil \beta_j \rceil)..h_j].$$

This brings us to the following domain reduction rule for inequality constraints:

LINEAR INEQUALITY 1

$$\frac{\langle \sum_{i \in POS} a_i x_i - \sum_{i \in NEG} a_i x_i \leq b \; ; \; x_1 \in [l_1..h_1], \ldots, x_n \in [l_n..h_n] \rangle}{\langle \sum_{i \in POS} a_i x_i - \sum_{i \in NEG} a_i x_i \leq b \; ; \; x_1 \in [l_1'..h_1'], \ldots, x_n \in [l_n'..h_n'] \rangle}$$

where for $j \in POS$

$$l_j' := l_j, \;\; h_j' := min(h_j, \lfloor \alpha_j \rfloor)$$

and for $j \in NEG$

$$l_j' := max(l_j, \lceil \beta_j \rceil), \;\; h_j' := h_j.$$

The domain reduction rule dealing with the linear inequalities of the form $x < y$ discussed in Subsection 3.2.6 is an instance of this rule.

6.4.2 Domain reduction rules for equality constraints

Each equality constraint can be equivalently written as two inequality constraints. By combining the corresponding domain reduction rules for these two inequality constraints we obtain a domain reduction rule for an equality constraint. More specifically, using the normalisation rules each equality constraint can be rewritten in the form

$$\sum_{i \in POS} a_i x_i - \sum_{i \in NEG} a_i x_i = b \tag{6.3}$$

where we adopt the conditions that follow (6.2) in the previous subsection.

Assume now the ranges

$$x_1 \in [l_1..h_1], \ldots, x_n \in [l_n..h_n].$$

We infer then both the ranges in the conclusion of the *LINEAR INEQUA-LITY 1* domain reduction rule and the ranges for the linear inequality

$$\sum_{i \in NEG} a_i x_i - \sum_{i \in POS} a_i x_i \leq -b,$$

which are

$$x_1 \in [l_1''..h_1''], \ldots, x_n \in [l_n''..h_n'']$$

where for $j \in POS$

$$l_j'' := max(l_j, \lceil \gamma_j \rceil), \ h_j'' := h_j$$

with

$$\gamma_j := \frac{b - \sum_{i \in POS - \{j\}} a_i h_i + \sum_{i \in NEG} a_i l_i}{a_j}$$

and for $j \in NEG$

$$l_j'' := l_j, \ h_j'' := min(h_j, \lfloor \delta_j \rfloor)$$

with

$$\delta_j := \frac{-b + \sum_{i \in POS} a_i h_i - \sum_{i \in NEG - \{j\}} a_i l_i}{a_j}$$

This yields the following domain reduction rule:

LINEAR EQUALITY

$$\frac{\langle \sum_{i \in POS} a_i x_i - \sum_{i \in NEG} a_i x_i = b \ ; \ x_1 \in [l_1..h_1], \ldots, x_n \in [l_n..h_n]\rangle}{\langle \sum_{i \in POS} a_i x_i - \sum_{i \in NEG} a_i x_i = b \ ; \ x_1 \in [l_1'..h_1'], \ldots, x_n \in [l_n'..h_n']\rangle}$$

where for $j \in POS$

$$l_j' := max(l_j, \lceil \gamma_j \rceil), \ h_j' := min(h_j, \lfloor \alpha_j \rfloor)$$

and for $j \in NEG$

$$l_j' := max(l_j, \lceil \beta_j \rceil), \ h_j' := min(h_j, \lfloor \delta_j \rfloor).$$

As an example of the use of the above domain reduction rule consider the CSP

$$\langle 3x - 5y = 4 \ ; \ x \in [0..9], y \in [1..8]\rangle,$$

depicted in Figure 6.3.

A straightforward calculation shows that $x \in [3..9]$, $y \in [1..4]$ are the

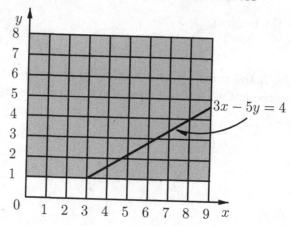

Fig. 6.3. Initial CSP

ranges in the conclusion of *LINEAR EQUALITY* rule. Another application of the rule yields the ranges $x \in [3..8]$ and $y \in [1..4]$ upon which the process stabilises. That is, the CSP $\langle 3x - 5y = 4 ; x \in [3..8], y \in [1..4]\rangle$, depicted in Figure 6.4, is closed under the applications of the *LINEAR EQUALITY* rule.

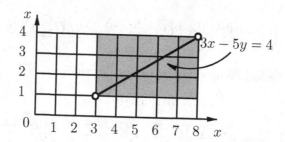

Fig. 6.4. Final CSP, after the applications of the *LINEAR EQUALITY* rule

Note that if in (6.3) there is only one variable, the *LINEAR EQUALITY* rule reduces to the following rule in which the constraint in the conclusion becomes solved and hence is deleted:

$$\frac{\langle ax = b ; x \in [l..h]\rangle}{\langle ; x \in \{\frac{b}{a}\} \cap [l..h]\rangle}$$

So, if a divides b and $l \leq \frac{b}{a} \leq h$, the domain expression $x = \frac{b}{a}$ is inferred, and otherwise a failure is reached. For instance, we have

$$\frac{\langle 4x = 19 ; x \in [0..100]\rangle}{\langle ; x \in \emptyset\rangle}$$

6.4.3 Rules for disequality constraints

The domain reduction rules for simple disequalities are very natural. First, note that the following rule

SIMPLE DISEQUALITY 1

$$\frac{\langle x \neq y \; ; \; x \in [a..b], y \in [c..d] \rangle}{\langle \; ; \; x \in [a..b], y \in [c..d] \rangle}$$

where $b < c$ or $d < a$, is an instance of the *DISEQUALITY 2* rule already discussed in Section 6.2. Following the convention introduced in Subsection 4.1.1 we dropped here the constraint from the conclusion of the proof rule.

Next, we adopt the following two rules that are instances of the *DISE-QUALITY 3* and *4* rules:

SIMPLE DISEQUALITY 2

$$\frac{\langle x \neq y \; ; \; x \in [a..b], y = a \rangle}{\langle \; ; \; x \in [a+1..b], y = a \rangle}$$

SIMPLE DISEQUALITY 3

$$\frac{\langle x \neq y \; ; \; x \in [a..b], y = b \rangle}{\langle \; ; \; x \in [a..b-1], y = b \rangle}$$

and similarly with $x \neq y$ replaced by $y \neq x$. Recall that the domain expression $y = a$ is a shorthand for $y \in [a..a]$.

To deal with disequality constraints that are not simple ones we use the following notation. Given a linear expression s and a sequence of ranges involving all the variables of s we denote by s^- the minimum s can take w.r.t. these ranges and by s^+ the maximum s can take w.r.t. these ranges. The considerations of Subsection 6.4.1 show how s^- and s^+ can be computed.

We now introduce the following transformation rule for non-simple disequality constraints:

DISEQUALITY TRANSFORMATION

$$\frac{\langle s \neq t \; ; \; \mathcal{DE} \rangle}{\langle x \neq t, \; x = s \; ; \; x \in [s^-..s^+], \mathcal{DE} \rangle}$$

where

- s is not a variable,
- x is a fresh variable,
- $\mathcal{DE}$ is a sequence of the ranges involving the variables present in s and t,
- s^- and s^+ are computed w.r.t. the ranges in $\mathcal{DE}$.

This rule was already mentioned in Section 4.1. The only difference is that here we use a different domain for the fresh variable x. We also introduce an analogous rule for the inequality $s \neq t$, where t is not a variable.

6.4.4 Rules for strict inequality constraints

Finally, to deal with the strict inequality constraints it suffices to use the transformation rules that rewrite $s < t$ into $s \leq t$, $s \neq t$, and similarly with $s > t$.

6.4.5 Shifting from intervals to finite domains

In our presentation we took care that all the rules preserved the property that the domains are intervals. In some constraint programming systems, such as ECL^{i}PS^e, this property is relaxed and, instead of finite intervals, finite sets of integers are used. To model the use of such finite domains it suffices to modify some of the rules introduced above.

In the case of inequality constraints we can use the following minor modification of the *LINEAR INEQUALITY 1* domain reduction rule:

LINEAR INEQUALITY 2

$$\frac{\langle \sum_{i \in POS} a_i x_i - \sum_{i \in NEG} a_i x_i \leq b \; ; \; x_1 \in D_1, \ldots, x_n \in D_n \rangle}{\langle \sum_{i \in POS} a_i x_i - \sum_{i \in NEG} a_i x_i \leq b \; ; \; x_1 \in D_1', \ldots, x_n \in D_n' \rangle}$$

where $D_1, \ldots, D_n$ are finite sets of integers and for $i \in [1..n]$ we have $D_i' := [l_i'..h_i'] \cap D_i$, where l_j' and h_j' are defined as in the *LINEAR INEQUALITY 1* domain reduction rule with $l_j := min(D_j)$ and $h_j := max(D_j)$.

An analogous modification of the *LINEAR EQUALITY* rule for the equality constraints is left to the reader. For the simple disequality constraint we rather use the *DISEQUALITY 3* and *4* rules of Section 6.2. So now, in contrast to the case of interval domains, an arbitrary element can be removed from a domain, not only the 'boundary' one.

This concludes our presentation of the proof rules that can be used to build a constraint solver for linear constraints over interval and finite domains. Such proof rules are present in one form or another within each constraint programming system that supports linear constraints over interval and finite integer domains.

6.4.6 Example: the *SEND + MORE = MONEY* puzzle

To illustrate use of the above rules for linear constraints over interval and finite domains, we analyse in detail the first formulation as a CSP of the *SEND + MORE = MONEY* puzzle introduced in Example 2.1 of Chapter 2. Recall that in this formulation we used a single equality constraint

$$
\begin{aligned}
1000 \cdot S & + 100 \cdot E + 10 \cdot N + D \\
+ \ 1000 \cdot M & + 100 \cdot O + 10 \cdot R + E \\
= 10000 \cdot M \ + \ 1000 \cdot O & + 100 \cdot N + 10 \cdot E + Y
\end{aligned}
$$

together with 28 simple disequality constraints $x \neq y$ for x, y ranging over the set $\{S, E, N, D, M, O, R, Y\}$, where x precedes y in the presented order, and with the range $[1..9]$ for S and M and the range $[0..9]$ for the other variables.

In typical constraint programming systems the above CSP is internally reduced to the one with the following domain expressions:

$$
S = 9, E \in [4..7], N \in [5..8], D \in [2..8],
$$
$$
M = 1, O = 0, R \in [2..8], Y \in [2..8]. \tag{6.4}
$$

We now show how this outcome can be formally derived using the rules we introduced.

First, using the normalisation rules we can rewrite the above equality to

$$
9000 \cdot M + 900 \cdot O + 90 \cdot N + Y - (91 \cdot E + D + 1000 \cdot S + 10 \cdot R) = 0.
$$

Applying the *LINEAR EQUALITY* domain reduction rule with the initial ranges we obtain the following sequence of new ranges:

$$
S = 9, E \in [0..9], N \in [0..9], D \in [0..9],
$$

$$
M = 1, O \in [0..1], R \in [0..9], Y \in [0..9].
$$

At this stage a subsequent use of the same rule yields no new outcome. However, by virtue of the fact that $M = 1$ we can now apply the *SIMPLE DISEQUALITY 3* rule to the disequality constraint $M \neq O$ to conclude that $O = 0$. Using now the facts that $M = 1, O = 0, S = 9$, the rules *SIMPLE DISEQUALITY 2* and *3* can be repeatedly applied to reduce the domains of the other variables. This yields the following new sequence of ranges:

$$
S = 9, E \in [2..8], N \in [2..8], D \in [2..8], M = 1, O = 0, R \in [2..8], Y \in [2..8].
$$

Now five successive iterations of the *LINEAR EQUALITY* rule yield the following sequences of shrinking ranges of E and N with other ranges unchanged:

$$E \in [2..7], N \in [3..8],$$

$$E \in [3..7], N \in [3..8],$$

$$E \in [3..7], N \in [4..8],$$

$$E \in [4..7], N \in [4..8],$$

$$E \in [4..7], N \in [5..8],$$

upon which the reduction process stabilises. At this stage the rules for disequalities are not applicable either. In other words, the CSP with the original constraints and the ranges (6.4) is closed under the applications of the normalisation rules, the *LINEAR EQUALITY* rule, and the *SIMPLE DISEQUALITY* rules *1*, *2* and *3*. So using these rules we reduced the original ranges to (6.4). The presented stabilising derivation, without counting the initial applications of the normalisation rules, consists of 24 steps.

Using the *VARIABLE ELIMINATION* rule of Section 4.1 and the normalisation rules the original equality constraint gets reduced to

$$90 \cdot N + Y - (91 \cdot E + D + 10 \cdot R) = 0.$$

Moreover, ten simple disequality constraints between the variables $E, N, D,$ R and Y are still present. The other eighteen simple disequality constraints are solved.

6.4.7 Bounds consistency

It is useful to realise that the rules introduced in this section are quite limited in their strength. For example, using them we cannot even solve the CSP

$$\langle x + y = 10, x - y = 0 \ ; \ x \in [0..10], y \in [0..10] \rangle$$

as it is closed under applications of the *LINEAR EQUALITY* rule of Subsection 6.4.2.

The point is that the domain reduction rules such as the *LINEAR EQUALITY* rule are in some sense 'orthogonal' to the rules that deal with algebraic manipulations and that can be expressed as transformation rules. The aim of the domain reduction rules is to reduce the domains and not to transform constraints. So it makes sense to clarify what these rules actually achieve. By means of example, we concentrate here on the *LINEAR EQUALITY* rule.

First note that the notion of hyper-arc consistency is not adequate to characterise this rule. Indeed, a CSP closed under the applications of the *LINEAR EQUALITY* rule does not need to be hyper-arc consistent. Take for example the CSP

$$\langle 3x - 5y = 4 \;;\; x \in [3..8],\, y \in [1..4]\rangle,$$

already discussed at the end of Subsection 6.4.2 and depicted in Figure 6.4. We already noted there that it is closed under the applications of the *LINEAR EQUALITY* rule. On the other hand, this CSP is not hyper-arc consistent since it has precisely two solutions: $x = 3, y = 1$ and $x = 8, y = 4$ and thus none with $x = 4$.

An even more revealing example is the following one. Consider the CSP

$$\langle 2x + 2y - 2z = 1 \;;\; x \in [0..1],\, y \in [0..1],\, z \in [0..1]\rangle.$$

One can show that it is closed under the applications of the *LINEAR EQUALITY* rule. Now, the equation $2x + 2y - 2z = 1$ has precisely six solutions in the unit cube formed by the real unit intervals for x, y and z, namely $(0,0.5,0)$, $(0.5,0,0)$, $(1,0,0.5)$, $(0,1,0.5)$, $(0.5,1,1)$ and $(1,0.5,1)$, see Figure 6.5. None of them is an integer solution. So this CSP is inconsistent.

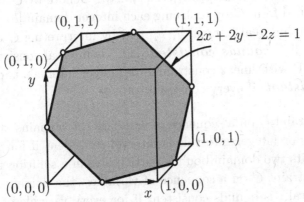

Fig. 6.5. A CSP with no integer solutions

On the other hand each variable bound, 0 and 1, participates in a solution to this equation over *reals*. This suggests an alternative notion of local consistency that uses a 'detour' through the intervals of reals. To define this notion we first introduce the following notation. Two reals a and b

determine the following real interval:

$$[a, b] := \{r \in \mathcal{R} \mid a \le r \le b\}.$$

In contrast, as already used throughout this section, two integers a and b, determine the following integer interval:

$$[a..b] = \{c \in \mathcal{Z} \mid a \le c \le b\}.$$

So for example, $\pi \in [3, 4]$ but $\pi \notin [3..4]$, since $[3..4] = \{3, 4\}$. The definition below applies to both types of intervals.

Definition 6.4

- Consider a constraint C on the variables $x_1, \ldots, x_n$ with the respective real interval domains $[l_1, h_1], \ldots, [l_n, h_n]$. We call C *interval consistent* if for every $i \in [1..n]$ there exist $d, e \in C$ such that $l_i = d[x_i]$ and $h_i = e[x_i]$.

  Similarly, we call a constraint C on the variables $x_1, \ldots, x_n$ with the respective integer interval domains $[l_1..h_1], \ldots, [l_n..h_n]$ *interval consistent* if for every $i \in [1..n]$ there exist $d, e \in C$ such that $l_i = d[x_i]$ and $h_i = e[x_i]$.

- A CSP the domains of which are real intervals or integer intervals is called *interval consistent* if every constraint of it is.

- Consider a linear constraint C on the variables $x_1, \ldots, x_n$ with the respective domains $[l_1..h_1], \ldots, [l_n..h_n]$. Denote by C^r the constraint obtained from C by replacing each integer domain $[l_i..h_i]$ by the corresponding real interval $[l_i, h_i]$ and by interpreting C over the reals. We call C *bounds consistent* if C^r is interval consistent.

- A CSP with linear constraints on integer intervals is called *bounds consistent* if every constraint of it is. □

So a constraint C on a sequence of variables the domains of which are all real intervals or integer intervals is interval consistent if for every variable of it each of its two domain bounds participates in a solution to C. In turn, a linear constraint C on a sequence of variables, the domains of which are integer intervals, is bounds consistent if for every variable of it each of its two domain bounds participates in a solution to the interpretation C^r of C on the real intervals.

The following example clarifies these notions.

Example 6.5

(i) Consider the CSP

$$\langle 3x - 5y = 4 \; ; \; x \in [3, 8], y \in [1, 4]\rangle.$$

Both $x = 3, y = 1$ and $x = 8, y = 4$ are solutions to it, so by the shape of these solutions this CSP is interval consistent. By definition the CSP

$$\langle 3x - 5y = 4 \; ; \; x \in [3..8], y \in [1..4]\rangle,$$

depicted in Figure 6.4 at the end of Subsection 6.4.2, is bounds consistent.

(ii) In contrast, the CSP

$$\langle 3x - 5y = 4 \; ; \; x \in [3, 10], y \in [1, 4]\rangle$$

is not interval consistent, since no solution to it exists with $x = 10$. Consequently, the CSP

$$\langle 3x - 5y = 4 \; ; \; x \in [3..10], y \in [1..4]\rangle,$$

depicted in Figure 6.6, is not bounds consistent and also not interval consistent.

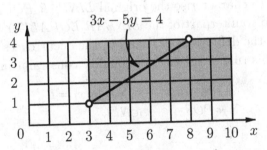

Fig. 6.6. A CSP that is not bounds consistent

(iii) Consider now the CSP

$$\langle 2x + 2y - 2z = 1 \; ; \; x \in [0, 1], y \in [0, 1], z \in [0, 1]\rangle.$$

already depicted in Figure 6.5. Previously we considered the same equation with the integer intervals $[0..1]$ instead of the real intervals $[0, 1]$. We already noted that the equation $2x + 2y - 2z = 1$ has precisely six solutions in the unit cube formed by the real unit intervals for x, y and z, namely $(0,0.5,0)$, $(0.5,0,0)$, $(1,0,0.5)$, $(0,1,0.5)$, $(0.5,1,1)$ and $(1,0.5,1)$. They show that each domain bound participates in a solution. So this CSP is interval consistent and by definition the originally considered CSP

$$\langle 2x + 2y - 2z = 1 \; ; \; x \in [0..1], y \in [0..1], z \in [0..1]\rangle$$

is bounds consistent. In contrast, this CSP is not interval consistent.   □

So the notion of bounds consistency is defined in an indirect way, by means of the notion of interval consistency. Note that interval consistency for linear constraints over integer intervals cannot be used to characterise the *LINEAR EQUALITY* rule. Indeed, we already mentioned that the CSP

$$\langle 2x + 2y - 2z = 1 \; ; \; x \in [0..1], y \in [0..1], z \in [0..1] \rangle$$

is closed under the applications of the *LINEAR EQUALITY* rule. Yet, as we just noticed, this CSP is not interval consistent. In the next subsection we show that bounds consistency is the right notion for characterising the *LINEAR EQUALITY* rule.

6.4.8 A characterisation of the *LINEAR EQUALITY* rule

To establish the appropriate result we proceed as follows. First we introduce a counterpart of the *LINEAR EQUALITY* rule that deals with the closed intervals of reals and provide its characterisation. Then we use this characterisation result to characterise the original *LINEAR EQUALITY* rule.

The mentioned counterpart of the *LINEAR EQUALITY* rule is obtained by deleting from the definitions of l'_j and h'_j the occurrences of the functions $\lceil \; \rceil$ and $\lfloor \; \rfloor$. So this rule deals with an equality constraint in the form

$$\sum_{i \in POS} a_i x_i - \sum_{i \in NEG} a_i x_i = b \qquad (6.5)$$

where

- a_i is a positive integer for $i \in POS \cup NEG$,
- x_i and x_j are different variables for $i \neq j$ and $i, j \in POS \cup NEG$,
- b is an integer,

and intervals of reals.

The rule in question has then the following form:

$$\mathcal{R}\text{-}LINEAR\ EQUALITY$$

$$\frac{\langle \sum_{i \in POS} a_i x_i - \sum_{i \in NEG} a_i x_i = b \; ; \; x_1 \in [l_1, h_1], \ldots, x_n \in [l_n, h_n] \rangle}{\langle \sum_{i \in POS} a_i x_i - \sum_{i \in NEG} a_i x_i = b \; ; \; x_1 \in [l^r_1, h^r_1], \ldots, x_n \in [l^r_n, h^r_n] \rangle}$$

where for $j \in POS$

$$l^r_j := max(l_j, \gamma_j), \; h^r_j := min(h_j, \alpha_j)$$

and for $j \in NEG$

$$l_j^r := max(l_j, \beta_j), \quad h_j^r := min(h_j, \delta_j).$$

Recall that $\alpha_j, \beta_j, \gamma_j$ and δ_j are defined in Subsection 6.4.2. For the purpose of the subsequent calculations recall that

$$\alpha_j = \frac{b - \sum_{i \in POS-\{j\}} a_i l_i + \sum_{i \in NEG} a_i h_i}{a_j}$$

and

$$\gamma_j = \frac{b - \sum_{i \in POS-\{j\}} a_i h_i + \sum_{i \in NEG} a_i l_i}{a_j}$$

It is straightforward to see that the $\mathcal{R}$-*LINEAR EQUALITY* rule, just as the *LINEAR EQUALITY* rule, is equivalence preserving. By considering now intervals of reals and not intervals of integers we obtain a weaker domain reduction, that is we obtain larger intervals in the rule conclusion. The reason is that we now also admit solutions with non-integer values, that is we now admit more solutions.

We need now the following lemma. We use here some self-explanatory notation concerning algebraic operations on sequences of the same length.

Note 6.6 (Convexity) *Consider an equality constraint of the form*

$$\sum_{i=1}^n a_i x_i = b$$

where $a_1, \ldots, a_n, b$ are integers. If $d = (d_1, \ldots, d_n)$ and $e = (e_1, \ldots, e_n)$ are two of its solutions over reals, then for any $\alpha \in [0, 1]$

- *$f := d + \alpha(e - d)$ is also a solution,*
- *for $i \in [1..n]$ we have*

$$f_i \in [d_i, e_i] \text{ if } d_i \leq e_i,$$

$$f_i \in [e_i, d_i] \text{ if } e_i \leq d_i,$$

where $f = (f_1, \ldots, f_n)$.

Proof Straightforward and left as Exercise 6.8. $\qquad\qquad\qquad\qquad\square$

Intuitively, the above note states that given two points in the n dimensional space $\mathcal{R}^n$ that represent solutions to an equality constraint, any point lying on the interval connecting these two points also represents a solution.

Moreover, each such point lies inside the parallelogram determined by these two points.

To characterise the $\mathcal{R}$-*LINEAR EQUALITY* rule we rely on the notion of hyper-arc consistency and use the Hyper-arc Consistency Lemma 6.1. Below, by a $\mathcal{R}$-**LINEQ CSP** we mean here a CSP the domains of which are intervals of reals and the constraints of which are linear equality constraints.

Theorem 6.7 ($\mathcal{R}$-LINEAR EQUALITY) *A non-failed $\mathcal{R}$-LINEQ CSP is hyper-arc consistent iff it is closed under the applications of the $\mathcal{R}$-LINEAR EQUALITY rule.*

That is, a non-failed $\mathcal{R}$-*LINEQ* CSP is hyper-arc consistent iff it is a final CSP in a stabilising derivation in which only the $\mathcal{R}$-*LINEAR EQUALITY* rule is applied.

Proof ($\Rightarrow$) It suffices to use the fact that the $\mathcal{R}$-*LINEAR EQUALITY* rule is an equivalence preserving domain reduction rule and apply the Hyper-arc Consistency Lemma 6.1.   .

($\Leftarrow$) Choose a constraint of the considered CSP. It is of the form (6.5) with the corresponding domain expressions

$$x_1 \in [l_1, h_1], \ldots, x_n \in [l_n, h_n].$$

Then for $j \in [1..n]$ we have

$$l_j^r = l_j \text{ and } h_j^r = h_j. \tag{6.6}$$

Fix now some $j \in [1..n]$. Assume that $j \in POS$. The case when $j \in NEG$ is analogous and is omitted. Choose some $d \in [l_j, h_j]$. We now show that d participates in a solution to the constraint (6.5). By (6.6) we have $l_j^r \le d \le h_j^r$, so by the definition of l_j^r and h_j^r we have $\gamma_j \le d \le \alpha_j$. Thus for some $\alpha \in [0, 1]$, namely for

$$\alpha := \frac{d - \gamma_j}{\alpha_j - \gamma_j},$$

we have $d = \gamma_j + \alpha(\alpha_j - \gamma_j)$.

Next, note that by the definition of α_j and γ_j we have both

$$\sum_{i \in POS - \{j\}} a_i l_i + a_j \alpha_j - \sum_{i \in NEG} a_i h_i = b$$

and

$$\sum_{i \in POS - \{j\}} a_i h_i + a_j \gamma_j - \sum_{i \in NEG} a_i l_i = b.$$

So we have two solutions to the constraint (6.5). By assumption the considered CSP is not failed, so each of its domains is non-empty, that is $l_i \leq h_i$ for $i \in [1..n]$. Thus by the Convexity Note 6.6 a solution $(d_1, \ldots, d_n)$ to the constraint (6.5) exists such that $d = d_j$ and $d_i \in [l_i, h_i]$ for $i \in [1..n]$.   □

We can return now to the original problem of characterising the *LINEAR EQUALITY* rule. It is the subject of the following theorem. By a **LINEQ CSP** we mean here a CSP the domains of which are intervals of integers and the constraints of which are linear equality constraints.

Theorem 6.8 (*LINEAR EQUALITY*) *A non-failed LINEQ CSP is bounds consistent iff it is closed under the applications of the LINEAR EQUALITY rule.*

That is, a non-failed *LINEQ* CSP is bounds consistent iff it is a final CSP in a stabilising derivation in which only the *LINEAR EQUALITY* rule is applied.

Proof Given a *LINEQ* CSP ϕ we denote by ϕ^r the $\mathcal{R}$-*LINEQ* CSP obtained from ϕ by replacing each integer domain $[l..h]$ by the corresponding interval $[l, h]$ of reals and by interpreting all constraints over the reals. Let ϕ be a non-failed *LINEQ* CSP and ϕ^r the corresponding $\mathcal{R}$-*LINEQ* CSP. Clearly ϕ^r is non-failed either. To prove the claim, in view of the $\mathcal{R}$-*LINEAR EQUALITY* Theorem 6.7, it suffices to establish the following two equivalences:

  (1) ϕ is bounds consistent iff ϕ^r is hyper-arc consistent,
  (2) ϕ is closed under the applications of the *LINEAR EQUALITY* rule iff ϕ^r is closed under the applications of the $\mathcal{R}$-*LINEAR EQUALITY* rule.

Proof of (1). By definition ϕ is bounds consistent iff ϕ^r is interval consistent.
($\Rightarrow$) By a simple application of the Convexity Note 6.6 to ϕ^r.
($\Leftarrow$) Immediate by the definition of ϕ^r.

Proof of (2). We first clarify the relationship between the applications of the *LINEAR EQUALITY* rule to $\mathcal{P}_1$ and the applications of the $\mathcal{R}$-*LINEAR EQUALITY* rule to $\mathcal{P}_1^r$.

Let $\mathcal{P}_2$ be the result of applying the *LINEAR EQUALITY* rule to $\mathcal{P}_1$ and $\mathcal{Q}_2$ the result of applying the $\mathcal{R}$-*LINEAR EQUALITY* rule to $\mathcal{Q}_1 := \mathcal{P}_1^r$. To better follow the reasoning we represent these four CSPs in the following form:

$$\frac{\mathcal{P}_1}{\mathcal{P}_2} \text{ versus } \frac{\mathcal{Q}_1}{\mathcal{Q}_2}.$$

To prove (2) it suffices to prove that

$$\mathcal{P}_1 = \mathcal{P}_2 \text{ iff } \mathcal{Q}_1 = \mathcal{Q}_2. \tag{6.7}$$

To start with, for two CSPs $\mathcal{P}'$ and $\mathcal{P}''$ with the same variables, let us write $\mathcal{P}' \subseteq \mathcal{P}''$ to denote the fact that the domains of $\mathcal{P}'$ are respective subsets of the domains of $\mathcal{P}''$. Then the following holds.

(i) $\mathcal{P}_2^r \subseteq \mathcal{Q}_2$.

This is due to the roundings resulting from the use of the $\lceil\rceil$ and $\lfloor\rfloor$ functions in the definition of the *LINEAR EQUALITY* rule;

(ii) $\mathcal{Q}_2 \subseteq \mathcal{Q}_1$.

This is because the $\mathcal{R}$-*LINEAR EQUALITY* rule is a domain reduction rule.

(iii) If the intervals of $\mathcal{Q}_2$ have integer bounds, then $\mathcal{P}_2^r = \mathcal{Q}_2$.

This is due to the fact that the roundings resulting from the use of the $\lceil\rceil$ and $\lfloor\rfloor$ functions in the definition of the *LINEAR EQUALITY* rule have no effect when applied to integer values.

We can now prove (6.7).

($\Rightarrow$) $\mathcal{P}_1 = \mathcal{P}_2$ implies $\mathcal{P}_1^r = \mathcal{P}_2^r$, which in turn implies by (i) $\mathcal{P}_1^r \subseteq \mathcal{Q}_2$, i.e., $\mathcal{Q}_1 \subseteq \mathcal{Q}_2$. So by (ii) $\mathcal{Q}_1 = \mathcal{Q}_2$.

($\Leftarrow$) $\mathcal{Q}_1 = \mathcal{Q}_2$ implies by the form of $\mathcal{Q}_1$ and (iii) $\mathcal{Q}_1 = \mathcal{P}_2^r$, i.e., $\mathcal{P}_1^r = \mathcal{P}_2^r$, which implies $\mathcal{P}_1 = \mathcal{P}_2$.
                                                                                    $\square$

For the $\mathcal{R}$-*LINEQ* CSPs we have to our disposal two natural notions of local consistency: the hyper-arc consistency and the interval consistency. The proof of item (1) above shows that for $\mathcal{R}$-*LINEQ* CSPs the notions of interval consistency and hyper-arc consistency in fact coincide.

In contrast, for the *LINEQ* CSPs we have to our disposal three natural notions of local consistency: the hyper-arc consistency, the interval consistency and the bounds consistency. It is clear from the definitions that hyper-arc consistency implies the interval consistency which in turn implies bounds consistency. However, all three notions differ. Indeed, we already noted that the CSP

$$\langle 3x - 5y = 4 \ ; \ x \in [3..8], \ y \in [1..4] \rangle$$

is not hyper-arc consistent and, as Example 6.5(i) shows, it is interval consistent. In turn, as Example 6.5(iii) shows, the CSP

$$\langle 2x + 2y - 2z = 1 \ ; \ x \in [0..1], y \in [0..1], z \in [0..1] \rangle$$

is not interval consistent but is bounds consistent.

6.5 Arithmetic constraints on integer intervals

Armed with the knowledge of how to deal with the linear constraints let us tackle now a more general class of constraints, that of the arithmetic constraints. To define them we add to the alphabet considered in the last section the binary function symbol '$\cdot$' written in an infix form.

That is, we use the alphabet that comprises

- two constants, 0 and 1,
- the unary minus function symbol '$-$',
- three binary function symbols, '$+$','$-$'and '$\cdot$', all written in the infix notation.

By an *arithmetic expression* we mean a term formed in this alphabet and by an *arithmetic constraint* a formula of the form

$$s \; op \; t,$$

where s and t are arithmetic expressions and $op \in \{<, \leq, =, \neq, \geq, >\}$. For example

$$x^5 \cdot y^2 \cdot z^4 + 3x \cdot y^3 \cdot z^5 \leq 10 + 4x^4 \cdot y^6 \cdot z^2 - y^2 \cdot x^5 \cdot z^4 \qquad (6.8)$$

is an arithmetic constraint. Here x^5 is an abbreviation for $x \cdot x \cdot x \cdot x \cdot x$ and similarly with the other expressions.

In what follows we consider the arithmetic constraints over domains that are integer intervals. We are interested in deriving appropriate domain reduction rules.

6.5.1 Domain reduction rules: first approach

We would like to follow the idea of Subsection 6.4.1 and compute the estimates based on the ranges' bounds. Now, however, we cannot in general rewrite a given inequality in such a way that the only occurrence of the selected variable is on the left-hand side of the inequality. We could ignore this difficulty and proceed as in the following example.

Consider the constraint

$$x^3y - x \leq 40$$

and the ranges $x \in [1..100]$ and $y \in [1..100]$. We can rewrite it as

$$x \leq \left\lfloor \sqrt[3]{\frac{40 + x}{y}} \right\rfloor \tag{6.9}$$

since x assumes integer values. The maximum value the expression on the right-hand side can take is $\lfloor \sqrt[3]{140} \rfloor$, so we conclude $x \leq 5$. By reusing (6.9), now with the information that $x \in [1..5]$, we conclude that the maximum value the expression on the right-hand side of (6.9) can take is actually $\lfloor \sqrt[3]{45} \rfloor$, from which it follows that $x \leq 3$.

In the case of y we can isolate it by rewriting the original constraint as $y \leq \frac{40}{x^3} + \frac{1}{x^2}$ from which it follows that $y \leq 41$, since by assumption $x \geq 1$. So we could reduce the domain of x to $[1..3]$ and the domain of y to $[1..41]$. This interval reduction is optimal, since $x = 1, y = 41$ and $x = 3, y = 1$ are both solutions to the original constraint $x^3 y - x \leq 40$.

However, for arbitrary inequality constraints this approach will often fail to achieve any domain reduction. To see this consider for instance the constraint

$$2x^5 \cdot y^2 \cdot z^4 - 4x^4 \cdot y^6 \cdot z^2 + 3x \cdot y^3 \cdot z^5 \leq 10 \tag{6.10}$$

and the ranges $x \in [-100..100], y \in [-100..100], z \in [-100..100]$.

If $y = 0$ or $z = 0$, then the above inequality is satisfied for any x and we do not achieve any reduction. So assume now that $y \neq 0$ and $z \neq 0$. Focusing on the first occurrence of x, we rewrite (6.10) as

$$2x^5 \cdot y^2 \cdot z^4 \leq 10 + 4x^4 \cdot y^6 \cdot z^2 - 3x \cdot y^3 \cdot z^5,$$

from which we conclude

$$x^5 \leq \frac{5}{y^2 \cdot z^4} + \frac{2x^4 \cdot y^4}{z^2} - \frac{3}{2}x \cdot y \cdot z.$$

By replacing each of the three summands on the right-hand side by the maximum value it can take we get

$$x^5 \leq 5 + 2 \cdot 100^8 + \frac{3}{2}100^3,$$

and consequently

$$x \leq \left\lfloor \sqrt[5]{5 + 2 \cdot 100^8 + \frac{3}{2}100^3} \right\rfloor .$$

But $\left\lfloor \sqrt[5]{5 + 2 \cdot 100^8 + \frac{3}{2}100^3} \right\rfloor > 100$ so we do not achieve any domain reduction for x, even assuming that $y \neq 0$ and $z \neq 0$. The problem is that when evaluating each of the summands on the right-hand side we also had to include in our analysis the variable x itself. This contributed to a substantial increase of the possible values these summands can take. A similar problem arises with the other variables and their occurrences in (6.10).

What is worse, this problem remains when we reduce the variable domains by means of the bisection mentioned in Section 3.2. In summary, if a variable has more than one occurrence in an arithmetic constraint, it will be quite common that no domain reduction will be achieved using the above approach (unless, of course, we reduce the domains to the singleton sets by means of the labeling, also mentioned in Section 3.2, and get rid of the variable occurrences by means of the *VARIABLE ELIMINATION* rule of Section 4.1 altogether).

In what follows we discuss two ways of overcoming this difficulty. In each of them we transform an arbitrary arithmetic constraint into a sequence of simpler ones for which we can derive the appropriate domain reduction rules.

6.5.2 Domain reduction rules: second approach

In this approach we limit our attention to a special type of polynomial constraints. To this end we fix some arbitrary linear ordering $\prec$ on the variables of the language. By a *monomial* we mean an integer or a term of the form

$$a \cdot x_1^{n_1} \cdot \ldots \cdot x_k^{n_k}$$

where $k > 0$, $x_1, \ldots, x_k$ are different variables ordered w.r.t. $\prec$, and a is a non-zero integer and $n_1, \ldots, n_k$ are positive integers. We call then $x_1^{n_1} \cdot \ldots \cdot x_k^{n_k}$ the *power product* of this monomial.

Next, by a *polynomial* we mean a term of the form

$$\Sigma_{i=1}^n m_i,$$

where $n > 0$, at most one monomial m_i is an integer, and the power products of the monomials $m_1, \ldots, m_n$ are pairwise different. Finally, by a *polynomial constraint* we mean an arithmetic constraint of the form $s \, op \, b$, where s is a polynomial, $op \in \{<, \leq, =, \neq, \geq, >\}$, and b is an integer. It is clear that by means of appropriate transformation rules we can transform each arithmetic constraint to a polynomial constraint. For example, assuming the ordering $x \prec y \prec z$ on the variables, the arithmetic constraint (6.8) can be transformed to the polynomial constraint (6.10).

To avoid the problems mentioned in the above discussion of the constraint

(6.10) we introduce an even more restricted class of constraints, the ones which are of the form $s \; op \; b$, where s is a polynomial in which each variable occurs at most once and where b is an integer. We call such a constraint a *simple polynomial constraint.* Using appropriate transformation rules we can rewrite each polynomial constraint into a sequence of simple polynomial constraints.

For example, we can rewrite the polynomial constraint (6.10) into the sequence

$$x_1 - x_2 + x_3 \leq 10, \quad 2x^5 \cdot y^2 \cdot z^4 - x_1 = 0,$$
$$4x^4 \cdot y^6 \cdot z^2 - x_2 = 0, \quad 3x \cdot y^3 \cdot z^5 - x_3 = 0. \tag{6.11}$$

We call then x_1, x_2, x_3 the *auxiliary* variables.

The restriction to the polynomials in which each variable occurs at most once allows us to compute the minimum s^- and the maximum s^+ such a polynomial s can take with respect to a sequence of ranges involving all its variables. Indeed, s^- and s^+ can be then computed by computing the minimum and the maximum for each of the monomials of s separately. The task of a systematic computing of the values of s^- and s^+ for a monomial s is left as Exercise 6.9.

Now, given a CSP with a single arithmetic constraint ϕ and a sequence of ranges involving all the variables used, we can transform it into the following CSP. The constraints are obtained by the above rewriting of ϕ into a sequence of simple polynomial constraints. The domain expressions are the original ranges augmented by the ranges of the form $z \in [t^- .. t^+]$, where z is an auxiliary variable that occurs in a constraint $t - z = 0$. Note that t is then a monomial. It is clear then that both CSPs are equivalent w.r.t. the sequence of the original variables.

We now reconsider the approach sketched in the previous subsection. To see that the restriction to simple polynomial constraints can make a difference let us return to the constraint (6.10) in the presence of the ranges $x \in [-100..100], y \in [-100..100]$ and $z \in [-100..100]$. After it gets transformed to the sequence of the constraints (6.11) no domain reduction is achieved for the resulting four simple polynomial constraints. But if through the bisection the domains of the variables get sufficiently small, the domains do get reduced. Indeed, consider for example the second constraint from (6.11), so $2x^5 \cdot y^2 \cdot z^4 - x_1 = 0$. Suppose that through the bisection we eventually reduce the original domain $[-2 \cdot 100^{11} .. 2 \cdot 100^{11}]$ of x_1 to $[-2 \cdot 100^{11} .. 2 \cdot h^5]$, where $h < 100$, and the domains of y and z to $[l_y..h_y]$ and $[l_z..h_z]$ such that $0 \notin [l_y..h_y]$ and $0 \notin [l_z..h_z]$. Then on the account of

$$x \leq \left\lfloor \sqrt[5]{\frac{x_1}{2y^2 \cdot z^4}} \right\rfloor$$

we can reduce the domain of x to $[-100..h]$.

Unfortunately, for arbitrary simple polynomial constraints we end up with an elaborate case analysis. Let us illustrate this point by means of an example. Consider the constraint

$$2x^4 + 3y^3 - 4z^2 \leq 1000 \qquad (6.12)$$

with the non-empty ranges $x \in [l_x..h_x], y \in [l_y..h_y], z \in [l_z..h_z]$. We can rewrite it as

$$x^4 \leq 500 - \frac{3}{2}y^3 + 2z^2.$$

Now note that $y \in [l_y..h_y]$ implies $y^3 \in [l_y^3..h_y^3]$. The situation is more complex for z^2, since the conclusion depends on the position of 0 w.r.t. the interval $[l_z..h_z]$. We get the following case distinction:

- If $l_z \geq 0$, then $z \in [l_z..h_z]$ implies $z^2 \in [l_z^2..h_z^2]$,
- If $h_z \leq 0$, then $z \in [l_z..h_z]$ implies $z^2 \in [h_z^2..l_z^2]$,
- If $l_z < 0$ and $h_z > 0$, then $z \in [l_z..h_z]$ implies $z^2 \in [0..max(l_z^2, h_z^2)]$.

By assumption $l_z < h_z$, so this case analysis covers all possibilities.

This implies that any value of x that satisfies (6.12) also satisfies the inequality

$$x^4 \leq 500 - \frac{3}{2}l_y^3 + 2h_z^2,$$

if $l_z \geq 0$, the inequality

$$x^4 \leq 500 - \frac{3}{2}l_y^3 + 2l_z^2,$$

if $h_z \leq 0$, and the inequality

$$x^4 \leq 500 - \frac{3}{2}l_y^3 + 2max(l_z^2, h_z^2),$$

if $l_z < 0$ and $h_z > 0$.

This allows us to conclude that no x satisfies (6.12) if one of the following three contingencies holds:

- $l_z \geq 0$ and $500 - \frac{3}{2}l_y^3 + 2h_z^2 < 0$,
- $h_z \leq 0$ and $500 - \frac{3}{2}l_y^3 + 2l_z^2 < 0$,
- $l_z < 0$ and $h_z > 0$ and $500 - \frac{3}{2}l_y^3 + 2max(l_z^2, h_z^2) < 0$.

In each case we can then reduce the interval $[l_x..h_x]$ to the empty one.

Otherwise, if $l_z \geq 0$ and $500 - \frac{3}{2}l_y^3 + 2h_z^2 \geq 0$, we can conclude that

$$-\left\lfloor \sqrt[4]{500 - \frac{3}{2}l_y^3 + 2h_z^2} \right\rfloor \leq x \leq \left\lfloor \sqrt[4]{500 - \frac{3}{2}l_y^3 + 2h_z^2} \right\rfloor$$

since x is to assume integer values, and thus reduce the interval $[l_x..h_x]$ to

$$[max(l_x, - \left\lfloor \sqrt[4]{500 - \frac{3}{2}l_y^3 + 2h_z^2} \right\rfloor)..min(h_x, \left\lfloor \sqrt[4]{500 - \frac{3}{2}l_y^3 + 2h_z^2} \right\rfloor)],$$

and analogously for the other two cases.

Similarly, we can rewrite (6.12) as

$$y^3 \leq \frac{1000}{3} - \frac{2}{3}x^4 + \frac{4}{3}z^2$$

To estimate the right-hand side we now need a double case analysis on x and z. This leads to nine cases, that we illustrate by a representative one.

If $l_x \geq 0$ and $h_z \leq 0$, we can conclude from the above inequality that

$$y^3 \leq \frac{1000}{3} - \frac{2}{3}l_x^4 + \frac{4}{3}l_z^2$$

and consequently

$$y \leq \left\lfloor \sqrt[3]{\frac{1000}{3} - \frac{2}{3}l_x^4 + \frac{4}{3}l_z^2} \right\rfloor$$

since y is to assume integer values. So in this case we can reduce the interval $[l_y..h_y]$ to $[l_y..min(\left\lfloor \sqrt[3]{\frac{1000}{3} - \frac{2}{3}l_x^4 + \frac{4}{3}l_z^2} \right\rfloor, h_y)]$.

The handling of the general case leads to an even more involved case analysis. In fact, the simple polynomial constraint (6.12) is actually not representative since each monomial on its left-hand side has only one variable. In the presence of monomials with more than one variable we get even more case distinctions. So the derivation of the domain reduction rules for simple polynomial constraints, while in principle straightforward, is by no means easy to present.

This extensive case analysis can be avoided if we use the integer interval arithmetic mentioned in Section 3.4. Instead of explaining its use for the simple polynomial constraints we rather further elaborate on the approach of Section 3.4 in which one focuses on a small set of 'atomic' arithmetic constraints.

6.5.3 Domain reduction rules: third approach

We call an arithmetic constraint **atomic** if it is in one of the following two forms:

- a linear constraint,
- $x \cdot y = z$.

It is easy to see that using appropriate transformation rules that involve auxiliary variables we can transform each arithmetic constraint to a sequence of atomic arithmetic constraints. The crucial rule is the following one:

$$\frac{\Sigma_{i=1}^n m_i \ op \ b}{\Sigma_{i=1}^n v_i \ op \ b, \ m_1 = v_1, \ldots, \ m_n = v_n}$$

where some m_i is not of the form ax_i and where $v_1, \ldots, v_n$ are auxiliary variables.

To compute the ranges of the auxiliary variables it is sufficient to know how to compute the values s^- and s^+ for a monomial s and a sequence of ranges involving all its variables. This task is left as Exercise 6.9.

Next, we focus on the reasoning for the multiplication constraint

$$x \cdot y = z$$

in the presence of the non-empty ranges $x \in D_x$, $y \in D_y$ and $z \in D_z$. To this end it is useful to extend the multiplication and division operations to the integer intervals, or more generally, to the sets of integers. Given two sets of integers X, Y we define their multiplication as follows:

$$X \cdot Y := \{x \cdot y \mid x \in X, y \in Y\}.$$

Note that for two integer intervals X, Y their multiplication $X \cdot Y$ does not need to be an interval. For example

$$[0..2] \cdot [1..2] = \{x \cdot y \mid x \in [0..2], y \in [1..2]\} = \{0, 1, 2, 4\}.$$

Consequently, to maintain the property that the domains of the variables are integer intervals, we introduce the following operation on the subsets of the set of the integers $\mathcal{Z}$:

$$int(X) := \begin{cases} \text{smallest integer interval containing } X & \text{if } X \text{ is finite,} \\ \mathcal{Z} & \text{otherwise.} \end{cases}$$

So by definition $int([0..2] \cdot [1..2]) = [0..4]$.

This brings us to the following domain reduction rule, in which to maintain the property that the domains are intervals we use the $int(.)$ operation.

MULTIPLICATION 1

$$\frac{\langle x \cdot y = z \ ; \ x \in D_x, y \in D_y, z \in D_z \rangle}{\langle x \cdot y = z \ ; \ x \in D_x, y \in D_y, z \in D_z \cap int(D_x \cdot D_y) \rangle}$$

As an example of its use consider the CSP

$$\langle x \cdot y = z \ ; \ x \in [0..2], y \in [1..2], z \in [4..6] \rangle.$$

An application of this rule reduces the domain of z to a singleton set since, as we already noticed, $int([0..2] \cdot [1..2]) = [0..4]$ and $[4..6] \cap [0..4] = [4..4]$.

To deal with the reduction of the domains of x and y of the constraint $x \cdot y = z$, we introduce the division of the integer intervals. A complication is that we have to deal with the division by zero. Therefore, given two sets of integers Z, Y we define their division as follows:

$$Z/Y = \{x \in \mathcal{Z} \mid \exists y \in Y \exists z \in Z \ x \cdot y = z\}.$$

Just as in the case of the interval multiplication, the result of the division of two integer intervals does not need to be an interval. Take for example $Z = [3..5]$ and $Y = [-1..2]$. Then

$$[3..5]/[-1..2] = \{-5, -4, -3, 2, 3, 4, 5\}.$$

Hence $int([3..5]/[-1..2]) = [-5..5]$. Note also that if $0 \in Y \cap Z$, then $Z/Y = \mathcal{Z}$. For example, $[-3..5]/[-1..2] = \mathcal{Z}$. Also, if $0 \notin Z$, then $Z/[0..0] = \emptyset$. We now introduce the following two domain reduction rules:

MULTIPLICATION 2

$$\frac{\langle x \cdot y = z \ ; \ x \in D_x, y \in D_y, z \in D_z \rangle}{\langle x \cdot y = z \ ; \ x \in D_x \cap int(D_z/D_y), y \in D_y, z \in D_z \rangle}$$

MULTIPLICATION 3

$$\frac{\langle x \cdot y = z \ ; \ x \in D_x, y \in D_y, z \in D_z \rangle}{\langle x \cdot y = z \ ; \ x \in D_x, y \in D_y \cap int(D_z/D_x), z \in D_z \rangle}$$

The way we defined the multiplication and the division of the integer intervals ensures that the *MULTIPLICATION* rules *1*, *2* and *3* are equivalence preserving. Consider for example the *MULTIPLICATION 2* rule. Take some $a \in D_x, b \in D_y$ and $c \in D_z$ such that $a \cdot b = c$. Then $a \in \{x \in \mathcal{Z} \mid \exists y \in D_y \exists z \in D_z \ x \cdot y = z\}$, so $a \in D_z/D_y$. Consequently $a \in D_x \cap (D_z/D_y)$ and a fortiori $a \in D_x \cap int(D_z/D_y)$. This shows that the *MULTIPLICATION 2* rule is equivalence preserving.

The following example shows an interaction between all three *MULTI-PLICATION* rules.

Example 6.9

(i) Consider the CSP

$$\langle x \cdot y = z \; ; \; x \in [1..20], y \in [9..11], z \in [155..161] \rangle. \qquad (6.13)$$

To facilitate the reading we underline the modified domains. An application of the *MULTIPLICATION 2* rule yields

$$\langle x \cdot y = z \; ; \; x \in \underline{[16..16]}, y \in [9..11], z \in [155..161] \rangle$$

since $[155..161]/[9..11]) = [16..16]$ (we shall return to this statement in Subsection 6.5.4) and $[1..20] \cap int([16..16]) = [16..16]$. Applying now the *MULTIPLICATION 3* rule we obtain

$$\langle x \cdot y = z \; ; \; x \in [16..16], y \in \underline{[10..10]}, z \in [155..161] \rangle$$

since $[155..161]/[16..16] = [10..10]$ and $[9..11] \cap int([10..10]) = [10..10]$. Next, by the application of the *MULTIPLICATION 1* rule we obtain

$$\langle x \cdot y = z \; ; \; x \in [16..16], y \in [10..10], z \in \underline{[160..160]} \rangle$$

since $[16..16] \cdot [10..10] = [160..160]$ and $[155..161] \cap int([160..160]) = [160..160]$.

So using all three multiplication rules we could solve the CSP (6.13).

(ii) Next, let us illustrate the reasoning in the presence of the integer intervals containing zero. Consider the CSP

$$\langle x \cdot y = z \; ; \; x \in [3..10], y \in [-2..2], z \in [-155..161] \rangle.$$

Using the *MULTIPLICATION 1* rule we obtain

$$\langle x \cdot y = z \; ; \; x \in [3..10], y \in [-2..2], z \in \underline{[-20..20]} \rangle$$

since $int([3..10] \cdot [-2..2]) = [-20..20]$ and $[-155..161] \cap [-20..20] = [-20..20]$. Now, however, the applications of the *MULTIPLICATION 1, 2* and *3* rules yield no change, since

- $[-20..20] = int([3..10] \cdot [-2..2])$,
- $[3..10] \subseteq int([-20..20]/[-2..2])$, as $int([-20..20]/[-2..2]) = \mathcal{Z}$,
- $[-2..2] \subseteq int([-20..20]/[3..10])$, as $int([-20..20]/[3..10]) = [-6..6]$.

So the last CSP is closed under the applications of all three *MULTIPLICATION* rules. □

As in the case of other classes of constraints studied in this chapter we would like to clarify what type of local consistency is achieved by means of the employed rules, in this case by the *MULTIPLICATION 1, 2* and *3* rules. To start with, note that the notions of interval and of bounds consistency introduced in Definition 6.4 for linear constraints trivially apply to the arithmetic constraints, as well.

However, we cannot characterise the *MULTIPLICATION* rules in terms of the interval consistency. Indeed, consider the CSP

$$\langle x \cdot y = z \; ; \; x \in [2..3], y \in [2..3], z \in [5..6] \rangle.$$

It is not interval consistent, as no solution exists with $z = 5$. A fortiori, it is not hyper-arc consistent. Yet, it is easy to see that it is closed under the applications of the *MULTIPLICATION 1, 2* and *3* rules since

- $[5..6] \subseteq int([2..3] \cdot [2..3])$ as $int([2..3] \cdot [2..3]) = [4..9]$, and
- $[2..3] \subseteq int([5..6]/[2..3])$ as $int([5..6]/[2..3]) = [2..3]$.

On the other hand this CSP is bounds consistent. For example for $z = 5$ we can take $x = 2$ and $y = 2.5$. Unfortunately, the *MULTIPLICATION* rules cannot be characterised in terms of the bounds consistency notion either. Indeed, consider the CSP

$$\langle x \cdot y = z \; ; \; x \in [-2..1], y \in [-3..10], z \in [8..10] \rangle.$$

It is not bounds consistent, since for $y = -3$ no real values $a \in [-2, 1]$ and $c \in [8, 10]$ exist such that $a \cdot (-3) = c$. Indeed, it is easy to check that $\{y \in \mathcal{R} | \exists \; x \in [-2, 1] \; \exists z \in [8, 10] \; x \cdot y = z\} = (-\infty, -4] \cup [8, \infty)$. However, this CSP is closed under the applications of the *MULTIPLICATION 1, 2* and *3* rules since

- $[8..10] \subseteq int([-2..1] \cdot [-3..10])$, as $int([-2..1] \cdot [-3..10]) = [-20..10]$,
- $[-2..1] \subseteq int([8..10]/[-3..10])$ as $int([8..10]/[-3..10]) \doteq [-10..10]$, and
- $[-3..10] \subseteq int([8..10]/[-2..1])$ as $int([8..10]/[-2..1]) = [-10..10]$.

The problem of an appropriate characterisation of the *MULTIPLICATION* rules remains then open.

Finally, let us clarify why we did not define the division of the sets of integers Z and Y by

$$Z/Y := \{z/y \in \mathcal{Z} \mid y \in Y, z \in Z, y \neq 0\}.$$

The reason is that in that case for any set of integers Z we would have $Z/\{0\} = \emptyset$. Consequently, if we adopted this definition of the division of the integer intervals, the resulting *MULTIPLICATION 2* and *3* rules would not be anymore equivalence preserving. Indeed, consider the CSP

$$\langle x \cdot y = z \; ; \; x \in [-2..1], y \in [0..0], z \in [-8..10] \rangle.$$

Then we would have $[-8..10]/[0..0] = \emptyset$ and consequently by the *MULTI-PLICATION 2* rule we could conclude

$$\langle x \cdot y = z \; ; \; x \in \emptyset, y \in [0..0], z \in [-8..10]\rangle.$$

So we reached a failed CSP while the original CSP is consistent.

6.5.4 Implementation of the third approach

Let us discuss now how the *MULTIPLICATION* rules of the third approach can be implemented. To this end we need to clarify how to implement the intersection operation on the integer intervals and the $int(.)$ closure of multiplication and the division operations on the integer intervals. The case when one of the intervals is empty is easy to deal with. So we assume that we deal with non-empty intervals, that is $a \le b$ and $c \le d$. First, it is easy to see that

$$[a..b] \cap [c..d] = [max(a, c)..min(b, d)].$$

So the interval intersection is straightforward to implement.

For the multiplication and the division operations first note that for the non-empty integer intervals $[a..b]$ and $[c..d]$

$$int([a..b] \cdot [c..d]) = [min(A)..max(A)],$$

where $A = \{a \cdot c, a \cdot d, b \cdot c, b \cdot d\}$. So the $int(.)$ closure of the interval multiplication can be efficiently implemented, as well. In fact, using an appropriate case analysis we can actually compute the bounds of $int([a..b] \cdot [c..d])$ directly in terms of the bounds of the constituent intervals.

In contrast, the $int(.)$ closure of the interval division is not so straightforward to compute. The reason is that, as we shall see in a moment, we cannot express the result in terms of some simple operations on the interval bounds.

Consider non-empty integer intervals $[a..b]$ and $[c..d]$. In analysing the outcome of $int([a..b]/[c..d])$ we distinguish the following cases.

Case 1. Suppose $0 \in [a..b]$ and $0 \in [c..d]$.
  Then by definition $int([a..b]/[c..d]) = \mathcal{Z}$. For example,

$$int([-1..100]/[-2..8]) = \mathcal{Z}.$$

Case 2. Suppose $0 \notin [a..b]$ and $c = d = 0$.

Then by definition $int([a..b]/[c..d]) = \emptyset$. For example,

$$int([10..100]/[0..0]) = \emptyset.$$

Case 3. Suppose $0 \notin [a..b]$ and $c < 0$ and $0 < d$.
It is easy to see that then

$$int([a..b]/[c..d]) = [-e..e],$$

where $e = max(|a|, |b|)$. For example,

$$int([-100..-10]/[-2..5]) = [-100..100].$$

Case 4. Suppose $0 \notin [a..b]$ and either $c = 0$ and $d \neq 0$ or $c \neq 0$ and $d = 0$.
Then $int([a..b]/[c..d]) = int([a..b]/([c..d] - \{0\}))$. For example

$$int([1..100]/[-7..0]) = int([1..100]/[-7..-1]).$$

This allows us to reduce this case to Case 5 below.

Case 5. Suppose $0 \notin [c..d]$.

This is the only case when we need to compute $int([a..b]/[c..d])$ indirectly.
First, observe that we have

$$int([a..b]/[c..d]) \subseteq [\lceil min(A) \rceil .. \lfloor max(A) \rfloor], \qquad (6.14)$$

where $A = \{a/c, a/d, b/c, b/d\}$.

However, the equality does not need to hold here. Indeed, note for example that $int([155..161]/[9..11]) = [16..16]$, whereas for $A = \{155/9, 155/11, 161/9, 161/11\}$ we have $\lceil min(A) \rceil = 15$ and $\lfloor max(A) \rfloor = 17$. The problem is that the value 16 is obtained by dividing 160 by 10 and none of these two values is an interval bound. Still, we can use the above inclusion (6.14) to approximate $int([a..b]/[c..d])$ using the integer interval $[\lceil min(A) \rceil .. \lfloor max(A) \rfloor]$. Then we search for the least $l \in [\lceil min(A) \rceil .. \lfloor max(A) \rfloor]$ such that

$$\exists y \in [c..d] \exists z \in [a..b] \, l \cdot y = z$$

starting at the low end of the interval, and for the greatest $h \in [\lceil min(A) \rceil .. \lfloor max(A) \rfloor]$ such that

$$\exists y \in [c..d] \exists z \in [a..b] \, h \cdot y = z$$

starting at the high end of the interval. This yields the integer interval $[l..h]$ which equals $int([a..b]/[c..d])$.

This completes the presentation of the third approach. This method is then pretty straightforward to explain. Also, it can be implemented in a simple and efficient way. However, there is a price to be paid for its simplicity. As Exercise 6.10 shows, it yields a weaker reduction of the domains than the first approach. This phenomenon is explained by the use of more auxiliary variables.

6.5.5 Shifting from intervals to finite domains

As in the case of the linear constraints on integer intervals we can easily modify the presented rules to the domains that are finite sets of integers. To this end it suffices to drop the use of the $int(.)$ operation. This leads to the following simple modifications of the *MULTIPLICATION* rules, where we assume now that D_x, D_y, D_z are finite sets of integers:

$$FD\text{-}MULTIPLICATION\ 1$$

$$\frac{\langle x \cdot y = z\ ;\ x \in D_x, y \in D_y, z \in D_z \rangle}{\langle x \cdot y = z\ ;\ x \in D_x, y \in D_y, z \in D_z \cap (D_x \cdot D_y) \rangle}$$

$$FD\text{-}MULTIPLICATION\ 2$$

$$\frac{\langle x \cdot y = z\ ;\ x \in D_x, y \in D_y, z \in D_z \rangle}{\langle x \cdot y = z\ ;\ x \in D_x \cap (D_z/D_y), y \in D_y, z \in D_z \rangle}$$

$$FD\text{-}MULTIPLICATION\ 3$$

$$\frac{\langle x \cdot y = z\ ;\ x \in D_x, y \in D_y, z \in D_z \rangle}{\langle x \cdot y = z\ ;\ x \in D_x, y \in D_y \cap (D_z/D_x), z \in D_z \rangle}$$

The *FD-MULTIPLICATION* rules achieve a better domain reduction than the *MULTIPLICATION* rules even if no non-interval domains are generated. To see this consider the CSP

$$\langle x \cdot y = z\ ;\ x \in [0..2], y \in [-1..2], z \in [3..4] \rangle.$$

Applying to it the *MULTIPLICATION 1* rule we do not get any reduction since $int([0..2] \cdot [-1..2]) = [-2..4]$ and $[3..4] \cap [-2..4] = [3..4]$. On the other hand, using the *FD-MULTIPLICATION 1* rule we can deduce that $z = 4$, since $[0..2] \cdot [-1..2] = \{-2, -1, 0, 1, 2, 4\}$ and $[3..4] \cap \{-2, -1, 0, 1, 2, 4\} = \{4\}$.

Also, for the CSP

$$\langle x \cdot y = z\ ;\ x \in [-2..1], y \in [-1..2], z \in [3..5] \rangle.$$

no reduction is achieved using the *MULTIPLICATION 2* rule, since, as already noted $int([3..5]/[-1..2]) = [-5..5]$ and $[-2..1] \cap [-5..5] = [-2..1]$.

On the other hand, as $[3..5]/[-1..2] = \{-5, -4, -3, 2, 3, 4, 5\}$, using the *FD-MULTIPLICATION 2* rule we can detect inconsistency, since $[-2..1] \cap \{-5, -4, -3, 2, 3, 4, 5\} = \emptyset$.

In fact, for the *FD-MULTIPLICATION* rules the following characterisation result holds.

Theorem 6.10 (*FD-MULTIPLICATION*) *A CSP $\langle x \cdot y = z \ ; \ x \in D_x, y \in D_y, z \in D_z \rangle$ with the domains being finite sets of integers is hyperarc consistent iff it is closed under the applications of the FD-MULTIPLICATION 1, 2 and 3 rules.*

Proof We have the following string of easy to check equivalences:

the CSP $\mathcal{P} := \langle x \cdot y = z \ ; \ x \in D_x, y \in D_y, z \in D_z \rangle$ is hyper-arc consistent

iff

$$D_z \subseteq D_x \cdot D_y, \ D_x \subseteq D_z/D_y \text{ and } D_y \subseteq D_z/D_x$$

iff

$\mathcal{P}$ is closed under the applications of the *FD-MULTIPLICATION 1, 2* and *3* rules.

$\square$

On the other hand, the construction of the sets $D_x \cdot D_y$ and D_z/D_y is certainly more costly than the construction of the corresponding integer intervals $int(D_x \cdot D_y)$ and $int(D_z/D_y)$. So the *FD-MULTIPLICATION* rules are less efficient to implement.

6.6 Arithmetic constraints on reals

In the previous section we studied arithmetic constraints on integer intervals. In the considered arithmetic expressions we allowed only integer constants. Here we consider arithmetic constraints that involve reals as constants and that are interpreted over, possibly open ended, intervals of reals.

We shall deal with them, as in Subsection 6.5.3, by transforming these constraints into a small set of 'atomic' arithmetic constraints and by dealing with these atomic constraints using appropriate domain reduction rules. As these rules achieve only a limited reduction of the considered intervals, this approach has to be augmented by splitting and search. In view of the possibly large size of the domains the appropriate form of splitting is bisection, using a middle value between the bounds, as already discussed in Subsection 3.2.4.

More formally, we define first the constraints and the domains over which they are interpreted. We use the alphabet that comprises

- each real number as a constant,
- three binary function symbols, '+','−'and '·', all written in the infix notation.

So the difference between this alphabet and the one used in Section 6.5 is that we allow now as constants all real numbers. As a result the unary minus function symbol '−' is not needed anymore. By an **arithmetic expression** we mean now a term formed in this alphabet and by an **arithmetic constraint** a formula of the form

$$s \; op \; t,$$

where s and t are arithmetic expressions and $op \in \{<, \leq, =, \neq, \geq, >\}$. For example

$$2.4 \cdot x^5 \cdot y^2 \cdot z^4 + 3.6 \cdot x \cdot y^3 \cdot z^5 \leq 10.1 + 4.2 \cdot x^4 \cdot y^6 \cdot z^2$$

is an arithmetic constraint.

To define the considered domains we first extend the set of reals $\mathcal{R}$ by two new elements, $-\infty$ and ∞. This yields the set

$$\mathcal{R}^+ := \mathcal{R} \cup \{-\infty, \infty\}.$$

We then extend the $<$ ordering from $\mathcal{R}$ to $\mathcal{R}^+$ by stipulating that for all $a \in \mathcal{R}$ we have $-\infty < a$ and $a < \infty$. Next, by an **extended real interval**, in short an **extended interval**, we mean an expression of the form

$$\langle a, b \rangle$$

where a and b are elements of $\mathcal{R}^+$. The extended interval $\langle a, b \rangle$ represents the set of all real numbers between a and b, including a if $a \notin \{-\infty, \infty\}$, and including b if $b \notin \{-\infty, \infty\}$. In other words, for $a, b \in \mathcal{R}^+$

$$\langle a, b \rangle = \{r \in \mathcal{R} | \ a \leq r \leq b\}.$$

In the boundary cases we have then for $a, b \in \mathcal{R}$

$$\langle a, a \rangle = \{a\},$$

$$\langle a, b \rangle = \{r \in \mathcal{R} | \ a \leq r \leq b\},$$

$$\langle -\infty, b \rangle = \{r \in \mathcal{R} | \ r \leq b\},$$

$$\langle a, \infty \rangle = \{r \in \mathcal{R} | \ a \leq r\},$$

$$\langle -\infty, \infty \rangle = \mathcal{R}.$$

So extended intervals include as special cases each real, represented as a singleton set, the set of reals $\mathcal{R}$, and the customary real intervals. If $a > b$, then $\langle a, b \rangle = \emptyset$ and we call such an extended interval *empty*. Also for $a, b \in \mathcal{R}$ the extended interval $\langle a, b \rangle$ coincides with the real interval $[a, b]$ considered in Subsection 6.4.7.

It is important to point out that we use here $-\infty$ and ∞ only for the purpose of a succinct representation. Note that for every extended interval I we have $I \subseteq \mathcal{R}$ and consequently $I \cap \{-\infty, \infty\} = \emptyset$. In what follows we use the extended intervals as the variable domains.

6.6.1 Interval arithmetic

To formulate the appropriate domain reduction rules we follow the third approach concerning the arithmetic constraints on the integer intervals discussed in Subsection 6.5.3. To deal with the matters in a systematic way we introduce first the arithmetic operations on extended intervals, or more generally on the sets of reals. Take the sets of reals X, Y. We define:

- addition:

$$X + Y := \{x + y \mid x \in X, y \in Y\},$$

- subtraction:

$$X - Y := \{x - y \mid x \in X, y \in Y\},$$

- multiplication:

$$X \cdot Y := \{x \cdot y \mid x \in X, y \in Y\},$$

- division:

$$X/Y := \{u \in \mathcal{R} \mid \exists x \in X \exists y \in Y \; u \cdot y = x\}.$$

Further, given a real r and $op \in \{+, -, \cdot, /\}$ we identify $r \, op \, X$ with $\{r\} \, op \, X$ and $X \, op \, r$ with $X \, op \, \{r\}$.

We shall return to this choice of the division operation at the end of this section. At this moment it is important to note that if $0 \in X \cap Y$, then $X/Y = \mathcal{R}$.

In the sequel we shall use the above operations, together with the intersection operation, on the extended intervals. The following observation is then of importance.

Note 6.11 (Intervals) *Suppose that X, Y are extended intervals and r a real. Then*

    (i) $X \cap Y$, $X + Y$, $X - Y$ and $X \cdot Y$ are extended intervals.

(ii) $X/\{r\}$ is an extended interval.

(iii) X/Y does not have to be an extended interval.

Proof (i) and (ii) The proof is left as Exercise 6.11.

(iii) We have for example

$$\langle 8, 10 \rangle / \langle -2, 1 \rangle = \langle -\infty, -4 \rangle \cup \langle 8, \infty \rangle.$$

The fact that the outcome is a disjoint union of extended intervals is caused here by the presence of 0 in the extended interval $\langle -2, 1 \rangle$. Actually, the division of the extended intervals does not even need to be a union of extended intervals. For example, we have

$$\langle 2, 16 \rangle / \langle -\infty, -2 \rangle = \{r \in \mathcal{R} | -8 \leq r < 0\}.$$

The fact that the outcome is the interval $[-8, 0]$ with 0 excluded is caused here by the presence of $-\infty$ as a bound. Note that $0 \notin \langle -\infty, -2 \rangle$. $\quad\square$

Consequently, to maintain the property that the domains of the variables are extended intervals, we introduce the following operation on the subsets of $\mathcal{R}$:

$$int(X) := \cap \{Y \in \mathcal{I} \mid X \subseteq Y\},$$

where $\mathcal{I}$ is the set of the extended intervals. So $int(X)$ is the smallest extended interval that contains the set of reals X. It is easy to see that $int(X)$ exists for every such X.

Note that the $int(.)$ operation differs from the one used in Subsection 6.5.3. Indeed, we have for example

$$int(\langle 8, 10 \rangle / \langle -2, 1 \rangle) = \langle -\infty, \infty \rangle,$$

while

$$int([8..10]/[-2..1]) = [-10..10].$$

6.6.2 Domain reduction rules

To deal with the arithmetic constraints on the extended intervals we follow the third approach to the arithmetic constraints on the integer intervals discussed in Subsection 6.5.3 and confine our attention to a small set of atomic constraints. Here we consider the following atomic constraints:

- an equality of the form

$$\sum_{i=1}^{n} a_i x_i = b,$$

where $n > 0$, $a_1, \ldots, a_n$ are non-zero reals, $x_1, \ldots, x_n$ are different variables, and b is a real,

- $x \neq y$,
- $x \cdot y = z$.

It is straightforward to see that using appropriate transformation rules each arithmetic constraint on the extended intervals can be transformed into a set of such atomic constraints. In particular, the arithmetic constraint constraint $s \geq t$ can be transformed first to $s - t + x = 0$, where x is a fresh variable with the domain $\langle -\infty, 0 \rangle$.

Then we introduce the domain reduction rules for the atomic constraints on the extended intervals. To better understand the first rule, note that from the equality

$$\sum_{i=1}^{n} a_i x_i = b$$

it follows that for $j \in [1..n]$ we have

$$x_j = \frac{b - \sum_{i \in [1..n] - \{j\}} a_i x_i}{a_j}.$$

This explains the format of the following rule parametrised by $j \in [1..n]$:

$\mathcal{R}$-LINEAR EQUALITY 1

$$\frac{\langle \sum_{i=1}^{n} a_i x_i = b ; \ x_1 \in D_1, \ldots, x_n \in D_n \rangle}{\langle \sum_{i=1}^{n} a_i x_i = b ; \ x_1 \in D_1', \ldots, x_n \in D_n' \rangle}$$

where

-

$$D_i' := D_i \text{ for } i \neq j,$$

-

$$D_j' := D_j \cap \frac{b - \sum_{i \in [1..n] - \{j\}} a_i \cdot D_i}{a_j}$$

This rule is essentially a generalisation of the $\mathcal{R}$-LINEAR EQUALITY rule of Subsection 6.4.8 to the extended intervals (though we chose here to reduce the variable domains one at a time). It is easy to see that the $\mathcal{R}$-LINEAR EQUALITY 1 is equivalence preserving. Indeed, suppose that for a sequence of reals $b_1, \ldots, b_n$ we have $b_i \in D_i$ for $i \in [1..n]$ and $\sum_{i=1}^{n} a_i b_i = b$. Then

$$b_j = \frac{b - \sum_{i \in [1..n] - \{j\}} a_i b_i}{a_j}$$

so

$$b_j \in \frac{b - \sum_{i\in[1..n]-\{j\}} a_i \cdot D_i}{a_j}$$

hence $b_j \in D'_j$.

For the case of the disequality $x \neq y$ we adopt the *DISEQUALITY 2* rule, that is,

$$\frac{\langle x \neq y \; ; \; x \in D_x, y \in D_y \rangle}{\langle \; ; \; x \in D_x, y \in D_y \rangle}$$

where $D_x \cap D_y = \emptyset$.

Finally, for the multiplication constraint we adopt the following domain reduction rules:

R-MULTIPLICATION 1

$$\frac{\langle x \cdot y = z \; ; \; x \in D_x, y \in D_y, z \in D_z \rangle}{\langle x \cdot y = z \; ; \; x \in D_x, y \in D_y, z \in D_z \cap D_x \cdot D_y \rangle}$$

R-MULTIPLICATION 2

$$\frac{\langle x \cdot y = z \; ; \; x \in D_x, y \in D_y, z \in D_z \rangle}{\langle x \cdot y = z \; ; \; x \in D_x \cap int(D_z/D_y), y \in D_y, z \in D_z \rangle}$$

R-MULTIPLICATION 3

$$\frac{\langle x \cdot y = z \; ; \; x \in D_x, y \in D_y, z \in D_z \rangle}{\langle x \cdot y = z \; ; \; x \in D_x, y \in D_y \cap int(D_z/D_x), z \in D_z \rangle}$$

So textually the *R-MULTIPLICATION 1* rule differs from the *MULTIPLICATION 1* rule of Subsection 6.5.3 only by the fact that the *int* operation is omitted, while the *R-MULTIPLICATION 2* and *3* rules are respectively identical to the *MULTIPLICATION 2* and *3* rules of Subsection 6.5.3. Of course, the *R-MULTIPLICATION* rules use different domains and a different interpretation of the *int* operation.

The way we defined the multiplication and the division of the extended intervals ensures that the above three rules are equivalence preserving. Consider for example the *MULTIPLICATION 3* rule. Take some $a \in D_x, b \in D_y$ and $c \in D_z$ such that $a \cdot b = c$. Then $b \in \{y \mid \exists x \in D_x \exists z \in D_z \; x \cdot y = z\}$ so $b \in D_z/D_x$ and a fortiori $b \in int(D_z/D_x)$. Consequently $b \in D_y \cap int(D_z/D_x)$.

The *R-MULTIPLICATION* rules behave differently than the *MULTIPLICATION* rules. To see it let us return to the CSPs considered in Example 6.9.

Example 6.12

(i) First, recall that using the *MULTIPLICATION* rules we could reduce the CSP

$$\langle x \cdot y = z \; ; \; x \in [1..20], y \in [9..11], z \in [155..161] \rangle$$

to

$$\langle x \cdot y = z \; ; \; x \in [16..16], y \in [10..10], z \in [160..160] \rangle.$$

Take now the corresponding CSP on the extended intervals, i.e.,

$$\langle x \cdot y = z \; ; \; x \in \langle 1, 20 \rangle, y \in \langle 9, 11 \rangle, z \in \langle 155, 161 \rangle \rangle.$$

Applying to it the *R-MULTIPLICATION 2* rule we obtain

$$\langle x \cdot y = z \; ; \; x \in \langle 155/11, 161/9 \rangle, y \in \langle 9, 11 \rangle, z \in \langle 155, 161 \rangle \rangle, \qquad (6.15)$$

since $\langle 155, 161 \rangle / \langle 9, 11 \rangle = \langle 155/11, 161/9 \rangle$ (which is approximately $\langle 14.0909, 17.8888 \rangle$) and $\langle 1, 20 \rangle \cap int(\langle 155/11, 161/9 \rangle) = \langle 155/11, 161/9 \rangle$.

Now, the CSP (6.15) is closed under the applications of the *R-MULTIPLICATION 1, 2* and *3* rules since

- $\langle 155, 161 \rangle \subseteq \langle 155/11, 161/9 \rangle \cdot \langle 9, 11 \rangle$, as

$$\langle 155/11, 161/9 \rangle \cdot \langle 9, 11 \rangle = \langle (155/11) \cdot 9, (161/9) \cdot 11 \rangle,$$

  which is approximately $\langle 126.8181, 196.7777 \rangle$,
- $\langle 155/11, 161/9 \rangle = \langle 155, 161 \rangle / \langle 9, 11 \rangle$,
- $\langle 9, 11 \rangle \subseteq int(\langle 155, 161 \rangle / \langle 155/11, 161/9 \rangle)$, as

$$\langle 155, 161 \rangle / \langle 155/11, 161/9 \rangle = \langle (155/161) \cdot 9, (161/155) \cdot 11 \rangle,$$

  which is approximately $\langle 8.6645, 11.4258 \rangle$.

So, in contrast to the case of the integer intervals, we cannot reduce now the domain of x to the single point interval $\langle 16, 16 \rangle$. This also shows that starting with a CSP with the intervals with the integer bounds the *R-MULTIPLICATION* rules can yield the intervals with non-integer bounds.

(ii) Next, recall that using the *MULTIPLICATION* rules we could reduce the CSP

$$\langle x \cdot y = z \; ; \; x \in [3..10], y \in [-2..2], z \in [-155..161] \rangle$$

to the CSP

$$\langle x \cdot y = z \; ; \; x \in [3..10], y \in [-2..2], z \in [-20..20] \rangle.$$

For the corresponding CSP on the extended intervals, i.e.,

$$\langle x \cdot y = z \ ; \ x \in \langle 3, 10 \rangle, y \in \langle -2, 2 \rangle, z \in \langle -155, 161 \rangle \rangle$$

we get an analogous outcome as in Example 6.9. Indeed, using the $\mathcal{R}$-*MULTIPLICATION 1* rule we get

$$\langle x \cdot y = z \ ; \ x \in \langle 3, 10 \rangle, y \in \langle -2, 2 \rangle, z \in \langle -20, 20 \rangle \rangle, \quad (6.16)$$

since $\langle 3, 10 \rangle \cdot \langle -2, 2 \rangle = \langle -20, 20 \rangle$ and $\langle -155..161 \rangle \cap \langle -20, 20 \rangle = \langle -20, 20 \rangle$. Now, the applications of the $\mathcal{R}$-*MULTIPLICATION 1, 2* and *3* rules yield no change, since

- $\langle -20, 20 \rangle = \langle 3, 10 \rangle \cdot \langle -2, 2 \rangle$,
- $\langle 3, 10 \rangle \subseteq int(\langle -20, 20 \rangle / \langle -2, 2 \rangle)$, as $\langle -20, 20 \rangle / \langle -2, 2 \rangle = \langle -\infty, \infty \rangle$,
- $\langle -2, 2 \rangle \subseteq int(\langle -20, 20 \rangle / \langle 3, 10 \rangle)$, as $\langle -20, 20 \rangle / \langle 3, 10 \rangle = \langle -20/3, 20/3 \rangle$.

So the CSP (6.16) is closed under the applications of all three $\mathcal{R}$-*MULTIPLICATION* rules.

(iii) As a final example let us illustrate the reasoning in the presence of the $-\infty$ bounds. Consider the CSP

$$\langle x \cdot y = z \ ; \ x \in \langle -\infty, -1 \rangle, y \in \langle -\infty, -2 \rangle, z \in \langle -\infty, 161 \rangle \rangle.$$

To facilitate the reading, as in Example 6.9, we underline the modified domains. Since $\langle -\infty, -1 \rangle \cdot \langle -\infty, -2 \rangle = \langle 2, \infty \rangle$ and $\langle -\infty, 161 \rangle \cap \langle 2, \infty \rangle = \langle 2, 161 \rangle$, we get using the $\mathcal{R}$-*MULTIPLICATION 1* rule

$$\langle x \cdot y = z \ ; \ x \in \langle -\infty, -1 \rangle, y \in \langle -\infty, -2 \rangle, z \in \underline{\langle 2, 161 \rangle} \rangle.$$

Now, note that $\langle 2, 161 \rangle / \langle -\infty, -1 \rangle = \{ r \in \mathcal{R} | -161 \le r < 0 \}$, so

$$int(\langle 2, 161 \rangle / \langle -\infty, -1 \rangle) = \langle -161, 0 \rangle$$

and consequently $\langle -\infty, -2 \rangle \cap int(\langle 2, 161 \rangle / \langle -\infty, -1 \rangle) = \langle -161, -2 \rangle$. Therefore applying to the last CSP the $\mathcal{R}$-*MULTIPLICATION 3* rule we get

$$\langle x \cdot y = z \ ; \ x \in \langle -\infty, -1 \rangle, y \in \underline{\langle -161, -2 \rangle}, z \in \langle 2, 161 \rangle \rangle.$$

Next, note that $\langle 2, 161 \rangle / \langle -161, -2 \rangle = \langle -80.5, -2/161 \rangle$ and

$$\langle -\infty, -1 \rangle \cap int(\langle -80.5, -2/161 \rangle) = \langle -80.5, -1 \rangle.$$

So applying to the last CSP the $\mathcal{R}$-*MULTIPLICATION 2* rule we get

$$\langle x \cdot y = z \ ; \ x \in \underline{\langle -80.5, -1 \rangle}, y \in \langle -161, -2 \rangle, z \in \langle 2, 161 \rangle \rangle. \quad (6.17)$$

Now, the CSP (6.17) is closed under the applications of all three $\mathcal{R}$-*MULTIPLICATION* rules. Indeed, we have

- $\langle 2, 161 \rangle \subseteq \langle -80.5, -1 \rangle \cdot \langle -161, -2 \rangle$, since

$$\langle -80.5, -1 \rangle \cdot \langle -161, -2 \rangle = \langle 2, 12960.5 \rangle,$$

- $\langle -80.5, -1 \rangle \subseteq int(\langle 2, 161 \rangle / \langle -161, -2 \rangle)$, since

$$\langle 2, 161 \rangle / \langle -161, -2 \rangle = \langle -80.5, -1 \rangle,$$

- $\langle -161, -2 \rangle \subseteq int(\langle 2, 161 \rangle / \langle -80.5, -1 \rangle)$, since

$$\langle 2, 161 \rangle / \langle -80.5, -1 \rangle = \langle -161, -2/80.5 \rangle.$$

So we succeeded to reduce the original CSP to the one with the real intervals.
□

Just like in the case of the arithmetic constraints on integer intervals it is not clear how to characterise the $\mathcal{R}\text{-}MULTIPLICATION$ rules using a local consistency notion. In Subsection 6.5.3 we showed that the $MULTI\text{-}PLICATION$ rules cannot be characterised in terms of bounds consistency and used for this purpose the CSP

$$\langle x \cdot y = z \ ; \ x \in [-2..1], y \in [-3..10], z \in [8..10] \rangle.$$

The corresponding CSP on the extended intervals, so

$$\langle x \cdot y = z \ ; \ x \in \langle -2, 1 \rangle, y \in \langle -3, 10 \rangle, z \in \langle 8, 10 \rangle \rangle,$$

provides an example that the $\mathcal{R}\text{-}MULTIPLICATION$ rules cannot be characterised using the interval consistency notion. (Recall that the notion of bounds consistency is appropriate only for CSPs on integer intervals.)

Indeed, this CSP is not interval consistent, since as already noted, for $y = -3$ no real values $a \in \langle -2, 1 \rangle$ and $c \in \langle 8, 10 \rangle$ exist such that $a \cdot (-3) = c$, because

$$\{y \mid \exists x \in \langle -2, 1 \rangle \ \exists z \in \langle 8, 10 \rangle \ x \cdot y = z\} = \langle -\infty, -4 \rangle \cup \langle 8, \infty \rangle.$$

On the other hand this CSP is closed under the applications of the $\mathcal{R}\text{-}MULTIPLICATION$ 1, 2 and 3 rules since

- $\langle 8, 10 \rangle \subseteq \langle -2, 1 \rangle \cdot \langle -3, 10 \rangle$ as $\langle -2, 1 \rangle \cdot \langle -3, 10 \rangle = \langle -20, 10 \rangle$,
- $\langle -2, 1 \rangle \subseteq int(\langle 8, 10 \rangle / \langle -3, 10 \rangle)$ as $\langle 8, 10 \rangle / \langle -3, 10 \rangle = \langle -\infty, -8/3 \rangle \cup \langle 0.8, \infty \rangle$, which implies $int(\langle 8, 10 \rangle / \langle -3, 10 \rangle) = \langle -\infty, \infty \rangle$,
- $\langle -3, 10 \rangle \subseteq int(\langle 8, 10 \rangle / \langle -2, 1 \rangle)$ as $\langle 8, 10 \rangle / \langle -2, 1 \rangle = \langle -\infty, -4, \rangle \cup \langle 8, \infty \rangle$, which implies $int(\langle 8, 10 \rangle / \langle -2, 1 \rangle) = \langle -\infty, \infty \rangle$.

$x+y$	$-\infty$	NR	0	PR	∞
$-\infty$	$-\infty$	$-\infty$	$-\infty$	$-\infty$	$\perp$
NR		NR	NR	$\mathcal{R}$	∞
0			0	PR	∞
PR				PR	∞
∞					∞

(left column label y)

$x-y$	$-\infty$	NR	0	PR	∞
$-\infty$	$\perp$	∞	∞	∞	∞
NR	$-\infty$	$\mathcal{R}$	PR	PR	∞
0	$-\infty$	NR	0	PR	∞
PR	$-\infty$	NR	NR	$\mathcal{R}$	∞
∞	$-\infty$	$-\infty$	$-\infty$	$-\infty$	$\perp$

(left column label y)

$x\cdot y$	$-\infty$	NR	0	PR	∞
$-\infty$	∞	∞	$\perp$	$-\infty$	$-\infty$
NR		PR	0	NR	$-\infty$
0			0	0	$\perp$
PR				PR	∞
∞					∞

(left column label y)

x/y	$-\infty$	NR	0	PR	∞
$-\infty$	$\perp$	0	0	0	$\perp$
NR	∞	PR	0	NR	$-\infty$
0	$\perp$	$\perp$	$\perp$	$\perp$	$\perp$
PR	$-\infty$	NR	0	PR	∞
∞	$\perp$	0	0	0	$\perp$

(left column label y)

Table 6.3. *Extension of the arithmetic operations to* $\mathcal{R}^+$

6.6.3 Implementation issues

To implement the approach just discussed we need to clarify how to implement the intersection and the arithmetic operations on the non-empty extended intervals. First we extend the arithmetic operations from $\mathcal{R}$ to $\mathcal{R}^+$. To this end we use Table 6.3. In this table the $\perp$ symbol indicates an undefined operation, PR denotes a positive real and NR a negative real, and the $\mathcal{R}$ indicates that the outcome can be an arbitrary real. Omitted entries are defined by symmetry. So for example $\infty + (-\infty)$ is undefined, $\infty/PR = \infty$, while $PR - NR$ can be an arbitrary real.

To deal with the intersection, addition and subtraction we can use the following simple observation.

Note 6.13 *Suppose that $\langle a, b \rangle$ and $\langle c, d \rangle$ are non-empty extended intervals. Then*

 (i) $\langle a, b \rangle \cap \langle c, d \rangle = \langle max(a, c), min(b, d) \rangle$.
 (ii) $\langle a, b \rangle + \langle c, d \rangle = \langle a + c, b + d \rangle$.
 (iii) $\langle a, b \rangle - \langle c, d \rangle = \langle a - d, b - c \rangle$. □

Note that since $\langle a, b \rangle$ and $\langle c, d \rangle$ are non-empty, we have $a \neq \infty, b \neq -\infty, c \neq \infty, d \neq -\infty$. So none of the used expressions $a+c, b+d, a-d, b-c$ can instantiate to one of the undefined expressions $\infty + (-\infty), (-\infty) + \infty, \infty - \infty$ or $(-\infty) - (-\infty)$. The proof follows by a simple case analysis depending on whether the bounds are an element of $\mathcal{R}$ or equals ∞ or $-\infty$ and is omitted.

This result provides us with a readily, simple and efficient implementation method of the intersection, addition and subtraction of the extended intervals. To deal with the multiplication and division operation we first need to classify the extended intervals depending on the position of 0 with respect to such an interval. The needed categories are listed in Table 6.4.

class of $\langle a, b \rangle$	at least one negative	at least one positive	signs of endpoints
M	yes	yes	$a < 0 \wedge b > 0$
Z	no	no	$a = 0 \wedge b = 0$
P	no	yes	$a \geq 0 \wedge b > 0$
P_0	no	yes	$a = 0 \wedge b > 0$
P_1	no	yes	$a > 0 \wedge b > 0$
N	yes	no	$a < 0 \wedge b \leq 0$
N_0	yes	no	$a < 0 \wedge b = 0$
N_1	yes	no	$a < 0 \wedge b < 0$

Table 6.4. *Classification of non-empty extended intervals*

The appropriate result for the multiplication operation requires only the categories P, M, N and Z of Table 6.4.

Theorem 6.14 (Multiplication) *Suppose that $\langle a, b \rangle$ and $\langle c, d \rangle$ are non-empty extended intervals. Then the result of $\langle a, b \rangle \cdot \langle c, d \rangle$ is provided in Table 6.5.*

□

Note that since $\langle a, b \rangle$ and $\langle c, d \rangle$ are non-empty, we have $a \neq \infty, b \neq -\infty, c \neq \infty, d \neq -\infty$. Consequently, none of the undefined expressions $0 \cdot \infty, 0 \cdot -\infty, -\infty \cdot 0$ or $\infty \cdot 0$ appears in Table 6.5. The proof follows by a tedious case analysis and is omitted. The number of cases can be reduced using symmetry laws, such as $x \cdot y = y \cdot x$, which allows us to derive the MP case from the PM case by interchanging a and c and interchanging b and d.

The corresponding result for the division operation requires in turn the categories P_0, P_1, M, N_0, N_1 and Z of Table 6.4.

Theorem 6.15 (Division) *Suppose that $\langle a, b \rangle$ and $\langle c, d \rangle$ are non-empty extended intervals. Then the result of $\langle a, b \rangle / \langle c, d \rangle$ is provided in Table 6.6.*

□

Again, since $\langle a, b \rangle$ and $\langle c, d \rangle$ are non-empty, none of the undefined expressions $-\infty/\infty, \infty/\infty, \infty/-\infty, -\infty/-\infty$ or $r/0$, where $r \in \mathcal{R}^+$, appears in

class of $\langle a, b \rangle$	class of $\langle c, d \rangle$	$\langle a, b \rangle \cdot \langle c, d \rangle$
P	P	$\langle a \cdot c, b \cdot d \rangle$
P	M	$\langle b \cdot c, b \cdot d \rangle$
P	N	$\langle b \cdot c, a \cdot d \rangle$
M	P	$\langle a \cdot d, b \cdot d \rangle$
M	M	$\langle min(a \cdot d, b \cdot c), max(a \cdot c, b \cdot d) \rangle$
M	N	$\langle b \cdot c, a \cdot c \rangle$
N	P	$\langle a \cdot d, b \cdot c \rangle$
N	M	$\langle a \cdot d, a \cdot c \rangle$
N	N	$\langle b \cdot d, a \cdot c \rangle$
Z	P, M, N, Z	$\langle 0, 0 \rangle$
P, M, N	Z	$\langle 0, 0 \rangle$

Table 6.5. *Case analysis for multiplication of non-empty extended intervals*

class of $\langle a, b \rangle$	class of $\langle c, d \rangle$	$\langle a, b \rangle / \langle c, d \rangle$
P_1	P_1	$\langle a/d, b/c \rangle - \{0\}$
P_1	P_0	$\langle a/d, \infty \rangle - \{0\}$
P_0	P_1	$\langle 0, b/c \rangle$
M	P_1	$\langle a/c, b/c \rangle$
N_0	P_1	$\langle a/c, 0 \rangle$
N_1	P_1	$\langle a/c, b/d \rangle - \{0\}$
N_1	P_0	$\langle -\infty, b/d \rangle - \{0\}$
P_1	M	$(\langle -\infty, a/c \rangle \cup \langle a/d, \infty \rangle) - \{0\}$
M, Z, P_0, N_0	M, Z, P_0, N_0	$\langle -\infty, +\infty \rangle$
N_1	M	$(\langle -\infty, b/d \rangle \cup \langle b/c, \infty \rangle) - \{0\}$
P_1	N_1	$\langle b/d, a/c \rangle - \{0\}$
P_1	N_0	$\langle -\infty, a/c \rangle - \{0\}$
P_0	N_1	$\langle b/d, 0 \rangle$
M	N_1	$\langle b/d, a/d \rangle$
N_0	N_1	$\langle 0, a/d \rangle$
N_1	N_1	$\langle b/c, a/d \rangle - \{0\}$
N_1	N_0	$\langle b/c, \infty \rangle - \{0\}$
Z	P_1, N_1	$\langle 0, 0 \rangle$
P_1, N_1	Z	$\emptyset$

Table 6.6. *Case analysis for division of non-empty extended intervals*

Table 6.6. The proof follows by a tedious case analysis and is omitted. Also here the number of cases can be reduced using appropriate symmetry laws. For example, the fact that $x/y = -(x/-y)$ allows us to derive the MN_1 case from the MP_1 case.

So, as already noted, the outcome of the division of two extended intervals does not have to be an extended interval. However, in the $\mathcal{R}$-MULTIPLICATION 2 and 3 rules we actually use the extended intervals $int(D_z/D_y)$ and $int(D_z/D_x)$ and these can be directly computed using Table 6.6.

Take for example the extended intervals $\langle 2, 16 \rangle$ and $\langle -\infty, -2 \rangle$. In the proof of the Intervals Note 6.11(iii) we noted that

$$\langle 2, 16 \rangle / \langle -\infty, -2 \rangle = \{r \in \mathcal{R} | - 8 \le r < 0\}.$$

This can be derived using Table 6.6 by noting that $\langle 2, 16 \rangle$ is of type P_1 and $\langle -\infty, -2 \rangle$ is of type N_1. In that case the entry

class of $\langle a, b \rangle$	class of $\langle c, d \rangle$	$\langle a, b \rangle / \langle c, d \rangle$
P_1	N_1	$\langle b/d, a/c \rangle - \{0\}$

applies and we conclude that

$$\langle 2, 16 \rangle / \langle -\infty, -2 \rangle = \langle 16/(-2), 2/(-\infty) \rangle - \{0\} = \langle -8, 0 \rangle - \{0\}.$$

Consequently, $int(\langle 2, 16 \rangle / \langle -\infty, -2 \rangle) = \langle -8, 0 \rangle$.

In conclusion, the above analysis of the intersection and the arithmetic operations on the extended intervals yields the necessary information for an efficient implementation of the rules introduced in the previous section.

6.6.4 Using floating-point intervals

In the presence of arithmetic operations on reals the rounding errors are unavoidable since in the computer hardware only a finite set of numbers, called the floating-point numbers, is supported. If we are interested in generating answers that are provably correct, we need to take care properly of these errors. This is done by generating answers in the form of domain expressions with small intervals with floating-point number bounds instead of in the form of reals. For example, assuming the existence of the floating-points for real numbers with five digits after the decimal point, if we wish to guarantee such an accuracy from the final results, we want to generate for the equation

$9 \cdot x^2 = 1$ over the interval $\langle -1, 1 \rangle$ two solutions, represented by the domain expressions $x \in \langle -0.33334, -0.33333 \rangle$ and $x \in \langle 0.33333, 0.33334 \rangle$.

Formally, we assume a fixed finite subset $\mathcal{F}$ of $\mathcal{R}^+$ containing $-\infty$ and ∞. We call the elements of $\mathcal{F}$ the **floating-point numbers**. By a **floating-point interval** we mean an extended interval

$$\langle a, b \rangle,$$

where a and b are floating-point numbers. To convert arbitrary sets of reals to floating-point intervals we introduce the following operation on the subsets of $\mathcal{R}$:

$$\Gamma(A) := \text{the least floating-point interval that contains } A.$$

Since $\{-\infty, \infty\} \subseteq \mathcal{F}$, $\Gamma(A)$ always exists. To ensure that the *R-MULTIPLI-CATION* rules do not cause rounding errors we modify them in such a way that instead of the extended intervals the floating-point intervals are used. This leads us to the following amended rules:

F-MULTIPLICATION 1

$$\frac{\langle x \cdot y = z \ ; \ x \in D_x, y \in D_y, z \in D_z \rangle}{\langle x \cdot y = z \ ; \ x \in D_x, y \in D_y, z \in D_z \cap \Gamma(D_x \cdot D_y) \rangle}$$

F-MULTIPLICATION 2

$$\frac{\langle x \cdot y = z \ ; \ x \in D_x, y \in D_y, z \in D_z \rangle}{\langle x \cdot y = z \ ; \ x \in D_x \cap \Gamma(D_z / D_y), y \in D_y, z \in D_z \rangle}$$

F-MULTIPLICATION 3

$$\frac{\langle x \cdot y = z \ ; \ x \in D_x, y \in D_y, z \in D_z \rangle}{\langle x \cdot y = z \ ; \ x \in D_x, y \in D_y \cap \Gamma(D_z / D_x), z \in D_z \rangle}$$

Since $\mathcal{F}$ is a subset of $\mathcal{R}^+$, we have $int(A) \subseteq \Gamma(A)$. This implies that the *F-MULTIPLICATION* rules are equivalence preserving, since the *R-MULTIPLICATION* rules are. A similar modification of the *R-LINEAR EQUALITY 1* rule is left to the reader.

We should still explain how to implement the new rules. This is done by providing an implementation of the operations $\Gamma(X+Y), \Gamma(X-Y), \Gamma(X \cdot Y)$ and $\Gamma(X/Y)$ for the floating-point intervals X, Y. To this end the formulas presented in the previous subsection for the implementation of the arithmetic operations on the extended intervals are appropriately modified so that the desired **outward rounding** effect takes place. More specifically, the outward rounding of an extended interval $\langle a, b \rangle$ is achieved by rounding a to the largest element of $\mathcal{F}$ which is smaller than or equal to a, and rounding b to the smallest element of $\mathcal{F}$ which is greater than or equal to b. This in turn is achieved by **directed rounding**, a facility available in the floating-point arithmetic. The details would take us too far afield. The interested reader may consult the bibliographic remarks at the end of this chapter.

6.6.5 Correctness and efficiency issues

There are a number of subtle points that underly the approach to the arithmetic constraints on reals here presented. Most of them are absent in the case of the arithmetic constraints on integer intervals. Let us discuss these matters in turn.

Interval Division Let us begin with the adopted definition of the division operation on the extended intervals. It deviates from the format of the other arithmetic operations on the extended intervals. In fact, originally the division operation for the extended intervals (or more precisely, for the real intervals) X and Y was defined by

$$X/Y := \{x/y \mid x \in X, y \in Y\},$$

where it is assumed that $0 \notin Y$. When $0 \in Y$ the expression X/Y is then undefined. Let us call it the **restricted division**. If we adopted in the formulation of the $\mathcal{R}$-*MULTIPLICATION* 2 and 3 rules the restricted division of the extended intervals, we would not be able to reduce the domain of x in the CSP

$$\langle x \cdot y = z \; ; \; x \in \langle -10, 20 \rangle, y \in \langle 0, 2 \rangle, z \in \langle 1, 5 \rangle \rangle.$$

In contrast, using the current formulation of the $\mathcal{R}$-*MULTIPLICATION* 2 rule we can reduce the domain of x to $\langle 0.5, 20 \rangle$ since $\langle 1, 5 \rangle / \langle 0, 2 \rangle = \langle 0.5, \infty \rangle$ and $\langle -10, 20 \rangle \cap int(\langle 0.5, \infty \rangle) = \langle 0.5, 20 \rangle$.

An occasionally used improvement in the definition of the restricted division consists of including the condition $y \neq 0$, that is, defining X/Y as follows:

$$X/Y := \{x/y \mid x \in X, y \in Y, y \neq 0\}.$$

Then X/Y is always defined. Let us call it the **functional division**. However, analogously as in Section 6.5, the functional division cannot be adopted to reason about arithmetic constraints. Indeed, if it were used in the $\mathcal{R}$-*MULTIPLICATION 2* and *3* rules, these rules would not be anymore equivalence preserving. To see this take the example from the end of Subsection 6.5.3, now reformulated as a CSP on the extended intervals, so the CSP

$$\langle x \cdot y = z \; ; \; x \in \langle -2, 1 \rangle, y \in \langle 0, 0 \rangle, z \in \langle -8, 10 \rangle \rangle.$$

Then we would have $\langle -8, 10 \rangle / \langle 0, 0 \rangle = \emptyset$ and consequently by the $\mathcal{R}$-*MULTIPLICATION 2* rule we could conclude

$$\langle x \cdot y = z \; ; \; x \in \emptyset, y \in \langle 0, 0 \rangle, z \in \langle -8, 10 \rangle \rangle.$$

Now, the second CSP is failed while the original one is consistent.

Additional Interval Operations When introducing the interval arithmetic we limited ourselves to four arithmetic operations. However, the laws of the interval arithmetic differ from the ones of the arithmetic and consequently the choice of the interval operations can be of consequence for the solving of the arithmetic constraints on reals. Consider for example the square operation defined for a set of reals X by:

$$X^2 = \{x^2 \mid x \in X\}.$$

Note that then $X^2 \subseteq X \cdot X$. However, the inclusion can be strict. For example $\langle -1, 2 \rangle^2 = \langle 0, 4 \rangle$, while $\langle -1, 2 \rangle \cdot \langle -1, 2 \rangle = \langle -2, 4 \rangle$. So if we interpret X^2 as $X \cdot X$ we obtain larger extended intervals which leads to a less efficient reasoning. In other words, it pays off to have an extended set of interval operations. We shall return to this matter in a moment.

Convergence In contrast to the arithmetic constraints on integer intervals, if we restrict our attention to the relevant rule applications, the termination of the considered derivations is not guaranteed. Indeed, take the obviously inconsistent CSP

$$\langle x - y = 1, y - x = 1 \; ; \; x \in \langle 0, \infty \rangle, y \in \langle 0, \infty \rangle \rangle$$

and consider a derivation in which the constraints are selected in an alternating fashion. Each time we can apply the $\mathcal{R}$-*LINEAR EQUALITY 1* rule and the domain expressions are successively modified to $x \in \langle 1, \infty \rangle$, $y \in \langle 2, \infty \rangle$, $x \in \langle 3, \infty \rangle$, $y \in \langle 4, \infty \rangle$ etc. and the derivation does not terminate.

In fact, termination is not guaranteed even if the considered intervals are bounded. To see this take the CSP

$$\langle x - y = 0, x - 2y = 0 \; ; \; x \in \langle 0, 100 \rangle, y \in \langle 0, 100 \rangle \rangle$$

and consider a derivation in which the constraints are selected in an alternating fashion. Again, each time we can apply the $\mathcal{R}$-*LINEAR EQUALITY 1* rule and the considered intervals asymptotically converge to $\langle 0, 0 \rangle$.

Once we move to the floating-point intervals this complication cannot arise. But due to the size of the floating-point intervals the number of possible deduction steps can still be large so the problem remains how to speed up the convergence to the final result.

Choice of atomic constraints It is also important to realise that the choice of the atomic constraints is crucial for the efficiency of the resulting approach to solving the arithmetic constraints. In general, when transforming a given arithmetic constraint into a sequence of atomic constraints, it is beneficial to introduce as few auxiliary variables as possible. For example, we could easily conclude from the CSP

$$\langle x^2 = z \; ; \; x \in \langle -\infty, \infty \rangle, z \in \langle -10, 9 \rangle \rangle$$

that $x \in \langle -3, 3 \rangle$ if we had to our disposal a natural domain reduction rule dealing with the constraint $x^2 = z$. In our case we need to introduce an auxiliary variable y and have to reason instead about the CSP

$$\langle x \cdot y = z, x = y \; ; \; x \in \langle -\infty, \infty \rangle, y \in \langle -\infty, \infty \rangle, z \in \langle -10, 9 \rangle \rangle,$$

which is closed under the applications of the adopted rules.

So it pays off to have an extended set of atomic constraints. Intuitively, a 'good' atomic constraint is the one which for each of its variables can be rewritten as a function of this variable. Such a rewriting leads to an appropriate domain reduction rule —see for instance the way we obtained the $\mathcal{R}$-*LINEAR EQUALITY 1* rule. For example, $x = y^3$ is a 'good' atomic constraint since it can be rewritten as $y = \sqrt[3]{x}$. In contrast, $x = 2y - 5y^7$ is not a 'good' atomic constraint since it is not clear how to rewrite it as a function of y.

Choice of transformations into atomic constraints The efficiency of the discussed approach also depends on the way the constraints are transformed into a sequence of atomic constraints. Consider for instance the clearly inconsistent CSP $\langle x - x = 1 \; ; \; x \in \langle 0, 100 \rangle \rangle$. The inconsistency can be detected directly by transforming the expression $x - x$ to 0. If instead we evaluate the expression $x - x$ using the interval arithmetic we obtain the interval $\langle -100, 100 \rangle$ and no inconsistency is detected (yet).

The problem is that in the interval arithmetic each occurrence of x is treated as a different variable. This phenomenon is called the **dependency**

problem. It becomes more explicit when we introduce auxiliary variables. For example, if we transform the above CSP to $\langle x - y = 1, x = y \, ; \, x \in \langle 0, 100 \rangle, y \in \langle -\infty, \infty \rangle \rangle$, we can first reduce the domain of y to $\langle 0, 100 \rangle$ using the *EQUALITY 2* rule and then the evaluation of the expression $x - y$ using the interval arithmetic yields $\langle -100, 100 \rangle$.

Choice of the function representation Finally, the efficiency of the underlying reasoning involving the interval arithmetic depends on the way we represent the functions. Consider the following three equivalent functions on reals:

$$f_1(x) := x^2 - x,$$

$$f_2(x) := (x - 0.5)^2 - 0.25,$$

$$f_3(x) := x \cdot (x - 1).$$

Then the corresponding interval extensions F_1, F_2 and F_3 of these functions are not equivalent. Indeed, we have

$$F_1(\langle 0, 2 \rangle) = \langle 0, 2 \rangle^2 - \langle 0, 2 \rangle = \langle -2, 4 \rangle,$$

$$F_2(\langle 0, 2 \rangle) = (\langle 0, 2 \rangle - 0.5)^2 - 0.25 = \langle -1, 2 \rangle,$$

$$F_3(\langle 0, 2 \rangle) = \langle 0, 2 \rangle \cdot (\langle 0, 2 \rangle - 1) = \langle -2, 2 \rangle,$$

where for an extended interval X we interpreted X^2 as $X \cdot X$. So the second function, F_2, yields the smallest interval. This is another instance of the dependence problem: note that the variable x occurs twice in the definition of f_1 and f_3, while only once in f_2.

The choice of the interval operations is also of direct relevance here. Indeed, $\{f_2(x) \mid x \in \langle 0, 2 \rangle\} = \langle -0.25, 2 \rangle$, so the interval produced by F_2 is not optimal. However, if we extend the interval arithmetic by the square operation X^2 and use it in the evaluation of $F_2(\langle 0, 2 \rangle)$, we do get the optimal interval $\langle -0.25, 2 \rangle$, since then $\langle -0.5, 1.5 \rangle^2 = \langle 0, 2.25 \rangle$.

One of the challenges of the interval arithmetic is to find the 'best' function representations in the sense that they yields the smallest intervals for the interval extensions. This task is of clear importance for solving arithmetic constraints on reals.

6.7 Arithmetic equations over reals

In this section we discuss an alternative approach to the one adopted in the previous section. It deals with the same constraints as in the previous section with the restriction that we allow only the equality '=' relation. We call these constraints **arithmetic equations**. Moreover, we assume that all variables range over the set of reals. So we do not consider other forms of extended intervals.

In contrast to the other incomplete constraint solvers discussed in this chapter, the one discussed here is not based on the domain reduction rules but rather on the transformation rules. We simply adopt the rules of the *LIN* proof system of Section 4.3 by means of which we defined two complete constraint solvers for linear equations on reals. To be able to apply these rules in this wider context we extend the normalisation and standardisation procedures to the arithmetic expressions and the arithmetic equations.

Assume a predermined ordering $\prec$ on the considered variables. Recall that in Subsection 6.5.2 we defined a *monomial* as an integer or a term of the form

$$n \cdot x_1^{n_1} \cdot \ldots \cdot x_k^{n_k}$$

where $k > 0$, $x_1, \ldots, x_k$ are different variables ordered w.r.t. $\prec$, and n is a non-zero integer and $n_1, \ldots, n_k$ are positive integers. We called $x_1^{n_1} \cdot \ldots \cdot x_k^{n_k}$ the *power product* of the monomial and defined a *polynomial* as a term of the form

$$\Sigma_{i=1}^n m_i,$$

where $n > 0$, at most one monomial m_i is an integer, and the power products of the monomials $m_1, \ldots, m_n$ are pairwise different.

Using appropriate transformation rules each arithmetic expression s can be rewritten to a uniquely defined polynomial that we denote by $norm(s)$. Also, each arithmetic equation e can be reduced to a unique **polynomial equation**, which is a constraint of the form $s = b$, where s is a polynomial and b is an integer. We call then $s = b$ the **normal form of** e and say that e **normalises to** $s = b$.

Finally, we reuse in this wider context the standardisation procedure defined by

$$stand(s = t) := norm(s) = norm(t).$$

After these preparations we can reinterpret the rules of the *LIN* as rules for arithmetic equations by interpreting the notions of normalisation and standardisation in this wider context. Clearly, these generalisations of the rules of the *LIN* system do not suffice to solve the considered constraints. Still, they can be useful, as the following example shows.

Example 6.16 Consider the following set of arithmetic equations:

$$
\begin{aligned}
x_0 &= 1 \\
y_0 &= 2 \\
x_0 x_1 + y_1 y_0 &= 0 \\
x_1 + y_1 &= (x_0 - y_0)(2x_0 + y_0 + 1) \\
x_1 x_2 + y_1 y_2 &= 0 \\
x_2 + y_2 &= (x_1 - y_1)(2x_1 + y_1 + 1)
\end{aligned}
$$

In the derivation below we repeatedly use the *SUBSTITUTION* rule, each time selecting a successive equation, starting with the first one, and each time using the remaining equations as E. For convenience let us restate this rule here:

$$SUBSTITUTION$$

$$
\frac{s = v,\; E}{x = t,\; stand(E\{x/t\})}
$$

where $x = t$ is a pivot form of $s = v$.

The first two applications result in substituting x_0 by 1 and y_0 by 2 in the last four equations. This yields following set of equations:

$$
\begin{aligned}
x_0 &= 1 \\
y_0 &= 2 \\
x_1 + 2y_1 &= 0 \\
x_1 + y_1 &= -5 \\
x_1 x_2 + y_1 y_2 &= 0 \\
x_2 + y_2 &= 2x_1^2 - x_1 y_1 + x_1 - y_1^2 - y_1
\end{aligned}
$$

The third equation is now linear and $x_1 = -2y_1$ is one of its pivot forms. So again by the *SUBSTITUTION* rule we get

$$
\begin{aligned}
x_0 &= 1 \\
y_0 &= 2 \\
x_1 &= -2y_1 \\
-y_1 &= -5 \\
-2x_2 y_1 + y_1 y_2 &= 0 \\
x_2 + y_2 &= 9y_1^2 - 3y_1
\end{aligned}
$$

Choosing now the fourth equation we use its pivot form $y_1 = 5$ and transform the above set to the following one:

$$
\begin{aligned}
x_0 &= 1 \\
y_0 &= 2 \\
x_1 &= -10 \\
y_1 &= 5 \\
-10x_2 + 5y_2 &= 0 \\
x_2 + y_2 &= 210
\end{aligned}
$$

The fifth equation is now linear and $y_2 = 2x_2$ is one of its pivot forms. Its use yields the following set of equations:

$$
\begin{aligned}
x_0 &= 1 \\
y_0 &= 2 \\
x_1 &= -10 \\
y_1 &= 5 \\
y_2 &= 2x_2 \\
3x_2 &= 210
\end{aligned}
$$

Finally, using the last equation we transform the above set into

$$
\begin{aligned}
x_0 &= 1 \\
y_0 &= 2 \\
x_1 &= -10 \\
y_1 &= 5 \\
y_2 &= 140 \\
x_2 &= 70
\end{aligned}
$$

So by repeated applications of the *SUBSTITUTION* rule we succeeded to solve the initial set of equations in spite of the fact that four out of six equations were not linear. $\square$

We could strengthen the *SUBSTITUTION* rule by applying it to any arithmetic equation that can be rewritten to a form $x = t$, where x does not occur in t. Such a stronger form of the rule would allow us to solve for example the following set of two equations:

$$ x - y^2 = 1, \quad xy - y^3 + 1 = z. $$

Even with such a modification the above three proof rules clearly form an incomplete constraint solver, since using them we cannot even solve quadratic equations, for example $x^2 - 2x + 1$. Even worse, we cannot detect that equations such as $x^2 = -1$ have no solution. Of course, one could augment this constraint solver by rules allowing us to solve quadratic equations in one variable. But this would not help us to solve more complex equations such as $2 \cdot x^5 - 5 \cdot x^4 + 5 = 0$ already discussed in Example 2.5 of Section 2.3. So there is no natural way to extend this solver to a complete one.

6.8 Summary

In this chapter we discussed in detail six incomplete constraint solvers. They dealt with:

- the equality and disequality constraints,
- Boolean constraints,
- the linear constraints over integer intervals and over finite integer domains,
- the arithmetic constraints over integer intervals,
- the arithmetic constraints over extended real intervals, and
- the arithmetic equations over reals.

In each case we introduced the corresponding constraint solver by means of the proof rules and in the first three ones we clarified what type of local consistency is achieved by each of them. In the first two cases this was done by means of a characterisation in terms of the notions of local consistency already discussed in Chapter 5. So the first two constraint solvers can be viewed as implementations of these notions of local consistency for constraints defined respectively in the language with exclusively equality and disequality symbols, and in the language of Boolean constraints.

To obtain such a characterisation for linear constraints over integer intervals we had to introduce a new notion of local consistency, called bounds consistency. In the case of the arithmetic constraints over integer intervals and over reals no characterisation result is available. Finally, for the case of the arithmetic equations over reals the reader is referred to the bibliographic remarks at the end of this chapter for a reference to the appropriate characterisation result.

6.9 Exercises

Exercise 6.1 Prove that each of the transformation rules of Subsection 6.3.1 is equivalence preserving w.r.t. to the sequence of the variables of the premise.

Exercise 6.2 Prove that every derivation in the proof system that consists of the transformation rules of Subsection 6.3.1 is finite.

Exercise 6.3 Prove that every derivation in the proof system $BOOL$ is finite.

Exercise 6.4 Consider the proof system $BOOL'$ given in Table 6.7.

EQU $1\text{-}4$	as in the system $BOOL$	
NOT $1\text{-}4$	as in the system $BOOL$	
AND $1'$	$x \wedge y = z, x = 1 \rightarrow z = y$	
AND $2'$	$x \wedge y = z, y = 1 \rightarrow z = x$	
AND $3'$	$x \wedge y = z, z = 1 \rightarrow x = 1$	
AND 4	as in the system $BOOL$	
AND 5	as in the system $BOOL$	
AND $6'$	$x \wedge y = z, z = 1 \rightarrow y = 1$	
OR 1	as in the system $BOOL$	
OR $2'$	$x \vee y = z, x = 0 \rightarrow z = y$	
OR $3'$	$x \vee y = z, y = 0 \rightarrow z = x$	
OR $4'$	$x \vee y = z, z = 0 \rightarrow x = 0$	
OR 5	as in the system $BOOL$	
OR $6'$	$x \vee y = z, z = 0 \rightarrow y = 0$	

Table 6.7. *Proof system $BOOL'$*

Note that the rules AND $1\text{-}3$ of $BOOL$ are replaced by the rules AND $1'$ and AND $2'$ of $BOOL'$ and the rules OR $2\text{-}4$ of $BOOL$ are replaced by the rules OR $2'$ and OR $3'$ of $BOOL'$. Also, the rule AND 6 of $BOOL$ is split in $BOOL'$ into two rules, AND $3'$ and AND $6'$ and analogously for the rules OR 6 of $BOOL$ and OR $3'$ and OR $6'$ of $BOOL'$.

(i) Prove that if a non-failed Boolean CSP is closed under the applications of the rules of the proof system $BOOL'$, then it is hyper-arc consistent.

(ii) Show that the converse result does not hold.

    Hint. Take the CSP $\langle x \wedge y = z \; ; \; x = 1, y \in \{0,1\}, z \in \{0,1\}\rangle$.

(iii) Call a Boolean CSP **limited** if none of the following four CSPs forms a subpart of it:

- $\langle x \wedge y = z \; ; \; x = 1, y \in \{0,1\}, z \in \{0,1\}\rangle$,
- $\langle x \wedge y = z \; ; \; x \in \{0,1\}, y = 1, z \in \{0,1\}\rangle$,
- $\langle x \vee y = z \; ; \; x = 0, y \in \{0,1\}, z \in \{0,1\}\rangle$,

- $\langle x \vee y = z \; ; \; x \in \{0,1\}, y = 0, z \in \{0,1\}\rangle$.

Prove that if a non-failed Boolean CSP is limited and hyper-arc consistent, then it is closed under the applications of the rules of the proof system $BOOL'$.

Exercise 6.5 We introduced in Table 6.2 two rules for the exclusive disjunction XOR. Find the remaining four rules and prove the counterpart of the $BOOL$ Theorem 6.3 for the proof system XOR consisting of these six proof rules.

Exercise 6.6 Consider the transformation rules given in Table 6.8 that deal with the exclusive disjunction XOR.

$XOR\ 1$	$x \oplus y = z, x = 1 \to \neg y = z$
$XOR\ 2$	$x \oplus y = z, x = 0 \to y = z$
$XOR\ 3$	$x \oplus y = z, y = 1 \to \neg x = z$
$XOR\ 4$	$x \oplus y = z, y = 0 \to x = z$
$XOR\ 5$	$x \oplus y = z, z = 1 \to \neg x = y$
$XOR\ 6$	$x \oplus y = z, z = 0 \to x = y$

Table 6.8. *Different proof rules for XOR*

Consider the proof system XOR' resulting from adding to these rules the EQU 1-4 and NOT 1-4 proof rules of the $BOOL$ system.

(i) Prove that if a non-failed Boolean CSP is closed under the applications of the rules of the proof system XOR', then it is hyper-arc consistent.

(ii) Show that the converse result does not hold.
   Hint. Take the CSP $\langle x \oplus y = z \; ; \; x = 1, y \in \{0,1\}, z \in \{0,1\}\rangle$.

(iii) Suggest a restriction on the considered CSPs for which the counterpart of the $BOOL$ Theorem 6.3 can be proved for the proof system XOR'.
   Hint. See Exercise 6.4.

Exercise 6.7 Provide transformation rules that transform each linear expression of Section 6.4 to the form

$$\Sigma_{i=1}^{n} a_i x_i + b,$$

where $n \geq 0$, $a_1, \ldots, a_n$ are non-zero integers, $x_1, \ldots, x_n$ are different variables, and b is an integer. Prove that every derivation in the resulting proof system is finite.

Exercise 6.8 Prove the Convexity Note 6.6.

Exercise 6.9 Compute the minimum s^- and the maximum s^+ a monomial s can take with respect to a sequence of ranges involving all its variables. *Hint.* Introduce the interval power operation X^n, where $n \geq 2$. Look at the characterisation of the integer interval $int([a..b] \cdot [c..d])$ given in Subsection 6.5.4.

Exercise 6.10 Find an arithmetic inequality constraint for which the third approach of Section 6.5 yields a strictly weaker domain reduction than the first one.
Hint. Consider the constraint $x^3 \leq 1000$ and the range $x \in [1..1000]$.

Exercise 6.11 Prove the Intervals Note 6.11(i) and (ii).

Exercise 6.12 Formulate appropriate domain reduction rules for the constraint $x^2 = y$ on integer intervals and on reals and suggest their implementations.
Hint. Introduce the operations of a square and of a square root of an integer interval and of an extended real interval.

Exercise 6.13 Consider Table 6.6 that defines the result of the division for non-empty extended intervals. Provide examples of the extended intervals for each case in which the outcome is not an extended interval.

6.10 Bibliographic remarks

The proof rules in the style of those constituting the proof system *BOOL* have been used for a long time. In McAllester [1980] they are explained informally; in McAllester [1990] they are called *Boolean constraint propagation*. In Simonis [1989] such rules are formulated explicitly and used to generate tests for combinatorial circuits. More recently, these rules were used in Codognet and Diaz [1996] as a basis for an efficient implementation of a Boolean constraint solver.

The proof system *BOOL'* from Exercise 6.4 is taken from the last paper though its *AND* rules already appear in Simonis [1989]. The proof system *BOOL* is a modification of *BOOL'* obtained in order to get the *BOOL*

Theorem 6.3 that characterises the notion of hyper-arc consistency in terms of these rules. Exercise 6.4 that shows that such a characterisation of hyper-arc consistency does not hold for the *BOOL'* system is from Apt [2000b]. The last paper also clarifies the relation between the proof system *BOOL* and the unit propagation, a form of propositional resolution (see, e.g. Zhang and Stickel [1996]) that is a component of the Davis–Putnam algorithm for the satisfiability problem (see Davis and Putnam [1960]). The inference problem discussed in Subsection 6.3.3 is from Frühwirth [1995].

The domain reduction rules *LINEAR INEQUALITY 1* and *LINEAR EQUALITY* are simple modifications of the domain reduction rule introduced in Davis [1987,page 306] that dealt with closed intervals of reals. These rules are well known in the area of integer programming under the name of 'preprocessing', see, e.g., Wolsey [1998,Section 7.6]. They were implemented in various constraint programming systems. The use of the *SEND + MORE = MONEY* puzzle to discuss the effect of these rules is from Van Hentenryck [1989,page 143].

The presentation in Section 6.4 is based on Apt [1998]. The $\mathcal{R}$-*LINEAR EQUALITY* Theorem 6.7 generalises a corresponding result stated in Davis [1987,page 326] for the more limited case of so-called unit coefficient constraints. The notion of bounds consistency was introduced in a number of papers, for example Van Hentenryck, Saraswat and Deville [1998]. The terminology here adopted follows Marriott and Stuckey [1998]. A similar notion was introduced in Lhomme [1993] for the case of constraints on reals. Harvey and Stuckey [2003] study how to improve the efficiency of the constraint solver discussed in Section 6.4 by means of different constraint representations.

The presentation in Section 6.5 is based on Apt and Zoeteweij [2003], where all three approaches to arithmetic constraints on integer intervals are explained in detail and compared by means of benchmarks. The third approach is inspired by a similar treatment of the polynomial constraints on reals based on the interval arithmetic, an intensely pursued research subject originated by Cleary [1987]. In particular, the *MULTIPLICATION* rules are analogues of the corresponding $\mathcal{F}$-*MULTIPLICATION* rules of Subsection 6.6.4 which are formulated explicitly, e.g., in van Emden [1999].

The research on the interval arithmetic and, more generally, interval analysis goes back to Moore [1966], where only real intervals were considered. In Hansen [1992] the analogues of the Multiplication Theorem 6.14 and the Division Theorem 6.15 for the multiplication and the restricted division of real intervals are presented. The dependency problem discussed in Subsection 6.6.5 and the corresponding examples are taken from these two references.

The contribution of Cleary [1987] was to combine the interval arithmetic with constraint propagation and splitting. Also extended intervals were used there. This approach was realised in the BNR-Prolog language, see, e.g., Older and Vellino [1993]. It was further elaborated in the works of E. Hyvŏnen, see, e.g. Hyvŏnen [1992]. This approach was also generalised to other domains in Benhamou and Older [1997] (originally published in 1993) where a unified treatment of Boolean constraints and arithmetic constraints on integers and reals was provided. This research was followed by Benhamou, McAllester and Van Hentenryck [1994], where a constraint programming language Newton was proposed based on a new local consistency notion, called *box consistency*, appropriate for polynomial constraints on reals. In turn, the research on Newton eventually led to Numerica, a modeling language of Van Hentenryck [1997] for solving non-linear constraints on reals and constrained optimization problems on reals. In the Declic language of Benhamou, Goualard and Granvilliers [1997] a cooperation is achieved between the approach described in Section 6.6 and the one based on box consistency.

This line was research was pursued independently by Russian researchers. This led to the system UniCalc, the first prototype of which was realised already in 1987. For an early description of it see Babichev et al. [1993]. In most of these works the presentation also includes a discussion of an appropriate constraint propagation algorithm that achieves a specific notion of local consistency. In our set up such algorithms are discussed separately, in Chapter 7.

The systematic account of the arithmetic operations on the extended intervals and their implementation is from Hickey, Ju and van Emden [2001]. The exception is that, for the reasons explained in Subsection 6.6.5, we use here a different division operation, due to Ratz [1996], where the Division Theorem 6.15 limited to the real intervals is established. The relevance of the so defined division operation for solving constraints on reals was clarified in Hickey, van Emden and Wu [1998]. The Tables 6.3, 6.4, 6.5 and (here appropriately modified) Table 6.6 are taken from Hickey, Ju and van Emden [2001]. The proofs of the Multiplication Theorem 6.14 and the Division Theorem 6.15 and the formulas for computing the floating-point intervals $\Gamma(X + Y), \Gamma(X - Y), \Gamma(X \cdot Y)$ and $\Gamma(X/Y)$ (for the functional division operation) are provided there. In Colmerauer [2001] a direct account of the domain reduction for the multiplication constraint $x \cdot y = z$ on real intervals can be found. It corresponds to the $\mathcal{F}$-*MULTIPLICATION* rules of Subsection 6.6.4.

The CSP $\langle x - y = 0, x - 2y = 0 \; ; \; x \in \langle 0, 100 \rangle, y \in \langle 0, 100 \rangle \rangle$ used in

Subsection 6.6.5 to illustrate possible divergence in case of constraints on reals is taken from Davis [1987, page 304].

The *SUBSTITUTION* rule, considered in Section 6.7 in the wider context of arithmetic equations, is discussed in Colmerauer [1993]. Example 6.16 is taken from this paper. In this paper a characterisation result is provided for a constraint solver for arithmetic equations over reals obtained by augmenting the three rules of the *LIN* system by a transformation rule that systematically rewrites the arithmetic equations into the ones that are either linear or of the form $x \cdot y = z$, where x, y, z are different variables. The strengthened form of the *SUBSTITUTION* rule mentioned at the end of Section 6.7 is discussed in Jaffar et al. [1993].

Many other approaches were proposed to deal with the incomplete constraint solvers here discussed. In Benhamou and Colmerauer [1993] one can find a number of alternative approaches dealing with the Boolean constraints and with the arithmetic constraints on reals. Jaffar and Maher [1994] discuss other examples of complete and incomplete constraint solvers. The subject of solving constraints on reals has been attracting a continuing, large, attention in the literature. Various approaches are discussed in Benhamou, Goualard and Granvilliers [2000], where one can find further references to this area.

6.11 References

K. R. APT
[1998] A proof theoretic view of constraint programming, *Fundamenta Informaticae*, 33, pp. 263–293. Available via `http://arXiv.org/archive/cs/`.

[2000b] Some remarks on Boolean constraint propagation, in: *New Trends in Constraints*, K. R. Apt, A. C. Kakas, E. Monfroy, and F. Rossi, eds., vol. 1865 of Lecture Notes in Artificial Intelligence, Springer-Verlag, pp. 91 – 107. Available via `http://arXiv.org/archive/cs/`.

K. R. APT AND P. ZOETEWEIJ
[2003] A comparative study of arithmetic constraints on integer intervals, in: *Proceedings of the 2003 ERCIM Workshop on Constraints*, MTA SZTAKI. Available via `http://www.cwi.nl/~apt`.

A. B. BABICHEV, O. B. KADYROVA, T. P. KAHEVAROVA, A. S. LESHCHENKO, AND A. L. SEMENOV
[1993] UniCalc, a novel approach to solving systems of algebraic equations, *Interval Computations*, N2, pp. 29 – 47.

F. BENHAMOU AND A. COLMERAUER
[1993] eds., *Constraint Logic Programming: Selected Research*, The MIT Press.

F. BENHAMOU, F. GOUALARD, AND L. GRANVILLIERS
[1997] Programming with the Declic language, in: *Proceedings of the Second Workshop on Interval Constraints (October 1997, Port-Jefferson, NY)*.

[2000] Interval constraints: Results and perspectives, in: *New Trends in Constraints*, K. R. Apt, A. C. Kakas, E. Monfroy, and F. Rossi, eds., vol. 1865 of Lecture Notes in Artificial Intelligence, Springer-Verlag, pp. 1–16.

F. BENHAMOU, D. A. MCALLESTER, AND P. VAN HENTENRYCK
[1994]   CLP(intervals) revisited, in: *Proceedings of the 1994 International Logic Programming Symposium*, M. Bruynooghe, ed., The MIT Press, pp. 124–138.

F. BENHAMOU AND W. OLDER
[1997]   Applying interval arithmetic to real, integer and Boolean constraints, *Journal of Logic Programming*, 32, pp. 1–24.

J. G. CLEARY
[1987]   Logical arithmetic, *Future Computing Systems*, 2, pp. 125–149.

P. CODOGNET AND D. DIAZ
[1996]   A simple and efficient Boolean constraint solver for constraint logic programming, *Journal of Automated Reasoning*, 17, pp. 97–128.

A. COLMERAUER
[1993]   Naive solving of non-linear constraints, in: *Constraint Logic Programming: Selected Research*, F. Benhamou and A. Colmerauer, eds., The MIT Press, pp. 89–112.
[2001]   Solving the multiplication constraint in several approximation spaces, in: *17th International Conference on Logic Programming, (ICLP 2001)*, P. Codognet, ed., vol. 2237 of Lecture Notes in Computer Science, Springer-Verlag, p. 1. The transparencies of the lecture are at `http://www.lim.univ-mrs.fr/~colmer/Transparents/Paphos01/paphosps.zip`.

E. DAVIS
[1987]   Constraint propagation with interval labels, *Artificial Intelligence*, 32, pp. 281–331.

M. DAVIS AND H. PUTNAM
[1960]   A computing procedure for quantification theory, *Journal of the ACM*, 7, pp. 201–215.

T. FRÜHWIRTH
[1995]   Constraint Handling Rules, in: *Constraint Programming: Basics and Trends*, A. Podelski, ed., LNCS 910, Springer-Verlag, pp. 90–107. (Châtillon-sur-Seine Spring School, France, May 1994).

E. HANSEN
[1992]   *Global Optimization Using Interval Analysis*, Marcel Dekker.

W. HARVEY AND P. J. STUCKEY
[2003]   Improving linear constraint propagation by changing constraint representation, *Constraints*, 8, pp. 173–207.

T. J. HICKEY, Q. JU, AND M. H. VAN EMDEN
[2001]   Interval arithmetic: from principles to implementation, *Journal of the ACM*, 48, pp. 1038–1068.

T. J. HICKEY, M. H. VAN EMDEN, AND H. WU
[1998]   A unified framework for interval constraints and interval arithmetic, in: *Proceedings of the Fourth International Conference on Principles and Practice of Constraint Programming (CP'98)*, M. J. Maher and J.-F. Puget, eds., vol. 1520 of Lecture Notes in Computer Science, Springer-Verlag, pp. 250–264.

E. HYVÖNEN
[1992]   Constraint reasoning based on interval arithmetic. The tolerance propagation approach, *Artificial Intelligence*, 58, pp. 71–112.

J. JAFFAR AND M. J. MAHER
[1994]   Constraint logic programming: a survey, *Journal of Logic Programming*, 19/20, pp. 503–581.

J. JAFFAR, M. J. MAHER, P. J. STUCKEY, AND R. H. C. YAP
[1993]   Projecting CLP($\mathcal{R}$) constraints, *New Generation Computing*, 11, pp. 449–469.

O. LHOMME
[1993]   Consistency techniques for numeric CSPs, in: *Proceedings of the International Joint Conference on Artificial Intelligence (IJCAI-93)*, pp. 232–238.

K. MARRIOTT AND P. J. STUCKEY
[1998]   *Programming With Constraints: An Introduction*, The MIT Press.

D. A. McALLESTER
  [1980]   An outlook on truth maintenance. MIT, Artificial Intelligence Laboratory, AI Memo
           No. 551.
  [1990]   Truth maintenance, in: *AAAI-90: Proceedings 8th National Conference on Artificial
           Intelligence*, pp. 1109–1116.

R. E. MOORE
  [1966]   *Interval Analysis*, Prentice-Hall, Englewood Cliffs, NJ.

W. OLDER AND A. VELLINO
  [1993]   Constraint arithmetic on real intervals, in: *Constraint Logic Programming: Selected
           Research*, F. Benhamou and A. Colmerauer, eds., The MIT Press, pp. 175–195.

D. RATZ
  [1996]   *Inclusion Isotone Extended Interval Arithmetic*, tech. rep., University of Karlsruhe.
           Report No. D-76128 Karlsruhe.

H. SIMONIS
  [1989]   Test generation using the Constraint Logic Programming language CHIP, in: *ICLP'89:
           Proceedings 6th International Conference on Logic Programming*, G. Levi and
           M. Martelli, eds., The MIT Press, pp. 101–112.

M. H. VAN EMDEN
  [1999]   The logic programming paradigm in numerical computation, in: *The Logic Program-
           ming Paradigm*, K. R. Apt, V. W. Marek, M. Truszczyński, and D. S. Warren, eds.,
           Springer-Verlag, pp. 257–276.

P. VAN HENTENRYCK
  [1989]   *Constraint Satisfaction in Logic Programming*, The MIT Press.
  [1997]   *Numerica: A Modeling Language for Global Optimization*, The MIT Press.

P. VAN HENTENRYCK, V. SARASWAT, AND Y. DEVILLE
  [1998]   Design, implementation, and evaluation of the constraint language cc(fd), *Journal of
           Logic Programming*, 37, pp. 139–164. Special Issue on Constraint Logic Programming
           (P. J. Stuckey and K. Marriot, Eds.).

L. A. WOLSEY
  [1998]   *Integer Programming*, John Wiley and Sons.

H. ZHANG AND M. STICKEL
  [1996]   An efficient algorithm for unit propagation, in: *Proceedings of the Fourth International
           Symposium on Artificial Intelligence and Mathematics*, Ft. Lauderdale, Florida.

Constraint propagation algorithms

T HE ALGORITHMS THAT achieve local consistency are called constraint propagation algorithms. In the literature, perhaps to confuse newcomers entering the field, several other names have also been used. In fact, we found the following alternative names for these algorithms: consistency, local consistency, local propagation, consistency enforcing, Waltz, filtering and narrowing algorithms. The aim of this chapter is to discuss various constraint propagation algorithms. These algorithms form a crucial ingredient of the generic procedure SOLVE of Figure 3.1 from Section 3.2 that can be used to solve a given CSP.

Sometimes a CSP can already be solved solely by means of a constraint propagation algorithm. Examples are furnished by some of the results proved in Chapter 5, namely the Consistency 2 Theorem 5.48, the Directional Arc Consistency Theorem 5.49, and the Directional Path Consistency

Theorem 5.50. Another example is provided by the crossword puzzle of Example 2.8. We saw at the end of Section 5.2 that the CSP that represents this puzzle can be solved by transforming it to an equivalent arc consistent CSP. So arc consistency turned out to be sufficient to find a solution to this CSP.

When introducing in Chapter 5 several local consistency notions we characterised them by means of proof rules of the proof theoretic framework of Section 4.1. Also in Chapter 6 we defined some incomplete constraint solvers using rules. This makes it possible to enforce the discussed local consistency notions and to implement these incomplete constraint solvers in a simple way, by generating stabilising derivations in the sense of Definition 4.5.

However, in specific situations several possibilities arise. Take for example the CSP of Example 2.8 that deals with the crossword puzzle. To transform it into an arc consistent CSP we should repeatedly use the *ARC CONSISTENCY* rules *1* and *2*. Denote now by $(\underline{i}, j)$ the fact that we apply the *ARC CONSISTENCY 1* rule to the constraint $C_{i,j}$ representing the intersection of the positions i and j and by $(i, \underline{j})$ the fact that we apply the *ARC CONSISTENCY 2* rule to the constraint $C_{i,j}$. Then at the beginning we can remove

- on the account of $(\underline{1}, 2)$: SAILS, SHEET, STEER from domain of x_1,
- on the account of $(\underline{1}, 3)$: LASER, SHEET from domain of x_1,
- on the account of $(1, \underline{2})$: HOSES, LASER from domain of x_2,
- on the account of $(1, \underline{3})$: HOSES, LASER from domain of x_3,

and so on. In fact, since there are twelve constraints, there are twenty four ways to start the derivation. So it is clear that even in this simple example there are many intrinsically different derivations and it is not straightforward to characterise their outcome.

In general, when considering such rules and resulting derivations we are interested in answering the following questions:

- How to schedule the applications of the rules so that the resulting derivations are stabilising?
- How to avoid (at a low cost) irrelevant, i.e., redundant, applications of the rules?
- Is the outcome of the stabilising derivations unique, and if yes, how can it be characterised?

When studying these questions it is preferable to deal with them at an appropriate level of generality so that we can draw conclusions concerning arbitrary rules here considered and not only the *ARC CONSISTENCY* rules. To this end we consider generic iteration algorithms on partial orderings. The aim of these algorithms is to compute a common fixpoint of a given set of functions. These functions correspond to the proof rules and their common fixpoint corresponds to a CSP closed under the applications of these rules. The partial ordering is determined by the considered local consistency notion or by the analysed incomplete constraint solver.

We explain these matters systematically as follows. First, in Section 7.1, we introduce generic iteration algorithms for arbitrary partial orderings and for Cartesian products of partial orderings. Then in Section 7.2 we explain how these algorithms relate to CSPs. Intuitively, each component of the considered Cartesian product ordering corresponds to a specific variable domain or to a specific constraint.

In the remaining part of the chapter we instantiate the algorithms of Section 7.1 to obtain specific constraint propagation algorithms. In Section 7.3 we obtain in this way a straightforward algorithm for node consistency. Then, in Sections 7.4, 7.5 and 7.6 we apply this framework to derive, respectively, algorithms for arc consistency, hyper-arc consistency, and directional arc consistency. These four algorithms modify the domains of the variables.

In the subsequent four sections, 7.7, 7.8, 7.9 and 7.10, we derive in a similar way algorithms for, respectively, path consistency, directional path consistency, k-consistency and relational consistency. These four algorithms modify the constraints.

Finally, in Section 7.11 we discuss how the algorithms of Section 7.1 can be used to implement incomplete constraint solvers, in particular those discussed in Chapter 6.

7.1 Generic iteration algorithms

7.1.1 Iterations

We begin by recalling some elementary notions concerning relations and orderings.

Definition 7.1 We call a binary relation R on a set D

- *reflexive* if $(a, a) \in R$ for all $a \in D$,
- *irreflexive* if $(a, a) \notin R$ for all $a \in D$,
- *antisymmetric* if for all $a, b \in D$ whenever $(a, b) \in R$ and $(b, a) \in R$ then $a = b$,

- *transitive* if for all $a, b, c \in D$ whenever $(a, b) \in R$ and $(b, c) \in R$ then also $(a, c) \in R$.

By a *partial ordering* we mean a pair $(D, \sqsubseteq)$ consisting of a set D and a reflexive, antisymmetric and transitive relation $\sqsubseteq$ on D. Given a partial ordering $(D, \sqsubseteq)$ an element d of D is called the *least* element if $d \sqsubseteq e$ for all $e \in D$.

By a *strict partial ordering* we mean a pair $(D, \sqsubset)$ consisting of a set D and an irreflexive and transitive relation $\sqsubset$ on D. We call a strict partial ordering $(D, \sqsubset)$ *well-founded* if no infinite sequence of elements $d_0, d_1, \ldots$ of D exists such that $d_{i+1} \sqsubset d_i$ for $i \geq 0$. $\qquad\square$

A typical example of a partial ordering is the set $\mathcal{N}$ of natural numbers with the $\leq$ relation. Two other examples of partial orderings will be repeatedly used in this chapter.

Example 7.2

(i) Given a set D denote by $\mathcal{P}(D)$ the set of all subsets of D. It is easy to check that $(\mathcal{P}(D), \supseteq)$ is a partial ordering, where $\supseteq$ is the reversed subset relation.

(ii) Consider the Cartesian product $\mathcal{P}(D_1) \times \cdots \times \mathcal{P}(D_n)$ with the elements ordered by the componentwise reversed subset ordering $\supseteq$. So

$$(X_1, \ldots, X_n) \supseteq (Y_1, \ldots, Y_n) \text{ iff } X_i \supseteq Y_i \text{ for } i \in [1..n].$$

This yields the partial ordering $(\mathcal{P}(D_1) \times \cdots \times \mathcal{P}(D_n), \supseteq)$. $\qquad\square$

If we use the set $\mathcal{N}$ of natural numbers with the $<$ relation instead, we obtain a strict partial ordering. Strict partial orderings will be needed only for the proofs of termination. In what follows we shall study iterations of functions on a partial ordering.

Definition 7.3 Consider a partial ordering $(D, \sqsubseteq)$ with the least element $\perp$ and a finite set of functions $F := \{f_1, \ldots, f_k\}$ on D.

- We say that a sequence $d_0, d_1, d_2 \ldots$ of elements from D *eventually stabilises at d* if for some $j \geq 0$ we have $d_i = d$ for $i \geq j$.
- By an *iteration of F* we mean a sequence $d_0, d_1, d_2 \ldots$ of elements from D defined inductively by

$$d_0 := \perp,$$

$$d_j := f_{n_j}(d_{j-1}),$$

where $j > 0$ and n_j is an element of $[1..k]$. We say then that the function f_{n_j} **is activated at step** j. $\square$

Throughout this chapter we omit brackets when writing repeated applications of functions to an argument. For example, given set of functions $F := \{f_1, f_2, f_3\}$, the following is an iteration of F in which each function f_i is activated at step $i + 3j$, for $j \geq 0$:

$$\bot, \; f_1(\bot), \; f_2 f_1(\bot), \; f_3 f_2 f_1(\bot), \; f_1 f_3 f_2 f_1(\bot), \; f_2 f_1 f_3 f_2 f_1(\bot), \ldots$$

The considered derivations and the constraint propagation algorithms will generate iterations of specific sets of functions. Such iterations correspond to derivations. In turn, iterations that eventually stabilise at a common fixpoint of the considered functions correspond to the stabilising derivations. So, as explained at the beginning of this chapter, we are interested in finding conditions under which these iterations eventually stabilise at a common fixpoint and under which they compute the same outcome. We identify such conditions by focusing on functions that satisfy some properties out of the following list.

Definition 7.4 Consider a partial ordering $(D, \sqsubseteq)$ and functions f and g on D.

- f is called **inflationary** if $x \sqsubseteq f(x)$ for all x.
- f is called **monotonic** if $x \sqsubseteq y$ implies $f(x) \sqsubseteq f(y)$ for all x, y.
- f is called **idempotent** if $ff(x) = f(x)$ for all x.
- We say that f and g **commute** if $fg(x) = gf(x)$ for all x.
- We say that f **semi-commutes with** g (**w.r.t.** $\sqsubseteq$) if $fg(x) \sqsubseteq gf(x)$ for all x.

$\square$

Let us start with the following simple observation that clarifies the role of monotonicity.

Lemma 7.5 (Stabilisation) *Consider a partial ordering $(D, \sqsubseteq)$ with the least element $\bot$ and a finite set F of monotonic functions on D.*

Suppose that an iteration of F eventually stabilises at a common fixpoint d of the functions from F. Then d is the least common fixed point of the functions from F.

Proof Let $d_0, d_1, \ldots$ be the iteration in question. For some $j \geq 0$ we have $d_i = d$ for $i \geq j$.

Take now a common fixpoint e of the functions from F. We prove that $d \sqsubseteq e$. It suffices to prove by induction on i that $d_i \sqsubseteq e$. The claim obviously holds for $i = 0$ since $d_0 = \bot$. Suppose it holds for some $i \geq 0$. We have $d_{i+1} = f_j(d_i)$ for some $j \in [1..k]$.

By the monotonicity of f_j and the induction hypothesis $f_j(d_i) \sqsubseteq f_j(e)$, so $d_{i+1} \sqsubseteq e$ since by assumption $f_j(e) = e$. □

We now establish a result that provides a way to compute the least common fixpoints in case the considered functions commute with each other.

Lemma 7.6 (Commutativity) *Consider a partial ordering $(D, \sqsubseteq)$ with the least element $\bot$. Let $F := \{f_1, \ldots, f_k\}$ be a finite set of functions on D such that*

- *each $f \in F$ is monotonic and idempotent,*
- *all $f \in F$ and $g \in F$ commute.*

Then for each permutation $\pi : [1..k] \to [1..k]$ $f_{\pi(1)} f_{\pi(2)} \cdots f_{\pi(k)}(\bot)$ is the least common fixpoint of the functions from F.

Proof First note that by commutativity

$$f_{\pi(1)} f_{\pi(2)} \cdots f_{\pi(k)}(\bot) = f_1 f_2 \cdots f_k(\bot),$$

so it suffices to establish the result for $f_1 f_2 \cdots f_k(\bot)$. Fix $i \in [1..k]$. On the account of commutativity and of idempotence of f_i we have the following string of equalities:

$$f_i f_1 f_2 \cdots f_k(\bot) = f_1 f_i f_2 \cdots f_k(\bot) = \cdots$$

$$= f_1 f_2 \cdots f_i f_i \cdots f_k(\bot) = f_1 f_2 \cdots f_k(\bot).$$

So $f_1 f_2 \cdots f_k(\bot)$ is a common fixpoint of the functions from F. This means that any iteration of F that starts with $\bot$, $f_k(\bot)$, $f_{k-1} f_k(\bot)$, $\ldots$, $f_1 f_2 \cdots f_k(\bot)$ eventually stabilises at $f_1 f_2 \cdots f_k(\bot)$. By the Stabilisation Lemma 7.5 we get the desired conclusion. □

In case we weaken the assumption of commutativity to semi-commutativity a weaker result holds.

Lemma 7.7 (Semi-commutativity) *Consider a partial ordering $(D, \sqsubseteq)$ with the least element $\bot$. Let $F := f_1, \ldots, f_k$ be a finite sequence of functions on D such that*

- *each f_i is monotonic, inflationary and idempotent,*
- *each f_i semi-commutes with f_j for $i > j$, that is,*

$$f_i f_j(x) \sqsubseteq f_j f_i(x) \text{ for all } x. \tag{7.1}$$

Then $f_1 f_2 \cdots f_k(\perp)$ is the least common fixpoint of the functions from F.

Intuitively, the assumption (7.1) states that given a nested application of two considered functions, if we 'push inside' the function with a larger index, the value increases. For example $f_3 f_1(x) \sqsubseteq f_1 f_3(x)$.

Proof   Fix $i \in [1..k]$. By the assumption (7.1) and the idempotence of f_i we have the following string of inclusions:

$$f_i f_1 f_2 \cdots f_k(\perp) \sqsubseteq f_1 f_i f_2 \cdots f_k(\perp) \sqsubseteq \cdots$$

$$\sqsubseteq f_1 f_2 \cdots f_i f_i \cdots f_k(\perp) \sqsubseteq f_1 f_2 \cdots f_k(\perp).$$

By the inflationarity of f_i we also have

$$f_1 f_2 \cdots f_k(\perp) \sqsubseteq f_i f_1 f_2 \cdots f_k(\perp).$$

So $f_1 f_2 \cdots f_k(\perp)$ is a common fixpoint of the functions from F. As in the proof of the Commutativity Lemma 7.6 this implies by the Stabilisation Lemma 7.5 that $f_1 f_2 \cdots f_k(\perp)$ is the least common fixpoint of the functions from F. □

Finally, in case no information about commutativity or semi-commutativity is available, we can use the following result. Note that the assumption of idempotence is not used here. On the other hand, we restricted our attention to finite partial orderings.

Lemma 7.8 (Least Fixed Point) *Consider a finite partial ordering $(D, \sqsubseteq)$ with the least element $\perp$. Let F be a finite set of functions on D such that*

- *each $f \in F$ is monotonic and inflationary.*

*Call an iteration $d_0, d_1, d_2 \ldots$ of F **regular** if it satisfies the following property:*

> *for all $f \in F$ and $m \geq 0$ if $f(d_m) \neq d_m$,*
> *then f is activated at some step $> m$.*

Then any regular iteration of F eventually stabilises at the least common fixpoint of the functions from F.

Proof   Consider a regular iteration $\chi := d_0, d_1, d_2 \ldots$ of F. By assumption each function in F is inflationary, so $d_j \sqsubseteq d_{j+1}$ for $j \geq 0$. So, since D is finite, χ eventually stabilises at some d_m.

Suppose that d_m is not a common fixpoint of the functions from F. Then for some $f \in F$ we have $f(d_m) \neq d_m$. By the regularity of χ the function f is activated at some step $n > m$, i.e. $d_n = f(d_{n-1})$. But χ eventually stabilises at d_m, so $d_m = d_{n-1} = d_n$ and hence $f(d_m) = d_m$, which is a contradiction. So d_m is a common fixpoint of the functions from F. By the Stabilisation Lemma 7.5 d_m is in fact the least common fixpoint. $\square$

7.1.2 Algorithms for arbitrary partial orderings

We fix now a partial ordering $(D, \sqsubseteq)$ with the least element $\bot$ and a set of functions $F := \{f_1, \ldots, f_k\}$ on D. We are interested in computing the least common fixpoint of the functions from F using the results established in the previous section. We begin with the following completely straightforward algorithm in which each function in F is applied exactly once, in an arbitrary order.

DIRECT ITERATION algorithm

```
d := ⊥;
G := F;
WHILE G ≠ ∅ DO
   choose g ∈ G;
   d := g(d);
   G := G − {g}
END
```

The following immediate consequence of the Commutativity Lemma 7.6 holds.

Corollary 7.9 (DIRECT ITERATION) *Suppose that $(D, \sqsubseteq)$ is a partial ordering with the least element $\bot$. Let F be a finite set of monotonic and idempotent functions on D that commute with each other. Then the DIRECT ITERATION algorithm terminates and computes in d the least common fixpoint of the functions from F.* $\square$

Next, we consider the following algorithm in which, again, each function in $F := \{f_1, \ldots, f_k\}$ is applied exactly once, though this time in a specific order.

SIMPLE ITERATION algorithm

```
d := ⊥;
FOR i := k TO 1 BY −1 DO
   d := f_i(d)
END
```

Then the following result is an immediate consequence of the Semi-Commutativity Lemma 7.7.

Corollary 7.10 (SIMPLE ITERATION) *Suppose that* $(D, \sqsubseteq)$ *is a partial ordering with the least element* $\perp$. *Let* $F := f_1, \ldots, f_k$ *be a finite sequence of monotonic, inflationary and idempotent functions on* D *such that* (7.1) *holds. Then the* SIMPLE ITERATION *algorithm terminates and computes in* d *the least common fixpoint of the functions from* F. □

Finally, we consider the situation in absence of the commutativity and semi-commutativity assumptions. The algorithm we now present will be a basis for developing most of the constraint propagation algorithms.

GENERIC ITERATION algorithm

```
d := ⊥;
G := F;
WHILE G ≠ ∅ DO
   choose g ∈ G;
   IF d ≠ g(d) THEN
      G := G ∪ update(G, g, d);
      d := g(d)
   ELSE
      G := G − {g}
   END
END
```

where for all G, g, d

A $\{f \in F - G \mid f(d) = d \wedge fg(d) \neq g(d)\} \subseteq update(G, g, d)$.

Assumption **A** states that $update(G, g, d)$ contains at least all the functions from $F - G$ for which d is a fixpoint but $g(d)$ is not. So at each loop iteration if $d \neq g(d)$, such functions are added to the set G. Otherwise the function g is removed from G.

An obvious example of an *update* function that satisfies assumption **A** is

$$update(G, g, d) := \{f \in F - G \mid f(d) = d \wedge fg(d) \neq g(d)\}.$$

However, this choice of *update* is expensive to compute because for each function f in $F - G$ we would have to compute the values $fg(d)$ and $f(d)$. In practice, we are interested in some approximations from above of this *update* function that are easy to compute. We shall discuss this matter in the next section.

The following result clarifies the status of this algorithm.

Theorem 7.11 (GENERIC ITERATION) *Suppose that* $(D, \sqsubseteq)$ *is a finite partial ordering with the least element* $\perp$. *Let* F *be a finite set of monotonic and inflationary functions on* D. *Then every execution of the* GENERIC IT-ERATION *algorithm terminates and computes in* d *the least common fixpoint of the functions from* F.

Proof   To prove termination we consider the lexicographic ordering of the strict partial orderings $(D, \sqsupset)$ and $(\mathcal{N}, <)$, defined on the elements of $D \times \mathcal{N}$ by

$$(d_1, n_1) <_{lex} (d_2, n_2) \text{ iff } d_1 \sqsupset d_2 \text{ or } (d_1 = d_2 \text{ and } n_1 < n_2).$$

We use here the inverse ordering $\sqsupset$ defined by: $d_1 \sqsupset d_2$ iff $d_2 \sqsubseteq d_1$ and $d_2 \neq d_1$. By assumption $(D, \sqsubseteq)$ is finite, so the $(D \times \mathcal{N}, <_{lex})$ ordering is well-founded, i.e., no infinite $<_{lex}$-descending sequence of pairs from $D \times \mathcal{N}$ exists.

Given a finite set G we denote by *card* G the number of its elements. By assumption all functions in F are inflationary, so with each WHILE loop iteration of the algorithm the pair

$$(d, card\, G)$$

strictly decreases in this ordering $<_{lex}$. Indeed, we have either $g(d) \sqsupset d$ or $g(d) = d$ and in the latter case the cardinality of the set G decreases, since g is then removed from it. The termination is now the consequence of the well-foundedness of $<_{lex}$.

To prove the second claim consider the predicate I defined by:

$$I := \forall f \in F - G \, f(d) = d.$$

Note that I is established by the assignment $G := F$. Moreover, it is easy to check that by virtue of the assumption **A** I is preserved by each WHILE loop iteration. Thus I is an invariant of the WHILE loop of the algorithm. Hence upon its termination

$$(G = \emptyset) \wedge I$$

holds, that is

$$\forall f \in F \; f(d) = d.$$

By the Stabilisation Lemma 7.5 d is the least common fixpoint of the functions from F.

□

In Exercise 7.1 we clarify the relation between the GENERIC ITERATION algorithm and the Least Fixpoint Lemma 7.8. In some sense, this algorithm can be viewed as a realisation of this lemma.

7.1.3 Algorithms for Cartesian products of partial orderings

In the applications we study the iterations are carried out on a partial ordering that is a Cartesian product of the partial orderings. The precise definition is as follows.

Definition 7.12 Consider partial orderings $(D_i, \sqsubseteq_i)$, for $i \in [1..n]$. Put $D := D_1 \times \cdots \times D_n$ and define for two elements $(d_1, \ldots, d_n)$ and $(e_1, \ldots, e_n)$

$$(d_1, \ldots, d_n) \sqsubseteq (e_1, \ldots, e_n) \text{ iff } d_i \sqsubseteq_i e_i \text{ for } i \in [1..n].$$

Then we call $(D, \sqsubseteq)$ the **Cartesian product of the partial orderings** $(D_1, \sqsubseteq_1), \ldots, (D_n, \sqsubseteq_n)$.

□

We fix now till the end of this section a partial ordering $(D, \sqsubseteq)$ that is the Cartesian product of some partial orderings $(D_i, \sqsubseteq_i)$, for $i \in [1..n]$, each with the least element $\perp_i$. So $D = D_1 \times \cdots \times D_n$ and $(\perp_1, \ldots, \perp_n)$ is the least element of D.

Further, we assume that each function from F depends from and affects only certain components of D. To be more precise we introduce a simple notation and terminology.

Definition 7.13 Consider a sequence of partial orderings $(D_1, \sqsubseteq_1), \ldots, (D_n, \sqsubseteq_n)$.

- By a **scheme** (on n) we mean a growing sequence of different elements from $[1..n]$.

- Given a scheme $s := i_1, \ldots, i_l$ on n we denote by $(D_s, \sqsubseteq_s)$ the Cartesian product of the partial orderings $(D_{i_1}, \sqsubseteq_{i_1}), \ldots, (D_{i_l}, \sqsubseteq_{i_l})$.
- Given a function f on D_s we say that f is **with scheme** s and say that f **depends on** i if i is an element of s.
- Given an n-tuple $d := d_1, \ldots, d_n$ from D and a scheme $s := i_1, \ldots, i_l$ on n we denote by $d[s]$ the tuple $d_{i_1}, \ldots, d_{i_l}$. In particular, for $j \in [1..n]$ $d[j]$ is the j-th element of d. □

Consider now a function f with scheme s. We extend it canonically to a function f^+ from D to D by putting for $d \in D$

$$f^+(d) := e,$$

where $e[s] = f(d[s])$ and $e[n-s] = d[n-s]$, and where $n-s$ is the scheme obtained by removing from $1, \ldots, n$ the elements of s. We call f^+ the **canonic extension** of f to the domain D.

So $f^+(d_1, \ldots, d_n) = (e_1, \ldots, e_n)$ implies $d_i = e_i$ for any i not in the scheme s of f. Informally, we can summarise it by saying that f^+ does not change the components on which it does not depend. This is what we meant above by stating that each considered function affects only certain components of D.

Let us reformulate now the algorithms of the previous section for the case of the functions with schemes. First, we need the following modification of our definitions.

Definition 7.14 Consider a sequence of partial orderings $(D_1, \sqsubseteq_1), \ldots, (D_n, \sqsubseteq_n)$ and their Cartesian product $(D, \sqsubseteq)$. Take two functions with schemes, f and g.

- We say that f and g **commute** if f^+ and g^+ commute, that is if

$$f^+ g^+(d) = g^+ f^+(d)$$

for all $d \in D$.
- We say that f **semi-commutes with** g (**w.r.t.** $\sqsubseteq$) if f^+ semi-commutes with g^+ w.r.t. $\sqsubseteq$, that is if

$$f^+ g^+(d) \sqsubseteq g^+ f^+(d)$$

for all $d \in D$. □

Consider now the Cartesian product $(D, \sqsubseteq)$ of the partial orderings and a finite set F_0 of functions with schemes. So F_0 uniquely determines the set of functions $F := \{f^+ \mid f \in F_0\}$ on D.

To start with we have the following counterpart of the DIRECT ITERATION algorithm.

DIRECT ITERATION FOR COMPOUND DOMAINS algorithm (DICD)

$d := (\perp_1, \ldots, \perp_n);$
$G := F_0;$
WHILE $G \neq \emptyset$ DO
     choose $g \in G;$
     $d[s] := g(d[s])$, where s is the scheme of $g;$
     $G := G - \{g\}$
END

The following counterpart of the DIRECT ITERATION Corollary 7.9 then holds.

Corollary 7.15 (DICD) *Suppose that* $(D, \sqsubseteq)$ *is a partial ordering that is a Cartesian product of n partial orderings, each with the least element $\perp_i$ with $i \in [1..n]$. Let F_0 be a finite set of functions with schemes.*

Suppose that all functions in F_0 are monotonic, idempotent and commute with each other. Then the DICD algorithm terminates and computes in d the least common fixpoint of the functions from $F := \{f^+ \mid f \in F_0\}$. $\square$

Next, we have the following counterpart of the SIMPLE ITERATION algorithm.

SIMPLE ITERATION FOR COMPOUND DOMAINS algorithm (SICD)

$d := (\perp_1, \ldots, \perp_n);$
FOR $i := k$ TO 1 BY -1 DO
     $d[s_i] := f_i(d[s_i])$, where s_i is the scheme of f_i
END

The following counterpart of the SIMPLE ITERATION Corollary 7.10 clarifies its status.

Corollary 7.16 (SICD) *Suppose that* $(D, \sqsubseteq)$ *is a partial ordering that is a Cartesian product of n partial orderings, each with the least element $\perp_i$ with $i \in [1..n]$. Let $F_0 := f_1, \ldots, f_k$ be a finite set of functions with schemes.*

Suppose that all functions in F_0 are monotonic, inflationary and idempotent such that each f_i semi-commutes with f_j for $i > j$, that is,

$$f_i^+ f_j^+(d) \sqsubseteq f_j^+ f_i^+(d) \text{ for all } d.$$

Then the SICD *algorithm terminates and computes in d the least common fixpoint of the functions from* $F := \{f^+ \mid f \in F_0\}$. □

Finally, let us consider the GENERIC ITERATION algorithm. When all considered functions are of the form f^+ we can use a simple definition of the *update* function justified by the following observation.

Note 7.17 (Update) *Suppose that each function in F is of the form f^+. Then the following function update satisfies the assumption* **A***:*

$$update(G, g^+, d) := \{f^+ \in F \mid f \text{ depends on an } i \text{ such that } d[i] \neq g^+(d)[i]\}.$$

Proof Suppose that $f^+(d) = d$ and $f^+(e) \neq e$. Then $f(d[s]) = d[s]$ and $f(e[s]) \neq e[s]$, where s is the scheme of f. So $d[s] \neq e[s]$, that is, d differs from e on a component i that is in the scheme s of f. In other words, f depends on i such that $d[i] \neq e[i]$.

Take now $f^+ \in F - G$ such that $f^+(d) = d$ and $f^+(g^+(d)) \neq g^+(d)$. By the above f depends on some i such that $d[i] \neq g^+(d)[i]$, i.e., $f^+ \in update(G, g^+, d)$. So we proved the assumption **A**. □

This, together with the GENERIC ITERATION algorithm, yields the following algorithm in which we introduced a variable d' to hold the value of $g^+(d)$, and used the above definition of *update*.

GENERIC ITERATION FOR COMPOUND DOMAINS algorithm (CD)

$d := (\perp_1, \ldots, \perp_n)$;
$d' := d$;
$G := F_0$;
WHILE $G \neq \emptyset$ DO
   choose $g \in G$;
   $d'[s] := g(d[s])$, where s is the scheme of g;
   IF $d'[s] \neq d[s]$ THEN
      $G := G \cup \{f \in F_0 \mid f \text{ depends on an } i \text{ in } s \text{ such that } d[i] \neq d'[i]\}$;
      $d[s] := d'[s]$
   ELSE
      $G := G - \{g\}$
   END
END

The following corollary to the GENERIC ITERATION Theorem 7.11 and the Update Note 7.17 summarises the correctness of this algorithm.

Corollary 7.18 (CD) *Suppose that* $(D, \sqsubseteq)$ *is a finite partial ordering that is a Cartesian product of n partial orderings, each with the least element $\perp_i$ with $i \in [1..n]$. Let F_0 be a finite set of functions with schemes.*

Suppose that all functions in F_0 are monotonic and inflationary. Then every execution of the CD algorithm terminates and computes in d the least common fixpoint of the functions from $F := \{f^+ \mid f \in F_0\}$.   □

7.2 From partial orderings to CSPs

Recall that our aim is to derive various constraint propagation algorithms. To be able to apply the results of the previous section we need to relate various abstract notions that we used there to constraint satisfaction problems. The framework of the previous section involved:

- Partial orderings with the least elements;

    These will be determined by the original CSP and the studied local consistency notion. Given a CSP $\langle C_1, \ldots, C_k \; ; \; x_1 \in D_1, \ldots, x_n \in D_n \rangle$ shall use here two partial orderings.

    The first one will be the already mentioned in Example 7.2 Cartesian product of the partial orderings $(\mathcal{P}(D_i), \supseteq)$, where $i \in [1..n]$. Recall that for a set D, $\mathcal{P}(D)$ denotes the set of all subsets of D. The second one will be the Cartesian product of the partial orderings $(\mathcal{P}(C_i), \supseteq)$, where $i \in [1..k]$. So in both cases we use the componentwise ordering $\supseteq$.

    To deal with the node consistency, arc consistency, hyper-arc consistency and directional arc consistency notions we shall use the first ordering, and to deal with path consistency, directional path consistency, k-consistency and relational consistency notions we shall use the second ordering.

- Monotonic and inflationary functions with schemes;

    These will correspond to the domain reduction rules and specific transformation rules that we used in Chapter 5 to characterise the considered local consistency notions. Each scheme will correspond to the variables used in the first partial ordering or to the constraints used in second partial ordering.

- Common fixpoints;

    These will correspond to the CSPs that satisfy the considered notion of local consistency.

So the considered functions with schemes will be now used in the presence of the componentwise ordering $\supseteq$. The following straightforward observation will then be useful.

Note 7.19 *Consider a function f on a Cartesian product $\mathcal{P}(E_1) \times \cdots \times$ $\mathcal{P}(E_m)$. Given two sequences $\mathbf{X} := (X_1, \ldots, X_m)$ and $\mathbf{Y} := (Y_1, \ldots, Y_m)$ from $\mathcal{P}(E_1) \times \cdots \times \mathcal{P}(E_m)$ we write $\mathbf{X} \subseteq \mathbf{Y}$ to denote the fact that $X_i \subseteq Y_i$ for all $i \in [1..m]$.*

- *f is inflationary w.r.t. the componentwise ordering $\supseteq$ if for all $\mathbf{X} \in \mathcal{P}(E_1) \times \cdots \times \mathcal{P}(E_m)$ we have $f(\mathbf{X}) \subseteq \mathbf{X}$.*
- *f is monotonic w.r.t. the componentwise ordering $\supseteq$ if $\mathbf{X} \subseteq \mathbf{Y}$ implies $f(\mathbf{X}) \subseteq f(\mathbf{Y})$ for all $\mathbf{X}, \mathbf{Y} \in \mathcal{P}(E_1) \times \cdots \times \mathcal{P}(E_m)$.* $\square$

In other words, f is monotonic w.r.t. $\supseteq$ iff it is monotonic w.r.t. $\subseteq$. This reversal of the set inclusion of course does not hold for the inflationarity notion.

7.3 A node consistency algorithm

We now begin the presentation of the specific constraint propagation algorithms. In this section we consider the node consistency notion. Fix a CSP $\mathcal{P}$ with the sequence $D_1, \ldots, D_n$ of the domains. We consider the Cartesian product of the partial orderings $(\mathcal{P}(D_i), \supseteq)$, where $i \in [1..n]$. The elements of this compound ordering are thus sequences $X_1, \ldots, X_n$ of respective subsets of the domains $D_1, \ldots, D_n$ ordered componentwise by the reversed subset ordering $\supseteq$. The sequence $D_1, \ldots, D_n$ is the least element in this ordering.

Next, recall the following domain reduction rule that we used in Section 5.1 to characterise the node consistency notion:

$$\text{NODE CONSISTENCY}$$
$$\frac{\langle C \; ; \; x \in D \rangle}{\langle C' \; ; \; x \in C \cap D \rangle}$$

where C is a unary constraint on x.

We explain how it can be interpreted as a function on the Cartesian product $\mathcal{P}(D_1) \times \cdots \times \mathcal{P}(D_n)$. This is quite straightforward since this rule can be viewed as a function that maps the old domain to the new domain. Indeed, given a unary constraint C on the variable x with the domain D the NODE CONSISTENCY rule can be viewed as the following function π_0 on $\mathcal{P}(D)$:

$$\pi_0(X) := X \cap C.$$

So π_0^+ is a function on $\mathcal{P}(D_1) \times \cdots \times \mathcal{P}(D_n)$.

This brings us to the following characterisation of the notion of node consistency in terms of fixpoints. The second part of this lemma will allow us to employ the DICD algorithm discussed in Section 7.1.

Lemma 7.20 (Node Consistency)

(i) *A CSP* $\langle \mathcal{C} \; ; \; x_1 \in D_1, \ldots, x_n \in D_n \rangle$ *that does not contain the false constraint* $\perp$ *is node consistent iff* $(D_1, \ldots, D_n)$ *is a common fixpoint of all functions* π_0^+ *associated with the unary constraints from* $\mathcal{C}$.

(ii) *All functions* π_0 *associated with a unary constraint* C *are*

- *monotonic w.r.t. the componentwise ordering* $\supseteq$,
- *idempotent,*
- *commute with each other.*

Proof   (i) is a direct consequence of the Node Consistency Note 5.3. The proof of (ii) is left as Exercise 7.4.   □

Let us instantiate now the DICD algorithm with the set of functions

$$F_0 := \{ f \mid f \text{ is the } \pi_0 \text{ function associated with a unary constraint of } \mathcal{P} \}$$

and each $\perp_i$ equal to D_i.

Call the resulting algorithm the NODE algorithm. The following result summarises its properties.

Theorem 7.21 (NODE Algorithm) *Consider a CSP* $\mathcal{P} := \langle \mathcal{C} \; ; \; x_1 \in D_1, \ldots, x_n \in D_n \rangle$ *that does not contain the false constraint* $\perp$.

The NODE *algorithm always terminates. Let* $\mathcal{P}'$ *be the CSP determined by* $\mathcal{P}$ *and the sequence of the domains computed in d. Then*

(i) $\mathcal{P}'$ *is node consistent,*

(ii) $\mathcal{P}'$ *is equivalent to* $\mathcal{P}$.

Proof   The termination and (i) are immediate consequences of the DICD Corollary 7.15 and of the Node Consistency Lemma 7.20.

To prove (ii) note that the final CSP $\mathcal{P}'$ can be equally obtained by means of repeated applications of the *NODE CONSISTENCY* rule. This rule is equivalence preserving so the claim follows by the Equivalence Lemma 4.2.
                                                                                 □

Item (i) corresponds to the statement in DICD Corollary 7.15 that the final value computed by the algorithm is a fixpoint of the considered functions. The fact that this value is actually the least fixpoint of the considered functions yields the following stronger conclusion. Consider all node consistent CSPs that are of the form $\langle \mathcal{C}' \; ; \; x_1 \in D_1', \ldots, x_n \in D_n' \rangle$ where $D_i' \subseteq D_i$ for $i \in [1..n]$ and the constraints in $\mathcal{C}'$ are the restrictions of the constraints in $\mathcal{C}$ to the domains $D_1', \ldots, D_n'$. Then among these CSPs $\mathcal{P}'$ has the largest domains. Analogous statements hold for the other constraint propagation algorithms discussed in this chapter.

As a final step we reformulate the NODE algorithm so that it deals with the considered CSP directly. We do this by representing the effect of the applications of the functions π_0 on the corresponding domains as assignments. This yields the following representation of this algorithm.

NODE algorithm

$S_0 := \{C \mid C \text{ is a unary constraint from } \mathcal{C}\};$
$S := S_0;$
WHILE $S \neq \emptyset$ DO
    choose $C \in S$; suppose C is on x_i;
    $D_i := C \cap D_i;$ % apply the function π_0 associated with C
    $S := S - \{C\}$
END

7.4 An arc consistency algorithm

In this section we provide an analogous account for the arc consistency notion, though the resulting algorithm will be an instance of a different generic algorithm. Again, fix a CSP $\mathcal{P}$ with the sequence $D_1, \ldots, D_n$ of the domains and consider the Cartesian product of the partial orderings $(\mathcal{P}(D_i), \supseteq)$, where $i \in [1..n]$. As before, the sequence $D_1, \ldots, D_n$ is the least element in this ordering.

Next, recall the following two domain reduction rules that we used in Section 5.2 to characterise the arc consistency notion, where C is a binary constraint on x, y:

ARC CONSISTENCY 1

$$\frac{\langle C \ ; \ x \in D_x, y \in D_y \rangle}{\langle C \ ; \ x \in D'_x, y \in D_y \rangle}$$

where $D'_x := \{a \in D_x \mid \exists b \in D_y \ (a, b) \in C\}$,

ARC CONSISTENCY 2

$$\frac{\langle C \ ; \ x \in D_x, y \in D_y \rangle}{\langle C \ ; \ x \in D_x, y \in D'_y \rangle}$$

where $D'_y := \{b \in D_y \mid \exists a \in D_x \ (a, b) \in C\}$.

We explain how they can be interpreted as functions on the Cartesian product $\mathcal{P}(D_1) \times \cdots \times \mathcal{P}(D_n)$. Given a binary constraint C on the variables x and y with the respective domains D_x and D_y, the *ARC CONSISTENCY rule 1* can be viewed as the following function π_1 on $\mathcal{P}(D_x) \times \mathcal{P}(D_y)$:

$$\pi_1(X, Y) := (X', Y),$$

where $X' := \{a \in X \mid \exists b \in Y \ (a, b) \in C\}$, and the *ARC CONSISTENCY rule 2* as the following function π_2 on $\mathcal{P}(D_x) \times \mathcal{P}(D_y)$:

$$\pi_2(X, Y) := (X, Y'),$$

where $Y' := \{b \in Y \mid \exists a \in X \ (a, b) \in C\}$.

Both π_1^+ and π_2^+ are functions on $\mathcal{P}(D_1) \times \cdots \times \mathcal{P}(D_n)$. This brings us to the following characterisation of the notion of arc consistency in terms of fixpoints.

Lemma 7.22 (Arc Consistency)
    (i) *A CSP $\langle \mathcal{C} \ ; \ x_1 \in D_1, \ldots, x_n \in D_n \rangle$ is arc consistent iff $(D_1, \ldots, D_n)$ is a common fixpoint of all functions π_1^+ and π_2^+ associated with the binary constraints from $\mathcal{C}$.*
    (ii) *Each projection function π_i associated with a binary constraint C is*
        • *inflationary w.r.t. the componentwise ordering $\supseteq$,*
        • *monotonic w.r.t. the componentwise ordering $\supseteq$.*

Proof   (i) is a direct consequence of the Arc Consistency Note 5.6. (ii) follows from Exercise 7.3.   □

In general, the π_i functions associated with different binary constraints do not commute or semi-commute, see Exercise 7.9. So we cannot employ here the DICD or the SICD algorithms of Section 7.1. However, we can still use the CD algorithm. The second part of the above lemma will then be of use. Let us instantiate now the CD algorithm with the set of functions

$F_0 := \{f \mid f \text{ is } \pi_1 \text{ or } \pi_2 \text{ function associated with a binary constraint of } \mathcal{P}\}$

and each $\perp_i$ equal to D_i.

Call the resulting algorithm the ARC algorithm. The following result summarises its properties. Here and elsewhere we call a CSP **finite** if all its domains (and therefore all its constraints) are finite.

Theorem 7.23 (ARC Algorithm) *Consider a finite CSP $\mathcal{P} := \langle \mathcal{C} \ ; \ x_1 \in D_1, \ldots, x_n \in D_n \rangle$.*

The ARC algorithm always terminates. Let $\mathcal{P}'$ be the CSP determined by $\mathcal{P}$ and the sequence of the domains computed in d. Then *(i)* $\mathcal{P}'$ *is arc consistent,*

(ii) $\mathcal{P}'$ *is equivalent to* $\mathcal{P}$.

Proof The termination and *(i)* are immediate consequences of the CD Corollary 7.18 and of the Arc Consistency Lemma 7.22.

To prove *(ii)* note that the final CSP $\mathcal{P}'$ can be equally obtained by means of repeated applications of the *ARC CONSISTENCY* rules *1* and *2*. Each of these rules is equivalence preserving so the claim follows by the Equivalence Lemma 4.2. $\square$

Let us reformulate now the ARC algorithm so that it deals with the considered CSP directly. Recall from Section 5.5 that for a binary relation R, $R^T = \{(b, a) \mid (a, b) \in R\}$. First, we represent the set of functions F_0 equivalently as the set of the π_1 functions of the constraints or relations from the set

$$S_0 := \{C \mid C \text{ is a binary constraint from } \mathcal{C}\}$$
$$\cup \ \{C^T \mid C \text{ is a binary constraint from } \mathcal{C}\}.$$

Consider now the corresponding instance of the CD algorithm. We represent the effect of the applications of the functions π_1 on the corresponding domains as assignments. This yields the following representation of the ARC algorithm.

ARC algorithm

$$S_0 := \{C \mid C \text{ is a binary constraint from } \mathcal{C}\}$$
$$\cup \ \{C^T \mid C \text{ is a binary constraint from } \mathcal{C}\};$$
$$S := S_0;$$
WHILE $S \neq \emptyset$ DO
    choose $C \in S$; suppose C is on x_i, x_j;
    $D_i := \{a \in D_i \mid \exists b \in D_j \ (a, b) \in C\}$; % apply π_1 associated with C
    IF D_i changed THEN
        $S := S \cup \{C' \in S_0 \mid C' \text{ is on } y, z \text{ where } y \text{ is } x_i \text{ or } z \text{ is } x_i\}$
    ELSE
        $S := S - \{C\}$
    END
  END

7.5 A hyper-arc consistency algorithm

A similar analysis allows us to derive a hyper-arc consistency algorithm. Recall that this notion was characterised in Section 5.3 using the the following proof rule parametrised by a constraint C on the variables $x_1, \ldots, x_k$ and $i \in [1..k]$:

HYPER-ARC CONSISTENCY

$$\frac{\langle C \; ; \; x_1 \in D_1, \ldots, x_k \in D_k \rangle}{\langle C \; ; \; x_1 \in D_1, \ldots, x_{i-1} \in D_{i-1}, x_i \in D_i', x_{i+1} \in D_{i+1}, \ldots, x_k \in D_k \rangle}$$

where

$$D_i' := \{a \in D_i \mid \exists d \in C \; a = d[x_i]\}.$$

Also this rule can also be viewed as a function. Indeed, given a constraint C on the variables $x_1, \ldots, x_k$ with respective domains $D_1, \ldots, D_k$, we can view for each $i \in [1..k]$ the *HYPER-ARC CONSISTENCY* rule as the function π_i on $\mathcal{P}(D_1) \times \cdots \times \mathcal{P}(D_k)$ defined by

$$\pi_i(X_1, \ldots, X_k) := (X_1, \ldots, X_{i-1}, X_i', X_{i+1}, \ldots, X_k)$$

where

$$X_i' = \{a \in X_i \mid \exists d \in C \cap (X_1 \times \cdots \times X_k) \, (a = d[x_i])\}.$$

In other words,

$$X_i' = \{d[x_i] \mid d \in X_1 \times \cdots \times X_k \text{ and } d \in C\}.$$

Each such function π_i is associated with a specific constraint C.

Note that when C is a binary constraint, the π_1 and π_2 functions coincide with the π_1 and π_2 functions introduced in the previous section. Just as in the case of arc consistency we can characterise the notion of hyper-arc consistency in terms of fixpoints of the π_i functions.

Lemma 7.24 (Hyper-arc Consistency)
   (i) *A CSP* $\langle C \; ; \; x_1 \in D_1, \ldots, x_n \in D_n \rangle$ *is hyper-arc consistent iff* $(D_1, \ldots, D_n)$ *is a common fixpoint of all functions* π_i^+ *associated with the constraints from* C.
   (ii) *Each projection function* π_i *associated with a constraint* C *is*

   - *inflationary w.r.t. the componentwise ordering* $\supseteq$,
   - *monotonic w.r.t. the componentwise ordering* $\supseteq$.

Proof   (i) is a direct consequence of the Hyper-arc Consistency Note 5.9. (ii) follows directly from Exercise 7.3. $\square$

Fix now a CSP $\mathcal{P}$. By instantiating the CD algorithm with

$$F_0 := \{f \mid f \text{ is a } \pi_i \text{ function associated with a constraint of } \mathcal{P}\}$$

and with each $\perp_i$ equal to D_i we get the HYPER-ARC algorithm that enjoys the same properties as the ARC algorithm and that we list in the following theorem. The proof is analogous to that of the ARC Algorithm Theorem 7.23 and is omitted.

Theorem 7.25 (HYPER-ARC Algorithm) *Consider a finite CSP $\mathcal{P} :=$* $\langle \mathcal{C} \; ; \; x_1 \in D_1, \ldots, x_n \in D_n \rangle.$

The HYPER-ARC algorithm always terminates. Let $\mathcal{P}'$ be the CSP determined by $\mathcal{P}$ and the sequence of the domains computed in d. Then

 (i) *$\mathcal{P}'$ is hyper-arc consistent,*

 (ii) *$\mathcal{P}'$ is equivalent to $\mathcal{P}$.*

□

7.6 A directional arc consistency algorithm

Let us return now to the notion of directional arc consistency defined in Section 5.4. To derive an algorithm that achieves this local consistency notion we characterise it first in terms of fixpoints of appropriate functions. To this end, given a $\mathcal{P}$ and a linear ordering $\prec$ on its variables, as in Section 5.4, we rather reason in terms of the related CSP $\mathcal{P}_\prec$. The following is a counterpart of the Arc Consistency Lemma 7.22(i).

Lemma 7.26 (Directional Arc Consistency) *Consider a CSP $\mathcal{P}$ with a linear ordering $\prec$ on its variables. Let $\mathcal{P}_\prec := \langle \mathcal{C} \; ; \; x_1 \in D_1, \ldots, x_n \in D_n \rangle.$ Then*

 (i) *$\mathcal{P}$ is directionally arc consistent w.r.t. $\prec$ iff $(D_1, \ldots, D_n)$ is a common fixpoint of the functions π_1^+ associated with the binary constraints from $\mathcal{P}_\prec$.*

 (ii) *Each projection function π_i associated with a binary constraint is idempotent.*

 (iii) *Consider two binary constraints of $\mathcal{P}_\prec$, C_1 on x, z and C_2 on v, y, where $y \preceq z$. Then the π_1 function of C_1 semi-commutes with the π_1 function of C_2 w.r.t. the componentwise ordering $\supseteq$, that is, for all $(X_1, \ldots, X_n) \in \mathcal{P}(D_1) \times \cdots \times \mathcal{P}(D_n)$*

$$f_{x,z}^+ f_{v,y}^+ (X_1, \ldots, X_n) \supseteq f_{v,y}^+ f_{x,z}^+ (X_1, \ldots, X_n),$$

where we denoted the π_1 function of C_1 by $f_{x,z}$ and the π_1 function of C_2 by $f_{v,y}$.

Proof   The proof is left as Exercise 7.5. □

Consider now a CSP $\mathcal{P}$ with a linear ordering $\prec$ on its variables and the corresponding CSP $\mathcal{P}_\prec$. To be able to apply the above lemma we order the π_1 functions of the binary constraints of $\mathcal{P}_\prec$ in an appropriate way. Assume for simplicity that the original CSP $\mathcal{P}$ is standardised, that is, that there exists precisely one constraint on each subsequence x, y of its variables. The same holds then for $\mathcal{P}_\prec$. Suppose that $\mathcal{P}_\prec := \langle \mathcal{C} \; ; \; x_1 \in D_1, \ldots, x_n \in D_n \rangle$. So $x_1 \prec x_2 \prec \cdots \prec x_n$. Denote the unique constraint of $\mathcal{P}_\prec$ on x_i, x_j by $C_{i,j}$.

Consider now the sequence of the π_1 functions corresponding to the following ordering of the binary constraints of $\mathcal{P}_\prec$:

$C_{1,n}, \quad C_{2,n}, \quad \ldots, C_{n-2,n}, C_{n-1,n},$

$C_{1,n-1}, C_{2,n-1}, \ldots, C_{n-2,n-1},$

$\ldots$

$C_{1,2}.$

So in this ordering the constraints on some y and x_n are listed first, followed by the constraints on some y and x_{n-1}, etc, and ending with the constraint $C_{1,2}$.

Then, given two such π_1 functions, f and g, if f precedes g in this ordering, then f is associated with a constraint $C_{i,j}$ and g is associated with a constraint $C_{k,l}$ where $l \leq j$, i.e. $x_l \preceq x_j$. So by virtue of the Directional Arc Consistency Lemma 7.26(iii) f semi-commutes with g w.r.t. the componentwise ordering $\supseteq$.

We now instantiate the SICD algorithm by the above-defined sequence of the π_1 functions and each $\perp_i$ equal to the domain D_i of the variable x_i. We obtain then the following algorithm, where we reformulated the applications of the functions π_1 as assignments on the corresponding variable domains.

DIRECTIONAL ARC CONSISTENCY algorithm (DARC)

```
FOR j := n TO 2 BY −1 DO
  FOR i := 1 TO j − 1 DO
    D_i := {a ∈ D_i | ∃ b ∈ D_j (a,b) ∈ C_{i,j}}  % apply π_1 associated with C_{i,j}
  END
END
```

This algorithm enjoys the following properties.

Theorem 7.27 (DARC Algorithm) *Consider a standardised CSP $\mathcal{P}$ with a linear ordering $\prec$ on its variables. Let $\mathcal{P}_\prec := \langle \mathcal{C} \; ; \; x_1 \in D_1, \ldots, x_n \in D_n \rangle$.*

The DARC algorithm always terminates. Let $\mathcal{P}'$ be the CSP determined by $\mathcal{P}_\prec$ and the sequence of the computed domains. Then

(i) $\mathcal{P}'$ is directionally arc consistent w.r.t. $\prec$,

(ii) $\mathcal{P}'$ is equivalent to $\mathcal{P}_{\prec}$.

Proof   The termination and (i) are immediate consequences of the SICD Corollary 7.16 for the SICD algorithm and of the Directional Arc Consistency Lemma 7.26.

The proof of (ii) is analogous to that of the ARC Algorithm Theorem 7.23(ii) and is omitted.   □

Note that in contrast to the ARC Algorithm Theorem 7.23 we do not need to assume here that the CSP is finite.

7.7 A path consistency algorithm

In this and the next three sections we deal with algorithms that modify the constraints. Here we derive an algorithm that achieves path consistency. In Section 5.5 this notion was defined for normalised CSPs, i.e., CSPs in which on each pair of variables at most one constraint exists. To keep the notational complications to minimum we limit ourselves to even more limited CSPs, the ones that are standardised. (We shall return to this matter at the end of this section.) Recall from Definition 5.14 that a CSP is standardised if for each pair x, y of variables a unique constraint on x, y exists. Below we denote this unique constraint on x, y by $C_{x,y}$.

So consider a standardised CSP $\mathcal{P}$ with the binary constraints $C_1, \ldots, C_k$. For the partial ordering we choose now the Cartesian product of the partial orderings $(\mathcal{P}(C_i), \supseteq)$, where $i \in [1..k]$. Recall from Section 5.5 that the notion of path consistency was characterised by means of the following three rules:

$$PATH\ CONSISTENCY\ 1$$

$$\frac{C_{x,y}, C_{x,z}, C_{y,z}}{C'_{x,y}, C_{x,z}, C_{y,z}}$$

where the constraint $C'_{x,y}$ on the variables x, y is defined by

$$C'_{x,y} := C_{x,y} \cap C_{x,z} \cdot C^T_{y,z},$$

$$PATH\ CONSISTENCY\ 2$$

$$\frac{C_{x,y}, C_{x,z}, C_{y,z}}{C_{x,y}, C'_{x,z}, C_{y,z}}$$

where the constraint $C'_{x,z}$ on the variables x, z is defined by

$$C'_{x,z} := C_{x,z} \cap C_{x,y} \cdot C_{y,z},$$

PATH CONSISTENCY 3

$$\frac{C_{x,y}, \; C_{x,z}, \; C_{y,z}}{C_{x,y}, \; C_{x,z}, \; C'_{y,z}}$$

where the constraint $C'_{y,z}$ on the variables y, z is defined by

$$C'_{y,z} := C_{y,z} \cap C^T_{x,y} \cdot C_{x,z}.$$

Each of these rules can be identified with a function. Indeed, given a subsequence x, y, z of the variables of $\mathcal{P}$ each of these rules can be viewed as a function on $\mathcal{P}(C_{x,y}) \times \mathcal{P}(C_{x,z}) \times \mathcal{P}(C_{y,z})$. The *PATH CONSISTENCY* rule *1* corresponds to the function

$$f^z_{x,y}(P, Q, R) := (P', Q, R),$$

where

$$P' := P \cap Q \cdot R^T,$$

the *PATH CONSISTENCY* rule *2* corresponds to the function

$$f^y_{x,z}(P, Q, R) := (P, Q', R),$$

where

$$Q' := Q \cap P \cdot R,$$

while the *PATH CONSISTENCY* rule *3* corresponds to the function

$$f^x_{y,z}(P, Q, R) := (P, Q, R'),$$

where

$$R' := R \cap P^T \cdot Q.$$

Now, $(f^z_{x,y})^+$, $(f^y_{x,z})^+$ and $(f^x_{y,z})^+$ are functions on $\mathcal{P}(C_1) \times \cdots \times \mathcal{P}(C_k)$. Since we wish to use the CD algorithm of Section 7.1, we need the following counterpart of the Arc Consistency Lemma 7.22.

Lemma 7.28 (Path Consistency)

   (i) *A standardised CSP $\mathcal{P}$ with the binary constraints $C_1, \ldots, C_k$ is path consistent iff $(C_1, \ldots, C_k)$ is a common fixpoint of all functions $(f^z_{x,y})^+$, $(f^y_{x,z})^+$ and $(f^x_{y,z})^+$ associated with the subsequences x, y, z of the variables of $\mathcal{P}$.*

   (ii) *The functions $f^z_{x,y}$, $f^y_{x,z}$ and $f^x_{y,z}$ are*

- *inflationary w.r.t. the componentwise ordering $\supseteq$,*
- *monotonic w.r.t. the componentwise ordering $\supseteq$.*

Proof (i) is a direct consequence of the Path Consistency Note 5.21. (ii) follows directly from Exercise 7.3. □

In general, the $f_{x,y}^z$ functions do not commute or semi-commute, so we cannot use the DICD or the SICD algorithm to characterise path consistency. Still we can use the CD algorithm. To this end we instantiate this algorithm with the set of functions

$$F_0 := \{f \mid x, y, z \text{ is a subsequence of the variables of } \mathcal{P} \text{ and}$$
$$f \in \{f_{x,y}^z, f_{x,z}^y, f_{y,z}^x\}\},$$

$n := k$ and each $\perp_i$ equal to C_i.

Call the resulting algorithm the PATH algorithm. It enjoys the following properties.

Theorem 7.29 (PATH Algorithm) *Consider a standardised CSP $\mathcal{P}$ with the binary constraints $C_1, \ldots, C_k$. Assume that $C_1, \ldots, C_k$ are finite.*

The PATH algorithm always terminates. Let $\mathcal{P}'$ be the CSP obtained from $\mathcal{P}$ by replacing the sequence of its binary constraints by the sequence of the binary constraints computed in d. Then

(i) *$\mathcal{P}'$ is path consistent,*
(ii) *$\mathcal{P}'$ is equivalent to $\mathcal{P}$.*

Proof The proof is analogous to that of the ARC Algorithm Theorem 7.23 and is left to the reader. □

Note that in contrast to the ARC Algorithm Theorem we do not need to assume that the CSP is finite, but only that its binary constraints are finite.

As in the case of the ARC algorithm we now rewrite the PATH algorithm so that it deals with the considered standardised CSP $\mathcal{P}$ directly. Because of the use of the $f_{x,y}^z$ functions the outcome is somewhat more complex. First, given two variables x and y we write $x \prec y$ if x appears before y in the sequence of the variables of $\mathcal{P}$. Each function of the form $f_{x,y}^u$ where $x \prec y$ and $u \notin \{x, y\}$ can be identified with the sequence x, u, y of the variables. (Note that the 'relative' position of u w.r.t. x and y is not fixed, so x, u, y does not have to be a subsequence of the variables of $\mathcal{P}$.)

This allows us to identify the set of functions F_0 with the set

$$V_0 := \{(x, u, y) \mid x, y, u \text{ are different variables of } \mathcal{P} \text{ and } x \prec y\}.$$

Next, given two variables x, y of $\mathcal{P}$ such that $x \prec y$, we introduce the following set of triples of different variables of $\mathcal{P}$:

$$
\begin{aligned}
V_{x,y} := \ & \{(x, y, u) \mid x \prec u\} \\
\cup \ & \{(y, x, u) \mid y \prec u\} \\
\cup \ & \{(u, x, y) \mid u \prec y\} \\
\cup \ & \{(u, y, x) \mid u \prec x\} \\
\cup \ & \{(x, u, y)\}.
\end{aligned}
$$

So $V_{x,y}$ is the subset of V_0 that consists of the triples that contain x and y. This corresponds to the set of functions in one of the following forms: $f_{x,u}^y, f_{y,u}^x, f_{u,y}^x, f_{u,x}^y$ and $f_{x,y}^u$. (The sixth form, $f_{y,x}^u$, is excluded since we assumed that $x \prec y$.)

After these preparations we reformulate the PATH algorithm as follows, where initially $E_{x,y} = C_{x,y}$.

PATH algorithm

$V_0 := \{(x, u, y) \mid x, y, u$ are different variables of $\mathcal{P}$ and $x \prec y$;
$V := V_0$;
WHILE $V \neq \emptyset$ **DO**
    choose $p \in V$; suppose $p = (x, u, y)$;
    apply $f_{x,y}^u$ to its current domains;
    IF $E_{x,y}$ changed **THEN**
        $V := V \cup V_{x,y}$
    ELSE
        $V := V - \{p\}$
    END
END

Here the phrase 'apply $f_{x,y}^u$ to its current domains' can be made more precise if the 'relative' position of u w.r.t. x and y is known. By way of example suppose that $u \prec x, y$. Then $f_{x,y}^u$ is defined on $\mathcal{P}(C_{u,x}) \times \mathcal{P}(C_{u,y}) \times \mathcal{P}(C_{x,y})$ by

$$
f_{x,y}^u(E_{u,x}, E_{u,y}, E_{x,y}) := (E_{u,x}, E_{u,y}, E_{x,y} \cap E_{u,x}^T \cdot E_{u,y})
$$

and the above phrase 'apply $f_{x,y}^u$ to its current domains' represents the assignment

$$
E_{x,y} := E_{x,y} \cap E_{u,x}^T \cdot E_{u,y}.
$$

In our presentation we only considered standardised CSPs. This restriction can be lifted as follows. Every normalised CSP $\mathcal{P}$ can be trivially transformed to an equivalent standardised CSP by adding for each subsequence x, y for which no constraint on x, y exists a constraint on x, y that equals the Cartesian product of the domains of the variables x and y. Then we can transform this standardised CSP to a path consistent CSP $\mathcal{P}'$ using the PATH algorithm. The CSP $\mathcal{P}'$ can be viewed as the outcome of the PATH algorithm applied to the original CSP $\mathcal{P}$. By virtue of the PATH Algorithm Theorem 7.29 $\mathcal{P}'$ is equivalent to $\mathcal{P}$.

7.8 A directional path consistency algorithm

In this section we deal with the notion of directional path consistency defined in Section 5.6. As in the previous section we limit our attention to the standardised CSPs. Given such a standardised CSP $\mathcal{P}$ we characterise it in terms of fixpoints using the CSP $\mathcal{P}_\prec$. In the latter CSP the variables are ordered according to $\prec$ and on every pair of variables a unique constraint exists.

The following is a counterpart of the Directional Arc Consistency Lemma 7.26. We use here the functions $f^z_{x,y}$ defined in Section 7.7.

Lemma 7.30 (Directional Path Consistency) *Consider a standardised CSP $\mathcal{P}$ with a linear ordering $\prec$ on its variables. Let $C_1, \ldots, C_k$ be the binary constraints of $\mathcal{P}_\prec$. Then*

    (i) *$\mathcal{P}$ is directionally path consistent w.r.t. $\prec$ iff $(C_1, \ldots, C_k)$ is a common fixpoint of all functions $(f^z_{x,y})^+$ such that $x \prec y \prec z$.*

    (ii) *The functions $f^z_{x,y}$, $f^y_{x,z}$ and $f^x_{y,z}$ are idempotent.*

    (iii) *Suppose that $x_1 \prec y_1 \prec z$, $x_2 \prec y_2 \prec u$, and $u \preceq z$. Then the function $f^z_{x_1,y_1}$ semi-commutes with the function $f^u_{x_2,y_2}$ w.r.t. the componentwise ordering $\supseteq$, that is, for all $(X_1, \ldots, X_k) \in \mathcal{P}(C_1) \times \cdots \times \mathcal{P}(C_k)$*

$$(f^z_{x_1,y_1})^+ (f^u_{x_2,y_2})^+ (X_1, \ldots, X_k) \supseteq (f^u_{x_2,y_2})^+ (f^z_{x_1,y_1})^+ (X_1, \ldots, X_k).$$

Proof   The proof is left as Exercise 7.6.   □

To obtain an algorithm that achieves directional path consistency we now instantiate appropriately the SICD algorithm. Consider a standardised CSP $\mathcal{P}$ with a linear ordering $\prec$ on its variables and the corresponding CSP $\mathcal{P}_\prec$. To be able to apply the above lemma we order appropriately the $f^t_{r,s}$ functions, where the variables r, s, t are such that $r \prec s \prec t$. Namely, we put $f^z_{x_1,y_1}$ before $f^u_{x_2,y_2}$ if $u \prec z$.

More precisely, let $x_1, \ldots, x_n$ be the sequence of the variables of $\mathcal{P}_\prec$. So $x_1 \prec x_2 \prec \cdots \prec x_n$. We can then order the functions $f^{x_m}_{x_k,x_l}$ as follows:

$$f^{x_n}_{x_1,x_2},$$
$$f^{x_n}_{x_1,x_3}, \quad f^{x_n}_{x_2,x_3},$$
$$\cdots,$$
$$f^{x_n}_{x_1,x_{n-1}}, f^{x_n}_{x_2,x_{n-1}}, \ldots, f^{x_n}_{x_{n-3},x_{n-1}} \, f^{x_n}_{x_{n-2},x_{n-1}},$$
$$f^{x_{n-1}}_{x_1,x_2},$$
$$f^{x_{n-1}}_{x_1,x_3}, \quad f^{x_{n-1}}_{x_2,x_3},$$
$$\cdots$$
$$f^{x_{n-1}}_{x_1,x_{n-2}}, f^{x_{n-1}}_{x_2,x_{n-2}}, \ldots, f^{x_{n-1}}_{x_{n-3},x_{n-2}},$$
$$\cdots,$$
$$f^{x_3}_{x_1,x_2}.$$

Then by virtue of the Directional Path Consistency 7.30(iii) if the function f precedes the function g in this sequence, then f semi-commutes with g w.r.t. the componentwise ordering $\supseteq$.

We now instantiate the SICD algorithm by the above-defined sequence of functions and each $\perp_i$ equal to the constraint C_i. By rewriting the applications of the functions $f^{x_m}_{x_i,x_j}$ as assignments this algorithm can be rewritten as the following triple FOR loop. As before we denote the unique constraint of $\mathcal{P}_\prec$ on x_i, x_j by $C_{i,j}$.

DIRECTIONAL PATH CONSISTENCY algorithm (DPATH)

```
FOR m := n TO 3 BY −1 DO
  FOR j := 2 TO m − 1 DO
    FOR i := 1 TO j − 1 DO
```
$$C_{i,j} := C_{i,j} \cap C_{i,m} \cdot C^T_{j,m} \quad \text{% apply the function } f^{x_m}_{x_i,x_j}$$
```
    END
  END
END
```

Apart from of the different choice of the constituent partial orderings and the functions with schemes, this algorithm is identical to the DARC of the previous section. Consequently, the DPATH algorithm enjoys analogous properties as the DARC algorithm. They are summarised in the following theorem.

Theorem 7.31 (DPATH Algorithm) *Consider a standardised CSP $\mathcal{P}$ with a linear ordering $\prec$ on its variables.*

The DPATH algorithm always terminates. Let $\mathcal{P}'$ be the CSP obtained from $\mathcal{P}_\prec$ by replacing the sequence of its binary constraints by the sequence of the binary constraints computed in it. Then

(i) $\mathcal{P}'$ is directionally path consistent w.r.t. $\prec$,

(ii) $\mathcal{P}'$ is equivalent to $\mathcal{P}_\prec$. $\square$

As in the case of the DArc Algorithm Theorem 7.27 we do not need to assume here that the CSP is finite. Also, as in the previous section we can lift the restriction to the standardised CSPs in a straightforward way.

7.9 A k-consistency algorithm

Let us turn our attention to the notion of k-consistency. In our presentation we rely on the notation introduced in Section 5.7, where this notion was defined. To obtain an algorithm that enforces this local consistency notion we proceed in the familiar by now four steps:

- we identify the relevant partial ordering,
- we reformulate the proof rule(s) characterising the notion as functions on a specific partial ordering,
- we establish the necessary properties of these functions,
- we instantiate the CD algorithm by the adopted partial ordering and by these functions.

In our presentation we limit ourselves to regular CSPs. Recall that a CSP is regular if for each sequence of its variables X a unique constraint on X exists, denoted by C_X, and that, as the Equivalence Note 5.16 shows, every CSP is equivalent to a regular CSP.

So consider a regular CSP $\mathcal{P}$ with the constraints $C_1, \ldots, C_n$. For the partial ordering we choose the Cartesian product of the partial orderings $(\mathcal{P}(C_i), \supseteq)$, where $i \in [1..n]$. In Section 5.7 we characterised the notion of k-consistency by means of the following rule:

$$k\text{-}CONSISTENCY$$

$$\frac{C_X}{C_X \cap \Pi_X(\overline{C_{X,y}})}$$

parametrised by all subsequences X of $k-1$ variables and a variable y that does not occur in X.

Next, we explain how this rule can be interpreted as a function on $\mathcal{P}(C_1) \times \cdots \times \mathcal{P}(C_n)$. This is a bit more complicated than in the case of other rules so far considered. Fix a subsequence X of $k-1$ variables and a variable y that does not occur in X and consider the sequence $C_X, C'_1, \ldots, C'_m$ of the constraints of $\mathcal{P}$, each on a different subsequence of X, y. Recall that C_X is the unique constraint on the sequence X of variables. The $k\text{-}CONSISTENCY$

rule corresponds then to the function $f_{X,y}$ on $\mathcal{P}(C_X) \times \mathcal{P}(C_1') \times \cdots \times \mathcal{P}(C_m')$ defined by

$$f_{X,y}(Q, Q_1, \ldots, Q_m) := (Q', Q_1, \ldots, Q_m),$$

where

$$Q' := Q \cap \Pi_X(Q_1 \bowtie \cdots \bowtie Q_m).$$

Intuitively, $f_{X,y}$ removes from its first argument the tuples that cannot be extended to an instantiation with the domain X, y that satisfies all the constraints $Q_1, \ldots, Q_m$. The canonic extension $f_{X,y}^+$ of $f_{X,y}$ is then a function on $\mathcal{P}(C_1) \times \cdots \times \mathcal{P}(C_n)$. We have then the following counterpart of the characterisation results provided in the previous sections.

Lemma 7.32 (k-Consistency) *Fix $k \geq 1$. Consider a regular CSP $\mathcal{P}$ with the constraints $C_1, \ldots, C_n$.*

> (i) *If $(C_1, \ldots, C_n)$ is a common fixpoint of all functions $f_{X,y}^+$ for all sub-sequences X of $k - 1$ variables of $\mathcal{P}$ and all variables y not in X, then $\mathcal{P}$ is k-consistent.*
>
> (ii) *The functions $f_{X,y}$ are*
>
> - *inflationary w.r.t. the componentwise ordering $\supseteq$,*
> - *monotonic w.r.t. the componentwise ordering $\supseteq$.*

Proof   (*i*) is a direct consequence of the k-Consistency Note 5.36. (*ii*) follows directly from Exercise 7.3. $\square$

Note that in contrast to the previous characterisation results of this chapter we only have here an implication. This is a consequence of an observation made in Section 5.7 after the k-Consistency Note 5.36. Still this result is sufficient for our purposes because we have to our disposal an algorithm that computes common fixpoints. Indeed, we can instantiate the CD algorithm with the set of functions

$$F_0 := \{f_{X,y} \mid X \text{ is a subsequence of variables of } \mathcal{P} \text{ of length } k - 1 \text{ and } y \text{ is not in } X\}$$

and each $\perp_i$ equal to C_i.

The resulting algorithm, that we call the k-CONSISTENCY algorithm, enjoys the following properties.

Theorem 7.33 (k-CONSISTENCY Algorithm) *Fix $k \geq 1$. Consider a regular CSP $\mathcal{P}$ with the constraints $C_1, \ldots, C_n$. Assume that $C_1, \ldots, C_n$ are finite.*

The k-CONSISTENCY algorithm always terminates. Let $\mathcal{P}'$ be the CSP obtained from $\mathcal{P}$ by replacing the sequence of its constraints by the sequence of the constraints computed in d. Then

(i) $\mathcal{P}'$ is k-consistent,

(ii) $\mathcal{P}'$ is equivalent to $\mathcal{P}$.

Proof The proof is analogous to that of the ARC Algorithm Theorem 7.23 and is left to the reader. $\qquad\square$

In the k-CONSISTENCY algorithm from each constraint on $k-1$ variables repeatedly tuples are removed that cannot be extended to a k-consistent instantiation. We can modify this algorithm by also removing tuples that extend inconsistent instantiations. This process can be described by means of the following proof rule:

$$k\text{-}CONSISTENCY\ 1$$

$$\frac{C_X}{C_X \cap \overline{C_X}}$$

It is straightforward to see that this rule is equivalence preserving. Indeed, it is an abbreviation of the following rule, where $C_1, \ldots, C_n$ are all constraints on a subsequence of the variables X:

$$\frac{\langle C_X, C_1, \ldots, C_n\ ;\ \mathcal{DE}\rangle}{\langle C'_X, C_1, \ldots, C_n\ ;\ \mathcal{DE}\rangle}$$

where $C'_X := C_X \cap (C_1 \bowtie \cdots \bowtie C_n)$.

Consider now a solution d of the CSP in the premise of the rule. Then both $d \in C_X$ and $d \in C_1 \bowtie \cdots \bowtie C_n$. So d is a solution of the CSP in the conclusion of the rule.

Since the notion of k-consistency was characterised in the k-Consistency Note 5.36 solely in terms of the k-CONSISTENCY rule, this rule is redundant. However, once we translate it into a function (or actually a set of functions since this rule is parametrised by a sequence X of the variables) we are brought to a useful revision of the k-CONSISTENCY algorithm.

This translation is obtained in the expected way. Given a sequence X of the variables of $\mathcal{P}$ let $C_X, C'_1, \ldots, C'_m$ be the sequence of the constraints of $\mathcal{P}$, each on a different subsequence of X. Then the k-CONSISTENCY 1 rule corresponds to the following function g_X on $\mathcal{P}(C_X) \times \mathcal{P}(C'_1) \times \cdots \times \mathcal{P}(C'_m)$:

$$g_X(Q, Q_1, \ldots, Q_m) := (Q', Q_1, \ldots, Q_m),$$

where

$$Q' := Q \cap (Q_1 \bowtie \cdots \bowtie Q_m).$$

As before it is straightforward to prove that the functions g_X are inflationary and monotonic w.r.t. the componentwise ordering $\supseteq$.

We can then in the familiar by now way instantiate the CD algorithm with the set of functions F_0 that consists of all functions of the type $f_{X,y}$ and g_X, where X is a subsequence of $k-1$ variables of $\mathcal{P}$ and y is not in X. The resulting algorithm enjoys the same properties as the k-CONSISTENCY algorithm.

7.10 A relational consistency algorithm

Finally, let us return to the notion of relational consistency introduced in Section 5.9. Recall from there that given a sequence of constraints $C_1, \ldots, C_m$ we denote by $Var(C_1, \ldots, C_m)$ the set of variables that are used in them. Recall also that the (i, m)-relational consistency for regular CSPs was there characterised by means of the following RELATIONAL (i, m)-CONSISTENCY rule parametrised by a sequence of constraints $C_1, \ldots, C_m$ and a subsequence X of $Var(C_1, \ldots, C_m)$ of length i:

RELATIONAL (i, m)-CONSISTENCY

$$\frac{C_X}{C_X \cap \Pi_X(C_1 \bowtie \cdots \bowtie C_m)}$$

where C_X is the unique constraint on the sequence X of variables.

The details of the presentation are analogous to the one of the previous section. First, we reformulate this rule as a function. To this end fix a regular CSP $\mathcal{P}$ with the constraints $E_1, \ldots, E_n$. Then for each sequence of constraints $C_1, \ldots, C_m$ and a subsequence X of $Var(C_1, \ldots, C_m)$ the RELATIONAL (i, m)-CONSISTENCY rule corresponds to the function $f_{C_1,\ldots,C_m,X}$ on $\mathcal{P}(C_X) \times \mathcal{P}(C_1) \times \cdots \times \mathcal{P}(C_m)$ defined by

$$f_{C_1,\ldots,C_m,X}(Q, Q_1, \ldots, Q_m) := (Q', Q_1, \ldots, Q_m),$$

where

$$Q' := Q \cap \Pi_X(Q_1 \bowtie \cdots \bowtie Q_m).$$

So $f_{C_1,\ldots,C_m,X}$ removes from its first argument the tuples that cannot be extended to an instantiation that satisfies all the constraints $Q_1, \ldots, Q_m$. The canonic extension $f^+_{C_1,\ldots,C_m,X}$ of $f_{C_1,\ldots,C_m,X}$ is then a function on $\mathcal{P}(E_1) \times \cdots \times \mathcal{P}(E_n)$. We have then the following characterisation result which is a counterpart of the k-Consistency Lemma 7.32 of the previous section.

Lemma 7.34 (Relational Consistency) *Fix $i, m \geq 0$. Consider a regular CSP $\mathcal{P}$ with the constraints $E_1, \ldots, E_n$.*

(i) *If $(E_1, \ldots, E_n)$ is a common fixpoint of all functions $f^+_{C_1, \ldots, C_m, X}$ for all subsequences $C_1, \ldots, C_m$ of the constraints and all subsequences X of $Var(C_1, \ldots, C_m)$ of length i, then $\mathcal{P}$ is relationally (i, m)-consistent.*

(ii) *The functions $f_{C_1, \ldots, C_m, X}$ are*

- *inflationary w.r.t. the componentwise ordering $\supseteq$,*
- *monotonic w.r.t. the componentwise ordering $\supseteq$.*

Proof   (i) is a direct consequence of the k-Consistency Note 5.36. (ii) follows directly from Exercise 7.3.   □

As the final step we instantiate the CD algorithm with the set of functions

$$F_0 := \{f_{C_1, \ldots, C_m, X} \mid C_1, \ldots, C_m \text{ is a subsequence of constraints and } X \text{ is a subsequence of } Var(C_1, \ldots, C_m) \text{ of length } i\}$$

and each $\perp_i$ equal to E_i.

Call the resulting algorithm the RELATIONAL (i, m)-CONSISTENCY algorithm. Its properties are summarised in the following theorem.

Theorem 7.35 (RELATIONAL (i, m)-CONSISTENCY Algorithm) *Fix $i, m \geq 0$. Consider a regular CSP $\mathcal{P}$ with the constraints $E_1, \ldots, E_n$. Assume that $E_1, \ldots, E_n$ are finite.*

The RELATIONAL (i, m)-CONSISTENCY algorithm always terminates. Let $\mathcal{P}'$ be the CSP obtained from $\mathcal{P}$ by replacing the sequence of its constraints by the sequence of the constraints computed in d. Then

(i) *$\mathcal{P}'$ is relationally (i, m)-consistent,*

(ii) *$\mathcal{P}'$ is equivalent to $\mathcal{P}$.*

Proof   The proof is analogous to that of the ARC Algorithm Theorem 7.23 and is left to the reader.   □

7.11 Implementations of incomplete constraint solvers

So far we dealt with the constraint propagation algorithms that enforce specific local consistency notions separately. Thanks to the adopted presentation these algorithms can be combined in a straightforward way. For example, suppose that we wish to enforce both arc and path consistency.

Then we simply instantiate the CD algorithm with the Cartesian product of the partial orderings used in Sections 7.4 and 7.7 and the set of functions that consists of the projection functions π_1 and the $f_{x,y}^z$ functions.

As already mentioned at the beginning of this chapter, the constraint propagation algorithms can also be used to implement specific incomplete constraint solvers that are defined by means of proof rules of Section 4.1. All that is needed is to check that the functions that represent the used rules are monotonic and inflationary w.r.t. some ordering. Then we can instantiate the CD algorithm by these functions.

In case an incomplete constraint solver is defined by means of the domain reduction rules it suffices to take the familiar by now componentwise reversed subset ordering $\supseteq$. Then each domain reduction rule when viewed as a function on the domains of the used variables is inflationary. Also, as Exercise 7.3 shows, monotonicity is ensured if the domains (respectively, the constraints) in the conclusion of a rule are obtained from the domains (respectively, the constraints) in the premise of the rule using a combination of the following operations on relations:

- union and intersection,
- transposition operation '$.^T$',
- composition operation '$. \cdot ..$',
- join operation $\bowtie$,
- projection functions π_i and Π_X, and
- removal of an element.

This vast repertoire of operations is sufficient to describe the domain reduction rules that we considered so far. In particular, it allows us to deal with the domain reduction rules used in Chapter 6 to describe the incomplete constraint solvers for:

- equality and disequality constraints,
- Boolean constraints, and
- linear constraints over integer intervals and finite integer domains,
- arithmetic constraints over integer intervals and over finite integer domains, and
- arithmetic constraints over reals.

By instantiating the generic CD algorithm by the domain reduction rules that define an incomplete constraint solver we provide then an implementation of this solver to which the conclusions of the CD Corollary 7.18 apply.

For an example of such an implementation see Exercise 7.12. If the considered functions satisfy some other properties listed in Definition 7.4, we can use the simpler DICD and SICD algorithms.

In general, however, we also need to deal with transformation rules that are part of an incomplete solver. For some specific transformation rules we can still use the generic framework of Section 7.1 to reason about them. An example are the *PATH CONSISTENCY* rules *1, 2* and *3* that were studied in Section 7.7. More generally, this framework can be used for the transformation rules to which Exercise 7.3 is applicable.

Also, for the transformation rules for Boolean constraints presented in Subsection 6.3.1 an ad hoc reasoning suffices to prove the desired results —see Exercise 6.2 of Chapter 6. The same holds for the normalisation rules for the linear constraints that we omitted in our presentation in Section 6.4 —see Exercise 6.7 of Chapter 6.

In principle the transformation rules can be arbitrarily complex and to reason in a systematic way about termination and uniqueness of the outcome of the resulting derivations one needs to rely on the term rewriting techniques, see, e.g., Baader and Nipkow [1998]. These techniques fall outside the scope of this book.

Further, note that the algorithms that are instantiations of the DICD and CD algorithms of Section 7.1 are non-deterministic. In spite of it, the result of their computations is always the same. By presenting such algorithms as non-deterministic ones we abstract from irrelevant details and provide a possibility for implementing the underlying scheduler of the considered functions separately. All that is needed is a data structure that supports three operations: selection, addition and deletion of an element. For example, we can use here a queue. This turns these algorithms into deterministic ones without affecting the stated properties (though see in this respect Exercise 7.2). In specific situations one can exploit additional properties of the scheduled functions to derive more efficient algorithms. Examples of such improvements are provided in Exercises 7.9 and 7.10.

Finally, let us note that it does not make sense to enforce the considered notion of local consistency if during the computation of the corresponding constraint propagation algorithm a failed CSP (that is, a CSP with an empty domain or an empty constraint) is reached. Indeed, all the considered algorithms maintain equivalence during the computation. So if a failed CSP is reached, we can readily conclude that the original CSP is inconsistent and might as well terminate the computation. Consider an example. Take the

CSP

$$\langle x = y, y < z \; ; \; x \in [50..100], y \in [0..20], z \in [0..10] \rangle.$$

Applying the *ARC CONSISTENCY* rule *1* to the first constraint we reduce the domain of x to the empty set. The resulting CSP is not yet arc consistent though it is failed. We might at this moment terminate the computation instead of carrying it on till an arc consistent CSP is reached (which in this case will have all variable domains empty). Such a modification can be easily incorporated into the ARC algorithm. Indeed, it suffices to change the condition of the WHILE loop to $S \neq \emptyset$ AND $\forall i \in [1..n] \, D_i \neq \emptyset$. Similar modifications can me made to the other considered constraint propagation algorithms. The resulting algorithms achieve a weaker property than their original versions. Namely, they transform the original CSP to the one that is either locally consistent or failed. As just explained, it is sufficient to our purposes.

7.12 Summary

In this chapter we studied various constraint propagation algorithms. These are algorithms that achieve local consistency. In fact, for each local consistency notion there exists an algorithm that enforces it in the sense that it transforms a given CSP to an equivalent one that is locally consistent.

The adopted presentation allowed us to introduce the constraint propagation algorithms as instances of simple generic iteration algorithms. This simplified the reasoning about correctness of these algorithms and clarified their nature. More specifically, this presentation allowed us to reason about these algorithms in two stages. First, we considered generic iteration algorithms on partial orderings and proved their correctness in an abstract setting. Then we instantiated these algorithms with concrete partial orderings and functions and obtained in this way specific constraint propagation algorithms. Because of its generality, the adopted approach can be used to model several other constraint propagation algorithms. Here we presented the constraint propagation algorithms that achieve

- node consistency,
- arc consistency,
- hyper-arc consistency,
- directional arc consistency,
- path consistency,
- directional path consistency.
- k-consistency,

- relational consistency.

We also showed how the discussed generic iteration algorithms can be used to implement incomplete constraint solvers.

7.13 Exercises

Exercise 7.1 Adopt the assumptions of the GENERIC ITERATION Theorem 7.11. Consider a terminating computation of the GENERIC ITERATION algorithm. Extend the sequence of values for d computed by it to an arbitrary iteration χ of F. Prove that χ is regular in the sense of the Least Fixpoint Lemma 7.8.

Exercise 7.2 Call an iteration *chaotic* if each function is activated in it infinitely often. We say that a function f is *eventually irrelevant for an iteration* $d_0, d_1, \ldots$ if for some $m \geq 0$ we have $f(d_j) = d_j$ for all $j \geq m$. Call an iteration *semi-chaotic* if each function that is activated in it finitely often is eventually irrelevant.

(i) Consider a finite partial ordering $(D, \sqsubseteq)$ with the least element $\bot$. Let F be a finite set of functions on D such that

- each $f \in F$ is monotonic and inflationary.

Prove that every semi-chaotic (and hence every chaotic) iteration of F eventually stabilises at the least common fixpoint of the functions from F.

(ii) Show that not all iterations generated by the infinite executions of the GENERIC ITERATION algorithm are semi-chaotic.

(iii) Consider the following modification of the GENERIC ITERATION algorithm that involves the queues. We denote here the empty queue by **empty**, and the head and the tail of a non-empty queue Q respectively by **head**(Q) and **tail**(Q). Finally, for a set S and a queue Q, the operation **enqueue**(S, Q) enqueues in an arbitrary order all the elements of S in Q.

GENERIC ITERATION WITH A QUEUE algorithm

```
d := ⊥;
Q := empty;
enqueue(F, Q);
WHILE Q ≠ empty DO
    g := head(Q);
```

```
    IF d ≠ g(d) THEN
        enqueue(update(Q, g, d), Q);
        d := g(d)
    ELSE
        Q := tail(Q)
    END
END
```

where for all Q, g, d

A $\{f \in F - Q \mid f(d) = d \wedge fg(d) \neq g(d)\} \subseteq update(Q, g, d)$.

(We identify here Q with the set of its elements.)

Prove that all iterations generated by the infinite executions of the GENERIC ITERATION WITH A QUEUE algorithm are semi-chaotic.

Exercise 7.3 Suppose that the domains in the conclusion of a rule are obtained from the domains in the premise of the rule using a combination of the following operations on relations:

- union and intersection,
- transposition operation '.^{T}',
- composition operation '. · ..',
- join operation ⋈,
- projection functions π_i and Π_X, and
- removal of an element.

Prove that each such rule viewed as a function on the domains of the used variables is monotonic w.r.t. the componentwise ordering $\supseteq$.

Hint. Prove that each of these operations is monotonic w.r.t. the componentwise ordering $\supseteq$ (or equivalently, as Note 7.19 shows, w.r.t. the componentwise ordering $\subseteq$).

Exercise 7.4 Prove the Node Consistency Lemma 7.20(*ii*).

Exercise 7.5 Prove the Directional Arc Consistency Lemma 7.26.

Exercise 7.6 Prove the Directional Path Consistency Lemma 7.30.

Exercise 7.7 Consider the following modification of the GENERIC ITERA-TION algorithm:

GENERIC ITERATION WITH IDEMPOTENT FUNCTIONS algorithm (GII)

$d := \bot$;
$G := F$;
WHILE $G \neq \emptyset$ DO
   choose $g \in G$;
   IF $d \neq g(d)$ THEN
      $G := G \cup update(G, g, d)$;
      $d := g(d)$
   END;
   $G := G - \{g\}$
END

where $update(G, g, d)$ satisfies the assumption **A** of Section 7.1. So here, in contrast to the GENERIC ITERATION algorithm, the selected function g is removed unconditionally. Prove the following counterpart of the GENERIC ITERATION Theorem 7.11:

Suppose that $(D, \sqsubseteq)$ is a finite partial ordering with the least element $\bot$. Let F be a finite set of monotonic, inflationary and idempotent functions on D. Then every execution of the GII algorithm terminates and computes in d the least common fixpoint of the functions from F.

Hint. Prove that $I := \forall f \in F - G \ f(d) = d$ is an invariant of the WHILE loop.

Exercise 7.8 Suppose that for each g the set of functions $Comm(g)$ from F is such that each element of $Comm(g)$ commutes with g. Prove that if $update(G, g, d)$ satisfies the assumption **A**, then so does the function $update(G, g, d) - Comm(g)$.

Exercise 7.9 Consider two binary constraints C and E.

  (i) Show that the π_1 function of C and the π_2 function of E do not need to commute.
    Hint. Consider the variables x and y with the corresponding domains $D_x := \{a, b\}$, $D_y := \{c, d\}$ and the constraints $C := \{(a, c), (b, d)\}$ and $E := \{(a, d)\}$, both on x, y.

  (ii) Show that the functions π_1 of C and of E do not need to commute.
    Hint. Consider the variables x, y, z with the corresponding domains $D_x := \{c, d\}$, $D_y := \{a, b\}$, $D_z := \{b\}$, and the constraint $C := \{(a, b)\}$ on y, z and $E := \{(c, a), (d, b)\}$ on x, y.

  (iii) Prove that the functions π_1 and π_2 of the constraint C commute.

(iv) Suppose that C is on the variables x, y and E on the variables x, z. Prove that the functions π_1 of C and of E commute.

(v) Combine this information with Exercise 7.8 to obtain the following modified version of the ARC algorithm that is an instance of the GII algorithm of Exercise 7.7:

AC-3 algorithm

$S_0 := \{C \mid C \text{ is a binary constraint from } \mathcal{C}\}$
     $\cup \ \{C^T \mid C \text{ is a binary constraint from } \mathcal{C}\};$
$S := S_0;$
WHILE $S \neq \emptyset$ DO
    choose $C \in S$; suppose C is on x_i, x_j;
    $D_i := \{a \in D_i \mid \exists b \in D_j \ (a, b) \in C\};$
    IF D_i changed THEN
       $S := S \cup \{C' \in S_0 \mid C' \text{ is on the variables } y, x_i \text{ where } y \not\equiv x_j\}$
    END;
    $S := S - \{C\}$
END

Note the difference with respect to the ARC algorithm in the second assignment to S, which is there

$$S := S \cup \{C' \in S_0 \mid C' \text{ is on the variables } y, z$$
$$\text{where } y \text{ is } x_i \text{ or } z \text{ is } x_i\}.$$

Exercise 7.10

(i) Consider a standardised CSP involving among others the variables x, y, z, u. Prove that the functions $f^z_{x,y}$ and $f^u_{x,y}$ commute.

(ii) Combine this information with Exercise 7.8 to obtain the following modified version of the PATH algorithm that is an instance of the GII algorithm of Exercise 7.7, where $U_{x,y}$ is the following set of triples of different variables of $\mathcal{P}$:

$$U_{x,y} := \{(x, y, u) \mid x \prec u\} \cup \{(y, x, u) \mid y \prec u\}$$
$$\cup \ \{(u, x, y) \mid u \prec y\} \cup \{(u, y, x) \mid u \prec x\}.$$

PC-2 algorithm

$V_0 := \{(x, u, y) \mid x, y, u \text{ are different variables of } \mathcal{P} \text{ and } x \prec y\};$
$V := V_0;$
WHILE $V \neq \emptyset$ DO
    choose $p \in V$; suppose $p = (x, u, y);$
    apply $f^u_{x,y}$ to its current domains;

IF $E_{x,y}$ changed THEN
    $V := V \cup U_{x,y}$
END;
    $V := V - \{p\}$
END

Note the difference with respect to the PATH algorithm in the second assignment to V which amounts there to:

$$V := V \cup U_{x,y} \cup \{(x,u,y) \mid u \notin \{x,y\}\}.$$

Exercise 7.11 Give an example of a domain reduction rule which when viewed as a function is not idempotent.
Hint. Consider the *LINEAR EQUALITY* rule of Section 6.4 and the CSP

$$\langle 3x - 5y = 4 \; ; \; x \in [0..9], y \in [1..8] \rangle$$

considered in Subsection 6.4.2.

Exercise 7.12 Provide an algorithm that transforms a *LINEQ* CSP (that is, a CSP the domains of which are integer intervals and the constraints of which are linear equality constraints) into one that is bounds consistent or failed.
Hint. Given an integer interval $[l..h]$ let $\mathcal{F}([l..h])$ be the set of all integer subintervals of $[l..h]$. Associate with the original *LINEQ* CSP $\langle \mathcal{C} \; ; \; x_1 \in [l_1..h_1],\ldots,x_n \in [l_n..h_n] \rangle$ the Cartesian product of the partial orderings $(\mathcal{F}([l_1..h_1]), \supseteq),\ldots,(\mathcal{F}([l_n..h_n]), \supseteq)$. Then use the *LINEAR EQUALITY* Theorem 6.8 to characterise non-failed *LINEQ* CSPs that are bounds consistent in terms of fixpoints and proceed as in the case of the arc consistency.

7.14 Bibliographic remarks

The first explicit constraint propagation algorithm, a path consistency algorithm, appeared in Montanari [1974], an article in which the notion of path consistency was defined. Then, in the context of analysis of polyhedral scenes discussed in Example 2.11, another constraint propagation algorithm was proposed in Waltz [1975]. In Mackworth [1977], an article in which the notion of arc consistency was introduced, Waltz' algorithm was explained in more general terms of CSPs with binary constrains. Also, the arc consistency algorithm AC-3 and the path consistency algorithm PC-2 were introduced, where the latter was modeled upon the former.

The HYPER-ARC algorithm is from Davis [1987]. In turn, the directional arc consistency algorithm DARC and the directional path consistency algorithm DPATH are from Dechter and Pearl [1988], the paper in which the notions of directional arc and directional path consistency were introduced. In Cooper [1989] an algorithm that achieves k-consistency was discussed. The modification of the k-CONSISTENCY algorithm described in Section 7.9 that involves the k-*CONSISTENCY 1* rule captures the main features of this algorithm.

The quest for a uniform framework for constraint propagation algorithms has a long history going back to Mackworth [1977]. The following additional references should be mentioned here. In Montanari and Rossi [1991] a general relaxation algorithm was proposed and it was showed that arc consistency and path consistency algorithms can be obtained by instantiating this algorithm. The idea that the meaning of a constraint is a function (on a constraint store) with some algebraic properties was put forward in Saraswat, Rinard and Panangaden [1991], where the properties of being inflationary (called there extensive), monotonic and idempotent were singled out.

A presentation of constraint propagation algorithms in terms of scheduling of specific functions can be traced back to Benhamou, McAllester and Van Hentenryck [1994], where the monotonicity, inflationarity and idempotence were identified as important properties in the context of constraints for reals. In Benhamou and Older [1997] this approach was considered for constraints on reals, integers and Boolean constraints.

In Benhamou [1996] and Telerman and Ushakov [1996] relevance of generic iteration algorithms for constraint programming was pointed out and it was noted that for specific functions these algorithms compute the same value independently of the order of the applications of the functions used. In turn, the relevance of the chaotic iterations for constraint propagation algorithms was independently noticed in van Emden [1997] and Fages, Fowler and Sola [1998]. In the latter paper a generic iteration algorithm was formulated and proved correct for the functions defined in Benhamou and Older [1997] and it was shown that the limit of the constraint propagation process for these functions is their greatest common fixpoint in the componentwise subset ordering $\subseteq$.

This work was further generalised in Apt [1999] to a study of specific constraint propagation algorithms obtained as instances of generic iteration algorithms on Cartesian products of partial orderings. In this paper a more complete overview of the history of constraint propagation algorithms can be found. The presentation of this chapter is based on Apt [2000a] where the presentation starts with an arbitrary partial ordering and where the use of chaotic iterations is dropped because of the focus on constraint propagation algorithms that always terminate.

The proofs of the claims stated in Exercises 7.5–7.10 can be found there, while Exercise 7.2 and its proof can be found in Apt [1999]. The GENERIC ITERATION algorithm was inspired by a similar algorithm of Monfroy and Réty [1999] that in turn builds on Apt [1999]. Monfroy and Réty studied a distributed version of this algorithm. It can be used as a basis for deriving in a uniform way distributed local consistency algorithms.

More recently, this work was continued in Gennari [2000] and Gennari [2001], where more advanced algorithms for achieving arc consistency, hyper-arc consistency, path consistency and k-consistency were modeled as instances of generic iteration algorithms.

7.15 References

K. R. APT
[1999]   The essence of constraint propagation, *Theoretical Computer Science*, 221, pp. 179–210. Available via `http://arXiv.org/archive/cs/`.
[2000a]   The role of commutativity in constraint propagation algorithms, *ACM Transactions on Programming Languages and Systems*, 22, pp. 1002–1036. Available via `http://arXiv.org/archive/cs/`.

F. BAADER AND T. NIPKOW
[1998]   *Term Rewriting and All That*, Cambridge University Press, Cambridge, UK.

F. BENHAMOU
[1996]   Heterogeneous constraint solving, in: *Proceeding of the Fifth International Conference on Algebraic and Logic Programming (ALP 96)*, M. Hanus and M. Rodriguez-Artalejo, eds., Lecture Notes in Computer Science 1139, Springer-Verlag, Berlin, pp. 62–76.

F. BENHAMOU, D. A. MCALLESTER, AND P. VAN HENTENRYCK
[1994]   CLP(intervals) revisited, in: *Proceedings of the 1994 International Logic Programming Symposium*, M. Bruynooghe, ed., The MIT Press, pp. 124–138.

F. BENHAMOU AND W. OLDER
[1997]   Applying interval arithmetic to real, integer and Boolean constraints, *Journal of Logic Programming*, 32, pp. 1–24.

M. C. COOPER
[1989]   An optimal k-consistency algorithm, *Artificial Intelligence*, 41, pp. 89–95.

E. DAVIS
[1987]   Constraint propagation with interval labels, *Artificial Intelligence*, 32, pp. 281–331.

R. DECHTER AND J. PEARL
[1988]   Network-based heuristics for constraint-satisfaction problems, *Artificial Intelligence*, 34, pp. 1–38.

F. FAGES, J. FOWLER, AND T. SOLA
[1998]   Experiments in reactive constraint logic programming, *Journal of Logic Programming*, 37, pp. 185–212.

R. GENNARI
[2000]   Arc consistency via subsumed functions, in: *Proceedings of Computational Logic 2000 (CL2000)*, J. Lloyd, ed., Lecture Notes in Artificial Intelligence 1861, Springer-Verlag, Berlin, pp. 358–372.
[2001]   General schema for constraint propagation, *Joint Bulletin of of the Novosibirsk Computing Center and Institute of Informatics Systems. Series: Computer Science*, 16, pp. 25–40.

A. MACKWORTH

[1977]   Consistency in networks of relations, *Artificial Intelligence*, 8, pp. 99–118.

E. MONFROY AND J.-H. RÉTY

[1999]   Chaotic iteration for distributed constraint propagation, in: *Proceedings of the 14th ACM Symposium on Applied Computing, ACM SAC'99, Scientific Computing Track*, J. Carroll, H. Haddad, D. Oppenheim, B. Bryant, and G. Lamont, eds., ACM Press, San Antonio, Texas, USA, March, pp. 19–24.

U. MONTANARI

[1974]   Networks of constraints: fundamental properties and applications to picture processing, *Information Science*, 7, pp. 95–132. Also Technical Report, Carnegie Mellon University, 1971.

U. MONTANARI AND F. ROSSI

[1991]   Constraint relaxation may be perfect, *Artificial Intelligence*, 48, pp. 143–170.

V. SARASWAT, M. RINARD, AND P. PANANGADEN

[1991]   Semantic foundations of concurrent constraint programming, in: *Proceedings of the Eighteenth Annual ACM Symposium on Principles of Programming Languages (POPL'91)*, pp. 333–352.

V. TELERMAN AND D. USHAKOV

[1996]   Data types in subdefinite models, in: *Artificial Intelligence and Symbolic Mathematical Computations*, Lecture Notes in Computer Science 1138, Springer-Verlag, Berlin, pp. 305–319.

M. H. VAN EMDEN

[1997]   Value constraints in the CLP scheme, *Constraints*, 2, pp. 163–184.

D. L. WALTZ

[1975]   Generating semantic descriptions from drawings of scenes with shadows, in: *The Psychology of Computer Vision*, P. H. Winston, ed., McGraw Hill, pp. 19–91.

8

Search

A S EXPLAINED IN the previous chapter, the purpose of the constraint propagation algorithms is to achieve some form of local consistency. In general these algorithms are not sufficient for finding a solution to a CSP. For instance, as already noted in Example 5.5, in the case of the n Queens Problem, where $n \geq 4$, nothing is gained by employing an arc consistency algorithm because this CSP is already arc consistent. In such situations a progress can be achieved only by splitting the current CSP $\mathcal{P}$ into two or more CSPs the union of which is equivalent to $\mathcal{P}$ in the sense of Definition 3.3. Such a split in general is obtained either by splitting a domain or by splitting a constraint.

So the general pattern consists of an alternating use of constraint propagation and splitting. This leads to what we call search trees. The purpose of this chapter is to discuss the search trees and the most common algorithms used to explore them. We call these algorithms search algorithms. Conceptually, while reading this chapter, it is helpful to have in mind the following slogan:

Search Algorithm = Search Tree + Exploration Algorithm.

The above equation is supposed to suggest that each search algorithm *can be viewed* as an exploration algorithm of a search tree and *not* that each such algorithm first constructs a search tree and then explores it. In fact, the considered search trees are constructed 'on the fly', during the execution of the exploration algorithm.

In our presentation we do not exploit this equation to the full extent, in that we confine our presentation to the **top-down search algorithms**, also called **depth-first search algorithms**. In these algorithms one repeatedly expands a node at the lowest level in the tree until a failure arises, upon which one returns (backtracks) to a higher level at which one resumes the node expansion. In the next chapter, we offer a short account of alternative forms of search algorithms.

We begin our presentation by introducing in the next section a very general notion of a search tree that is sufficient to describe the alternation between arbitrary forms of constraint propagation and splitting. Then in Section 8.2 we discuss the most common type of search trees, that we call labeling trees. They are obtained using the labeling method of Section 3.2 as splitting and a domain reduction method as constraint propagation. To illustrate these trees we discuss in Section 8.3 in detail three types of labeling trees for the CSP that represents the *SEND + MORE = MONEY* puzzle of Example 2.1.

Next, in Section 8.4, we discuss the labeling trees that result from choosing three specific forms of constraint propagation. This way we obtain

- forward checking,
- partial look ahead, and
- maintaining arc consistency (MAC), sometimes called full look ahead,

search trees.

After this exposition of the search trees we move on to a presentation of the search algorithms, more specifically the top-down search algorithms. In Section 8.5 we present in turn

- the BACKTRACK-FREE search algorithm,
- the BACKTRACK-FREE WITH CONSTRAINT PROPAGATION search algorithm,
- the BACKTRACK search algorithm, and

- the BACKTRACK WITH CONSTRAINT PROPAGATION search algorithm.

Then, in Section 8.6 we discuss three specialisations of the last search algorithm, for the

- forward checking,
- partial look ahead, and
- MAC

search trees. In Section 8.7 we turn our attention to the search algorithms for constrained optimization problems introduced in Section 2.6. We discuss in turn

- the BRANCH AND BOUND search algorithm,
- the BRANCH AND BOUND WITH CONSTRAINT PROPAGATION search algorithm, and
- the BRANCH AND BOUND WITH CONSTRAINT PROPAGATION AND COST CONSTRAINT search algorithm.

Next, in Section 8.8, we discuss various heuristics that are useful in the context of search algorithms for the labeling trees.

The search algorithms discussed in Sections 8.5–8.8 all deal with the labeling trees. Most of these algorithms can also be formulated for arbitrary search trees. We conclude the exposition by discussing in Section 8.9 an example of such an algorithm: an abstract branch and bound algorithm for arbitrary search trees.

8.1 Search trees

First, we provide a formal definition of a search tree. Here and elsewhere in this chapter we assign to each node in a tree a *level* as follows. The root is at the level 0 and the direct descendants of a node at the level i are all at the level $i + 1$.

Definition 8.1 Consider a CSP $\mathcal{P}$ with a sequence of variables X. By a *search tree for* $\mathcal{P}$ we mean a finite tree such that

- its nodes are CSPs,
- its root is $\mathcal{P}$,
- the nodes at an even level have exactly one direct descendant,
- if $\mathcal{P}_1, \ldots, \mathcal{P}_m$, where $m \geq 1$, are direct descendants of $\mathcal{P}_0$, then the union of $\mathcal{P}_1, \ldots, \mathcal{P}_m$ is equivalent w.r.t. X to $\mathcal{P}_0$. $\qquad \square$

So a search tree is admittedly a very general notion. The idea is that:

- at the even levels the constraint propagation is applied to the current CSP,
- at the odd levels splitting is applied to the current CSP,

and that we continue to apply this procedure until we reach a leaf that is a 'manifestly solved' CSP or we reach leaves all of which are 'manifestly failed'. An example of a search tree in which we refer explicitly to constraint propagation and splitting is depicted in Figure 8.1.

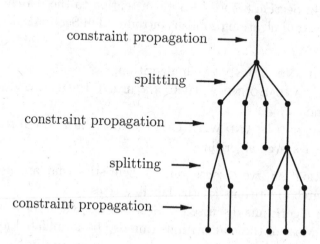

Fig. 8.1. A search tree for a CSP

The reference to 'manifestly' means that it is straightforward to generate all solutions to the CSP, in case it is 'manifestly solved', or to determine that no solution to it exists, in case it is 'manifestly failed'. This is an admittedly imprecise description analogous to the notion of a complete solver introduced at the beginning of Chapter 4. As we shall see in the next section different realisations of the notion of a 'manifestly failed' CSP lead to various types of search trees.

In the above definition constraint propagation and splitting are applied in an alternating fashion. Such a general definition allows us to model arbitrary forms of constraint propagation and of splitting. In fact, it even allows for a possibility that at each node a different form of constraint propagation or of splitting is applied. The splitting, as noted in Section 3.2, can consist either of splitting a constraint or of splitting a domain of a variable.

Since the root of the tree is at an even level, the constraint propagation is applied first to the original CSP $\mathcal{P}$. It is tempting to stipulate that the nodes at an odd level have at least two direct descendants, all obtained by means of splitting. However, for reasons that will become clear in the next section, we also want to admit here the border case when splitting reduces to a 'non-action', represented by a replication of the node.

The following simple result summarises the fundamental property of the search trees.

Note 8.2 (Search Tree) *Consider a $\mathcal{P}$ with a sequence of variables X. Suppose that $\mathcal{P}_1, \ldots, \mathcal{P}_m$ are the leaves of a search tree for $\mathcal{P}$. Then the union of $\mathcal{P}_1, \ldots, \mathcal{P}_m$ is equivalent w.r.t. X to $\mathcal{P}$.*

Proof   The proof is left as Exercise 8.1.   □

This note shows that given a CSP $\mathcal{P}$ and a search tree for it, when looking for a solution to $\mathcal{P}$ it is sufficient to look for a solution to one of the leaf CSPs.

Finally, note that we postulated nothing about the internal, i.e., non-leaf, nodes. These CSPs can be inconsistent or even failed. Such situations arise when, for example, the original CSP is inconsistent but this fact is detected only by means of deduction modeled by constraint propagation and case analysis modeled by splitting.

From now on we assume that all considered CSPs are finite, i.e., that their domains are finite.

8.2 Labeling trees

The most common form of splitting consists of the **labeling** of a domain of a variable. It corresponds to the labeling rule mentioned in Section 3.2. Informally, it consists of taking a variable, say x, and splitting its domain into singleton sets. Each such singleton set, say $\{a\}$, corresponds to a CSP in which the domain of the variable x is replaced by $\{a\}$. Equivalently, each such singleton set $\{a\}$ corresponds to an assignment of the value a to the variable x.

In this section we define several types of search trees for finite CSPs. For each of them:

- splitting consists of the labeling,
- constraint propagation consists of a domain reduction method.

We call such search trees **labeling trees**. An alternative exposition would lead to the **enumeration trees** that result from using the enumeration rule of Section 3.2 instead of labeling. So the enumeration trees, in contrast to the labeling trees, are binary. Our focus on the labeling trees instead of on the enumeration trees is motivated by the fact that in the next chapter we shall more often refer to the labeling than to the enumeration.

As we shall see, in a number of situations it will be possible to define the labeling trees in a simpler way, without using nodes that are CSPs.

8.2.1 Complete labeling trees

We begin by discussing the labeling trees in case no constraint propagation is present. Then the nodes at the odd levels, that correspond to the outcome of the constraint propagation, can be ignored and the resulting tree can be simplified by removing them. Further, the search tree can be defined directly in terms of instantiations, without introducing any CSPs. The formal definition is as follows.

Definition 8.3 Consider a CSP $\mathcal{P}$. Let $x_1, \ldots, x_n$ be the sequence of its variables linearly ordered by $\prec$. By a **complete labeling tree associated with $\mathcal{P}$ and $\prec$** we mean a tree such that

- the direct descendants of the root are of the form (x_1, d),
- the direct descendants of a node (x_j, d), where $j \in [1..n-1]$, are of the form (x_{j+1}, e),
- its branches determine all the instantiations with the domain $\{x_1, \ldots, x_n\}$.

□

To clarify the relation between this definition and Definition 8.1 let us associate with each complete labeling tree a unique search tree as follows. To start with, we associate with the root of the complete labeling tree the original CSP $\mathcal{P}$. Then with each node (x_k, d_k) with the path $\{(x_1, d_1), \ldots, (x_k, d_k)\}$ leading to it we associate a unique CSP obtained from $\mathcal{P}$ by modifying the domains of the variables $x_1, \ldots, x_k$ to, respectively, $\{a_1\}, \ldots, \{a_k\}$, and by restricting the constraints $\mathcal{P}$ to these new domains. Finally, to accommodate for the constraint propagation, which is here the 'identity action', we expand each node r to an arc with the node r at each end. So a complete labeling tree can be viewed as a simplified representation of the search tree with the trivial constraint propagation and the labeling as the splitting method. A complete labeling tree is also a 'compact' way of representing all possible instantiations.

In the case of complete labeling trees both 'manifestly solved' and 'manifestly failed' CSPs are with all domains being singleton sets. So we detect the status of a CSP only after we have applied labeling to all of its variables.

Note that the complete labeling tree associated with a CSP depends on the way we order its variables.

Example 8.4 Consider the following CSP:

$$\langle x < y, y < z \; ; \; x \in \{1, 2, 3\}, y \in \{2, 3\}, z \in \{1, 2, 3\}\rangle.$$

If we order its variables as $x \prec y \prec z$, then we get the complete labeling tree depicted in Figure 8.2, while for the ordering $x \prec z \prec y$ we get the complete labeling tree depicted in Figure 8.3. □

Note that the first complete labeling tree has 28 nodes, while the second one 31 nodes. In contrast, both of them have the same number of leaves, namely 18. So the size of the complete labeling tree depends on the variable ordering. In fact, we can be more precise. .

Note 8.5 (Labeling) *Fix a CSP with non-empty domains. Let $x_1, \ldots, x_n$ be the sequence of its variables linearly ordered by $\prec$ and $D_1, \ldots, D_n$ the corresponding domains.*

(i) *The number of nodes in the complete labeling tree associated with $\prec$ equals*

$$1 + \Sigma_{i=1}^n (\Pi_{j=1}^i |D_j|),$$

where $|A|$ denotes the cardinality of the set A.

(ii) *The number of leaves in the complete labeling tree associated with $\prec$ equals*

$$\Pi_{j=1}^n |D_j|,$$

so it does not depend on the variable ordering.

(iii) *The labeling tree has the least number of nodes if the variables are ordered by their domain sizes in the increasing order.*

Proof
(i) Recall that we assumed that the root of a tree is at the level 0 and the direct descendants of a node at the level i are all at the level $i + 1$. A direct proof by induction shows that the number of nodes at the level i is $\Pi_{j=1}^i |D_j|$. This proves the claim.

(ii) All the leaves are at the level n, so the proof of (i) provides their number.

(iii) If we transpose in the ordering $\prec$ the variables x_{j+1} and x_{j+2}, then the number of nodes in the labeling tree changes by

$$(\Pi_{k=1}^j |D_k|) \cdot (|D_{j+2}| - |D_{j+1}|).$$

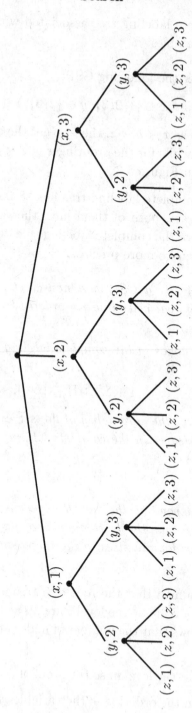

Fig. 8.2. The complete labeling tree for the ordering $x \prec y \prec z$

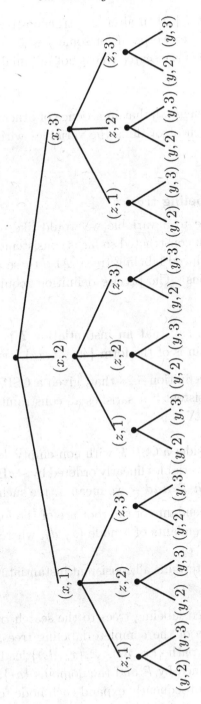

Fig. 8.3. The complete labeling tree for the ordering $x \prec z \prec y$

Thus if $|D_{j+2}| < |D_{j+1}|$, then after this transposition the size of the search tree decreases. In other words, if for some $j \in [0..n-2]$ we have $|D_{j+1}| > |D_{j+2}|$, then the size of the search tree is not minimal. This proves the claim. □

This observation suggests that in absence of other information it is useful to select in the search algorithms the variables with the smallest domains first.

8.2.2 Reduced labeling trees

By assigning a value to a variable we would like to do it in such a way that the instantiation constructed so far is consistent. This leads to labeling trees that we call reduced labeling trees. Also these trees can be defined in terms of instantiations. The precise definition requires an introduction of an auxiliary notion.

Definition 8.6 We say that an instantiation I is **along the ordering** $x_1, \ldots, x_n$ if its domain is of the form $\{x_1, \ldots, x_j\}$ for some $j \in [1..n]$. □

Recall now from Definition 5.28 that, given a CSP, an instantiation with the domain X is consistent if it satisfies all constraints on the subsequences of the variables from X.

Definition 8.7 Consider a CSP $\mathcal{P}$ with non-empty domains. Let $x_1, \ldots, x_n$ be the sequence of its variables linearly ordered by $\prec$. By a **reduced labeling tree associated with $\mathcal{P}$ and $\prec$** we mean a tree such that

- the direct descendants of the root are of the form (x_1, d),
- the direct descendants of a node (x_j, d), where $j \in [1..n-1]$, are of the form (x_{j+1}, e),
- its branches determine all consistent instantiations along the ordering $x_1, \ldots, x_n$. □

To relate the reduced labeling trees to the search trees we proceed analogously as in the case of the complete labeling trees. That is, with each node (x_k, d_k) with the path $\{(x_1, d_1), \ldots, (x_k, d_k)\}$ leading to it we associate a unique CSP determined by $\mathcal{P}$ and the domains $\{a_1\}, \ldots, \{a_k\}$ of the variables $x_1, \ldots, x_k$, and subsequently expand each node to an arc. It is easy to see that the resulting tree is a search tree.

So a reduced labeling tree can be viewed as a simplified representation of the search tree in which the splitting consists of the labeling limited to those values for which the instantiation constructed so far remains consistent. The fact that we consider only consistent instantiations reflects the view that we consider now a CSP as 'manifestly failed' earlier than in the complete labeling trees, namely at the moment a consistent instantiation is generated that cannot be consistently extended to the next variable.

Just as the complete labeling tree, the reduced labeling tree associated with a CSP depends on the way we order its variables. For different variable orderings we can obtain radically different trees.

Example 8.8 Consider again the CSP of Example 8.4, so

$$\langle x < y, y < z \ ; \ x \in \{1,2,3\}, y \in \{2,3\}, z \in \{1,2,3\} \rangle$$

and the already considered two variable orderings: $x \prec y \prec z$ and $x \prec z \prec y$. For the first one we get the reduced labeling tree depicted in Figure 8.4, while for the second one we get the reduced labeling tree depicted in Figure 8.5. □

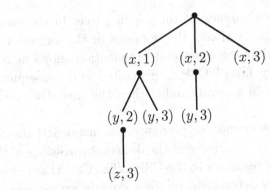

Fig. 8.4. The reduced labeling tree for the ordering $x \prec y \prec z$

The size of the reduced labeling tree depends not only on the size of the variable domains but also on the considered constraints. Therefore, in general it is quite complicated to compute its size.

Note that in the definitions of a complete labeling tree and of a reduced labeling tree we ignored the ordering between the direct descendants. Of course, in figures such as the above ones it is not possible to abstract from such an ordering. We ordered in them the direct descendants according to the value of the chosen elements.

In general, the ordering between the direct descendants matters for the search algorithms employed because they visit the nodes in a specific order. However, except for the backtrack-free search algorithms, the outcome of

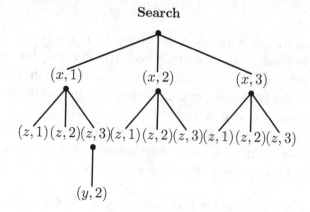

Fig. 8.5. The reduced labeling tree for the ordering $x \prec z \prec y$

the considered algorithms does not depend on this ordering. Therefore, in each of them the elements will be selected in a non-deterministic way.

8.2.3 *prop* labeling trees

We now move on to the discussion of the labeling trees in the presence of a constraint propagation. It affects the domains of the variables not yet considered. The idea is that the constraint propagation allows us to detect earlier that a 'manifestly failed' CSP is generated and consequently the resulting search trees are in general smaller than the ones discussed in the previous subsections.

To discuss such trees we cannot anymore use just instantiations. Still, we can represent each node by a sequence of the domain expressions of the considered variables, without resorting to the CSPs. The CSP that corresponds to such a node is uniquely determined by these domain expressions and the original CSP $\mathcal{P}$: its constraints are obtained by restricting the constraints of $\mathcal{P}$ to the listed domains.

Further, since we now wish to include an arbitrary constraint propagation in the form of a domain reduction, we do not anymore delete the nodes at the odd level. In fact, we now wish to model the fact that successive variable instantiations are intertwined with the applications of the constraint propagation. From now on we assume for simplicity that the linear ordering $\prec$ on the variables coincides with the ordering used in the definition of the considered CSP.

Consider a CSP $\mathcal{P} := \langle \mathcal{C} \; ; \; x_1 \in D_1, \ldots, x_n \in D_n \rangle$. We assume a fixed form of constraint propagation $prop(i)$ in the form of a domain reduction, parametrised by a value $i \in [0..n-1]$. The value i determines the sequence $x_{i+1}, \ldots, x_n$ of the variables to the domains of which $prop(i)$ is applied.

That is, given a sequence of the current variable domains $E_1, \ldots, E_n$, the constraint propagation $prop(i)$ transforms only the domains $E_{i+1}, \ldots, E_n$. The outcome of $prop(i)$ depends on the original constraints $\mathcal{C}$ of $\mathcal{P}$ and on the domains $E_1, \ldots, E_i$. Because we discuss here labeling trees, at the moment the constraint propagation $prop(i)$ is carried out, the domains $E_1, \ldots, E_i$ are all singleton sets.

Let us provide now the formal definition of the search trees we are interested in.

Definition 8.9 Assume a fixed form of constraint propagation $prop(i)$ in the form of a domain reduction as explained above. Consider a CSP $\mathcal{P} := \langle \mathcal{C} \; ; \; x_1 \in D_1, \ldots, x_n \in D_n \rangle$. By a **prop labeling tree associated with** $\mathcal{P}$ we mean a tree such that

- its nodes are sequences of the domain expressions $x_1 \in E_1, \ldots, x_n \in E_n$,
- its root is the sequence $x_1 \in D_1, x_2 \in D_2, \ldots, x_n \in D_n$,
- each node at a level $2i$ with $i \in [0..n]$ is of the form

$$x_1 \in \{d_1\}, \ldots, x_i \in \{d_i\}, x_{i+1} \in E_{i+1}, \ldots, x_n \in E_n.$$

If $i = n$, this node is a leaf. Otherwise, it has exactly one direct descendant,

$$x_1 \in \{d_1\}, \ldots, x_i \in \{d_i\}, x_{i+1} \in E'_{i+1}, \ldots, x_n \in E'_n,$$

where $E'_j \subseteq E_j$ for $j \in [i+1..n]$, obtained by means of the constraint propagation $prop(i)$,

- each node at a level $2i + 1$ with $i \in [0..n-1]$ is of the form

$$x_1 \in \{d_1\}, \ldots, x_i \in \{d_i\}, x_{i+1} \in E_{i+1}, \ldots, x_n \in E_n.$$

If $E_j = \emptyset$ for some $j \in [i+1..n]$, this node is a leaf. Otherwise it has direct descendants of the form

$$x_1 \in \{d_1\}, \ldots, x_i \in \{d_i\}, x_{i+1} \in \{d\}, x_{i+2} \in E_{i+2}, \ldots, x_n \in E_n,$$

for all $d \in E_{i+1}$ such that the instantiation $\{(x_1, d_1), \ldots, (x_i, d_i), (x_{i+1}, d)\}$ is consistent. This set of direct descendants can be a singleton set or empty.

We call a leaf a **success node** if it is at the level $2n$ and a **failed node** (or a **failure**) if it is at a level $< 2n$. □

Let us now clarify some elements of this definition. Given the node at level 0, i.e., the tree root, we call $x_1, \ldots x_n$ its future variables. Given a node at level 1 or 2 we call x_1 its current variable and $x_2, \ldots x_n$ its future variables. Next, given a node at level 3 or 4 we call x_1 its past variable, x_2 its current variable and $x_3, \ldots x_n$ its future variables. And so on.

More formally, given a node $x_1 \in E_1, \ldots, x_n \in E_n$ at level $2i - 1 \geq 0$ or $2i \geq 0$,

- if $i \in [2..n-1]$, we call $x_1, \ldots x_{i-1}$ its **past variables**,
- if $i \in [1..n]$, we call x_i its **current variable**, and
- if $i \in [0..n-1]$, we call $x_{i+1}, \ldots x_n$ its **future variables**.

As an example assume a CSP $\mathcal{P}$ with three variables, x_1, x_2 and x_3. Consider a *prop* labeling tree associated with $\mathcal{P}$ depicted in Figure 8.6 together with the listing of its levels and the corresponding past, current, and future variables. We disregard here the structure of the nodes. According to the above terminology A, B, C and D are failed nodes, while E and F are success nodes.

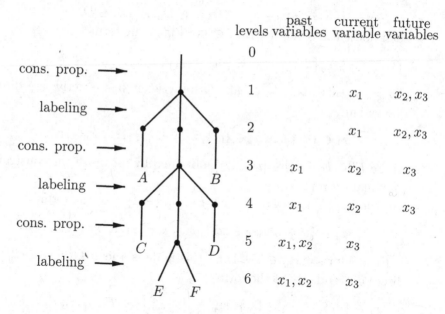

Fig. 8.6. A *prop* labeling tree

Note that the domains of the past variables are all singleton sets. Further, if a node is at a level $2i$ with $i \in [0..n-1]$, the constraint propagation *prop* is applied to it. More precisely, $prop(i)$ is applied to the CSP uniquely determined by the original CSP and the domain expressions of the node. Its outcome is represented by a new sequence of the domain expressions. The constraint propagation $prop(i)$ affects only the domains of the future variables. A node at an even level $2i$ with $i \in [0..n]$ is a leaf if and only if $i = n$. Such a node corresponds to a success in the sense that it determines a solution to the considered CSP.

By incrementing the level from $2i$ to $2i + 1$ the current variable changes from x_i to x_{i+1}. So at each odd level a node with a new current variable is considered. A node at a level $2i + 1$ is a leaf in one of two cases:

- the domain of the current variable x_{i+1} or of a future variable is empty,
- the instantiation $\{(x_1, d_1), \ldots, (x_i, d_i)\}$ cannot be consistently extended to the variable x_{i+1}.

In both cases the node corresponds to a 'manifestly failed' CSP. The first contingency is due to the use of the constraint propagation and is new with respect to the previous subsection in which we considered the reduced labeling trees.

If the node at the level $2i + 1$ is not a leaf, the labeling is applied to the current variable, x_{i+1}, but only those elements in its domain are selected for which the instantiation constructed so far remains consistent. This is analogous to the case of the reduced labeling trees.

It is straightforward to see that each *prop* labeling tree corresponds to a unique search tree. In this correspondence *prop(i)* is the constraint propagation used at the even levels. *prop(i)* maintains equivalence w.r.t. the original set of variables and reduces the variable domains. This correspondence allows us to draw the following important conclusion on the account of the Search Tree Note 8.2.

Note 8.10 (*prop* Labeling Tree) *Consider a finite CSP $\mathcal{P}$ and a prop labeling tree $\mathcal{T}$ associated with $\mathcal{P}$. A node of the form $x_1 \in \{d_1\}, \ldots, x_n \in \{d_n\}$ is a leaf of $\mathcal{T}$ iff $(d_1, \ldots, d_n)$ is a solution to $\mathcal{P}$.* □

This means that given a finite CSP $\mathcal{P}$, all solutions to it can be found by exploring an arbitrary *prop* labeling tree associated with $\mathcal{P}$. The appropriate algorithms will be presented in Section 8.5. As mentioned at the beginning of this chapter, these algorithms do not actually explore the *prop* labeling trees, but rather construct them during their execution. The execution then corresponds to an exploration of the constructed *prop* labeling tree.

8.3 An example: *SEND + MORE = MONEY*

The reduced labeling trees and the *prop* labeling trees can be substantially smaller than the complete labeling trees. To illustrate the amount of savings that can be achieved when using them we return now to the $SEND + MORE = MONEY$ puzzle introduced in Example 2.1 of Chapter 2.

Let us discuss now the corresponding labeling trees. So we take as the CSP the one in which we have one equality constraint

$$
\begin{aligned}
& 1000 \cdot S \;+\; 100 \cdot E \;+\; 10 \cdot N \;+\; D \\
+\; & 1000 \cdot M \;+\; 100 \cdot O \;+\; 10 \cdot R \;+\; E \\
=\; 10000 \cdot M \;+\; 1000 \cdot O \;+\; 100 \cdot N \;+\; 10 \cdot E \;+\; Y
\end{aligned}
$$

and 28 simple disequality constraints $x \neq y$ for x, y ranging over the set $\{S, E, N, D, M, O, R, Y\}$ where x precedes y in the alphabetic order, and with the domain $[1..9]$ for S and M and the domain $[0..9]$ for the other six variables.

The complete labeling tree associated with this CSP and the displayed ordering on the variables is huge: its total number of leaves is $9^2 \cdot 10^6 = 81\,000\,000$. Its initial fragment is depicted in Figure 8.7. Here and below we use some self-explanatory simplifications in the representation of the nodes.

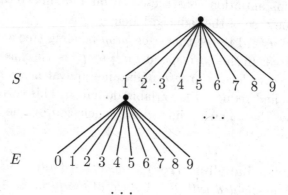

Fig. 8.7. The complete labeling tree for the $SEND + MORE = MONEY$ CSP

The reduced labeling tree is substantially smaller. Using the inside information that this CSP has exactly one solution we can conclude that the total number of leaves in this tree is $10 \cdot 9 \cdot 8 \cdot 7 \cdot 6 \cdot 5 \cdot 4 - 2 \cdot (9 \cdot 8 \cdot 7 \cdot 6 \cdot 5 \cdot 4) = 483\,840$. This represents a gain of 99.4% with respect to the complete labeling tree. Its initial fragment is depicted in Figure 8.8. Note that the number of direct descendants for the node marked by E is now 9.

The effect of constraint propagation is seen in a dramatic way by considering the *prop* labeling tree where for *prop* we take the constraint propagation for linear constraints over the integer intervals, discussed in Section 6.4. We showed there that this constraint propagation reduces the initial domains of

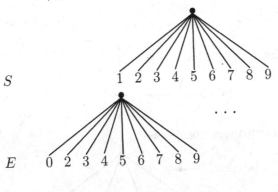

Fig. 8.8. The reduced labeling tree for the *SEND + MORE = MONEY* CSP

the considered variables to

$$S = 9, E \in [4..7], N \in [5..8], D \in [2..8], M = 1, O = 0, R \in [2..8], Y \in [2..8],$$

where $X = a$ is the shorthand for $X \in \{a\}$.

This means that this sequence of domain expressions is the direct descendant of the original sequence of domain expressions. It is now easy to construct the actual tree. It is depicted in Figure 8.9. This *prop* labeling tree has just four leaves. The labeling of each variable except E is applied to a singleton set. Consequently, each node at an odd level different from 3 has none or exactly one direct descendant.

8.4 Instances of *prop* labeling trees

In this section we instantiate the definition of a *prop* labeling tree by successively stronger forms of a constraint propagation *prop(i)* commonly used in the context of search. For each specific form of the constraint propagation *prop(i)* we just need to clarify how for each non-leaf node

$$x_1 \in \{d_1\}, \ldots, x_i \in \{d_i\}, x_{i+1} \in E_{i+1}, x_n \in E_n$$

at a level $2i$ the new domains $E'_{i+1}, \ldots, E'_n$ are defined.

8.4.1 Forward checking

To illustrate this constraint propagation method consider the n Queens Problem discussed in Example 2.2 of Chapter 2 for $n = 5$. Assume its formalisation in the form of a standardised CSP, that is a CSP in which for

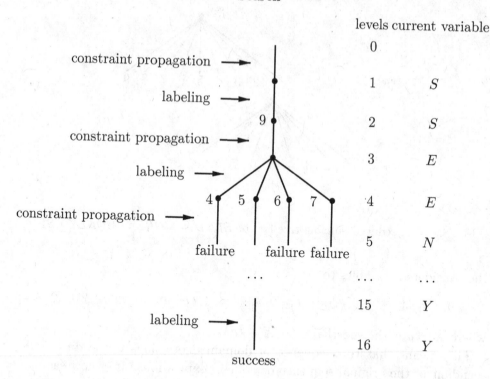

Fig. 8.9. The *prop* labeling tree for the *SEND + MORE = MONEY* CSP

each pair x, y of variables a unique constraint on x, y exists. So this CSP is of the form

$$\langle \mathcal{C} \; ; \; x_1 \in [1..5] \ldots, x_5 \in [1..5] \rangle,$$

where for every pair x_i, x_j of variables with $i \neq j$ the unique constraint on x_i, x_j is the conjunction of the following three constraints:

- $x_i \neq x_j$,
- $x_i - x_j \neq i - j$,
- $x_i - x_j \neq j - i$,

discussed in Example 2.2.

We represent such a CSP as the empty 5×5 chess board depicted in Figure 8.10. Recall that in the adopted representation of this problem the queens are supposed to be placed in different columns, so here a–e. That is, each column corresponds to a variable domain. For example the d column corresponds to the domain $[1..5]$ of the variable x_4. Figure 8.10 then corresponds with the root

$$x_1 \in [1..5], x_2 \in [1..5], x_3 \in [1..5], x_4 \in [1..5], x_5 \in [1..5]$$

of a *prop* labeling tree associated with this CSP.

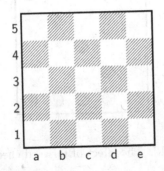

Fig. 8.10. The empty 5 × 5 chess board

Suppose now that we place the first queen at the field **a1**. We depict it by Figure 8.11. This figure corresponds with the following direct descendant of the root in the discussed *prop* labeling tree:

$$x_1 \in \{1\}, x_2 \in [1..5], x_3 \in [1..5], x_4 \in [1..5], x_5 \in [1..5].$$

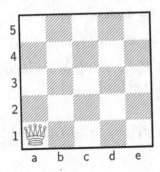

Fig. 8.11. First queen placed at **a1**

Then we mark in the other columns the fields that come under attack. This leads to a situation depicted in Figure 8.12. This situation corresponds to a removal of the marked elements from the domains of the variables representing the other queens. Note that in this way no solution is lost. Figure 8.12 corresponds with the following unique direct descendant of the previous node in the discussed *prop* labeling tree:

$$x_1 \in \{1\}, x_2 \in \{3, 4, 5\}, x_3 \in \{2, 4, 5\}, x_4 \in \{2, 3, 5\}, x_5 \in \{2, 3, 4\}.$$

More generally, we consider the columns in the alphabetic order and after placing a queen at a field we mark in the still to be considered columns the fields that come under attack. This process can be formalised as a form of

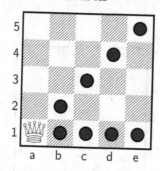

Fig. 8.12. The effect of forward checking

constraint propagation called ***forward checking***. It was not discussed so far as it is closely intertwined with the search process.

The corresponding trees are called **FORWARD CHECKING** search trees. They are defined as follows.

Definition 8.11 Consider a CSP $\mathcal{P} := \langle \mathcal{C} \ ; \ x_1 \in D_1, \ldots, x_n \in D_n \rangle$. By a **FORWARD CHECKING** search tree we mean a *prop* labeling tree associated with $\mathcal{P}$, where for each non-leaf node

$$x_1 \in \{d_1\}, \ldots, x_i \in \{d_i\}, x_{i+1} \in E_{i+1}, x_n \in E_n$$

at a level $2i$ the domains $E'_{i+1}, \ldots, E'_n$ of its unique direct descendant are defined by putting for $j \in [i+1..n]$

$$E'_j := \{e \in E_j \mid \{(x_1, d_1), \ldots, (x_i, d_i), (x_j, e)\} \text{ is consistent}\}. \qquad (8.1)$$

$\square$

So in the *FORWARD CHECKING* search tree, given a current variable x_i, each domain of a future variable x_j is revised by taking into account the constraints on the subsequences of $x_1, \ldots, x_i, x_j$. As an example, we depict in Figure 8.13 the *FORWARD CHECKING* search tree for the CSP

$$\langle x < y, y < z \ ; \ x \in \{1, 2, 3\}, y \in \{2, 3\}, z \in \{1, 2, 3\} \rangle$$

introduced in Example 8.4.

In the *FORWARD CHECKING* search tree for each future variable x_j only the constraints relating x_j with the past or current variables are considered. By taking subsequently into account *also* the constraints on the subsequences of the sequence $x_{i+1}, \ldots, x_n$ of the future variables we obtain stronger forms of constraint propagation. In the next two subsections we define two such types of constraint propagation.

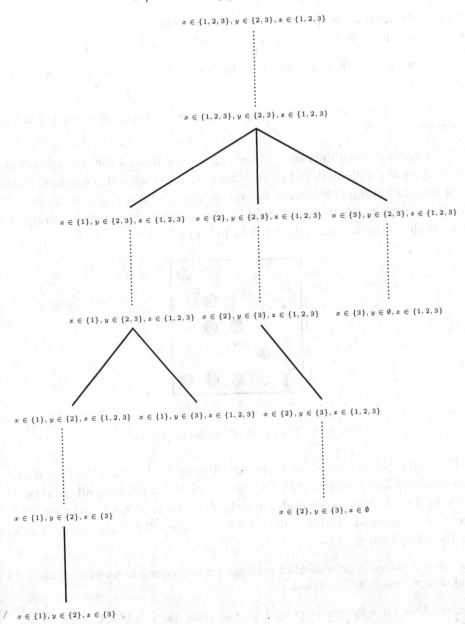

Fig. 8.13. The *FORWARD CHECKING* search tree for the CSP of Example 8.4

8.4.2 Partial look ahead

As in Subsection 8.4.1 we illustrate the approach first by means of the 5 Queens Problem. Let us reconsider the situation depicted in Figure 8.12, so after

- in the column a the queen is placed at the field a1,
- in the columns b–d the fields under attack are marked.

We now repeatedly mark any field in the columns b–d with the following property:

if a queen is placed at this field, then in some *later* column all unmarked fields come under attack.

Marking each such field corresponds to the removal of the corresponding element from the domain of the variable associated with this column. Note that no solution is lost this way. Indeed, no queen can be placed at a marked field, since otherwise no queen could be placed the later, 'offensive', column. This leads to the situation depicted in Figure 8.14.

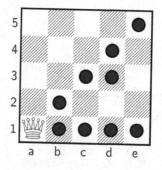

Fig. 8.14. The effect of partial look ahead

The difference between this figure and Figure 8.12 is that the field d3 is now marked. The reason is that if a queen is placed at d3, then all unmarked fields in the column e come under attack. After d3 is marked, no other field needs to be marked. Indeed, at this moment the following property holds for the columns b–d:

if a queen is placed at an unmarked field, then in any later column some unmarked field does not come under attack.

For example, if a queen is placed at the unmarked field c4, then in the column d the field d2 does not come under attack and in the column e the field e3 does not come under attack. In other words, if a queen is placed at c4, then in the column d a queen can be placed at d2 and in the column e a queen can be placed at e3.

This procedure can be formalised by imposing directional arc consistency on the CSP resulting from applying the forward checking. The whole process can be defined as another form of constraint propagation, called *partial look ahead*. The corresponding trees, called **PARTIAL LOOK AHEAD** search trees, are defined as follows.

Definition 8.12 Consider a CSP $\mathcal{P} := \langle \mathcal{C} \; ; \; x_1 \in D_1, \ldots, x_n \in D_n \rangle$. By a **PARTIAL LOOK AHEAD** search tree we mean a *prop* labeling tree associated with $\mathcal{P}$, where for each non-leaf node

$$x_1 \in \{d_1\}, \ldots, x_i \in \{d_i\}, x_{i+1} \in E_{i+1}, x_n \in E_n$$

at a level $2i$ the domains $E'_{i+1}, \ldots, E'_n$ of its unique direct descendant are first defined by means of the forward checking, i.e., using (8.1) for $j \in [i+1..n]$. If all of them are non-empty, we consider the CSP

$$\mathcal{P}_i := \langle \mathcal{C}' \; ; \; x_{i+1} \in E'_{i+1}, \ldots, x_n \in E'_n \rangle, \tag{8.2}$$

where the constraints $\mathcal{C}'$ are uniquely determined by the constraints of $\mathcal{P}$ on the subsequences of $x_{i+1}, \ldots, x_n$ and the domains $E'_{i+1}, \ldots, E'_n$, and redefine these domains by imposing on $\mathcal{P}_i$ the directional arc consistency w.r.t. the ordering $x_{i+1} \prec \ldots \prec x_n$ by means of any directional arc consistency algorithm. $\qquad\qquad\square$

As an example, we depict in Figure 8.15 the **PARTIAL LOOK AHEAD** search tree for the CSP

$$\langle x < y, y < z \; ; \; x \in \{1, 2, 3\}, y \in \{2, 3\}, z \in \{1, 2, 3\} \rangle$$

from Example 8.4. So this tree is smaller than the corresponding *FORWARD CHECKING* search tree depicted in Figure 8.13. This is due to the fact that the constraint propagation is now stronger.

8.4.3 Maintaining arc consistency (MAC)

An even stronger form of constraint propagation than the one used in the *PARTIAL LOOK AHEAD* search trees, albeit defined only for binary constraints, is obtained by imposing arc consistency on the future variables. This leads to the notion called **MAC**, an abbreviation for **Maintaining Arc Consistency**. In the literature *MAC* is alternatively called **ARC CONSISTENCY LOOK AHEAD** or **FULL LOOK AHEAD**.

To explain the intuition behind this method let us return to our running example, the 5 Queens Problem. Suppose that we strengthen the procedure discussed in Subsection 8.4.2 to the following one. After placing the first queen at the field **a1** and removing the fields under attack in the other columns we perform the following action. We repeatedly mark any field in the columns **b-d** with the following property:

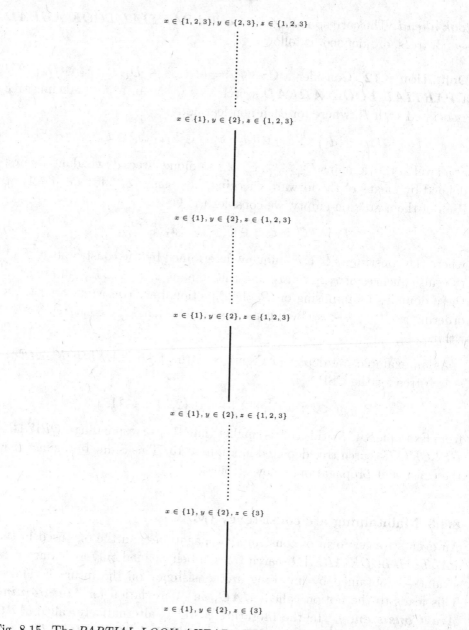

Fig. 8.15. The *PARTIAL LOOK AHEAD* search tree for the CSP of Example 8.4

if a queen is placed at this field, then in some other column from b-d all unmarked fields come under attack.

The difference between this procedure and the one described in the previous subsection is that we drop now the qualification '*later*' when referring to the other columns. This leads to the situation depicted in Figure depicted in Figure 8.16.

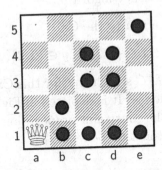

Fig. 8.16. The effect of maintaining arc consistency (MAC)

The difference between this figure and Figure 8.14 is that the field c4 is now also marked. The reason is that if a queen is put at c4, then all unmarked fields in the column b come under attack. In Subsection 8.4.2 only the impact of placing a queen on the *later* columns was considered, so the consequences of placing a queen in the c column on the b column were not analysed.

After c4 and d3 are marked, no other field needs to be marked. Indeed, at this moment the following holds for the columns b-d:

if a queen is placed at an unmarked field, then in any other column from b-d some unmarked field does not come under attack.

This procedure can be formalised by imposing arc consistency on the CSP resulting from applying the forward checking. The corresponding trees, called **MAC** search trees, are defined analogously as the *PARTIAL LOOK AHEAD* search trees.

Definition 8.13 Consider a CSP $\mathcal{P} := \langle \mathcal{C} \; ; \; x_1 \in D_1, \ldots, x_n \in D_n \rangle$. By a **MAC** search tree we mean a *prop* labeling tree associated with $\mathcal{P}$, where for each non-leaf node

$$x_1 \in \{d_1\}, \ldots, x_i \in \{d_i\}, x_{i+1} \in E_{i+1}, x_n \in E_n$$

at a level $2i$ the domains $E'_{i+1}, \ldots, E'_n$ of its unique direct descendant are first defined by means of the forward checking, i.e., using (8.1) for $j \in [i + 1..n]$. If all of them are non-empty, we consider the CSP

$$\mathcal{P}_i = \langle \mathcal{C}' \; ; \; x_{i+1} \in E'_{i+1}, \ldots, x_n \in E'_n \rangle$$

defined in (8.2) and uniquely determined by $\mathcal{P}$ and the domains $E'_{i+1}, \ldots, E'_n$, and redefine the domains $E'_{i+1}, \ldots, E'_n$ by imposing on $\mathcal{P}_i$ the arc consistency, by means of any arc consistency algorithm. $\square$

As an example, let us return to the CSP

$$\langle x < y, y < z \; ; \; x \in \{1,2,3\}, y \in \{2,3\}, z \in \{1,2,3\} \rangle$$

from Example 8.4. The MAC search tree for this CSP is reduced to a single path consisting of seven nodes. It is depicted in Figure 8.17. So in this case the initial application of the constraint propagation led to a reduction of all the domains to the singleton sets.

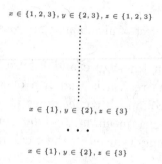

$$x \in \{1,2,3\}, y \in \{2,3\}, z \in \{1,2,3\}$$

$$x \in \{1\}, y \in \{2\}, z \in \{3\}$$

$$x \in \{1\}, y \in \{2\}, z \in \{3\}$$

Fig. 8.17. The MAC search tree for the CSP of Example 8.4

8.5 Search algorithms for the labeling trees

Now that we have defined search trees and their most common types for the case of the labeling let us turn to the search algorithms. The aim of these algorithms is to find a solution or all solutions to a CSP, or to report that no such solution exists. In case of the constrained optimisation problems these algorithms look for an optimal or all optimal solutions. In what follows we discuss several search algorithms for the labeling trees. The strategy employed by the first two algorithms is correct only for specific finite CSPs, while the other ones are correct for all finite CSPs. Conceptually, each of these algorithms looks for a solution by performing a depth-first search in an appropriate type of labeling tree defined in the previous two sections.

In all the algorithms we assume for simplicity that the linear ordering $\prec$

on the variables coincides with the ordering used in the definition of the considered CSP $\mathcal{P} := \langle \mathcal{C} \; ; \; x_1 \in D_1, \ldots, x_n \in D_n \rangle$. We also assume two further unanalysed types `elements` and `domain` and use the array D of the type `ARRAY [1..n] OF domain` to represent the sequence of the domains $D_1, \ldots, D_n$. A solution, if it exists, is produced in the global array `inst` of the type `ARRAY [1..n] OF elements`. Finally, we abbreviate the statement

'the instantiation $\{(x_1, \mathtt{inst}[1]), \ldots, (x_{j-1}, \mathtt{inst}[j-1]), (x_j, \mathtt{d})\}$
is consistent'

to `cons(inst,j,d)`.

When discussing the algorithms we assume that the elements in each numeric domain are chosen in the increasing order. This will allow us to relate these algorithms to the discussed labeling trees. These algorithms are written using the MODULA-2 syntax that should be self-explanatory. Let us recall that in MODULA-2 there are two types of parameters: the customary call-by-value parameter, and the call-by-variable parameter, distinguished by the `VAR` prefix. The actual call-by-value parameters can be arbitrary expressions of the given type, while the actual call-by-variable parameter can be only variables of the given type. The former cannot be changed, while the latter can. The call-by-value is modelled in C by using as an actual parameter a pointer to the considered variable.

8.5.1 Backtrack-free search

We begin with the simplest algorithm, called the BACKTRACK-FREE search algorithm. It attempts to construct a solution by starting with the empty instantiation and by successively trying to extend it to a consistent instantiation defined on the next variable in the assumed linear ordering. If by proceeding this way the final variable gets instantiated, a solution is found. Otherwise a failure is reported. The algorithm is presented in Figure 8.18. It is formulated in such a way that it will be easy to modify it to obtain other search algorithms.

The BACKTRACK-FREE search algorithm performs search in the reduced labeling trees. More precisely, the following result holds.

Theorem 8.14 (Backtrack-free Search) *The* BACKTRACK-FREE *search algorithm constructs in an initial segment of the array* `inst` *the leftmost branch of the corresponding reduced labeling tree and sets the variable* `success` *to* `TRUE` *if this branch represents a solution.* $\square$

```
MODULE backtrack_free;
TYPE domains =  ARRAY [1..n] OF domain;
     instantiation = ARRAY [1..n] OF elements;
VAR inst: instantiation;
PROCEDURE backtrack_free(j: INTEGER; D: domains;
                         VAR success: BOOLEAN);
BEGIN
  WHILE D[j] <> {} AND NOT success DO
    choose d from D[j];
    D[j] := D[j] - {d};
    IF cons(inst,j,d) THEN
      inst[j] := d;
      success := (j = n);
      IF NOT success THEN
        j := j+1
      END
    END
  END
END backtrack_free;
BEGIN
  success := FALSE;
  backtrack_free(1,D,success)
END backtrack_free;
```

Fig. 8.18. BACKTRACK-FREE search algorithm

The proofs of this and the analogous subsequent results proceed by induction on the number of variables. Most of these proofs are straightforward. They are left as Exercises.

In the case of the labeling tree of Figure 8.4 the BACKTRACK-FREE search algorithm proceeds along the leftmost branch of the tree and constructs in inst a solution that corresponds to the consistent instantiation $\{(x,1),(y,2),(z,3)\}$. Note that this branch is not the leftmost branch in the corresponding complete labeling tree Figure 8.2. In turn, in the case of the labeling tree of Figure 8.5 the BACKTRACK-FREE algorithm produces an initial segment of inst that corresponds to the instantiation $\{(x,1),(z,1)\}$ and thus fails to find a solution.

So in general the BACKTRACK-FREE search algorithm does not find a solution if one exists. On the other hand this algorithm is efficient — it runs in time $O(\sum_{i=1}^{n} |D_i|)$, where $|D_i|$ denotes the cardinality of the domain D_i. So it is of interest to find conditions which guarantee that the BACKTRACK-FREE search algorithm finds a solution if it exists. The following theorem is an example of such a result. It provides such conditions in terms of the concepts introduced in Sections 5.8 and 5.10.

Theorem 8.15 (Backtrack-free Search II) *Consider a CSP which is strongly $(k + 1)$-consistent and the graph of which has width k. Then for some variable ordering the* BACKTRACK-FREE *search algorithm constructs a solution if it exists and otherwise it reports a failure by setting the variable* success *to* FALSE.

Proof If some domain is empty, then no solution exists and the BACKTRACK-FREE search algorithm terminates with success set to FALSE. Otherwise the construction employed in the proof of the Consistency 2 Theorem 5.48 coincides with a successful execution of the BACKTRACK-FREE search algorithm. □

8.5.2 Backtrack-free search with constraint propagation

It is easy to modify the BACKTRACK-FREE search algorithm so that a constraint propagation in the form of domain reduction is incorporated into it. We represent the constraint propagation symbolically by means of the procedure prop with the signature

```
PROCEDURE prop(j: INTEGER; VAR D: domains;
               VAR failure: BOOLEAN);
```

Given an array D of the type ARRAY [1..n] OF domain representing the sequence of the variable domains and $j \in [1..n]$, the procedure call prop(j,D, failure) creates a local copy D' of D, modifies the domains D[j+1], ..., D[n] and if one of these domains becomes empty, it sets the variable failure to TRUE (independently of its initial value) and copies D' back to D. We modify then the procedure backtrack_free backtrack_free_prop. The resulting search algorithm is presented in Figure 8.19.

The difference is in the presence of the calls prop(0,D,failure) and prop(j,D,failure) and the use of the test NOT failure before the call backtrack_free_prop(1,D,success) and the assignment j := j+1. The BACKTRACK-FREE WITH CONSTRAINT PROPAGATION search algorithm performs search in the *prop* labeling trees.

In contrast to the BACKTRACK-FREE search algorithm the BACKTRACK-FREE WITH CONSTRAINT PROPAGATION search algorithm performs search

```
MODULE backtrack_free_prop;
TYPE domains =  ARRAY [1..n] OF domain;
     instantiation = ARRAY [1..n] OF elements;
VAR inst: instantiation;
    failure: BOOLEAN;
PROCEDURE backtrack_free_prop(j: INTEGER; D: domains;
                                  VAR success: BOOLEAN);
BEGIN
  WHILE D[j] <> {} AND NOT success DO
    choose d from D[j];
    D[j] := D[j] - {d};
    IF cons(inst,j,d) THEN
      inst[j] := d;
      success := (j = n);
      IF NOT success THEN
        prop(j,D,failure);
        IF NOT failure THEN
          j := j+1
        END
      END
    END
  END
END backtrack_free_prop;
BEGIN
  success := FALSE;
  prop(0,D,failure);
  IF NOT failure THEN
    backtrack_free_prop(1,D,success)
  END
END backtrack_free_prop;
```

Fig. 8.19. BACKTRACK-FREE WITH CONSTRAINT PROPAGATION search algorithm

in a more complicated tree. Consequently, the outcome of this algorithm is more difficult to describe. The reason is that, in contrast to the reduced trees, in the *prop* labeling trees the failed nodes are explicitly present: they are generated as a result of the constraint propagation. So to define the outcome of the BACKTRACK-FREE WITH CONSTRAINT PROPAGATION search algorithm we perform the following sequence of operations on the corresponding *prop* labeling tree:

- remove all failed nodes;
  these removed nodes will not be visited by the algorithm,
- remove from the resulting tree all the leaves L with the following property:
  there exists a sibling of L lying to its right which is not a leaf;
  in the original tree these removed nodes will be visited by the algorithm,
  but will not be selected since their unique descendant in the original tree
  is a failed node,
- locate the leftmost leaf in the resulting tree. Call it the *final* node.

We can now state the desired result.

Theorem 8.16 (Backtrack-free with Constraint Propagation Search) *The* BACKTRACK-FREE WITH CONSTRAINT PROPAGATION *search algorithm constructs in an initial segment of the array* inst *an instantiation that corresponds to the final node of the corresponding prop labeling tree and sets the variable* success *to* TRUE *if this node is at level 2n.* □

8.5.3 Backtracking

The BACKTRACK-FREE and the BACKTRACK-FREE WITH CONSTRAINT PROPAGATION search algorithms are correct only for a limited class of finite CSPs. From now on we discuss the search algorithms that are correct for all finite CSPs.

Note that in the BACKTRACK-FREE search algorithm the choices of the elements d for which cons(inst,j,d) holds cannot be revoked: each time such a d is found it is permanently recorded in the array inst. The BACK-TRACK search algorithm is a modification of this strategy. Informally, if the search 'under' the node (j,d) does not succeed, another choice of d for the level j is attempted. This is realised by replacing the assignment j := j+1 by a recursive call of the algorithm which represents this search 'under' the node (j,d). The resulting algorithm is presented in Figure 8.20.

Note that in the BACKTRACK search algorithm the array D is passed as a call by value parameter. This is crucial for the proper functioning of the algorithm: then at each level of recursion only a local version of D is modified. The BACKTRACK search algorithm performs search in the reduced labeling trees. The following result summarises its behaviour.

```
MODULE backtrack;
TYPE domains =  ARRAY [1..n] OF domain;
     instantiation = ARRAY [1..n] OF elements;
VAR inst: instantiation;
PROCEDURE backtrack(j: INTEGER; D: domains;
                    VAR success: BOOLEAN);
BEGIN
  WHILE D[j] <> {} AND NOT success DO
    choose d from D[j];
    D[j] := D[j] - {d};
    IF cons(inst,j,d) THEN
      inst[j] := d;
      success := (j = n);
      IF NOT success THEN
        backtrack(j+1,D,success)
      END
    END
  END
END backtrack;
BEGIN
  success := FALSE;
  backtrack(1,D,success)
END backtrack;
```

Fig. 8.20. BACKTRACK search algorithm

Theorem 8.17 (Backtrack Search) *If a solution exists, the* BACKTRACK *search algorithm constructs in the array* inst *the leftmost branch of the corresponding reduced labeling tree that represents a solution. Otherwise it reports a failure by setting the variable* success *to* FALSE. ☐

8.5.4 Backtracking with constraint propagation

We now modify the BACKTRACK search algorithm so that a constraint propagation in the form of a domain reduction is incorporated into it. To this end we proceed analogously as in Subsection 8.5.2 and use the procedure prop with the signature

```
PROCEDURE prop(j: INTEGER; VAR D: domains;
               VAR failure: BOOLEAN);
```

The appropriate modification of the BACKTRACK search algorithm yields the algorithm presented in Figure 8.21.

```
MODULE backtrack_prop;
TYPE domains =  ARRAY [1..n] OF domain;
     instantiation = ARRAY [1..n] OF elements;
VAR inst: instantiation;
    failure: BOOLEAN;
PROCEDURE backtrack_prop(j: INTEGER; D: domains;
                        VAR success: BOOLEAN);

BEGIN
  WHILE D[j] <> {} AND NOT success DO
    choose d from D[j];
    D[j] := D[j] - {d};
    IF cons(inst,j,d) THEN
      inst[j] := d;
      success := (j = n);
      IF NOT success THEN
        prop(j,D,failure);
        IF NOT failure THEN
          backtrack_prop(j+1,D,success)
        END
      END
    END
  END
END backtrack_prop;
BEGIN
  success := FALSE;
  prop(0,D,failure);
  IF NOT failure THEN
    backtrack_prop(1,D,success)
  END
END backtrack_prop;
```

Fig. 8.21. BACKTRACK WITH CONSTRAINT PROPAGATION search algorithm

So in the BACKTRACK WITH CONSTRAINT PROPAGATION search algorithm we employ the constraint propagation embodied in the procedure call prop(j,D,failure) that precedes both the initial and the recursive call to the main procedure backtrack_prop. These calls are entered only if failure is not set to TRUE. The behaviour of this search algorithm is summarised by the following result analogous to the BACKTRACK Search Theorem 8.17.

Theorem 8.18 (Backtrack with Constraint Propagation Search) *If a solution exists, the* BACKTRACK WITH CONSTRAINT PROPAGATION *search algorithm constructs in the array* inst *the leftmost leaf of the corresponding prop labeling tree that represents a solution. Otherwise it reports a failure by setting the variable* success *to* FALSE.

□

8.6 Instances of backtracking with constraint propagation

We shall now use the last search algorithm as a template to derive three specialised search algorithms that are related to the *FORWARD CHECK-ING, PARTIAL LOOK AHEAD*, and *MAC* search trees defined in Section 8.4. Analogous specialisations of the BACKTRACK-FREE WITH CONSTRAINT PROPAGATION search algorithm are left to the reader.

8.6.1 Forward checking

The first one, called the FORWARD CHECKING search algorithm, is a specialisation of the BACKTRACK WITH CONSTRAINT PROPAGATION search algorithm in which the constraint propagation consists of the forward checking as explained in Subsection 8.4.1. To define it more precisely we use the following auxiliary procedure revise that uses the global array inst:

```
PROCEDURE revise(j,k: INTEGER; VAR D: domains);
BEGIN
    D[k] := {d ∈ D[k] | {(x_1,inst[1]),...,(x_j,inst[j]),(x_k,d)} is
                        a consistent instantiation}
END revise;
```

The prop procedure is now defined as follows.

```
PROCEDURE prop(j: INTEGER; VAR D: domains;
               VAR failure: BOOLEAN);
VAR k: INTEGER;
BEGIN
    failure := FALSE;
    k := j+1;
    WHILE k <> n+1 AND NOT failure DO
        revise(j,k,D);
```

```
   failure := (D[k] = {});
      k := k+1
   END
END prop;
```

So in case the domain of a future variable x_k becomes empty as a result of the call revise(j,k,D), the variable failure is set to TRUE and, as an optimisation, the revisions of the subsequent future variables are abandoned. In that case the call prop(j,D,failure) actually does not compute the new domains of all future variables as defined in the case of the *FORWARD CHECKING* search tree, but it does not matter since in that case in the search algorithm a backtracking takes place anyway.

The resulting FORWARD CHECKING search algorithm performs search in the *FORWARD CHECKING* search tree. The following result summarises its behaviour.

Theorem 8.19 (Forward Checking Search) *If a solution exists, the* FORWARD CHECKING *search algorithm constructs in the array* inst *the leftmost leaf of the corresponding FORWARD CHECKING tree that represents a solution. Otherwise it reports a failure by setting the variable* success *to* FALSE. $\square$

8.6.2 Partial look ahead

The next algorithm, called the PARTIAL LOOK AHEAD search algorithm, is another specialisation of the BACKTRACK WITH CONSTRAINT PROPAGATION search algorithm in which the constraint propagation consists of the partial look ahead as explained in Subsection 8.4.2.

We limit ourselves to its presentation for CSPs with only binary constraints. The extension to arbitrary CSPs is straightforward though one needs to revise in an appropriate way the DARC algorithm of Section 7.6 that imposes directional arc consistency. Below we use another, minor, modification of the DARC algorithm in which the algorithm also terminates, as soon as a variable domain becomes empty. In that case the variable failure is set to TRUE. In the algorithm below this modification of the DARC algorithm has the following signature:

```
PROCEDURE darc(i: INTEGER; VAR D: domains;
                  VAR failure: BOOLEAN);
```

The call darc(i,D,failure) invokes the abovementioned modification of the DARC algorithm for the CSP limited to the variables $x_i, \ldots, x_n$. In the prop procedure this procedure is invoked with the actual parameter j+1. The appropriate prop procedure is now defined as follows.

```
PROCEDURE prop(j: INTEGER; VAR D: domains;
                VAR failure: BOOLEAN);
VAR k: INTEGER;
BEGIN
  failure := FALSE;
  k := j+1;
  WHILE k <> n+1 AND NOT failure DO
    revise(j,k,D);
    failure := (D[k] = {});
    k := k+1
  END;
  IF NOT failure THEN
    darc(j+1,D,failure)
  END
END prop;
```

The resulting PARTIAL LOOK AHEAD search algorithm is related to the *PARTIAL LOOK AHEAD* search tree in the analogous way as the one formulated for the FORWARD CHECKING Search Theorem 8.19.

8.6.3 Maintaining arc consistency (MAC)

The final algorithm, called the MAC search algorithm, or the **full look ahead** search algorithm, is a specialisation of the BACKTRACK WITH CONSTRAINT PROPAGATION search algorithm in which the constraint propagation consists of the *MAC*, i.e., the *FULL LOOK AHEAD* procedure, as explained in Subsection 8.4.3.

To be more specific we use here a modification of the ARC algorithm of Section 7.4 in which the algorithm also terminates as soon as a variable domain becomes empty. In that case the variable failure is set to TRUE. In the algorithm this modification of the ARC algorithm has the following signature:

```
PROCEDURE arc(i: INTEGER; VAR D: domains;
                VAR failure: BOOLEAN);
```

The call arc(i,D,failure) invokes the just described modification of the ARC algorithm for the CSP limited to the variables $x_i, \ldots, x_n$. In the prop procedure this procedure is invoked with the actual parameter j+1. The appropriate `prop` procedure is defined in the same way as in the previous subsection: it suffices to replace the call `darc(j+1,D,failure)` by `arc(j+1,D,failure)`.

The resulting MAC search algorithm is related to the MAC search tree in the analogous way as the one formulated for the FORWARD CHECKING Search Theorem 8.19.

8.6.4 Searching for all solutions

It is straightforward to modify all the algorithms of the last two sections to the ones in which one searches for all solutions instead of for one. To this end it suffices in each algorithm to drop the condition `NOT success` from the `WHILE` loop and add after the assignment `success := (j = n)` the line

`IF success THEN PRINT(inst) END`

where `PRINT` is a procedure with the expected meaning. Further, the `success` variable is not needed anymore so one can replace it by a direct reference to the test `j = n`. In the case of the BACKTRACK search algorithm of Subsection 8.5.3 these modifications result in the algorithm presented in Figure 8.22.

The BACKTRACK-ALL search algorithm performs search in the reduced labeling tree. Its behaviour is summarised by the following theorem.

Theorem 8.20 (Backtrack-all Search) *The* BACKTRACK-ALL *search algorithm prints all instances of the array* inst *that represent a solution.* $\square$

In the next section we use this search algorithm as a basis for developing algorithms for the constrained optimization problems.

8.7 Search algorithms for finite constrained optimization problems

We now turn our attention to the constrained optimization problems originally introduced in Section 2.6. So we consider a CSP $\mathcal{P} := \langle \mathcal{C} \; ; \; x_1 \in D_1, \ldots, x_n \in D_n \rangle$ and assume a function $obj : Sol \to \mathcal{R}$ from the set Sol of all solutions to $\mathcal{P}$ to the set $\mathcal{R}$ of real numbers. We seek a solution d to $\mathcal{P}$ for which the value $obj(d)$ is maximal.

Recall from Section 3.2 that in typical instances of the constrained optimization problem we also have to our disposal a heuristic function h that allows us to efficiently approximate the value of obj from above. The idea is that the function h can be computed before all the variables are completely

```
MODULE backtrack_all;
TYPE domains =  ARRAY [1..n] OF domain;
     instantiation = ARRAY [1..n] OF elements;
VAR inst: instantiation;
PROCEDURE backtrack_all(j: INTEGER; D: domains);
BEGIN
  WHILE D[j] <> {} DO
    choose d from D[j];
    D[j] := D[j] - {d};
    IF cons(inst,j,d) THEN
      inst[j] := d;
      IF j = n THEN
        PRINT(inst)
      ELSE
        backtrack_all(j+1,D)
      END
    END
  END
END backtrack_all;
BEGIN
  backtrack_all(1,D)
END backtrack_all;
```

Fig. 8.22. BACKTRACK-ALL search algorithm

instantiated and that the resulting value provides an **upper bound** on the values of *obj* on *all* solutions that extend the current instantiation. This upper bound can then be used to abandon instantiations that cannot be extended to solutions with a larger value of the objective function *obj* than the one known so far. In general, the choice of the heuristic function h requires good insights into the considered constrained optimization problem.

In what follows we assume the existence of a function

$$h : \mathcal{P}(D_1) \times \cdots \times \mathcal{P}(D_n) \to \mathcal{R} \cup \{\infty\}$$

from the set of all set sequences $E_1, \ldots, E_n$ such that $E_1 \subseteq D_1, \ldots, E_n \subseteq D_n$ to the set of real numbers augmented with ∞ which satisfies the following two properties, where we assume that the subset relation is extended componentwise to the sequences of sets denoted by $\bar{E}_1$ and $\bar{E}_2$:

Monotonicity If $\bar{E}_1 \subseteq \bar{E}_2$, then $h(\bar{E}_1) \leq h(\bar{E}_2)$,

Bound $obj(d_1, \ldots, d_n) \leq h(\{d_1\}, \ldots, \{d_n\})$.

These properties are obvious specialisations of the corresponding two properties postulated in Section 3.2 to the situation in which splitting consists of the labeling.

In what follows we present three search algorithms that allow us to look for a solution to thus formulated constrained optimization problem. We limit our attention to finite CSPs and assume that the splitting consists of the labeling. These algorithms employ the same principle, called **branch and bound**, which explains their names. We represent in them the functions *obj* and *h* by means of the procedures `obj` and `h` with the signatures

```
PROCEDURE obj(inst: instantiation): REAL;
```

```
PROCEDURE h(inst: instantiation; j: INTEGER; D: domains): REAL;
```

The intention is that the call `h(inst,j,D)` returns the value of the function *h* on the sequence (`{inst[1]}`, ..., `{inst[j]}`, `D[j+1]`, ..., `D[n]`).

8.7.1 Branch and bound

The first algorithm, called BRANCH AND BOUND search algorithm, is a modification of the BACKTRACK-ALL search algorithm of Subsection 8.6.4 and is presented in Figure 8.23.

Let us summarise the differences between the BRANCH AND BOUND search algorithm and the BACKTRACK-ALL search algorithm. First, we employ in the procedure two additional parameters, `solution`, to record the best solution, and `bound`, to maintain the best known value of the maximum we are looking for.

Second, when a solution is encountered, that is when `j = n` holds, it is not printed. Instead, if it is a solution with a higher value of the *obj* function, that is if `obj(inst) > bound` holds, the variable `bound` is updated and this solution is recorded in the variable `solution`.

Further, the recursive call is entered only if the test `h(inst,j,D) > bound` succeeds. Its purpose is to check whether this call can yield a solution with a higher value of the *obj* function than the one recorded in the variable `bound`. To put it negatively, if `h(inst,j,D) <= bound`, then by virtue of the **Monotonicity** and the **Bound** assumptions no solution extending the current instantiation can yield a value of the *obj* function higher than the one recorded in the variable `bound`.

The execution of the algorithm starts by initialising the `solution` variable

```
MODULE branch_and_bound;
TYPE domains =  ARRAY [1..n] OF domain;
     instantiation = ARRAY [1..n] OF elements;
VAR inst: instantiation;
PROCEDURE branch_and_bound(j: INTEGER; D: domains;
                              VAR solution: instantiation;
                              VAR bound: REAL);
BEGIN
  WHILE D[j] <> {} DO
    choose d from D[j];
    D[j] := D[j] - {d};
    IF cons(inst,j,d) THEN
      inst[j] := d;
      IF j = n THEN
        IF obj(inst) > bound THEN
          bound := obj(inst);
          solution := inst
        END
      ELSE
        IF h(inst,j,D) > bound THEN
          branch_and_bound(j+1,D,solution,bound)
        END
      END
    END
  END
END branch_and_bound;
BEGIN
  solution := NIL;
  bound := -infinity;
  branch_and_bound(1,D,solution,bound)
  END
END branch_and_bound;
```

Fig. 8.23. BRANCH AND BOUND search algorithm

to some value NIL assumed to be different from all solutions, and the bound
variable to the smallest possible value, represented by -infinity. The
following theorem summarises the behaviour of this algorithm.

Theorem 8.21 (Branch and Bound Search) *If a solution exists, the* BRANCH AND BOUND *search algorithm constructs in the array* solution *a solution with the largest obj value. Otherwise it reports a failure by setting the variable* solution *to* NIL. □

8.7.2 Branch and bound with constraint propagation

Next, we modify the BRANCH AND BOUND search algorithm by incorporating into it a constraint propagation. As in the case of the search algorithms presented in the previous section, we represent it by means of the procedure prop with the signature

```
PROCEDURE prop(j: INTEGER; VAR D: domains;
               VAR failure: BOOLEAN);
```

The appropriate modification results in the algorithm presented in Figure 8.24.

So we incorporated into the BRANCH AND BOUND WITH CONSTRAINT PROPAGATION search algorithm the same modifications as the ones that we used when transforming the BACKTRACK search algorithm into the BACKTRACK WITH CONSTRAINT PROPAGATION search algorithm. Namely, the recursive call is now entered only if the constraint propagation, represented by the call prop(j,D,failure), does not set the variable failure to TRUE and when the previously discussed test h(inst,j,D) > bound succeeds. This algorithm satisfies the same property as the one stated in the BRANCH AND BOUND Search Theorem 8.21.

8.7.3 Branch and bound with constraint propagation and cost constraint

In the final modification of the BRANCH AND BOUND search algorithm we incorporate into it, in addition to the constraint propagation, a *dynamic modification* of the considered CSP. More specifically, when the test obj(inst) > bound succeeds, apart from updating the variables bound and solution we also add the constraint $obj(x_1, \ldots, x_n) >$ bound to the set of considered constraints. We assume here that the function *obj* is definable in the language used to represent the constraints and that $obj(x_1, \ldots, x_n) >$ bound is a syntactically allowed constraint. This is for example the case when we consider linear constraints and when the function *obj* is linear.

The idea is that when the test obj(inst) > bound succeeds, we only need to look from now on for the solutions with a the *obj* value larger than the

```
MODULE branch_and_bound_prop;
TYPE domains =  ARRAY [1..n] OF domain;
     instantiation = ARRAY [1..n] OF elements;
VAR inst: instantiation;
    failure: BOOLEAN;
PROCEDURE branch_and_bound_prop(j: INTEGER; D: domains;
                                VAR solution: instantiation;
                                VAR bound: REAL);

BEGIN
  WHILE D[j] <> {} DO
    choose d from D[j];
    D[j] := D[j] - {d};
    IF cons(inst,j,d) THEN
      inst[j] := d;
      IF j = n THEN
        IF obj(inst) > bound THEN
          bound := obj(inst);
          solution := inst
        END
      ELSE
        prop(j,D,failure);
        IF NOT failure THEN
          IF h(inst,j,D) > bound THEN
            branch_and_bound_prop(j+1,D,solution,bound)
          END
        END
      END
    END
  END
END branch_and_bound_prop;
BEGIN
  solution := NIL;
  bound := -infinity;
  prop(0,D,failure);
  IF NOT failure THEN
    branch_and_bound_prop(1,D,solution,bound)
  END
END branch_and_bound_prop;
```

Fig. 8.24. BRANCH AND BOUND WITH CONSTRAINT PROPAGATION search algorithm

one just found and recorded in the variable bound. That is, we can impose the $obj(x_1, \ldots, x_n) >$ bound constraint on the set of the still to be generated solutions. This results in the algorithm presented in Figure 8.25.

To formulate the dynamic modification of the set of constraints we use in the procedure branch_and_bound_prop_obj of the BRANCH AND BOUND WITH CONSTRAINT PROPAGATION AND COST CONSTRAINT search algorithm a new parameter C of a further not analysed type constraints that represents the set of considered constraints. Note that C is passed as a call by variable parameter. This way the changes to the set of constraints are permanent. As with the previously considered algorithm, the BRANCH AND BOUND WITH CONSTRAINT PROPAGATION AND COST CONSTRAINT search algorithm satisfies the same property as the one stated in the BRANCH AND BOUND Search Theorem 8.21.

The last two search algorithms can be instantiated in a straightforward way by an arbitrary constraint propagation in the form of a domain reduction. In particular, they can be instantiated by the constraint propagation employed in the FORWARD CHECKING, PARTIAL LOOK AHEAD and MAC search algorithms. This leads to search algorithms that combine the features introduced in the last two sections.

8.8 Heuristics for search algorithms

When discussing in the last two sections the search algorithms we assumed that the constraint propagation and the split method is fixed. But even then some choices still remain. They are concerned with the selection of the variables and the selection of the values in the variables domains. In general it is very difficult, if not impossible, to predict their effect on the efficiency of search for a solution to a given CSP. Hence, in absence of further information, these choices are determined by means of various heuristics the effectiveness of which is assessed empirically.

Let us discuss now these choices for the case of the labeling trees. They can be naturally incorporated into any search algorithm discussed in the previous two sections.

8.8.1 Variable selection

This decision concerns the choice of the next variable for labeling. Two natural heuristics were proposed:

- Select a variable with the smallest domain.
  This choice is motivated by the Labeling Note 8.5 according to which

```
MODULE branch_and_bound_prop_obj;
TYPE domains =  ARRAY [1..n] OF domain;
     instantiation = ARRAY [1..n] OF elements;
VAR inst: instantiation;
    failure: BOOLEAN;
PROCEDURE branch_and_bound_prop_obj(j: INTEGER;
               VAR C: constraints; D: domains;
               VAR solution: instantiation; VAR bound: REAL);
BEGIN
  WHILE D[j] <> {} DO
    choose d from D[j];
    D[j] := D[j] - {d};
    IF cons(inst,j,d) THEN
      inst[j] := d;
      IF j = n THEN
        IF obj(inst) > bound THEN
          bound := obj(inst);
          solution := inst;
          C := C ∪ {obj(x_1,...,x_n) > bound}
        END
      ELSE
        prop(j,D,failure);
        IF NOT failure THEN
          IF h(inst,j,D) > bound THEN
            branch_and_bound_prop_obj(j+1,C,D,solution,bound)
          END
        END
      END
    END
  END
END branch_and_bound_prop_obj;
BEGIN
  solution := NIL;
  bound := -infinity;
  prop(0,D,failure);
  IF NOT failure THEN
    branch_and_bound_prop_obj(1,C,D,solution,bound)
  END
END branch_and_bound_prop_obj;
```

Fig. 8.25. BRANCH AND BOUND WITH CONSTRAINT PROPAGATION AND COST CONSTRAINT search algorithm

the size of the complete labeling tree is smallest when the variables are ordered by their domain sizes in the increasing order.

- Select a ***most constrained*** variable, i.e., a variable that appears in the largest number of constraints.

  A justification for this choice is provided by an observation that an instantiation of such a variable should yield a more effective domain reduction by means of the constraint propagation. For example, it can turn a non-linear equation to a linear one.

Additionally, if all the variable domains are numeric, we can use the following heuristics:

- Select a variable with the smallest difference between its domain bounds.

  Note that this does not have to be a variable with the smallest domain: take for instance the variable x with the domain $\{0, 1, 2\}$ and the variable y with the domain $\{0, 100\}$.

All three heuristics are instances of the so-called ***first-fail*** principle according to which when faced with a choice one tries first an alternative that most likely leads to a failure.

It is important to note that the above selection principles are ***dynamic*** in the sense that at each level the selection is made anew. Now, to keep the definition simple, we assumed that the labeling trees and the *prop* labeling trees are defined with respect to ***a fixed in advance*** variable ordering. To properly account for the dynamic selection principle this definition should be modified so that at each odd level the new current variable is determined dynamically.

8.8.2 Value selection

When presenting the search algorithms we assumed that the elements in each variable domain are selected in a non-deterministic way. In practice a number of natural choices arise. In case of search algorithms for constrained optimization problems the following heuristics is helpful:

- select a value for which the heuristic function yields the highest outcome.

If the heuristic function is well chosen (that is, approximates reasonably well the *obj* function), such a value is then 'most promising'. To be more specific, in the BRANCH AND BOUND search algorithm and its two modifications, assuming j < n, we choose an element d from the domain D[j] for which cons(inst,j,d) holds and for which, after the assignment inst[j]

:= d, the value of h(inst,j,D) is the highest. So this heuristic calls for a simple subsidiary computation.

Further, when discussing numeric domains, the following natural choices arise when selecting the next value in a domain:

- select the smallest value,
- select the largest value,
- select the middle value.

The first two heuristics are obvious. The third one is motivated by the observation that in some circumstances the choice of the middle value can lead to a more effective constraint propagation. For example, it has been noted that this heuristics is beneficial for the CSP formalising the n Queens Problem presented in Example 2.2.

8.9 An abstract branch and bound algorithm

We started this chapter by defining in Section 8.1 arbitrary search trees. Then, after discussing the labeling trees we presented the search algorithms for them. Let us close now the loop by discussing briefly the search algorithms for the arbitrary search trees. In these trees the constraint propagation is modeled by means of a transition from even to odd levels. So we should confine our attention to three search algorithms BACKTRACK-FREE WITH CONSTRAINT PROPAGATION, BACKTRACK WITH CONSTRAINT PROPAGATION, and BRANCH AND BOUND WITH CONSTRAINT PROPAGATION. We now present the last algorithm in an abstract form, leaving the presentation of the other two, simpler ones, as Exercise 8.11.

We fix a finite search tree T and represent it by means of an array children of some further unanalysed type searchtree that given a CSP P yields in children[P] the set of its direct descendants in T. Also, we assume a further unanalysed type CSP. Further, we assume a function next that will be applied to a CSP at an even level to access its only direct descendant, using the instruction R := next(P).

We also assume that a CSP is a leaf of T if and only if it is 'manifestly solved' or 'manifestly failed'. To test the status of a CSP we assume the existence of two procedures, solved which returns the truth value of the statement 'the CSP is 'manifestly solved' ', and failed which returns the truth value of the statement 'the CSP is 'manifestly failed' '.

Finally, we model the optimization by assuming the existence of an obj function that given a 'manifestly solved' CSP returns its objective value being a real value. We look in the search tree T for a 'manifestly solved'

CSP with a maximal `obj` value. To this end we employ a heuristic function h that assigns to each CSP P in $\mathcal{T}$ a real value and assume two properties of the functions `obj` and `h`:

- if R is a direct descendant of P, then $h(R) \leq h(P)$,
- if P is a 'manifestly solved' CSP, then $obj(P) \leq h(P)$.

The algorithm is presented in Figure 8.26. For its proper functioning it is essential that the `children` parameter is passed by value, so that the modifications performed during the recursive call are carried out only on its local version.

The following theorem summarises the behaviour of this algorithm.

Theorem 8.22 (Abstract Branch and Bound Search) *Call a CSP* P *'manifestly solved' if* `solved(P)` *holds. If in the considered search tree with the root* `Pinit` *a 'manifestly solved' CSP exists, the* ABSTRACT BRANCH AND BOUND *search algorithm returns in* P *such a CSP with the largest* `obj` *value. Otherwise it reports a failure by setting the variable* `solution` *to* NIL.

$\square$

This theorem holds for arbitrary CSPs, in particular for the ones with infinite domains. The ABSTRACT BRANCH AND BOUND search algorithm can be specialised in many ways by choosing the definitions of a 'manifestly solved' and of a 'manifestly failed' CSP, and by selecting the split method, the form of constraint propagation, the *obj* function, and the heuristic function.

As an illustration of its use let us return to the approach of computing optimal solutions to polynomial constraints on integer intervals subject to a polynomial objective function that we discussed in Section 3.4. We used there a specific *obj* function, defined a specific split method in the form of a bisection, and defined constraint propagation and the heuristic function *h* using interval arithmetic on integers. To complete the details of the ABSTRACT BRANCH AND BOUND search algorithm we define a CSP to be 'manifestly solved' if it is solved and all its domains are singletons, and 'manifestly failed' if it is failed.

Note also that by considering the finite CSPs with the splitting defined as the labeling and by defining 'manifestly solved' as 'a solved CSP with the domains being singleton sets' we obtain the already discussed constrained optimization problem for finite CSPs and the BRANCH AND BOUND WITH CONSTRAINT PROPAGATION search algorithm.

It is difficult to define heuristics for arbitrary search trees. This can be

```
MODULE abstract_branch_and_bound;
PROCEDURE abstract_branch_and_bound(children: searchtree;
                    VAR solution: CSP; VAR bound: REAL);
BEGIN
  WHILE children[P] <> {} DO
    choose R from children[P];
    children[P] := children[P] - {R};
    IF NOT failed(R) THEN
      P := R;
      IF solved(P) THEN
        IF obj(P) > bound THEN
          bound := obj(P);
          solution := P
      END
    ELSE
      P := next(P);
      IF NOT failed(P) THEN
        IF h(P) > bound THEN
            abstract_branch_and_bound(children,solution,bound)
        END
      END
    END
  END
END
END abstract_branch_and_bound;
BEGIN
  solution := NIL;
  bound := -infinity;
  P := next(Pinit);
  IF NOT failed(P) THEN
    abstract_branch_and_bound(children,solution,bound)
  END
END abstract_branch_and_bound;
```

Fig. 8.26. ABSTRACT BRANCH AND BOUND search algorithm

done for some specific cases of splitting and constraint propagation. For
example, the variable selection heuristics defined in Section 8.8 can be also

used when splitting consists of bisecting the domain of the current variable with a numeric domain using a middle value between the bounds.

8.10 Summary

In this chapter we studied search algorithms. To this end we first introduced search trees that result from an alternating use of constraint propagation and splitting. Then we presented the search algorithms as algorithms that explore the search trees.

The bulk of the presentation dealt with the search trees obtained when the labeling is used as the splitting method. We called them the labeling trees. We presented three types of the labeling trees that result from choosing a specific form of constraint propagation:

- forward checking,
- partial look ahead, and
- maintaining arc consistency (MAC),

and presented several search algorithms for these trees, namely

- the backtrack-free search algorithm,
- the backtrack search algorithm,

and their modifications that involve constraint propagation.

Also, we discussed various search algorithms for constrained optimization problems, the aim of which is to find an optimal solution. These algorithms rely on

- the branch and bound principle.

We presented the search algorithms for the labeling trees in a uniform way, by successive minor modifications. This allowed us to clarify how these algorithms are related to each other. We also explained how the search algorithms for the labeling trees can be combined with a number of heuristics that are concerned with the variable and value selection. Finally, we argued that the basic search algorithms can also be presented for arbitrary search trees.

8.11 Exercises

Exercise 8.1 Prove the Search Tree Note 8.2.

Exercise 8.2 Suppose that all constraints of the considered CSP are unary or binary. Show that the *FORWARD CHECKING* search tree can then be defined using the following, simpler, definition of the domains $E'_{i+1}, \ldots, E'_n$:

$$E'_j := E_j - \{e \in E_j \mid \text{ for some constraint } C \text{ on } x_i \text{ and } x_j \;\; (d_i, e) \notin C\},$$

where $j \in [i+1..n]$.

Exercise 8.3 Prove the BACKTRACK-FREE Search Theorem 8.14.
Hint Use here and in Exercises 8.4–8.9 induction on the number of variables.

Exercise 8.4 Prove the BACKTRACK-FREE WITH CONSTRAINT PROPAGATION Search Theorem 8.16.

Exercise 8.5 Prove the BACKTRACK Search Theorem 8.17.

Exercise 8.6 Prove the BACKTRACK WITH CONSTRAINT PROPAGATION Search Theorem 8.18.

Exercise 8.7 Prove the FORWARD CHECKING Search Theorem 8.19.

Exercise 8.8 Prove the BACKTRACK-ALL Search Theorem 8.20.

Exercise 8.9 Prove the BRANCH AND BOUND Search Theorem 8.21.

Exercise 8.10 Prove the ABSTRACT BRANCH AND BOUND Search Theorem 8.22.
Hint Use induction on the number of nodes.

Exercise 8.11 Present the BACKTRACK-FREE WITH CONSTRAINT PROPAGATION and the BACKTRACK WITH CONSTRAINT PROPAGATION search algorithms for the arbitrary search trees.

8.12 Bibliographic remarks

Many of the algorithms discussed in this chapter embody standard techniques that were used in artificial intelligence and combinatorial optimization before the advent of constraint programming.

More specifically, the BACKTRACK and the BRANCH AND BOUND search algorithms are informally described Golomb and Baumert [1965]. In Bitner and Reingold [1975], a non-recursive algorithmic description of the BACKTRACK search algorithm is provided. According to this paper the backtrack technique dates back at least to the end of the nineteenth century, when it was used by Lucas [1891] to thread mazes, and the recursive formulation of the algorithm, that we adopted here, appeared first in Tarjan [1972].

The BRANCH AND BOUND search algorithm was also introduced in Dakin [1965] in the context of integer programming. Its modification to the BRANCH AND BOUND WITH CONSTRAINT PROPAGATION search algorithm has its roots in the incorporation of so-called cuts into the branch and bound algorithm for integer programming. (Cuts are valid linear inequalities with integer coefficients that can be deduced from a given set of such inequalities. Their use corresponds to an application of constraint propagation.)

The Backtrack-free Search II Theorem 8.15 is from Freuder [1982]. Much research went on into identifying other structural properties of constraints guaranteeing that backtrack-free search is sufficient to determine consistency, see in particular van Beek and Dechter [1995] and Sam-Haroud and Faltings [1996].

The FORWARD CHECKING search algorithm was originally introduced in McGregor [1979], for binary constraints. Bessière et al. [2002] show that this algorithm admits several generalisations to non-binary constraints. The PARTIAL LOOK AHEAD search algorithm is due to Haralick and Elliot [1980]. The MAC search algorithm was proposed in Gaschnig [1974] under the name of FULL LOOK AHEAD. The name MAC comes from Sabin and Freuder [1994], a paper in which the original conclusions of Haralick and Elliot [1980] favouring partial look ahead over full look ahead were critically assessed. The most constrained variable heuristic is mentioned in Bitner and Reingold [1975]. The *first-fail* principle was formulated in Haralick and Elliot [1980].

A detailed survey of the backtracking algorithms for constraint satisfaction problems is given in Dechter and Frost [2002]. This survey focuses on the so-called **look back methods** (sometimes called *intelligent backtracking*) that we did not consider here.

8.13 References

C. BESSIÈRE, P. MESEGUER, E. C. FREUDER, AND J. LARROSA
  [2002]   On forward checking for non-binary constraint satisfaction, *Artificial Intelligence*, 141, pp. 205–224.

J. J. BITNER AND E. M. REINGOLD
  [1975]   Backtrack programming techniques, *Communications of the ACM*, 18, pp. 651–656.

R. J. DAKIN
  [1965]   A tree search algorithm for mixed integer programming problems, *The Computer Journal*, 8, pp. 250–255.

R. DECHTER AND D. FROST
  [2002]   Backjump-based backtracking for constraint satisfaction problems, *Artificial Intelligence*, 136, pp. 147–188.

E. C. FREUDER

[1982]   A sufficient condition for backtrack-free search, *Journal of the ACM*, 29, pp. 24–32.

J. GASCHNIG

[1974]   A constraint satisfaction method for inference making, in: *Proceedings of the 12th Annual Allerton Conference on Circuit and System Theory*, Urbana-Champaign, IL, pp. 866–874.

S. W. GOLOMB AND L. D. BAUMERT

[1965]   Backtrack programming, *Journal of the ACM*, 12, pp. 516–524.

R. M. HARALICK AND G. L. ELLIOT

[1980]   Increasing tree search efficiency for constraint satisfaction problems, *Artificial Intelligence*, 14, pp. 263–313.

E. LUCAS

[1891]   *Récréations Mathématiques*, Gauthier Villar, Paris, second ed.

J. J. MCGREGOR

[1979]   Relational consistency algorithms and their application in finding subgraph and graph isomorphism, *Information Science*, 19, pp. 229–250.

D. SABIN AND E. C. FREUDER

[1994]   Contradicting conventional wisdom in constraint satisfaction, in: *Proceedings ECAI'94*, Amsterdam, pp. 125–129.

D. SAM-HAROUD AND B. FALTINGS

[1996]   Consistency techniques for continuous constraints, *Constraints*, 1, pp. 85–118.

R. TARJAN

[1972]   Depth-first search and linear graph algorithms, *SIAM Journal on Computing*, 1, pp. 146–160.

P. VAN BEEK AND R. DECHTER

[1995]   On the minimality and global consistency of row-convex constraint networks, *Journal of the ACM*, 42, pp. 543–561.

9

Issues in constraint programming

I N THE PREVIOUS chapters we discussed various aspects of constraint programming. We did it by concentrating on the relevant ingredients of this programming style separately. In principle we could put them together using the general framework of Section 3.2. There are, however, other issues that naturally arise when one tries to incorporate these techniques in a programming language or system. In this chapter we shall discuss these matters and also shed light on the resulting programming style. At the same time we shall provide a short summary of various research topics currently pursued in constraint programming.

We discuss in turn the issues concerned with modeling (in Section 9.1), constraint programming languages (in Section 9.2), constraint propagation (in Section 9.3), constraint solvers (in Section 9.4), search (in Section 9.5) and over-constrained problems (in Section 9.6). Finally, at the end of the chapter, in the bibliographic remarks, we provide pointers to a number of useful surveys that should allow the reader to embark on research in constraint programming. As the final bibliography is just 'next door' we do not list the, rather extensive, list of references at the end of this chapter.

9.1 Modeling

Recall that in Chapter 1 we formulated the following principle:

Constraint programming is about a formulation of the problem as a constraint satisfaction problem and about solving it by means of domain specific or general methods.

As already stated, the first task, that is, the problem formulation, is called modeling. We noted in Chapter 2 that it is quite common that a given problem admits several natural representations. To choose among them requires proper understanding of the underlying alternatives and occasionally some good insights. Even then it is difficult to draw hard conclusions.

9.1.1 Choosing the right variables

This matter can be illustrated even by such a simple example as the *SEND + MORE = MONEY* puzzle of Example 2.1. We provided there a number of different representations of this problem. Let us concentrate now on the issue of representing the relevant equality constraints. In the first representation we used the variables S, E, N, D, M, O, R, Y. The variables S and M had as the domain the integer interval $[1..9]$ and the remaining six variables the integer interval $[0..9]$. We used the equality constraint

$$
\begin{aligned}
1000 \cdot S \quad &+ \quad 100 \cdot E \quad + \quad 10 \cdot N \quad + \quad D \\
+ \quad 1000 \cdot M \quad &+ \quad 100 \cdot O \quad + \quad 10 \cdot R \quad + \quad E \\
= 10000 \cdot M \quad + \quad 1000 \cdot O \quad &+ \quad 100 \cdot N \quad + \quad 10 \cdot E \quad + \quad Y
\end{aligned}
$$

combined with 28 disequality constraints $x \neq y$ for x, y ranging over the set $\{S, E, N, D, M, O, R, Y\}$ with x preceding y in the presented order.

We noted in Section 6.4 that using the domain reduction rules for the linear constraints on integer intervals we can reduce the original domains to

$$S = 9, E \in [4..7], N \in [5..8], D \in [2..8], M = 1, O = 0, R \in [2..8], Y \in [2..8].$$

The alternative representation of this problem used the auxiliary 'carry' variables C_1, C_2, C_3, C_4 ranging over $[0..1]$ and the following five equality constraints:

$$D + E = 10 \cdot C_1 + Y,$$

$$C_1 + N + R = 10 \cdot C_2 + E,$$

$$C_2 + E + O = 10 \cdot C_3 + N,$$

$$C_3 + S + M = 10 \cdot C_4 + O,$$

$$C_4 = M.$$

It turns out that the same domain reduction rules for the linear constraints on integer intervals yield now a weaker domain reduction. Indeed, one can check that the original domains of the S, E, N, D, M, O, R, Y variables reduce now to

$$S = 9, E \in [2..8], N \in [2..8], D \in [2..8], M = 1, O = 0, R \in [2..8], Y \in [2..8].$$

So the second representation yields initially a weaker constraint propagation. In fact, the *prop* labeling tree corresponding with the first representation and depicted in Figure 8.9 of Section 8.3 has 23 nodes and the unique solution is found by the BACKTRACK WITH CONSTRAINT PROPAGATION search algorithm of Subsection 8.5.4 after visiting 19 nodes. In contrast, for the second representation the corresponding *prop* labeling tree has 29 nodes and the unique solution is found by the BACKTRACK WITH CONSTRAINT PROPAGATION search algorithm of Subsection 8.5.4 after visiting 23 nodes. So the first representation turns out to be more efficient.

However, for the *GERALD + DONALD = ROBERT* alphametic problem, mentioned in the bibliographic remarks of Chapter 2, the situation is reverse. The representation of the corresponding equality constraint without the carries leads to a *prop* labeling tree with 16651 nodes and the unique solution is found by the BACKTRACK WITH CONSTRAINT PROPAGATION search algorithm of Subsection 8.5.4 after visiting 13795 nodes. In contrast, the representation with the carries results in a substantially smaller *prop* labeling tree, with 869 nodes, and the unique solution is found by the BACKTRACK WITH CONSTRAINT PROPAGATION search algorithm of Subsection 8.5.4 after visiting 791 nodes.

This shows that it is not easy to determine in advance whether it is better to use the original constraints or to introduce auxiliary variables and transform the constraints to simpler ones.

9.1.2 Choosing the right constraints

Recall from Chapter 2 that given a sequence of variables $x_1, \ldots, x_n$ with respective domains $D_1, \ldots, D_n$ the `all_different` constraint was defined by

$$\texttt{all\_different}(x_1, \ldots, x_n) := \{(d_1, \ldots, d_n) \mid d_i \neq d_j \text{ for } i \neq j\}.$$

Semantically `all_different`$(x_1, \ldots, x_n)$ is equivalent to the conjunction

$$\bigwedge_{i=1}^{n-1} \bigwedge_{j=i+1}^{n} x_i \neq x_j,$$

that is to say, the corresponding CSPs are equivalent. So it may seem that the use of `all_different`$(x_1, \ldots, x_n)$ instead of the above disequality constraints is just a matter of syntactic convenience. Indeed, it is easy to check that in the above example of the *SEND + MORE = MONEY* puzzle the same domain reduction is achieved when using the disequality constraints or the `all_different` constraint.

However, in general, this does not need to be the case. Consider for instance the obviously inconsistent CSP

$$\langle \texttt{all\_different}(x_1, x_2, x_3) \; ; \; x_1 \in \{1, 2\}, x_2 \in \{1, 2\}, x_3 \in \{1, 2\} \rangle.$$

Note that this CSP is not hyper-arc consistent. In fact, the constraint `all_different`(x_1, x_2, x_3) is here empty. We can detect the inconsistency by transforming this CSP to an equivalent one that is hyper-arc consistent and the domains of which are all empty.

Let us take now an alternative representation of this CSP by means of the disequality constraints:

$$\langle x_1 \neq x_2, x_1 \neq x_3, x_2 \neq x_3 \; ; \; x_1 \in \{1, 2\}, x_2 \in \{1, 2\}, x_3 \in \{1, 2\} \rangle.$$

Then this CSP is obviously hyper-arc consistent (or, equivalently, arc consistent, since all constraints are binary). So hyper-arc consistency is insufficient to detect that this CSP is inconsistent. To determine inconsistency we have to resort to other forms of local consistency discussed in Chapter 5, like path consistency or relational consistency. However, in general, the corresponding constraint propagation algorithms are too inefficient, so they are not provided in specific implementations of the constraint programming languages.

In contrast, the appropriate domain reduction rule for the `all_different` constraint can be efficiently implemented. Namely, as shown by Régin [1994], the hyper-arc consistency for this constraint can be achieved in $O(k\, n^{3/2})$ time, where k is the size of the maximum domain and n is the number of variables. The algorithm employs an efficient algorithm for computing a maximal matching in bipartite graphs.

We now continue a discussion of this constraint in the context of other constraints. To illustrate the point let us return to the Zebra puzzle introduced in Example 2.3. We mentioned there two ways of representing the disequalities. The first one consisted of an explicit listing of all fifty of them. The second one involved five uses of the all_different constraint, each time applied to five variables.

We shall now study the impact of these two choices in conjunction with another, less obvious, choice concerning the formalisation of the following three constraints that rely on the absolute difference function:

- The Norwegian lives next door to the blue house:
  $|\texttt{norwegian} - \texttt{blue}| = 1$,
- The fox is in the house next to the doctor's: $|\texttt{fox} - \texttt{doctor}| = 1$,
- The horse is in the house next to the diplomat's:
  $|\texttt{horse} - \texttt{diplomat}| = 1$.

One way to represent these constraints is by means of the disjunctive constraints mentioned in Section 3.2 and take care of them by means of the splitting rule there mentioned. So for example the constraint $|\texttt{norwegian} - \texttt{blue}| = 1$ would be rewritten as a disjunctive constraint

$$\texttt{norwegian} - \texttt{blue} = 1 \lor \texttt{norwegian} - \texttt{blue} = -1.$$

In the alternative representation we use the binary constraint difference1 on the variables x and y with the respective integer domains D_x and D_y, defined by

$$\texttt{difference1}(x,y) = \{(a,b) \mid |a - b| = 1\},$$

together with two rules that define constraint propagation for this constraint. In these rules for a set of integers D, as in Section 3.4,

$$D + \{-1, 1\} := \{a + 1 \mid a \in D\} \cup \{a - 1 \mid a \in D\}.$$

difference1–1

$$\frac{\langle \texttt{difference1}(x,y)\ ;\ x \in D_x, y \in D_y \rangle}{\langle \texttt{difference1}(x,y)\ ;\ x \in D'_x, y \in D_y \rangle}$$

where $D'_x = D_x \cap (D_y + \{-1, 1\})$,

difference1–2

$$\frac{\langle \texttt{difference1}(x,y)\ ;\ x \in D_x, y \in D_y \rangle}{\langle \texttt{difference1}(x,y)\ ;\ x \in D_x, y \in D'_y \rangle}$$

where $D'_y = D_y \cap (D_x + \{-1, 1\})$.

It is easy to see that both rules are equivalence preserving and that a CSP $\langle \texttt{difference1}(x,y)\ ;\ x \in D_x, y \in D_y \rangle$ is closed under their applications iff it is arc consistent. So in view of the Hyper-arc Consistency Lemma 6.1 of Section 6.1 these rules are optimal.

To see their use note for example that once we reduce the domain of the `norwegian` variable to 1 on the account of the `norwegian` $=1$ constraint, we can apply the second rule to

$$\langle\texttt{difference1(norwegian, blue)} \; ; \; \texttt{norwegian} = 1, \texttt{blue} \in [1..5]\rangle$$

and reduce it to

$$\langle\texttt{difference1(norwegian, blue)} \; ; \; \texttt{norwegian} = 1, \texttt{blue} = 2\rangle.$$

This reduction does not take place in the first representation for which the constraint propagation rests only on the *LINEAR EQUALITY* rule of Section 6.4 adapted for finite integer domains.

An equivalent approach consists of replacing each constraint $|x - y| = 1$ by the linear constraint $x - y = z$, where for each constraint z is a new variable with the initial domain $\{-1, 1\}$.

The accumulated impact of different representations of the puzzle is illustrated in Table 9.1 in which the size of the corresponding binary search tree for the enumeration splitting method of Section 3.2 and the first-fail heuristic of Section 8.8 is listed.

using	all_different	disequality constraints
disjunctive constraints	43	55
difference1 constraints	25	33

Table 9.1. *Sizes of search trees for the Zebra puzzle*

So choosing the `all_different` and the `difference1` constraints yields the smallest search tree. While this does not prove that this combination yields the most efficient solution, it does illustrate the consequences of various choices.

9.1.3 Choosing the right representation

Of course, the above presented examples are very simplistic. Still, they illustrate an obvious yet important point that, because of constraint propagation, different problem representations lead to search trees of different sizes. In general, this size is a good measure of the complexity of the problem representation. So we are interested in a problem representation that, together with the selected form of constraint propagation, yields the smallest search tree. While the right choice is in general difficult to predict, a number of common sense observations can be made.

Before we make them let us list some more realistic examples that show how modeling affects the efficiency. They can be found in the following three publications, where a CSP representation of a non-trivial problem was compared with a customary IP (integer programming) representation:

- A *Microcode Label Assignment Problem* (Van Hentenryck [1989])

  – CSP representation: 187 finite integer domain variables,
  – IP representation: 2024 Boolean variables,

- A *Packing Problem* (Bockmayr and Kasper [1998])

  – CSP representation: 7 finite integer domain variables, 2 constraints,
  – IP representation: 42 Boolean variables, 18 constraints,

- A *Golf Scheduling Problem* (Darby-Dowman and Little [1998])

  – CSP representation: 176 variables,
  – IP representation 1: 2574 variables,
  – IP representation 2: 592 variables.

This illustrates dramatic differences between alternative ways of modeling a problem. In each case the use of the CSP representation and of the constraint programming techniques turned out to be more efficient.

In general, it is preferable to use representations that involve less variables and simpler constraints for which constraint propagation is readily available. Another rule of thumb is that constraint propagation techniques that require less preprocessing (that often relies on the introduction of auxiliary variables) are often more powerful and thus preferable, since they reduce the search space better. Further, one should be aware that the use of disjunctive constraints can lead to an inefficient representation, since their processing can generate a large search space.

As already stated in Chapter 3 modeling is more an art than science. Consequently, the above guidelines have to be taken with a grain of salt. Probably, for each rule of thumb one can find an exception. The choice of heuristics for problem modeling is a subject of an ongoing research in constraint programming.

In general, it also pays off to use constraints for which we have to our disposal efficient domain reduction algorithms. This leads us to the subject of global constraints.

9.1.4 Global constraints

A *global constraint* is a name customarily used to describe a complex (that is, 'complicated', in an informal sense) constraint, with the number of variables often being a parameter. An appropriate constraint propagation for a global constraint is then taken care of by means of a special purpose algorithm. Modeling by means of global constraints is therefore more efficient than relying on the general purpose constraint propagation algorithms.

A typical example of a global constraint is the already discussed `all_different` constraint. In the literature several other global constraints were proposed together with customised constraint propagation algorithms. The most known of them is the `cumulative` constraint of Aggoun and Beldiceanu [1993] used to formalise various optimization problems that can be expressed as scheduling problems involving tasks with starting times, durations, and resource consumption. This constraint involves the following variables ranging over the natural numbers:

- $S_1, \ldots, S_n$ that denote the starting times of the tasks,
- $D_1, \ldots, D_n$ that denote the durations of these tasks,
- $R_1, \ldots, R_n$ that denote the resource consumption of these tasks,
- L that denotes the limit that is not exceeded at any point of time by the sum of the resource consumption of all active tasks.

Formally, this constraint is defined as follows, where the variables $S_1, \ldots, S_n$, $D_1, \ldots, D_n, R_1, \ldots, R_n, L$ range over the natural numbers:

$$\texttt{cumulative}([S_1, \ldots, S_n], [D_1, \ldots, D_n], [R_1, \ldots, R_n], L) :=$$
$$\{([s_1, \ldots, s_n], [d_1, \ldots, d_n], [r_1, \ldots, r_n], l) \mid \forall t \; \textstyle\sum_{\{i \mid s_i \leq t \leq s_i + d_i - 1\}} r_i \leq l\}.$$

Here a task i is **active** at time point t if $s_i \leq t \leq s_i + d_i - 1$. So the expression $\sum_{\{i \mid s_i \leq t \leq s_i + d_i - 1\}} r_i$ represents the sum of the resource consumption of all active tasks at time point t.

The appropriate constraint propagation algorithm employs the so-called edge-finding technique that attempts to check whether some task has to be placed before or after a set of other tasks. If yes, then the domain of the starting time variable of this task is appropriately reduced. This constraint, together with the corresponding constraint propagation algorithm, is available in several constraint programming systems.

Another example is the following **sortedness** constraint defined on integer intervals (or more generally, on finite intervals of linear orderings):

`sortedness([`$X_1, \ldots, X_n$`], [`$Y_1, \ldots, Y_n$`]) := {(([`$d_1, \ldots, d_n$`], [`$e_1, \ldots, e_n$`])` |
$[e_1, \ldots, e_n]$ is the sorted permutation of $[d_1, \ldots, d_n]$}.

It was introduced in Older, Swinkels and van Emden [1995] and was successfully used to formulate and solve job-shop scheduling type problems. In Bleuzen-Guernalec and Colmerauer [2000] an $O(n \, log \, n)$ constraint propagation algorithm was proposed that reduces the initial intervals to minimal ones without affecting the constraint.

9.2 Constraint programming languages

Constraint programming has been realised in a number of programming languages and systems. Some of these systems are restricted to handling of specific constraints by fixed domain specific methods. To this category belong the *modeling languages* for mathematical programming, such as AMPL (A Modeling Language for Mathematical Programming) or GAMS (the General Algebraic Modeling System), designed for modeling and solving various optimization problems arising in the operations research. They generate matrices that can be passed to various packages (often called solvers), like CPLEX or MINOS, that support linear programming and certain nonlinear programming problems.

Then the interactive computer algebra systems, such as MATLAB or Reduce, usually provide support for various numerical calculations, including operations on vectors and matrices, simplifications of algebraic expressions in the presence of trigonometric and other standard functions, symbolic integration and differentiation, and factorisations of polynomials. In particular, they provide support for solving various forms of polynomial equations, including linear equations, and some nonlinear constraints on reals. Some of them, like Maple or Mathematica, are full fledged programming languages which support interaction with sophisticated numeric symbolic algebra packages.

In what follows we rather focus on the programming languages built around the general framework of Section 3.2. They are characterised by a built-in constraint propagation for various constraints, notably the Boolean constraints, the linear constraints on integer domains, and selected global constraints, by some form of 'general purpose' constraint propagation (for example arc consistency on finite domains), and by the presence of several built-ins for constructing various forms of search. In these languages the constraints are handled by adding them to the *constraint store* to which various constraint solvers are attached.

Intuitively, a constraint store can be viewed as an internal CSP maintained by the program. If the added constraint is in a specific form (for example, it is a linear constraint on finite integer domains), the appropriate constraint solver (in this case, the incomplete constraint solver for linear constraints on finite integer domains, discussed in Section 6.4) is triggered on the corresponding part of the constraint store (in this case, the set of linear constraints on finite integer domains) augmented by the new constraint. Upon termination the 'obviously solved' constraints are removed from the constraint store. If the constraint store becomes a failed CSP, a backtracking takes place. The addition of a constraint store to the customary memory store results in a ***two-level architecture*** that is a distinguishing feature of constraint programming.

To deal with the constraints one also needs to represent and manipulate variables present in them. We call them below ***constraint variables***. These variables are unknowns in the mathematical sense, so the customary C-like or Pascal-like variables that are used to capture the changing, but known quantities, cannot be used to model them. Basically, two approaches were proposed to deal with this problem.

9.2.1 Constraint logic programming

The most popular solution involves an extension of the logic programming paradigm by means of the constraints. This can be done in a natural way since the logic programming paradigm, in contrast to the other programming paradigms, supports the notion of a ***logical variable***, a variable to which one can assign terms, so expressions possibly containing variables. So in this approach the constraint variables are modeled as logical variables.

From the constraint programming perspective a unification algorithm, for example the MARTELLI–MONTANARI algorithm described in Section 4.2, is a complete constraint solver built into Prolog. It allows us to solve equations on terms. To deal with other constraints one needs to add other constraint solvers to the language.

Additionally, Prolog and other logic programming languages support automatic backtracking, through the use of multiple clauses with the same relation (i.e., the same procedure) in the clause head. This provides a good starting base for implementing backtracking in the presence of constraints.

This approach to constraint programming through logic programming has been pioneered by Alain Colmerauer in a series of successors to Prolog, Prolog II till Prolog IV, see, e.g., Colmerauer [1990] for a description of Prolog III and http://prologianet.univ-mrs.fr/societe/PrologIV/

`New_index.html` for information on Prolog IV. In parallel, a number of other languages extending Prolog were proposed, starting with the CHIP programming language, see Dincbas et al. [1988] and for a more extensive coverage Van Hentenryck [1989], that introduced constraint programming on finite domains, and CLP($\mathcal{R}$), see Jaffar et al. [1992], that provided support for solving constraints on reals. CHIP in turn led to a (n ongoing) development of the ECL^{i}PS^e system, see, e.g., Wallace, Novello and Schimpf [1997] and `http://www-icparc.doc.ic.ac.uk/eclipse/`. Another system with similar functionalities is SICStus Prolog, see `http://www.sics.se/sicstus/`. The last two systems include now some constraint programming languages developed separately. All mentioned systems were successfully used in several application domains.

These developments led to creation of an area called ***constraint logic programming*** (CLP). On the theoretical side they were captured in an elegant way in the influential CLP(X) scheme of Jaffar and Lassez [1987] of which CLP($\mathcal{R}$) is an implemented instance. In this scheme the unification mechanism of logic programming is replaced by the more general mechanism of constraint solving and the substitution (that can be viewed as the logic programming counterpart of the state) is replaced by the constraint store. To illustrate the resulting programming style consider the following ECL^{i}PS^e program (that coincides with the original CHIP version) solving the *SEND + MORE = MONEY* problem of Example 2.1:

```
send(List):-                                          %  1
    List = [S,E,N,D,M,O,R,Y],                         %  2
    [E,N,D,O,R,Y] :: [0..9],                          %  3
    [S,M]:: [1..9],                                   %  4
    alldifferent(List),                               %  5
            1000*S + 100*E + 10*N + D                 %  6
        + 1000*M + 100*O + 10*R + E                   %  7
  #= 10000*M + 1000*O + 100*N + 10*E + Y,             %  8
    labeling(List).                                   %  9
```

It consists of a declaration of the procedure **send**. In line 2 the argument variable LIST is assigned to the list of eight variables, S,E,N,D,M,O,R,Y. In lines 3 and 4 the domains of these variables are declared. Lines 5–8 introduce two constraints. `alldifferent` is a built-in that corresponds to the all_different constraint, while #= denotes the equality constraint on finite domains. Finally, in line 9, the labeling combined with the backtrack search with the built-in constraint propagation is triggered by the `labeling` built-in.

The reader can appreciate the utmost simplicity of this program. More-over, this program is efficient since its execution automatically triggers the constraint propagation for linear constraints on finite domains, discussed in detail in Subsection 6.4.6. The corresponding search tree is depicted in Figure 8.9 of Section 8.3. The BACKTRACK WITH CONSTRAINT PROPAGATION search initiated by the `labeling` built-in finds the unique solution after only one backtracking.

Research on constraint logic programming led to a further research on **concurrent constraint programming** (CCP) languages, in which the processes interact with the constraint store by means of the primitive **ask** and **tell** constraints, see Saraswat [1993]. This provided a powerful, abstract, view of constraint programming.

The CCP paradigm was incorporated into the multi-paradigm constraint programming language Oz, see, e.g., Smolka [1995], that was used in several applications including planning, scheduling, and natural language processing. Research on Oz led to a creation of the Mozart Programming System, an advanced development platform for various distributed applications, see `http://www.mozart-oz.org`.

Another multi-paradigm programming language supporting constraint programming is Claire, see, e.g., Caseau, Josset and Laburthe [2002]. It was successfully used for solving various combinatorial optimization problems including scheduling, routing, and time-tabling.

9.2.2 ILOG solver

Another solution to the problem of representing the constraint variables was realised in the ILOG solver, a constraint-based optimization engine, see, e.g., ILOG [2003]. It is based on modeling the constraint satisfaction problems in C++ using classes. This led to a development of an extensive class library that supports constraint programming. The constraint variables are modeled as objects and are manipulated by means of special methods provided by the given class. As an illustration of this approach, here is the ILOG solver version 5.1 program that solves the *SEND + MORE = MONEY* puzzle:

```
#include <ilsolver/ilosolverint.h>              % 1
ILOSTLBEGIN                                      % 2

int main(){                                      % 3
  IloEnv env;                                    % 4
```

```
IloModel model(env);                                          % 5
IloIntVar S(env, 1, 9), E(env, 0, 9), N(env, 0, 9),          % 6
    D(env, 0, 9), M(env, 1, 9), O(env, 0, 9),                % 7
    R(env, 0, 9), Y(env, 0, 9);                              % 8

IloIntVarArray AllVars(env, 8, S, E, N, D, M, O, R, Y);      % 9

model.add( IloAllDiff(env, AllVars) );                       % 10
model.add(            1000*S + 100*E + 10*N + D              % 11
                  + 1000*M + 100*O + 10*R + E                % 12
          == 10000*M + 1000*O + 100*N + 10*E + Y);           % 13

IloSolver solver(model);                                     % 14
solver.solve(IloGenerate(env, AllVars));                     % 15

for (IloInt i=0; i<8; i++)                                   % 16
  solver.out() << solver.getValue(AllVars[i]) << " ";        % 17
solver.out() << endl;                                        % 18

env.end();                                                   % 19
return 0;                                                    % 20
}                                                            % 21
```

In lines 1 and 2 the appropriate solver is loaded and initialised. In line 4, inside the body of the **main** procedure, an environment **env** is created in which the memory management takes place and in line 5 the corresponding 'model' in which the constraints are variables are managed is declared. In lines 6–8 the finite domain variables are declared together with their domains and in line 9 these variables are packed into an array. The constraints are introduced in lines 10–13. In lines 14 and 15 a call to the solver is made and in lines 16–18 the solution is printed.

Currently, the ILOG solver is one of the engines of the ILOG Optimization Suite that incorporates various modeling languages and packages supporting mathematical programming and allows one to deal with a variety of optimization problems, see http://www.ilog.com/products/optimization/.

9.2.3 Generation of constraints

In the case of the *SEND + MORE = MONEY* problem the constraints could be simply written out explicitly. For less trivial problems we need to *generate* the appropriate constraints. In other words, we need to construct the appropriate CSP. An 'execution' of a constraint amounts to adding it to the constraint store, so the generation of the appropriate constraints can be realised using the customary control statements. Depending on the language this can be done in a more or less straightforward way.

For example, in OPL (Optimization Programming Language), a modeling language for mathematical programming and combinatorial optimization that provides support for constraint programming, see Van Hentenryck [1999], the Eight Queens Problem of Example 2.2 can be be solved using the following program:

```
int n = 8;
range Domain 1..n;
var Domain queen[Domain];
solve{
   forall(ordered i,j in Domain) {
      queen[i] <> queen[j];
      queen[i] <> queen[j]+j-i;
      queen[i] <> queen[j]+i-j
   };
};
```

Here, thanks to the `forall` statement and arrays of constraint variables present in the language, the appropriate 28 constraints are generated in a way closely resembling their original formulation. So the `forall` statement corresponds to the bounded universal quantifier. Another example showing how the constraints can be elegantly generated using recursion is given in Subsection 9.4.3.

9.3 Constraint propagation

When choosing between general purpose and domain specific constraint propagation, it is in general better to rely on the latter. The reason is that when limiting one's attention to a specific domain one can rely on additional properties which can lead to more efficient algorithms. This explains why global constraints and constraint solvers are useful.

Moreover, most of the constraint propagation algorithms are too costly to be used in practice. Consequently, in most constraint programming systems only the arc consistency and occasionally hyper-arc consistency are supported by means of the built-in algorithms. This explains the considerable amount of research that went into the study of the arc and hyper-arc consistency algorithms, see, e.g., Bessière and Régin [2001] and Zhang and Yap [2001].

The local consistency notions are useful if we wish to characterise constraint solvers or certain domain reduction rules. Examples are provided in Chapter 6. As another example consider the knapsack problem discussed in Example 2.12. In Trick [2001] a variant of this problem, called the **two sided knapsack constraint** is studied, in which the considered constraint is of the form

$$l \leq \sum_{i=1}^{n} a_i \cdot x_i \leq v,$$

where the variables $x_1, ..., x_n$ range over the domain $\{0, 1\}$. So the difference is that here also a lower bound for the total value of the selection is given. This constraint is a part of various integer programming problems. The author proposes an $O(nv^2)$ algorithm based on the dynamic programming techniques that enforces hyper-arc consistency on this constraint. It leads to a significantly more efficient way of dealing with this constraint than other approaches. On the account of the Hyper-arc Consistency Lemma 6.1 of Section 6.1 we know that the resulting domain reduction is optimal.

Further, some local consistency notions can be used to clarify the role and nature of certain methods used in computer science and applied mathematics. For example, as explained in Dechter and van Beek [1997], the notion of relational consistency and the resulting RELATIONAL (i, m)-CONSISTENCY rule of Section 5.9 generalise a number of approaches including the resolution rule mentioned in Chapter 3 and the GAUSSIAN ELIMINATION and FOURIER–MOTZKIN ELIMINATION algorithms discussed in Chapter 4.

Constraint propagation also allows us to better understand various techniques used in the area of combinatorial optimization, where it is common in the process of solving the original problem to derive and add specific constraints. In the terminology of Chapter 3 such constraints are implied constraints and their addition is an instance of constraint propagation. Various examples of such implied inequalities used to solve integer programming problems and the knapsack problem are discussed in Wolsey [1998].

In fact, constraint propagation lies at the heart of various efforts aiming at the integration of constraint programming and operations research. It is often implicitly present in the form of efficient constraint propagation algorithms developed for specific global constraints.

9.4 Constraint solvers

In a typical constraint programming system several constraint solvers are incorporated. They act as 'black boxes' that are automatically activated once a constraint that can be handled by them is encountered in the program text.

9.4.1 Building constraint solvers

If a constraint solver is not built into a programming system it can be added as a program written in a special purpose programming language. A successful example of such a language is the CHR language of Frühwirth [1995] that is integrated into the ECL^{i}PS^e programming system and SICStus Prolog. CHR stands for Constraint Handling Rules. It is a rule-based language built on top of Prolog that realises the CCP paradigm. Each CHR rule allows us to rewrite a given query into another one which is logically equivalent. Consequently, the CHR rules allow us to program in an elegant way the proof rules discussed in Section 4.1. The resulting program executions correspond to the failed or stabilising derivations there introduced. So in CHR various constraint solvers and some local consistency notions, for example path consistency, can be programmed by simply formalising the proof rules that define them.

For example, the *AND 1–6* domain reduction rules for the Boolean *AND* constraint presented in Section 6.3 can be written in CHR as follows:

```
and(1,1,Z) <=> Z=1.
and(1,Y,0) <=> Y=0.
and(X,1,0) <=> X=0.
and(0,Y,Z) <=> Z=0.
and(X,0,Z) <=> Z=0.
and(X,Y,1) <=> X=1, Y=1.
```

Such rules are automatically triggered when a constraint is encountered to which a rule can be applied. More complicated rules have guards that state conditions under which the rule can be applied. These rules can be defined using a subsidiary Prolog program. Originally, in the CHIP language, similar rules were present and called demon rules.

ECL^{i}PS^e and SICStus Prolog provide a number of low level mechanisms that allow us to write various forms of constraint propagation without the use of CHR rules. This makes it possible to implement CHR through a translation into ECL^{i}PS^e or SICStus Prolog. In turn, Mozart provides an interface to C++, called Constraint Propagator Interface (CPI), through which one can add new constraint solvers to the system. In the Claire language constraint solvers can be naturally programmed using event-based rules that are available together with a rule-based inference engine. They are compiled into procedural demons by translating them first to algebraic expressions over a relational algebra.

9.4.2 Incrementality

In Chapters 4 and 6 we defined constraint solvers as transformations of CSPs that maintain equivalence. But in reality the individual constraints are encountered in the program text on a 'one-by-one' basis and the actual constraint solvers deal with each newly encountered constraint separately, in the context of a constraint store that usually satisfies some property. For example, in the case of a complete constraint solver the corresponding constraints present in the constraint store are in some solved form. In turn, the incomplete constraint solvers usually achieve some form of local consistency. So the CSP formed by the corresponding constraints present in the constraint store satisfies this notion of local consistency at the moment a new constraint is added.

Taking such additional information into account makes it often possible to improve the efficiency of the constraint solver. The resulting solvers are called *incremental*. The complete constraint solvers discussed in Chapter 4 were all defined by means of proof rules and a scheduler that repeatedly applies them. As a result, the appropriate modification of these constraint solvers to incremental ones can be achieved by a simple modification of the scheduler.

For example, in the case of the term equations studied in Section 4.2, it suffices to modify the MARTELLI–MONTANARI algorithm by taking into account that the set of equations present in the constraint store is in solved form. More precisely, suppose that the constraint store equals $F := \{x_1 = t_1,$ $\ldots, x_n = t_n\}$ and that e is the new equation.

The incremental algorithm consists of three phases. In the first phase n applications of the *SUBSTITUTION* rule with the selected equation $x_i = t_i$ and E equal to the singleton set $\{e\{x_1/t_1\}\ldots\{x_{i-1}/t_{i-1}\}\}$ are performed. This amounts to 'interpreting' e in the 'context' of F. Note that these rule applications are not global in the terminology of Chapter 4. The second phase consists of applying the MARTELLI–MONTANARI algorithm to the singleton set consisting of the equation $e\{x_1/t_1\}\ldots\{x_n/t_n\}$. If this yields a set of equations $G := \{y_1 = s_1, \ldots, y_m = s_m\}$ in solved form, the third phase consists of m applications of the *SUBSTITUTION* rule with the selected equation $y_i = s_i$ and E equal to $F\{y_1/s_1\}\ldots\{y_{i-1}/s_{i-1}\}$. This amounts to interpreting F in the context of G. Otherwise, the algorithm terminates with failure.

Of course, such simple modifications are in general insufficient to turn more complex complete constraint solvers into incremental ones. The situation is different in the case of the incomplete constraint solvers. As explained in Section 7.11, these solvers usually can be, and often are, implemented using some generic iteration algorithm. These algorithms can be easily adjusted to an incremental form by starting the iteration with the functions associated with the newly added constraint.

9.4.3 Simplification of constraints

When manipulating constraints it is important to be able to output them in a form readable to the system user. To see the relevance of this issue consider the following problem that became a trademark of the CLP($\mathcal{R}$) system. We are interested in expressing the mortgage relationship between the following five variables:

  P (the principal),
  T (the length of loan in months),
  I (fixed, but compounded, monthly interest rate),
  B (outstanding balance at the end), and
  M (the monthly payment).

Mathematically, this relationship can be summarised by the following two equations, where we indicate the value of the principal P at time t by P_t:

$$P_0 = B,$$

$$P_{t-1} = P_t * (1 + I) - M, \text{ where } t \geq 1.$$

This translates into the following, remarkable in its simplicity, CLP($\mathcal{R}$) program:

```
mg(P, 0, I, P, M).


mg(P, T, I, B, M) :-
  T >= 1,
  mg(P*(1 + I) - M, T - 1, I, B, M).
```

This program can be used in a number of ways, including the request for expressing the relationship between the monthly payments (the variable M), the principal (the variable P), and the outstanding balance at the end (the

variable B). For example, the query mg(P, 360, 0.01, B, M), expressing
the information that the loan is for 360 months at 1% monthly interest rate
yields the following answer:

P = 0.0278167*B + 97.2183*M.

Internally, the execution of this query successively adds the above equations
to the constraint store, starting with the one for $t = 360$, where $P_{360} =$
P. Without constraint simplification the output would consist of all the
constraints referring to the local variables generated during the execution,
in particular to all 360 copies P_t, where $t \in [0..359]$, of the initial variable P.

In general, a simplification may involve elimination of certain variables
(which amounts to a projection of the constraint), a transformation of the
constraints to an accepted form (for example, to linear equations in normal
form), or an elimination of some function or relation symbols (for example,
of $\geq$ in the case of linear constraints) from the output constraints.

9.5 Search

9.5.1 Search in modeling languages

Mathematical modeling languages traditionally did not allow one to specify
search methods. Instead, special cases of constrained optimization problems were directly supported by means of specific algorithms that could be
activated by a language command. For example in the AMPL language
the linear programming problems can be solved directly, as in the following
self-explanatory program taken from Fourer, Gay and Kernigham [1993]:

```
var XB;
var XC;
maximize profit: 25 * XB + 30* XC;
subject to Time: (1/200) * XB + (1/140) * XC <= 40;
subject to B_limit: 0 <= XB <= 6000;
subject to C_limit: 0 <= XC <= 4000;

solve;
```

which is solved by calling the MINOS solver.

Such a direct access to an underlying linear programming package is nowa-
days present in many constraint programming languages. In a new generation of modelling languages search is programmable and various forms of
constraint propagation are present.

An example is the 2LP language (that stands for 'linear programming and logic programming') of McAloon and Tretkoff [1996] that integrates both fields using the technology of constraint logic programming. The language uses C syntax and has been designed for constraint programming in the area of combinatorial optimization. In 2LP there are two types of variables: the 'customary', programming, variables and the **continuous** variables (the name derives from their use in mathematics). The continuous variables vary over the real interval $[0, +\infty)$ and can be constrained only by imposing linear constraints on them, the addition of which triggers an internal SIMPLEX-based algorithm. So they are examples of constraint variables.

In contrast to the customary modeling languages 2LP, through its bidirectional link with C, also provides support for generating and solving more complex systems of linear constraints, including disjunctive constraints, and for programming complex forms of search.

Another language that extends the traditional modeling languages is the already mentioned OPL to which we shall return after discussing various search algorithms.

9.5.2 Depth-first search: backtracking and branch and bound

As clarified in Chapter 8, backtracking and branch and bound search, combined with various forms of constraint propagation, form two basic forms of the depth-first search. In many constraint programming languages these two forms of search are built-in. In fact, the constraint logic programming languages inherited from Prolog the reliance on the depth-first left-first search strategy. In CHIP the resulting built-in backtrack search is automatically combined with the built-in constraint propagation. It is triggered by the already mentioned `labeling` built-in that originated from CHIP. In addition, the user can specify forward checking and partial look ahead as a search strategy.

In turn, the branch and bound search is supported by means of another built-in. In ECL^{i}PS^e it is called `min_max` and is used as in the following program skeleton:

```
solveOpt(List):-
   declareFinDom(List),
   generateConsAndObj(List, Obj),
   min_max(labeling(List), Obj).
```

The call of `solveOpt` relation leads to a declaration of the finite domains for the variables listed in the `List` argument, followed by a generation of the constraints and of a (linear) objective function, and a branch and bound search with the built-in constraint propagation triggered by the call `min_max(labeling(List), Obj)`.

These and other constraint logic programming language also allow one to program in a simple way various heuristics, such as first-fail, that are used during the search. In some languages first-fail is a default heuristic. Such facilities are included in one way or another in most contemporary constraint programming languages.

In Claire so-called *versioning* allows one to program in a simple way various search strategies based on backtracking. A *version* is a virtual copy of the state of the objects. Versions are organised into a stack. The language provides an efficient support for creation and rollback of the versions.

9.5.3 Breadth-first search and limited discrepancy search

We considered here only one form of search: the top-down (or depth-first) search. Let us discuss now briefly alternative forms of search that are often used to solve constraint satisfaction problems and constrained optimization problems.

In the *breadth-first search* one explores the search tree layer by layer. A modification of this search includes the *best-first search* according to which one maintains a frontier of the tree and selects from it for expansion a node with the best value according to some heuristic function. The obvious complication is that the breadth-first search requires to maintain the increasingly growing list of generated nodes in the memory. Some variations avoid this problem by using a bounded amount of memory and combining the search with a limited form of backtracking.

Another alternative to the top-down search is the *limited discrepancy search* of Harvey and Ginsberg [1995]. This search is organised in a sequence of waves. Wave 0 follows the heuristic and for $i > 0$ wave i explores the solutions that can be reached if i deviations are made from the heuristic. Suppose for example that the search tree is binary and the heuristic is 'top-down, left-first'. Then in wave 0 the leftmost branch of the search tree is explored. In wave 1 the nodes are explored that lie on the branches in which precisely one 'turn' to the right is made. In general, in wave i the nodes are explored that lie on the branches in which precisely i 'turns' to the right are made.

9.5.4 Local search

Another important alternative to the top-down search is so-called *local search*, which is a generic name for a whole class of search algorithms. The local search algorithms operate on the leaves of a complete labeling tree. Their purpose is to find a solution to a CSP or to a constrained optimization problem by starting with an instantiation defined on all the variables (called in this context a *state*) and trying to improve its *quality* iteratively, by small (so local) changes, called *moves*. The quality of a state is defined by means of a *cost function*. Below we say that a state is *better* (respectively *worse*) if its quality is better (respectively worse) and assume that a solution (respectively, an optimal solution) is one of the *best* states. A simple example of a cost function is the number of constraints violated by the state. Then the quality of a solution is 0.

The basic ingredient of the local search is the notion of a *neighbourhood*, which is a function that assigns to each state I (i.e., an instantiation) a set of states, that are called the *neighbours* of I. An execution of a local search algorithm starts in an initial state, obtained by another technique or randomly, and enters a loop in which repeatedly a move is performed from a state to one of its neighbours. The final state is either a solution to the considered CSP (respectively, an optimal solution to a constrained optimization problem) or a 'stop' state that corresponds to an information that the CSP is inconsistent. Specific forms of local search are obtained by specifying the way the moves are chosen and the way the search is stopped.

An example of a local search is the *hill-climbing search*, which is actually a family of local search techniques, according to which in each move one selects the best neighbour among the better or equally good neighbours. The complication is that one can end in a *local minimum*, i.e., a state all neighbours of which are worse. Various modifications were proposed to solve this problem. They include randomised decisions to restart the search, to redefine the neighbourhood, or to select a move. One of them, called the *heuristic repair method*, or the *min-conflicts* heuristic, of Minton et al. [1992] proved to be highly successful. In this method one chooses randomly any variable that violates a constraint and selects for it a new value that minimises the number of violated constraints.

To illustrate this approach to search reconsider the n Queens Problem of Example 2.2 of Chapter 2 for $n = 5$. To solve it by means of the hill-climbing search we use the first representation of this problem as a CSP. So the states (or equivalently, the instantiations) are the sequences of 5 elements from the set [1..5]. Each state can be viewed as a placement of five queens on the 5×5

chess board so that no two queens are in the same column. For example, the state 3,4,5,2,1 is represented by Figure 9.1.

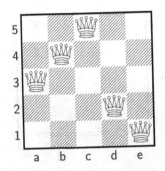

Fig. 9.1. Local search: the initial state

Given a state we associate with it the neighbourhood defined as the set of states that can be obtained from it by a single transposition. Graphically, this corresponds to an exchange of the row positions of two queens. For example, the state 4,3,5,2,1 represented by Figure 9.2 belongs to the neighbourhood of the state 3,4,5,2,1 represented by Figure 9.1. So each neighbour of a state can indeed be reached from it by a small change.

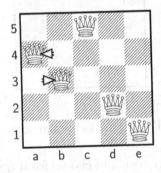

Fig. 9.2. A neighbour state

As a cost function, that yields a quality of a state, we choose the function counting the number of constraints violated by the state. For example, the quality of the state 3,4,5,2,1 represented by Figure 9.1 is 6 because six constraints are violated by it and the quality of the state 4,3,5,2,1 represented by Figure 9.2 is 2.

We consider now moves that improve the quality of a state, that is the ones that lead to a state with a lower value of the cost function. Then a solution to the 5 Queens Problem can be obtained by two moves from the initial state 3,4,5,2,1 represented by Figure 9.1: first to the state 4,3,5,2,1 represented by Figure 9.2 and then to the state 1,3,5,2,4 represented by Figure 9.3.

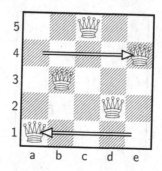

Fig. 9.3. A solution

Further, note that the state 4,1,5,2,3 represented by Figure 9.4 is a local minimum. Indeed, its quality is 2 and the quality of each of its neighbours is at least 2.

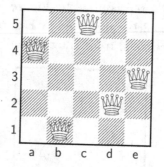

Fig. 9.4. A local minimum

If we now select the last queen and choose for it a value that minimises the number of violated constraints, then we end up with the sequence 4,1,5,2,5 depicted in Figure 9.5 for which the number of violated constraints is 1. So this way we could escape here from the local minimum.

An important variant of the hill-climbing search is the *tabu search*. In this search method in each move one selects the best neighbour, independently of the fact that it can be worse than that of the current state. This approach allows one to escape from local maxima, but can cause cycling among a set of states. To prevent cycling the so-called *tabu list* is maintained, which is the list of disallowed moves. This list stores the reverses of the last k accepted moves, where k is a, possibly dynamically, changing parameter of the method. Under some conditions, called *aspiration cri-*

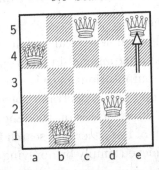

Fig. 9.5. An escape from the local minimum

teria, the tabu list restrictions can be overridden. An example of such a criterion is that the move leads to a significantly better state.

Another variant of the hill-climbing search in which the moves to worse neighbours are allowed is the **simulated annealing**. These moves are randomly selected. If a state is better, it is accepted. Otherwise it is accepted only with a probability less than 1. The probability exponentially decreases with the 'badness' of the move that is measured by comparing the quality of the old and new state. The probability also decreases with the 'temperature' that goes down according to a schedule defined in terms of the number of moves.

Breadth-first and local search techniques are discussed in many books on artificial intelligence or operations research, for example in Russell and Norvig [2003], where also the appropriate references can be found.

9.5.5 Search in constraint programming languages

Recall the following slogan that we stated at the beginning of Chapter 8:

Search Algorithm = Search Tree + Exploration Algorithm

and used to divide the chapter into two natural parts. Modern constraint programming languages increasingly move towards realising this slogan by separating the specification of the search tree from the specification of the exploration algorithm. So the same search tree can be explored by different exploration algorithms that can be programmed. The resulting framework goes beyond the basic framework for constrained programming introduced in Section 3.2 even though most of the techniques, like constraint propagation can be reused in it (for some forms of search) without any change.

This approach was pioneered in Oz. The language provides a library of predefined search methods (called **search engines**) and also allows one to program new search engines in a generic way. Schulte [1997], and more extensively Schulte [2002], shows how several search engines, including limited discrepancy search, can be programmed in Oz using the abstraction of the **computation spaces** (a computation space is essentially a constraint store with a set of concurrently operating constraint solvers, called **propagators**, attached to it) to which a direct access on the language level is provided.

This way the exploration of the generated search tree by a different exploration algorithm can be achieved simply by applying a different search engine to the program describing the problem. To illustrate this separation of the program statements that specify the search tree from the ones that specify the exploration algorithm consider the nondeterministic `choice` statement of Oz. It allows one to model and implement in a straightforward way the disjunctive constraints mentioned in Section 3.2. Consider for example the disjunctive constraint

$$\texttt{Start[task}_1] + \texttt{Duration[task}_1] \leq \texttt{Start[task}_2] \lor$$
$$\texttt{Start[task}_2] + \texttt{Duration[task}_2] \leq \texttt{Start[task}_1]$$

already mentioned in Section 3.2. It can be modeled in Oz as follows:

```
choice Start.task1 + Duration.task1 =<: Start.task2
[]      Start.task2 + Duration.task2 =<: Start.task1
end
```

where `Start` and `Duration` are declared as records of constraint variables. In this context the `choice` statement can be viewed as the logical disjunction.

Assume now that the underlying search engine is the depth-first search. Then the execution of the program attempts to find a solution with the first alternative added as a constraint and, upon failure, with the second alternative added. (The corresponding CHIP or ECL^{i}PS^e solution relies on Prolog's use of multiple clauses with the same relation in the clause head or the disjunction statement ';' also present in Prolog.) If, however, the selected search engine is the generic best-first search, the execution of the program will explore the generated search tree using the best-first search.

This approach to search was adopted in a somewhat different way in OPL. The language provides a large number of useful high-level abstractions that allow one to specify the search tree and, separately, to explore it by means of various built-in and programmable exploration strategies. They are described in detail in Van Hentenryck, Perron and Puget [2000]. To illustrate these facilities let us return to the OPL solution to the Eight Queens Problem presented in Section 9.2. The default search procedure triggered by the `solve` built-in is the depth-first left-first combined with the first-fail heuristic. If we combine this program with the following specification of the search:

```
search {
  forall(i in 1..n)
    tryall(v in 1..n)
      queen[i] = v;
};
```

then we change the default search procedure to the one in which to each queen `queen[i]` in turn a value from [1..n] is nondeterministically assigned. So the `tryall` statement corresponds to the bounded existential quantifier. If one adds now as the first line of the code the instruction `LDSearch(2)`, then the declared search procedure uses the limited discrepancy search with discrepancy increments of 2.

Let us mention in passing that Michel and Van Hentenryck [2002b] discuss a novel implementation of the limited discrepancy search for solving constraint satisfaction problems.

Another constraint programming language in which search can be programmed is ELAN, see e.g. Borovansky et al. [1998] or Kirchner and Ringeissen [1998] for its use for constraint programming and constraint solving. The program is a rewriting system that consists of conditional rewrite rules that are controlled by strategies. The strategies can be programmed by means of a small set of powerful primitives that include nondeterminism, iteration, and some selection strategies. ELAN is used to support the design of various rule-based algorithms such as constraints solvers, decision procedures, theorem provers, and algorithms expressed in logic programming languages, and to provide a modular framework for studying their combinations.

Further, as shown in Wallace and Schimpf [2002], the *repair* library of ECL^{i}PS^e allows one to develop effective hybrid algorithms. Finally, the already mentioned ILOG Solver also provides a number of built-in search strategies and high-level abstractions for programming new search strategies.

Among the frameworks and languages for supporting the development of local search algorithms we mention three elegant recent proposals. SALSA of Laburthe and Caseau [2002] is a language for specifying various search algorithms, including local and hybrid ones. It works in cooperation with a host programming language and can be implemented on top of constraint programming systems.

LOCAL++ of Schaerf, Cadoli and Lenzerini [2000] is an object-oriented framework for developing and implementing local search algorithms in C++. Its core consists of a hierarchy of solvers that comprise three forms of 'simple' local search: hill climbing, simulated annealing and tabu search, and two forms of composite local search. One can combine LOCAL++ with various widely available C++ libraries.

Finally, Michel and Van Hentenryck [2002a] propose an object-oriented architecture that supports local search. It consists of a declarative and search component. The first component specifies the properties of the solutions and the data structures that are maintained during the search, while the second component specifies the implementation of heuristics and meta-heuristics. This architecture was realised in the COMET language.

9.5.6 Biology-inspired approaches

Under this name we list two approaches in which search is performed using computation models inspired by biology.

An approach to solving CSPs based on the **neural networks** architecture was proposed in Davenport et al. [1994] in the form of an algorithm called GENET. This approach uses networks the nodes of which are very simple processors and the arcs of which have weights associated with them. At any moment, each node is in a state that is determined by means of simple operations that take into account the previous states of the nodes connected to it and by the weights associated with these arcs.

Assume for simplicity that the considered CSP is binary. The CSP is represented by a network the nodes of which correspond to the values of all variables and the arcs between nodes correspond to the constraints. The nodes representing a domain of one variable are grouped into a cluster and it is assumed that at each moment exactly one value in each cluster is 'turned on'. To each arc that violates a constraint an inhibitory link is attached. The network is initialised by assigning a fixed value to all weights that are associated with the arcs. The algorithm starts in a random state and repeatedly recomputes the new state by using the information on the weights of the neighbouring nodes. A stable state that is not a solution is exited by means of a change of the weights based on a learning strategy.

Finally, the **genetic algorithms** draw on an analogy with the evolution theory from which they borrow the terminology of **fitness** (the name used for the cost function), **recombination, mating, cross-over, population** and **mutation**. In these algorithms one derives new states by recombining two parent states using a mating function that produces a new state (or a pair of new states) corresponding to a cross-over (an exchange of the 'bits') of the parent states. The parent states are selected from a pool of states called population, taking into account their fitness. The new states are subjected to small random changes that model the mutation.

Eiben and Ruttkay [1997] discuss how the genetic algorithms can be specialised to solve CSPs and constrained optimization problems by defining the relevant functions in terms of CSPs concepts. For example, the fitness function can be defined in terms of the number of satisfied constraints or the number of variables that do not occur in the violated constraints. In turn, the cross-over and mutation operators can be defined using various heuristics for selecting a variable to be modified and a new value in its domain. Such specialisations of the relevant functions led to a considerable speed up of the convergence process.

Genetic algorithms have been successfully used in many areas including operations research, numerical analysis and electrical engineering. An example of a system that supports genetic algorithms is GENOCOP (Genetic Algorithm for Numerical Optimization for COnstrained Problems), see Michalewicz [1996]. It is a genetic algorithm-based program for constrained and unconstrained optimization problems involving linear constraints on reals.

In both approaches it is not guaranteed that a solution is found. In particular the algorithms may diverge. In specific applications this complication could often be overcome by an appropriate choice of the parameters that in particular ensured termination.

9.6 Over-constrained problems

We stated in Chapter 1 that the representation of a problem by means of constraints is very flexible because the constraints can be added, removed or modified. This comes particularly handy when a formalisation of a problem we would like to solve yields an inconsistent CSP. In many situations it simply means that the original problem needs to be reformulated. Such problems are usually called **over-constrained problems**, which indicates that some constraints may be dropped or that we should relax the requirement that all the constraints are to be satisfied.

This brings us to the subject of **soft constraints** which is a generic name for a variety of approaches that augment the CSP framework by allowing constraints to be partially satisfied. The problem consists then of finding the 'best' instantiation according to some criterion. These problems differ from the usual constrained optimization problems, because the optimization can be multi-objective and because constraint propagation in this context has to be reconsidered.

We shall now illustrate these approaches to over-constrained problems drawing on Rudová [2001], where they were applied to a study of a University timetabling problem. The problem deals with a given set of course offerings, each consisting of several courses. Each student is to enroll in one or more offerings having some small amount of choice among the proposed offerings.

The most natural formalisation of this problem should take into account the usual constraints stating that at most n courses can be scheduled at the same time, where n is the number of available rooms, and that for each offering its courses do not overlap in time.

If one also adopts the constraints that the courses selected by each of the students do not overlap in time, one can easily end up with a formalisation of the problem that has no solution. For the purpose of the subsequent discussion we denote the constraint that the courses $c_1, \ldots, c_m$ selected by a student do not overlap in time by $disjunctive(c_1, \ldots, c_m)$. It is a conjunction of the constraints $disj(c_i, c_j)$, where $1 \leq i < j \leq m$ and where each $disj(c_i, c_j)$ constraint states that the courses c_i and c_j do not overlap in time.

9.6.1 Partial, weighted and fuzzy CSPs

Instead of taking the rigid viewpoint that no solution exists to the discussed problem, one can either relax the problem by dropping some constraints (for example the ones referring to the students) or revise the formalisation by indicating which constraints are obligatory (sometimes called in this context *crisp constraints* or *hard constraints*) and which are optional.

In a general setting this is the subject of the work of Freuder and Wallace [1992] on *partial constraint satisfaction*. Instead of searching for a solution, when dealing with a partial CSP, one is willing to accept a solution that violates some of the constraints. If one searches for an instantiation that satisfies all the crisp constraints and as many optional constraints as possible, this problem is called *max-CSP*.

The BRANCH AND BOUND search algorithm discussed in Subsection 8.7.1 can be modified in a natural way to solve max-CSPs with finite domains. However, an addition of constraint propagation to this algorithm is not anymore so straightforward. The reason is that constraint propagation, when applied to optional constraints, may lead to a removal of values that could be retained in the final instantiation. Freuder and Wallace [1992] propose for max-CSPs a limited form of constraint propagation based on so-called *arc consistency counts*.

In the above timetabling problem, one could either try to maximise the number of satisfied original optional constraints (which amounts to maximising the number of students for which no course conflicts would arise), or to transform each *disjunctive* constraint to the corresponding set of *disj* constraints and maximise the number of satisfied resulting optional constraints. This would amount to minimising the total number of overlaps between the courses selected by the students.

Another approach consists of assigning to each constraint a 'weight' that represents the penalty incurred if the constraint is not satisfied. This approach leads to so-called **weighted CSPs**, for which the task is to find an instantiation for which the sum of the penalties is minimised. The max-CSP is a special case of the weighted CSPs, in which all the optional constraints have the same weight.

For example, in the above timetabling problem, for each pair of courses c_1 and c_2 selected by a student (so a pair of courses that are supposed not to overlap) we can assign to the corresponding constraint $disj(c_1, c_2)$ a weight that equals the number of optional *disjunctive* constraints in which such a pair appears and then replace each such *disjunctive* constraint by the corresponding set of the *disj* constraints. Then the task is to find an instantiation that satisfies all the obligatory constraints and for which the total sum of the weights of the violated *disj* constraints is minimal.

Yet another approach consists of assigning to each constraint C and instantiation I a 'degree of satisfaction' $sat(C, I)$, which is a value in the $[0, 1]$ real interval indicating the 'degree' that C is satisfied by I. If this value is 1, C is satisfied and if this value is 0, C is violated. This interpretation leads to **fuzzy CSPs** introduced in Dubois, Fargier and Prade [1993] and Ruttkay [1994]. In the most common interpretation of them the task is to find an instantiation I for which the minimum of $sat(C, I)$ with C ranging over all the constraints (which is the smallest degree of satisfaction for the instantiation I) is maximal.

To apply this approach to the above example we could assign to each optional constraint $disjunctive(c_1, \ldots, c_m)$ and instantiation I the percentage of the constituent $disj(c_i, c_j)$ constraints that are satisfied.

A combination of the last two approaches leads to a study of a combination of weighted and fuzzy CSPs, also considered in Rudová [2001].

9.6.2 Constraint hierarchies

Another way of dealing with over-constrained problem was proposed in Borning et al. [1987] and more extensively Borning, Freeman-Benson and Wilson [1992]. In this approach each constraint is labeled with a **strength value** drawn from a finite, linearly ordered set. A **constraint hierarchy** is a finite multiset of such labeled constraints. The constraint hierarchy can be naturally divided into a sequence $H_0, \ldots, H_n$ of levels by putting constraints with the same label into the same level. The constraints in the lowest level H_0 are considered to be the required (i.e., crisp) constraints.

We assume that for each constraint we have an **error function** that given an instantiation I indicates how nearly the constraint is satisfied. For example, the error function for the $x \leq y$ constraint on reals could be $max(0, x - y)$. Intuitively, a solution to a constraint hierarchy is then an instantiation that satisfies the required constraints and 'respects the hierarchy'. More formally, we define the notion of a solution parameterising it by the concept of a 'better' instantiation. We say that an instantiation I is a **solution to the constraint hierarchy** corresponding to $H_0, \ldots, H_n$ if

- I is a solution to H_0,
- no solution J of H_0 is 'better' than I.

The partial ordering 'better' on the instantiations can be defined in a number of ways. Each of them is called a **comparator**. They refer to the error functions. An example is the **locally_better** comparator defined as follows:

$locally\_better(I, J)$ holds iff for some $k > 0$

- $\forall i \in [1..k-1]\, \forall c \in H_i\ error(c, I) = error(c, J)$,
- $\forall c \in H_k\ error(c, I) \leq error(c, J)$,
- $\exists c \in H_k\ error(c, I) < error(c, J)$.

It is easy to see that if the CSP formed by the constraints in H_0 is consistent and has finitely many solutions (which is for example the case when all domains are finite), then the considered constraint hierarchy has a solution. Indeed, it suffices to choose from the solutions to H_0 any instantiation that is minimal in the 'better' ordering. To solve constraint hierarchies various algorithms were proposed, see, e.g., Borning and Freeman-Benson [1998]. They usually deal with simple constraints, like linear inequalities on reals, and employ a form of constraint propagation combined with planning techniques.

Constraint hierarchies are typically used in constraint-based interactive graphic systems, in particular in the user interface toolkits. But in principle they can also be employed to specify any over-constrained problem involving arithmetic constraints on finite domains or linear constraints on reals. For example, in Henz et al. [2003] the constraint hierarchies involving linear constraints on finite domains are used to model large airport gate allocation problems.

9.6.3 Generalisations

Such and other natural generalisations of the CSPs are studied in a uniform way in Schiex, Fargier and Verfaillie [1995], using the notion of a **valued CSP**, and in Bistarelli, Montanari and Rossi [1997], using the notion of **semiring-based constraint satisfaction**.

In the first approach a CSP is augmented with a **valuation structure** which is a linear ordering with the largest element $\top$ and the smallest element $\bot$, and an associative and commutative binary 'aggregation' operator. The $\top$ element expresses complete inconsistency, while $\bot$ expresses complete consistency. To each constraint its 'valuation' is associated, which is an element of the valuation structure denoting its importance. Then to each instantiation I a valuation is assigned, which is the aggregation of the valuations of the constraints that are violated by I. The task is then to find an instantiation with a minimum valuation. By choosing different valuation structures different generalisations of a CSP are obtained.

In the second approach a semiring contains two operations, $+$ and $\times$. The first operation is used to select the best solution among different instantiations, while the second operation corresponds to the join operation of Definition 5.34. We noted there that using join we can define the set of all solutions to a CSP. For each specific generalisation of a CSP an appropriate semiring is chosen. Its set specifies the values to be associated with each tuple of elements from the variable domains (for example $\{0,1\}$ for the customary CSPs and $[0,1]$ for the fuzzy CSPs) and its two operations are used to define the set of all solutions. Both approaches are compared in Bistarelli et al. [1996].

9.6.4 Reified constraints

Reified constraints are not soft constraints. But they are often used to deal with the max-CSPs, so it is natural to discuss them in this section.

Given a constraint c we introduce a fresh Boolean variable B and call $c \leftrightarrow B$ a **reified constraint**. Given a max-CSP with the optional constraints $c_1, \ldots, c_n$ we choose new Boolean variables $B_1, \ldots, B_n$ and consider instead the crisp reified constraints $c_1 \leftrightarrow B_1, \ldots, c_n \leftrightarrow B_n$. The task of solving the original max-CSP becomes now simply a constrained optimization problem with $\sum_{i=1}^{n} B_i$ as the objective function.

A complication is that the constraint propagation needs to be appropriately extended to the reified constraints. To see this note that a reified constraint $c \leftrightarrow B$ is equivalent to the disjunction $(c \wedge B) \vee (\neg c \wedge \neg B)$. So conceptually we can view a reified constraint as a disjunctive constraint.

(In practice they are dealt with more efficiently.) Then for each disjunct different proof rules have to be used. For example, if c is a linear equality constraint over integer intervals, then for the first disjunct the *LINEAR EQUALITY* rule of Section 6.4 is applicable, while for the second disjunct we need to use appropriate transformation rules and the *DISEQUALITY* rules of Section 6.4. Some constraint programming systems provide support for reified constraints.

9.7 Summary

The aim of this chapter was to put various aspects of constraint programming discussed in the previous chapters in a proper perspective. To this end we discussed in turn the issues concerned with

- modeling,

  by clarifying the impact of various problem representations on the efficiency,
- constraint programming languages,

  by explaining how the constraints and the variables present in them are represented in constraint programming languages, and by discussing the common features of these languages,
- constraint propagation,

  by explaining the implicit role played by it in some areas of computer science and applied mathematics,
- constraint solvers,

  by reflecting on their desired features from the point of view of efficiency and usability,
- search,

  by explaining what forms of search are commonly used to solve CSPs and constrained optimization problems and how they are realised in constraint programming languages, and
- over-constrained problems,

  by clarifying what approaches have been proposed to deal with the problems the formalisation of which yields an inconsistent CSP.

9.8 Bibliographic remarks

One of the aspects of modeling that increasingly attracts attention of the researchers is handling of symmetries in an efficient way. Various approaches that were proposed to deal with this subject are summarised in Flener et al. [2002], while recent contributions can be found in Flener and Pearson [2002].

van Hoeve [2001] surveys efficient constraint propagation algorithms for the `all_different` constraint with respect to various local consistency notions. Beldiceanu [2000] provides a classification scheme and a large inventory of global constraints. Wester [1999] is a collection of articles that describe the capabilities and limitations of various computer algebra systems.

Cohen [1990] is an early survey on constraint logic programming languages. Jaffar and Maher [1994] is a more recent and more extensive survey with emphasis on theory, implementation, and applications. It also includes an analysis of various desired aspects of constraint solvers and an account of constraint logic programming languages. Van Hentenryck and Saraswat [1996] is a useful summary of various research directions in constraint programming. Marriott and Stuckey [1998] is a solid introduction to constraint logic programming, both from the theoretical and practical point of view. It also contains a good account of incremental constraint solvers and an overview of various constraint programming languages. Information on and pointers to several constraint systems and languages can be found through the `constraints/systems/` link of the Constraints Archive website `http://www.cs.unh.edu/ccc/archive/` maintained by Peg Eaton.

In Simonis [1996] a classification of problems solved with constraint logic programming on finite domains is provided. The proposed scheme tries to clarify which types of problems can be effectively solved using this approach and which ones are best solved using the integer programming and local search techniques. Wallace [2002] discusses current directions in constraint logic programming, with pointers to works on hybrid algorithms. Schulte and Smolka [2002] is a web-based tutorial on constraint programming on finite domains in Oz that shows the benefits gained from using such techniques as the global constraints, exclusion of symmetries, implied constraints (called there redundant constraints) and reified constraints. Frühwirth [1998] provides a comprehensive survey of the use of the `CHR` language.

Useful bibliographic information and other web resources on local search techniques can be found through the website `http://people.freenet.de/Emden--Weinert/localsearch.html` maintained by Thomas Emden-Weinert.

Granvilliers, Monfroy and Benhamou [2001] survey the issues concerned with cooperation of constraint solvers with an emphasis on combinations of symbolic and interval methods. Jampel, Freuder and Maher [1996] is a collection of articles on a number of approaches to over-constrained CSPs.

Meseguer et al. [2003] is a more recent survey discussing fuzzy, lexicographic, probabilistic, weighted, and hierarchical CSPs. Finally, Barták [2002] is an informative on-line guide to constraint programming maintained by Roman Barták. It also contains many useful pointers to constraint resources available on the web.

Bibliography

A. AGGOUN AND N. BELDICEANU
[1993]   Extending CHIP in order to solve complex scheduling and placement problems, *Mathematical and Computer Modelling*, 17, pp. 57–73. *Cited on page* **358**.

J. F. ALLEN
[1983]   Maintaining knowledge about temporal intervals, *Communications of ACM*, 26, pp. 832–843. *Cited on page* **51**.

K. R. APT
[1998]   A proof theoretic view of constraint programming, *Fundamenta Informaticae*, 33, pp. 263–293. Available via http://arXiv.org/archive/cs/. *Cited on pages* **132, 249**.

[1999]   The essence of constraint propagation, *Theoretical Computer Science*, 221, pp. 179–210. Available via http://arXiv.org/archive/cs/. *Cited on pages* **296, 297**.

[2000a] The role of commutativity in constraint propagation algorithms, *ACM Transactions on Programming Languages and Systems*, 22, pp. 1002–1036. Available via http://arXiv.org/archive/cs/. *Cited on page* **296**.

[2000b] Some remarks on Boolean constraint propagation, in: *New Trends in Constraints*, K. R. Apt, A. C. Kakas, E. Monfroy, and F. Rossi, eds., vol. 1865 of Lecture Notes in Artificial Intelligence, Springer-Verlag, pp. 91 – 107. Available via http://arXiv.org/archive/cs/. *Cited on page* **249**.

K. R. APT AND P. ZOETEWEIJ
[2003]   A comparative study of arithmetic constraints on integer intervals, in: *Proceedings of the 2003 ERCIM Workshop on Constraints*, MTA SZ-TAKI. Available via http://www.cwi.nl/~apt. *Cited on page* **249**.

F. BAADER AND T. NIPKOW
[1998]   *Term Rewriting and All That*, Cambridge University Press, Cambridge, UK. *Cited on page* **289**.

F. BAADER AND J. H. SIEKMANN
[1994]   Unification theory, in: *Handbook of Logic in Artificial Intelligence and Logic Programming Vol. 2, Deduction Methodologies*, D. M. Gabbay, C. J. Hogger, and J. A. Robinson, eds., Oxford University Press, pp. 41–125. *Cited on page* **133**.

A. B. BABICHEV, O. B. KADYROVA, T. P. KAHEVAROVA, A. S. LESHCHENKO, AND A. L. SEMENOV

[1993] UniCalc, a novel approach to solving systems of algebraic equations, *Interval Computations*, N2, pp. 29 – 47. *Cited on page* **250**.

F. BACCHUS AND P. VAN BEEK

[1998] On the conversion between non-binary and binary constraint satisfaction problems, in: *AAAI-98: Proceedings of the 15th National Conference on Artificial Intelligence*, AAAI Press, Menlo Park. *Cited on page* **52**.

R. BARTÁK

[2002] On-line guide to constraint programming. Available via `http://kti.ms.mff.cuni.cz/~bartak/constraints/index.html`. *Cited on page* **386**.

N. BELDICEANU

[2000] *Global constraints as graph properties on structured network of elementary constaints of the same type*, Tech. Rep. T2000-01, Swedish Institute of Computer Science (SICS). Available via `http://www.sics.se/isl/cps/`. *Cited on page* **385**.

F. BENHAMOU

[1996] Heterogeneous constraint solving, in: *Proceeding of the Fifth International Conference on Algebraic and Logic Programming (ALP 96)*, M. Hanus and M. Rodriguez-Artalejo, eds., Lecture Notes in Computer Science 1139, Springer-Verlag, Berlin, pp. 62–76. *Cited on page* **296**.

F. BENHAMOU AND A. COLMERAUER

[1993] eds., *Constraint Logic Programming: Selected Research*, The MIT Press. *Cited on page* **251**.

F. BENHAMOU, F. GOUALARD, AND L. GRANVILLIERS

[1997] Programming with the `Declic` language, in: *Proceedings of the Second Workshop on Interval Constraints (October 1997, Port-Jefferson, NY)*. *Cited on page* **250**.

[2000] Interval constraints: Results and perspectives, in: *New Trends in Constraints*, K. R. Apt, A. C. Kakas, E. Monfroy, and F. Rossi, eds., vol. 1865 of Lecture Notes in Artificial Intelligence, Springer-Verlag, pp. 1–16. *Cited on page* **251**.

F. BENHAMOU, D. A. MCALLESTER, AND P. VAN HENTENRYCK

[1994] CLP(intervals) revisited, in: *Proceedings of the 1994 International Logic Programming Symposium*, M. Bruynooghe, ed., The MIT Press, pp. 124–138. *Cited on pages* **250**, **296**.

F. BENHAMOU AND W. OLDER

[1997] Applying interval arithmetic to real, integer and Boolean constraints, *Journal of Logic Programming*, 32, pp. 1–24. *Cited on pages* **250**, **296**.

C. BESSIÈRE, P. MESEGUER, E. C. FREUDER, AND J. LARROSA

[2002] On forward checking for non-binary constraint satisfaction, *Artificial Intelligence*, 141, pp. 205–224. *Cited on page* **349**.

C. BESSIÈRE AND J. C. RÉGIN

[2001] Refining the basic constraint propagation algorithm, in: *Proceedings of the International Joint Conference on Artificial Intelligence (IJCAI-01)*, Morgan Kaufmann, Seattle, WA, USA, pp. 309–315. *Cited on page* **365**.

S. BISTARELLI, H. FARGIER, U. MONTANARI, F. ROSSI, T. SCHIEX, AND
    G. VERFAILLIE
[1996]   Semiring-based CSPs and valued CSPs: basic properties and compari-
son, in: *Over-Constrained Systems*, M. Jampel, E. C. Freuder, and M. J.
Maher, eds., vol. 1106 of Lecture Notes in Computer Science, Springer,
pp. 111–150. *Cited on page* **383**.

S. BISTARELLI, U. MONTANARI, AND F. ROSSI
[1997]   Semiring-based constraint satisfaction and optimization, *Journal of the
ACM*, 44, pp. 201–236. *Cited on page* **383**.

J. J. BITNER AND E. M. REINGOLD
[1975]   Backtrack programming techniques, *Communications of the ACM*, 18,
pp. 651–656. *Cited on pages* **348, 349**.

N. BLEUZEN-GUERNALEC AND A. COLMERAUER
[2000]   Optimal narrowing of a block of sortings in optimal time, *Constraints*,
5, pp. 85–118. *Cited on page* **359**.

A. BOCKMAYR AND T. KASPER
[1998]   A unifying framework for integer and finite domain constraint programming, *INFORMS Journal on Computing*, 10, pp. 287 – 300. *Cited on
page* **357**.

A. BORNING, R. DUISBERG, B. FREEMAN-BENSON, A. KRAMER, AND
    M. WOOLF
[1987]   Constraint hierarchies, in: *OOPSLA '87*, Oct., pp. 48–60. *Cited on page*
381.

A. BORNING AND B. FREEMAN-BENSON
[1998]   Ultraviolet: a constraint satisfaction algorithm for interactive graphics,
Constraints, 3, pp. 9–32. *Cited on page* **382**.

A. BORNING, B. FREEMAN-BENSON, AND M. WILSON
[1992]   Constraint hierarchies, *Lisp and Symbolic Computation*, 5, pp. 223–270.
Cited on page **381**.

P. BOROVANSKY, C. KIRCHNER, H. KIRCHNER, P.-E. MOREAU, AND
    C. RINGEISSEN
[1998]   An Overview of ELAN, in: *Proceedings of the Second International Workshop on Rewriting Logic and its Applications*, C. Kirchner and H. Kirchner, eds., vol. 15 of Electronic Notes in Theoretical Computer Science,
Elsevier, Pont-à-Mousson (France), September. *Cited on pages* **176, 377**.

R. BOSCH
[1999]   Peaceably coexisting armies of queens, *OPTIMA (Newsletter of the
Mathematical Programming Society)*, 62, pp. 6–9. *Cited on page* **52**.

T. BY
[1997]   *Line Labelling by Meta-programming*, Tech. Rep. CS-97-07, University
of Sheffield. *Cited on page* **52**.

Y. CASEAU, F.-X. JOSSET, AND F. LABURTHE
[2002]   CLAIRE: Combining sets, search and rules to better express algorithms,
Theory and Practice of Logic Programming, 2, pp. 769–805. *Cited on
page* **362**.

C. Castro

[1998]   Building constraint satisfaction problem solvers using rewrite rules and strategies, *Fundamenta Informaticae*, 33, pp. 263–293. *Cited on page* **176**.

J. G. Cleary

[1987]   Logical arithmetic, *Future Computing Systems*, 2, pp. 125–149. *Cited on pages* **249, 250**.

M. B. Clowes

[1971]   On seeing things, *Artificial Intelligence*, 2, pp. 79–116. *Cited on page* **36**.

P. Codognet and D. Diaz

[1996]   A simple and efficient Boolean constraint solver for constraint logic programming, *Journal of Automated Reasoning*, 17, pp. 97–128. *Cited on page* **248**.

J. Cohen

[1990]   Constraint logic programming languages, *Communications of the ACM*, 33, pp. 52–68. *Cited on page* **385**.

A. G. Cohn and S. M. Hazarika

[2001]   Qualitative spatial representation and reasoning: an overview, *Fundamenta Informaticae*, 46, pp. 1–29. *Cited on page* **51**.

A. Colmerauer

[1990]   An introduction to Prolog III, *Communications of the ACM*, 33, pp. 69–90. *Cited on page* **360**.

[1993]   Naive solving of non-linear constraints, in: *Constraint Logic Programming: Selected Research*, F. Benhamou and A. Colmerauer, eds., The MIT Press, pp. 89–112. *Cited on page* **251**.

[2001]   Solving the multiplication constraint in several approximation spaces, in: *17th International Conference on Logic Programming, (ICLP 2001)*, P. Codognet, ed., vol. 2237 of Lecture Notes in Computer Science, Springer-Verlag, p. 1. The transparencies of the lecture are at http://www.lim.univ-mrs.fr/~colmer/Transparents/Paphos01/paphosps.zip. *Cited on page* **250**.

M. C. Cooper

[1989]   An optimal *k*-consistency algorithm, *Artificial Intelligence*, 41, pp. 89–95. *Cited on page* **296**.

R. J. Dakin

[1965]   A tree search algorithm for mixed integer programming problems, *The Computer Journal*, 8, pp. 250–255. *Cited on page* **349**.

K. Darby-Dowman and J. Little

[1998]   Properties of some combinatorial optimization problems and their effect on the performance of integer programming and constraint logic programming, *INFORMS Journal on Computing*, 10, pp. 276–286. *Cited on page* **357**.

A. J. Davenport, E. Tsang, C. J. Wang, and K. Zhu

[1994]   GENET: A connectionist architecture for solving constraint satisfaction problems by iterative improvement, in: *National Conference on Artificial Intelligence*, pp. 325–330. *Cited on page* **378**.

E. DAVIS
[1987]   Constraint propagation with interval labels, *Artificial Intelligence*, 32, pp. 281–331. *Cited on pages* **176, 249, 251, 295**.

M. DAVIS AND H. PUTNAM
[1960]   A computing procedure for quantification theory, *Journal of the ACM*, 7, pp. 201–215. *Cited on page* **249**.

R. DECHTER AND P. VAN BEEK
[1997]   Local and global relational consistency, *Theoretical Computer Science*, 173, pp. 283–308. *Cited on pages* **176, 365**.

R. DECHTER AND D. FROST
[2002]   Backjump-based backtracking for constraint satisfaction problems, *Artificial Intelligence*, 136, pp. 147–188. *Cited on page* **349**.

R. DECHTER AND J. PEARL
[1988]   Network-based heuristics for constraint-satisfaction problems, *Artificial Intelligence*, 34, pp. 1–38. *Cited on pages* **176, 296**.

M. DINCBAS, P. VAN HENTENRYCK, H. SIMONIS, A. AGGOUN, T. GRAF, AND F. BERTHIER
[1988]   The Constraint Logic Programming Language CHIP, in: *FGCS-88: Proceedings International Conference on Fifth Generation Computer Systems*, ICOT, Tokyo, pp. 693–702. *Cited on page* **361**.

A. DOLLAS, W. T. RANKIN, AND D. MCCRACKEN
[1998]   A new algorithm for Golomb ruler derivation and proof of the 19 mark rule, *IEEE Transactions on Information Theory*, pp. 379–382. *Cited on page* **52**.

D. DUBOIS, H. FARGIER, AND H. PRADE
[1993]   The calculus of fuzzy restrictions as a basis for flexible constraint satisfaction, in: *Proceedings 2nd IEEE Conference on Fuzzy Sets*, San Francisco, Mar. *Cited on page* **381**.

M. EGENHOFER
[1991]   Reasoning about binary topological relations, in: *Proceedings of the 2nd International Symposium on Large Spatial Databases (SSD)*, O. Günther and H.-J. Schek, eds., vol. 525 of Lecture Notes in Computer Science, Springer-Verlag, pp. 143–160. *Cited on page* **51**.

[1994a] Deriving the composition of binary topological relations, *Journal of Visual Languages and Computing*, 5, pp. 133–149. *Cited on page* **51**.

[1994b] Pre-processing queries with spatial constraints, *Photogrammetric Engineering & Remote Sensing*, 60, pp. 783–790. *Cited on page* **51**.

A. E. EIBEN AND Z. RUTTKAY
[1997]   Constraint satisfaction problems, in: *Handbook of Evolutionary Computation*, T. Bäck, D. B. Fogel, and Z. Michalewicz, eds., Institute of Physics Publishing and Oxford University Press, Bristol, New York, pp. C5.7:1–8. *Cited on page* **379**.

F. FAGES, J. FOWLER, AND T. SOLA
[1998]   Experiments in reactive constraint logic programming, *Journal of Logic Programming*, 37, pp. 185–212. *Cited on page* **296**.

B.-J. FALKOWSKI AND L. SCHMITZ

[1986]   A note on the queens' problem, *Information Processing Letters*, 23, pp. 39–46. *Cited on page* **51**.

P. FLENER, A. FRISCH, B. HNICH, Z. KIZILTAN, I. MIGUEL, J. PEARSON, AND T. WALSH

[2002]   Breaking row and column symmetries in matrix models, in: *Proceedings of the Eighth International Conference on Principles and Practice of Constraint Programming (CP '02)*, vol. 2470 of Lecture Notes in Computer Science, Springer-Verlag, pp. 462–477. *Cited on page* **385**.

P. FLENER AND J. PEARSON

[2002]   eds., *SymCon'02: The Second International Workshop on Symmetry in Constraint Satisfaction Problems*. Available via `http://www.it.uu.se/research/group/astra/SymCon02`. *Cited on page* **385**.

R. FOURER, D. M. GAY, AND B. W. KERNIGHAM

[1993]   *AMPL: A Modeling Language for Mathematical Programming*, The Scientific Press Series. *Cited on page* **369**.

J. FOURIER

[1827]   Analyse des travaux de l'Académie Royale des Sciences pendant l'année 1824, partie mathématique, *Histoire de l'Académie Royale des Sciences de l'Institut de France*, 7. English Translation (partially) in: D .A. Kohler, Translation of a report by Fourier on his work on linear inequalities, *Opsearch, 10*, 1973, pp. 38-42. *Cited on page* **133**.

E. C. FREUDER

[1978]   Synthesizing constraint expressions, *Communications of the ACM*, 21, pp. 958–966. *Cited on page* **176**.

[1982]   A sufficient condition for backtrack-free search, *Journal of the ACM*, 29, pp. 24–32. *Cited on pages* **176, 349**.

E. C. FREUDER AND R. WALLACE

[1992]   Partial constraint satisfaction, *Artificial Intelligence*, 58, pp. 21–70. *Cited on page* **380**.

T. FRÜHWIRTH

[1995]   Constraint Handling Rules, in: *Constraint Programming: Basics and Trends*, A. Podelski, ed., LNCS 910, Springer-Verlag, pp. 90–107. (Châtillon-sur-Seine Spring School, France, May 1994). *Cited on pages* **249, 366**.

[1998]   Theory and practice of Constraint Handling Rules, *Journal of Logic Programming*, 37, pp. 95–138. Special Issue on Constraint Logic Programming (P. J. Stuckey and K. Marriot, Eds.). *Cited on page* **385**.

M. GARDNER

[1979]   *Mathematical Circus*, Knopf. *Cited on page* **52**.

[1997]   *The Last Recreations: Hydras, Eggs, and Other Mathematical Mystifications*, Copernicus Books. *Cited on page* **52**.

J. GASCHNIG

[1974]   A constraint satisfaction method for inference making, in: *Proceedings of the 12th Annual Allerton Conference on Circuit and System Theory*, Urbana-Champaign, IL, pp. 866–874. *Cited on page* **349**.

R. GENNARI
  [2000] Arc consistency via subsumed functions, in: *Proceedings of Computa-
          tional Logic 2000 (CL2000)*, J. Lloyd, ed., Lecture Notes in Artificial
          Intelligence 1861, Springer-Verlag, Berlin, pp. 358–372. *Cited on page*
          297.
  [2001] General schema for constraint propagation, *Joint Bulletin of of the
          Novosibirsk Computing Center and Institute of Informatics Systems. Se-
          ries: Computer Science*, 16, pp. 25–40. *Cited on page* **297**.

S. W. GOLOMB AND L. D. BAUMERT
  [1965] Backtrack programming, *Journal of the ACM*, 12, pp. 516–524. *Cited on
          page* **348**.

L. GRANVILLIERS, E. MONFROY, AND F. BENHAMOU
  [2001] Symbolic-interval cooperation in constraint programming, in: *Proceed-
          ings of the 26th ACM International Symposium on Symbolic and Alge-
          braic Computation (ISSAC 2001)*, ACM Press, pp. 150–166. *Cited on
          page* **385**.

W. K. HALE
  [1980] Frequency assignment: theory and applications, in: *Proceedings of the
          IEEE Transactions on Vehicular Technology*, vol. 68, pp. 1497–1514.
          Cited on page **52**.

E. HANSEN
  [1992] *Global Optimization Using Interval Analysis*, Marcel Dekker. *Cited on
          page* **249**.

R. M. HARALICK AND G. L. ELLIOT
  [1980] Increasing tree search efficiency for constraint satisfaction problems, *Ar-
          tificial Intelligence*, 14, pp. 263–313. *Cited on page* **349**.

W. HARVEY AND P. J. STUCKEY
  [2003] Improving linear constraint propagation by changing constraint repre-
          sentation, *Constraints*, 8, pp. 173–207. *Cited on page* **249**.

W. D. HARVEY AND M. L. GINSBERG
  [1995] Limited discrepancy search, in: *Proceedings of the Fourteenth Inter-
          national Joint Conference on Artificial Intelligence (IJCAI-95); Vol.
          1*, C. S. Mellish, ed., Morgan Kaufmann, Montréal, Québec, Canada,
          pp. 607–615. *Cited on page* **371**.

M. HENZ, Y. F. LIM, S. C. LUA, X. P. SHI, J. P. WALSER, AND R. H. C.
          YAP
  [2003] Solving hierarchical constraints over finite domains with local search,
          Annals of Mathematics and Artificial Intelligence. To appear. *Cited on
          page* **382**.

J. HERBRAND
  [1971] *Logical Writings*, Reidel. W. D. Goldfarb, ed. *Cited on page* **132**.

T. J. HICKEY, Q. JU, AND M. H. VAN EMDEN
  [2001] Interval arithmetic: from principles to implementation, *Journal of the
          ACM*, 48, pp. 1038–1068. *Cited on page* **250**.

Bibliography

T. J. HICKEY, M. H. VAN EMDEN, AND H. WU

[1998] A unified framework for interval constraints and interval arithmetic, in: *Proceedings of the Fourth International Conference on Principles and Practice of Constraint Programming (CP'98)*, M. J. Maher and J.-F. Puget, eds., vol. 1520 of Lecture Notes in Computer Science, Springer-Verlag, pp. 250–264. *Cited on page* **250**.

W. J. VAN HOEVE

[2001] The alldifferent constraint: A survey, November. Submitted for publication. Available via `http://www.cwi.nl/~wjvh/papers/alldiff.ps.gz`. *Cited on page* **385**.

D. HUFFMAN

[1971] Impossible objects as nonsense sentences, in: *Machine Intelligence 6*, B. Meltzer and D. Mitchie, eds., pp. 295–323. *Cited on page* **36**.

E. HYVÖNEN

[1992] Constraint reasoning based on interval arithmetic. The tolerance propagation approach, *Artificial Intelligence*, 58, pp. 71–112. *Cited on page* **250**.

ILOG

[2003] Ilog white papers. Available via `http://www.ilog.com/products/optimization/papers.cfm`. *Cited on page* **362**.

J.-L. IMBERT

[1995] Fourier Elimination: which to choose, in: *Principles and Practice of Constraint Programming*, P. Van Hentenryck and V. Saraswat, eds., MIT Press, pp. 245–268. *Cited on page* **133**.

J. JAFFAR AND J.-L. LASSEZ

[1987] Constraint logic programming, in: *POPL'87: Proceedings 14th ACM Symposium on Principles of Programming Languages*, ACM, pp. 111–119. *Cited on page* **361**.

J. JAFFAR AND M. J. MAHER

[1994] Constraint logic programming: a survey, *Journal of Logic Programming*, 19/20, pp. 503–581. *Cited on pages* **251**, **385**.

J. JAFFAR, M. J. MAHER, P. J. STUCKEY, AND R. H. C. YAP

[1993] Projecting CLP($\mathcal{R}$) constraints, *New Generation Computing*, 11, pp. 449–469. *Cited on pages* **133**, **251**.

J. JAFFAR, S. MICHAYOV, P. J. STUCKEY, AND R. H. C. YAP

[1992] The CLP($\mathcal{R}$) language and system, *ACM Transactions on Programming Languages and Systems*, 14, pp. 339–395. *Cited on page* **361**.

M. JAMPEL, E. C. FREUDER, AND M. J. MAHER

[1996] eds., *Over-Constrained Systems*, vol. 1106 of Lecture Notes in Computer Science, Springer. *Cited on page* **385**.

C. KIRCHNER AND C. RINGEISSEN

[1998] Rule-based constraint programming, *Fundamenta Informaticae*, 34, pp. 225–262. *Cited on page* **377**.

F. LABURTHE AND Y. CASEAU

[2002] SALSA: A language for search algorithms, *Constraints*, 7, pp. 255–288. *Cited on page* **377**.

O. LHOMME
[1993] Consistency techniques for numeric CSPs, in: *Proceedings of the International Joint Conference on Artificial Intelligence (IJCAI-93)*, pp. 232–238. *Cited on page* **249**.

E. LUCAS
[1891] *Récréations Mathématiques*, Gauthier Villar, Paris, second ed. *Cited on page* **349**.

A. MACKWORTH
[1977] Consistency in networks of relations, *Artificial Intelligence*, 8, pp. 99–118. *Cited on pages* **176, 295, 296**.
[1992] Constraint satisfaction, in: *Encyclopedia of Artificial Intelligence*, S. C. Shapiro, ed., John Wiley and Sons, pp. 285–293. Volume 1. *Cited on pages* **51, 176**.

K. MARRIOTT AND P. J. STUCKEY
[1998] *Programming With Constraints: An Introduction*, The MIT Press. *Cited on pages* **133, 176, 249, 385**.

A. MARTELLI AND U. MONTANARI
[1982] An efficient unification algorithm, *ACM Transactions on Programming Languages and Systems*, 4, pp. 258–282. *Cited on page* **132**.

D. MCALLESTER
[1980] An outlook on truth maintenance. MIT, Artificial Intelligence Laboratory, AI Memo No. 551. *Cited on page* **248**.
[1990] Truth maintenance, in: *AAAI-90: Proceedings 8th National Conference on Artificial Intelligence*, pp. 1109–1116. *Cited on page* **248**.

K. MCALOON AND C. TRETKOFF
[1996] *Optimization and Computational*, John Wiley and Sons. *Cited on page* **370**.

J. J. MCGREGOR
[1979] Relational consistency algorithms and their application in finding subgraph and graph isomorphism, *Information Science*, 19, pp. 229–250. *Cited on page* **349**.

P. MESEGUER, N. BOUHMALA, T. BOUZOUBAA, M. IRGENS, AND
   M. SÁNCHEZ
[2003] Current approaches for solving over-constrained problems, *Constraints*, 8, pp. 9–39. *Cited on page* **386**.

Z. MICHALEWICZ
[1996] *Genetic Algorithms + Data Structures = Evolution Programs*, Springer-Verlag, Berlin, third ed. *Cited on page* **379**.

L. MICHEL AND P. VAN HENTENRYCK
[2002a] A constraint-based architecture for local search, in: *Proceedings of the 17th ACM conference on Object-oriented programming, systems, languages, and applications*, ACM Press, pp. 83–100. *Cited on page* **378**.
[2002b] A decomposition-based implementation of search strategies. To appear in ACM Transactions on Computational Logic. Available via http://www.acm.org/tocl. *Cited on page* **377**.

S. Minton, M. D. Johnston, A. B. Philips, and P. Laird
[1992] A heuristic repair method for constraint satisfaction and scheduling problems, *Artificial Intelligence*, 58, pp. 161–205. *Cited on page* **372**.

R. Mohr and G. Masini
[1988] Good old discrete relaxation, in: *Proceedings of the 8th European Conference on Artificial Intelligence (ECAI)*, Y. Kodratoff, ed., Pitman Publishers, pp. 651–656. *Cited on page* **176**.

E. Monfroy and J.-H. Réty
[1999] Chaotic iteration for distributed constraint propagation, in: *Proceedings of the 14th ACM Symposium on Applied Computing, ACM SAC'99, Scientific Computing Track*, J. Carroll, H. Haddad, D. Oppenheim, B. Bryant, and G. Lamont, eds., ACM Press, San Antonio, Texas, USA, March, pp. 19–24. *Cited on page* **297**.

U. Montanari
[1974] Networks of constraints: fundamental properties and applications to picture processing, *Information Science*, 7, pp. 95–132. Also Technical Report, Carnegie Mellon University, 1971. *Cited on pages* **176, 295**.

U. Montanari and F. Rossi
[1991] Constraint relaxation may be perfect, *Artificial Intelligence*, 48, pp. 143–170. *Cited on page* **296**.

R. E. Moore
[1966] *Interval Analysis*, Prentice-Hall, Englewood Cliffs, NJ. *Cited on page* **249**.

T. S. Motzkin
[1936] *Beiträge zur Theorie der linearen Ungleichungen*, PhD thesis, University of Zurich. *Cited on page* **133**.

E. Netto
[1901] *Lehrbuch der Çombinatorik*, Teubner, Stuttgart. *Cited on page* **51**.

W. Older, G. Swinkels, and M. H. van Emden
[1995] Getting to the real problem: experience with BNR Prolog in OR, in: *Proceedings of the Third International Conference on the Practical Application of Prolog (PAP '95)*, L. Sterling, ed., Alinmead Software Ltd, pp. 465–478. *Cited on page* **359**.

W. Older and A. Vellino
[1993] Constraint arithmetic on real intervals, in: *Constraint Logic Programming: Selected Research*, F. Benhamou and A. Colmerauer, eds., The MIT Press, pp. 175–195. *Cited on page* **250**.

C. H. Papadimitriou and K. Steiglitz
[1982] *Combinatorial Optimization: Algorithms and Complexity*, Prentice-Hall. *Cited on page* **131**.

M. S. Paterson and M. N. Wegman
[1978] Linear unification, *J. Comput. System Sci.*, 16, pp. 158–167. *Cited on page* **132**.

W. H. Press, B. P. Flannery, S. A. Teukolsky, and W. T. Vetterling
[1992] *Numerical Recipes in C : The Art of Scientific Computing*, Cambridge University Press, 2nd ed. *Cited on page* **133**.

D. A. RANDELL, A. G. COHN, AND Z. CUI
[1992] Computing transitivity tables: A challenge for automated theorem provers, in: *Proceedings CADE 11*, Springer, Berlin. *Cited on page* **51**.

D. RATZ
[1996] *Inclusion Isotone Extended Interval Arithmetic*, tech. rep., University of Karlsruhe. Report No. D-76128 Karlsruhe. *Cited on page* **250**.

J. C. RÉGIN
[1994] A filtering algorithm for constraints of difference in CSPs, in: *AAAI-94: Proceedings of the 12th National Conference on Artificial Intelligence*, pp. 362–367. *Cited on page* **354**.

J. A. ROBINSON
[1965] A machine-oriented logic based on the resolution principle, *J. ACM*, 12, pp. 23–41. *Cited on page* **132**.
[1992] Logic and logic programming, *Communications of ACM*, 35, pp. 40–65. *Cited on page* **133**.

H. RUDOVÁ
[2001] Soft scheduling, in: *Proceedings of the 2001 ERCIM Workshop on Constraints*, Charles University in Prague, Faculty of Mathematics and Physics. Available via `http://arXiv.org/abs/cs.AI/0106004`. *Cited on pages* **380, 381**.

S. RUSSELL AND P. NORVIG
[2003] *Artifical Intelligence: A Modern Approach*, Prentice-Hall, Englewood Cliffs, NJ, second ed. *Cited on pages* **51, 375**.

Z. RUTTKAY
[1994] Fuzzy constraint satisfaction, in: *Proceedings 1st IEEE Conference on Evolutionary Computing*, Orlando, pp. 542–547. *Cited on page* **381**.

D. SABIN AND E. C. FREUDER
[1994] Contradicting conventional wisdom in constraint satisfaction, in: *Proceedings ECAI'94*, Amsterdam, pp. 125–129. *Cited on page* **349**.

D. SAM-HAROUD AND B. FALTINGS
[1996] Consistency techniques for continuous constraints, *Constraints*, 1, pp. 85–118. *Cited on page* **349**.

V. SARASWAT
[1993] *Concurrent Constraint Programming*, The MIT Press. *Cited on page* **362**.

V. SARASWAT, M. RINARD, AND P. PANANGADEN
[1991] Semantic foundations of concurrent constraint programming, in: *Proceedings of the Eighteenth Annual ACM Symposium on Principles of Programming Languages (POPL'91)*, pp. 333–352. *Cited on page* **296**.

A. SCHAERF, M. CADOLI, AND M. LENZERINI
[2000] LOCAL++: A C++ framework for combinatorial search problems, *Software—Practice and Experience*, pp. 233–257. *Cited on page* **377**.

T. SCHIEX, H. FARGIER, AND G. VERFAILLIE
[1995] Valued constraint satisfaction problems: hard and easy problems, in: *IJCAI'95*, Montreal, Canada, pp. 631–637. *Cited on page* **383**.

A. SCHRIJVER

[1986] *Theory of Linear and Integer Programming,* John Wiley and Sons. *Cited on page* **133**.

C. SCHULTE

[1997] Programming constraint inference engines, in: *Proceedings of the Third International Conference on Principles and Practice of Constraint Programming (CP '97)*, G. Smolka, ed., vol. 1330 of Lecture Notes in Computer Science, Springer-Verlag, pp. 519–533. *Cited on page* **376**.

[2002] *Programming Constraint Services,* vol. 2302 of Lecture Notes in Computer Science, Springer. *Cited on page* **376**.

C. SCHULTE AND G. SMOLKA

[2002] Finite domain constraint programming in Oz. A tutorial, August. Version 1.2.4 (20020829). Available via `http://www.mozart-oz.org/documentation/fdt/index.html`. *Cited on page* **385**.

E. SCHWALB AND L. VILA

[1998] Temporal constraints: a survey, *Constraints*, 3, pp. 129–149. *Cited on page* **51**.

H. SIMONIS

[1989] Test generation using the Constraint Logic Programming language CHIP, in: *ICLP'89: Proceedings 6th International Conference on Logic Programming*, G. Levi and M. Martelli, eds., The MIT Press, pp. 101–112. *Cited on page* **248**.

[1996] A problem classification scheme for finite domain constraint solving, in: *Proceedings of the CP'96 workshop on Constraint Programming Applications*, Cambridge MA, pp. 1–26. Available via `http://www.cs.wfu.edu/~burg/CP96/cp96.html`. *Cited on page* **385**.

B. M. SMITH, K. E. PETRIE, AND I. P. GENT

[2002] Models and symmetry breaking. presented at the ECAI 2002 workshop W9 Modelling and Solving Problems with Constraints. available via `http://4c.ucc.ie/~tw/ecai02/smith.ps`. *Cited on page* **52**.

B. M. SMITH, K. STERGIOU, AND T. WALSH

[2000] Using auxiliary variables and implied constraints to model non-binary problems, in: *AAAI-00: Proceedings National Conference on Artificial Intelligence*, pp. 182–187. *Cited on page* **52**.

G. SMOLKA

[1995] The Oz programming model, in: *Computer Science Today*, J. van Leeuwen, ed., vol. 1000 of Lecture Notes in Computer Science, Springer-Verlag, pp. 324–343. *Cited on page* **362**.

R. TARJAN

[1972] Depth-first search and linear graph algorithms, *SIAM Journal on Computing*, 1, pp. 146–160. *Cited on page* **349**.

V. TELERMAN AND D. USHAKOV

[1996] Data types in subdefinite models, in: *Artificial Intelligence and Symbolic Mathematical Computations*, Lecture Notes in Computer Science 1138, Springer-Verlag, Berlin, pp. 305–319. *Cited on page* **296**.

M. TRICK
[2001] A dynamic programming approach for consistency and propagation for knapsack constraints, in: *Proceedings of the Third International Workshop on Integration of AI and OR Techniques in Constraint Programming for Combinatorial Optimization Problems (CPAIOR-01)*, pp. 113–124. Available via http://www.icparc.ic.ac.uk/cpAIOR01/. *Cited on page* 365.

E. TSANG
[1993] *Foundations of Constraint Satisfaction*, Academic Press. *Cited on page* xi.

P. VAN BEEK
[1992] Reasoning about qualitative temporal information, *Artificial Intelligence*, 58, pp. 297–326. *Cited on page* 51.

P. VAN BEEK AND R. DECHTER
[1995] On the minimality and global consistency of row-convex constraint networks, *Journal of the ACM*, 42, pp. 543–561. *Cited on page* 349.

M. H. VAN EMDEN
[1997] Value constraints in the CLP scheme, *Constraints*, 2, pp. 163–184. *Cited on page* 296.
[1999] The logic programming paradigm in numerical computation, in: *The Logic Programming Paradigm*, K. R. Apt, V. W. Marek, M. Truszczyński, and D. S. Warren, eds., Springer-Verlag, pp. 257–276. *Cited on page* 249.

P. VAN HENTENRYCK
[1989] *Constraint Satisfaction in Logic Programming*, The MIT Press. *Cited on pages* xi, 51, 249, 357, 361.
[1997] *Numerica: A Modeling Language for Global Optimization*, The MIT Press. *Cited on page* 250.
[1999] *The OPL Optimization Programming Language*, The MIT Press. *Cited on page* 364.

P. VAN HENTENRYCK, L. PERRON, AND J.-F. PUGET
[2000] Search and strategies in OPL, *ACM Transactions on Computational Logic*, 1, pp. 285–320. *Cited on page* 376.

P. VAN HENTENRYCK AND V. SARASWAT
[1996] Strategic directions in constraint programming, *ACM Computing Surveys*, 28, pp. 701–726. *Cited on page* 385.

P. VAN HENTENRYCK, V. SARASWAT, AND Y. DEVILLE
[1998] Design, implementation, and evaluation of the constraint language cc(fd), *Journal of Logic Programming*, 37, pp. 139–164. Special Issue on Constraint Logic Programming (P. J. Stuckey and K. Marriot, Eds.). *Cited on page* 249.

M. WALLACE
[2002] Constraint logic programming, in: *Computational Logic: Logic Programming and Beyond, Essays in Honour of Robert A. Kowalski, Part I*, A. C. Kakas and F. Sadri, eds., vol. 2407 of Lecture Notes in Computer Science, Springer, pp. 512–532. *Cited on page* 385.

M. WALLACE, S. NOVELLO, AND J. SCHIMPF

[1997]   *ECL^{i}PS^e: A Platform for Constraint Logic Programming*, tech. rep., IC-Parc, Imperial College, London. Available via `http://www.icparc.ic.ac.uk/eclipse/reports/index.html`. *Cited on pages* **52, 361**.

M. WALLACE AND J. SCHIMPF

[2002]   Finding the right hybrid algorithm – a combinatorial meta-problem, *Annals of Mathematics and Artificial Intelligence*, 34, pp. 259–269. *Cited on page* **377**.

T. WALSH

[2001]   *Relational Consistencies*, Tech. Rep. APES-28-2001, APES Research Group, January. Available from http://www.dcs.st-and.ac.uk/ apes/apesreports.html. *Cited on page* **176**.

D. L. WALTZ

[1975]   Generating semantic descriptions from drawings of scenes with shadows, in: *The Psychology of Computer Vision*, P. H. Winston, ed., McGraw Hill, pp. 19–91. *Cited on pages* **51, 295**.

M. J. WESTER

[1999]   ed., *Computer Algebra Systems*, John Wiley and Sons. *Cited on page* **385**.

P. H. WINSTON

[1992]   *Artificial Intelligence*, Addison-Wesley, third ed. *Cited on page* **51**.

L. A. WOLSEY

[1998]   *Integer Programming*, John Wiley and Sons. *Cited on pages* **249, 365**.

H. ZHANG AND M. STICKEL

[1996]   An efficient algorithm for unit propagation, in: *Proceedings of the Fourth International Symposium on Artificial Intelligence and Mathematics*, Ft. Lauderdale, Florida. *Cited on page* **249**.

Y. ZHANG AND R. H. C. YAP

[2001]   Making AC-3 an optimal algorithm, in: *Proceedings of the International Joint Conference on Artificial Intelligence (IJCAI-01)*, Morgan Kaufmann, Seattle, WA, USA, pp. 316–321. *Cited on page* **365**.

Author index

401

Subject index